HEIDEGGER
AND
AQUINAS

HEIDEGGER AND AQUINAS

An Essay on Overcoming Metaphysics

JOHN D. CAPUTO

New York
FORDHAM UNIVERSITY PRESS
1982

Printed in the United States of America

To
My Mother and Father
FLORENCE AGNES
and
PETER JOSEPH CAPUTO

Works of Heidegger

References will be indicated by means of the following abbreviations of the German titles of Heidegger's works, followed by the page number of the German edition and by the cross reference to the English translation. Thus *Weg.*² 45/3 means that I am quoting p. 45 of the Gesamtausgabe edition of *Wegmarken*, listed in the Bibliography, a translation of which is to be found on p. 3 of the English version listed immediately after it in the Bibliography. I have tried to make use of existing translations, and by consulting these translations, the reader will see for himself where I have adapted the translation or entirely retranslated it.

AED	*Aus der Erfahrung des Denkens*
EM	*Einführung in die Metaphysik*
FS²	*Frühe Schriften* (Gesamtausgabe)
FW	*Die Feldweg*
G	*Gelassenheit*
GP	*Grundprobleme der Phänomenologie* (Gesamtausgabe)
Holz.²	*Holzwege* (Gesamtausgabe)
ID	*Identität und Differenz*
K	*Die Technik und die Kehre*
N I, N II	*Nietzsche*
SD	*Zur Sache des Denkens*
SG	*Der Satz vom Grund*
SZ	*Sein und Zeit*
US	*Unterwegs zur Sprache*
VA	*Vorträge und Aufsätze*
WD	*Was heisst Denken?*
WdP	*Was ist das—die Philosophie?*
Weg.²	*Wegmarken* (Gesamtausgabe)
WG	*Vom Wesen des Grundes*

Works of Aquinas

Reference to the works of St. Thomas is standardized and does not involve the use of page numbers, either in Latin or in translation. Full bibliographical information on the Latin editions and English translations which I have used may be obtained from the Bibliography. As with Heidegger, I have tried to make use of existing translations.

Comp. theol.	*Compendium theologiae*
De ente	*De ente et essentia*
De pot.	*Quaestiones disputatae de potentia dei*
De spir. creat.	*Quaestiones disputatae de spiritualibus creaturis*
De ver.	*Quaestiones disputatae de veritate*
Exp. Boet. De Trin.	*Expositio super librum Boethii De Trinitate*
In Boet. De hebd.	*Expositio in librum Boethii De hebdomadibus*
In De causis	*In librum De causis expositio*
In Met.	*In duodecim libros Metaphysicorum Aristotelis expositio*
In Phys.	*In octo libros Physicorum Aristotelis expositio*
In I Sent.	*Scripta super libros Sententiarum, liber I*
In I Tim.	*Super epistolas s. Pauli lectura*
Quod.	*Quaestiones quodlibetales*
SCG	*Summa contra Gentiles*
ST	*Summa theologiae* (*theologica*)

In addition, I have supplied the reader with cross references, where useful, to the following anthology:

AR	*An Aquinas Reader.* Ed. Mary Clark. Garden City, N.Y.: Doubleday Image, 1972.

ACKNOWLEDGMENTS

I wish to thank Professor John Sallis, Chairman of the Department of Philosophy at Duquesne University, for the invitation which he and his department extended to me to spend the Fall 1978 semester at Duquesne as a Visiting Professor. During this time I taught a graduate course on Heidegger and Aquinas, the lectures of which gave shape to the first draft of this book. I am grateful, too, to the students in that class, in particular to Panos Alexakos and Tony Godzieba, whose contributions to this course were of considerable help to me.

I owe a debt of gratitude to Professor Albert Hofstadter for making available to me and my students the early draft of his translation of the crucial §§ 10–12 of *The Basic Problems of Phenomenology*.

I also wish to thank Professor Thomas Sheehan, of Loyola University in Chicago. I have profited greatly, not only from his excellent published writings on Heidegger, but also from our private correspondence, and, in particular, from his careful reading of the present manuscript.

My thanks to Rev. John O'Malley, o.s.a., Dean of the College of Arts and Sciences at Villanova University, Dr. James Cleary, Academic Vice President, and Dr. Bernard Downey, Graduate Dean, for their support in defraying the cost of typing this manuscript. Nor can I fail to mention the gracious and efficient work of our departmental secretary, Mrs. Sandy Shupard, who patiently and expeditiously typed the corrections and final drafts of this work.

I should also like to thank John Sallis, Editor of *Research in Phenomenology*, for permission to use parts of my "Language, Logic and Time," which appeared in *Research in Phenomenology*, 3 (1973), 147–55.

It is also a pleasure to acknowledge the help of Mary Beatrice Schulte, Editor at Fordham University Press, who edited the text of this book with such obvious care and professional expertise.

Finally, and most importantly, I thank my wife, Kathy, not only for her patience with the long hours which must necessarily be invested in a work such as this, but also for the design of the cover of the paperback edition.

Villanova University   JOHN D. CAPUTO

CONTENTS

HEIDEGGER
AND
AQUINAS

INTRODUCTION

The Thought of Being
and
the Metaphysics of *Esse*

THE PURPOSE OF THE PRESENT STUDY is to undertake a confrontation of the thought of Martin Heidegger and of Thomas Aquinas on the question of Being and the problem of metaphysics. Now, a "confrontation" which does no more than draw up a catalogue of common traits and points of difference is no more than a curiosity, an idle comparison which bears no fruit. What matters in a genuinely philosophical confrontation is that something be brought forth about the nature of things (*rerum natura*), about the matter to be thought (*Sache des Denkens*). Husserl's warning not to be concerned with philosophers and their philosophies rings truer than ever today, when the lines of philosophical communication threaten to be flooded with monographs and studies of this or that philosopher and of this or that "connection." I have no interest here in establishing such a connection between Heidegger and Aquinas, between this German philosopher who still today is popularly thought to be an atheist and this medieval theologian whose thought has always been held close to the bosom of the Catholic Church. What interests me is the *Sache*, the matter which presents itself for thought, which, in the case of these two thinkers, is the problem of Being and the nature of metaphysical knowledge. I have no interest in developing an expertise in Heidegger or Aquinas. What interests me is the problem of how Being can be thought.

And that is the point of this confrontation. For however widely separated these authors may be by historical setting and substantive concerns, Aquinas and Heidegger are philosophers of Being *par excellence*. And they each lay claim—or in the case of Aquinas his followers lay claim on his behalf—to a unique insight into Being, one which consigns the rest of the history of metaphysics to a kind of oblivion (*Vergessenheit*). The cutting edge of this confrontation lies in the fact that each thinker is included in the other's history of the oblivion of Being.

From the standpoint of St. Thomas the work of Gilson is especially pertinent, for Gilson defends the Thomistic thesis on Being historically. With a rare combination of historical erudition and philosophical insight (FS[2] 194), Gilson interprets the history of metaphysics as a series of more or less distorted conceptions of what Being means, of various attempts to substitute something other than Being for Being itself. Time and again, Gilson thinks, metaphysicians succumb to the inclination to reduce Being to the proportions of conceptual reason. The history of metaphysics is a sustained attempt to make Being something conceivable and definable. In Platonism Being is reduced to unity, and in Aristotelianism to substance; and in the long tradition from Avicenna to Hegel, Being becomes essence. It is only in St. Thomas that Being is taken precisely as Being, in all of its primordiality as Being. Thomas alone has the tenacity to stay purely in "the element of Being," as Heidegger once put it (*Weg.*[2] 316/196) and to think Being in terms of the existential act which is *esse*, the *actualitas omnium rerum*, the *perfectissimum omnium* (ST, I, 4, 1, ad 3).

Yet this is precisely what Heidegger holds about the "thought of Being." What Being means, Heidegger says, has fallen into neglect or oblivion (*Seinsvergessenheit*), precisely because the difference between Being and beings has been concealed. Being is everywhere reduced to the proportions of something entitative, of some being or other. In metaphysics Being is taken as εἶδος, οὐσία, *Gegenstand, Begriff, Wille*—and also as *actus, actualitas*. In every case Being itself is characterized in terms of a region of beings. Only the thought of Being (*Seinsdenken*) practiced by Heidegger resists this tendency and meditates Being as simple φύσις, as the sheer emergence into presence by which the being shows itself from itself.

But how can one conceivably include the metaphysics of *esse* in the history of an oblivion of Being? What possible sense can there be in speaking of a philosophy whose whole focus is on the existential act-of-being, the very act in virtue of which a thing is rather than is not, as somehow forgetful of Being? It is hard to imagine forgetfulness here, where everything turns on the doctrine of *esse*. Indeed, at the summit of this doctrine stands the notion of God, not as "a" being, but as subsistent Being itself, *ipsum esse subsistens*. Far from forgetting Being, everything in an existential metaphysics is focused on it.

Now, it is my opinion that an "existential" metaphysics in the Thomistic sense, in the sense of a philosophy which gives primacy to the act of existence, does not stand outside the scope of what Heidegger means by the oblivion of Being, that the "essentialism" criticized by Gilson and the "oblivion of Being" are not the same. No matter which principle gains the primacy, the understanding of Being in terms of essence and existence belongs to the oblivion in the Heideggerian sense. One cannot extricate the metaphysics of St. Thomas from this charge, in my opinion—not if one comes to grips with the fully radical meaning of Heidegger's critique, not if one really gets to the bottom of what he means. The usual response to Heidegger's critique which is made by the followers of St. Thomas seems to me too facile; it underestimates the radicality of Heidegger's criticisms.

For as his thought developed, Heidegger ceased to say that the problem with metaphysics is that it is preoccupied with beings to the neglect of Being. That is a misleading way to put it, one which does not get to the core of the issue. For Heidegger eventually came to the conclusion that the word "Being" belongs to the metaphysicians and that it could no longer do service for what he wanted to think, for the genuine matter to be thought. "Being" has been the subject of every metaphysical or, as he says, "onto-theo-logical" account of beings from Plato to Nietzsche. The real concern of thought is, not the Being of the metaphysicians, but that which grants Being as the subject matter of metaphysics. It is not the distinction between Being and beings which concerns Heidegger, but that which opens up this distinction in each and every metaphysical epoch. All metaphysics moves within the distinction between Being and beings, and in each case Being is thought as some kind of ground or cause of beings. This is clearly true of St. Thomas' metaphysics, which is centered on the distinction between pure subsistent Being, *esse subsistens*, and finite beings, *ens participatum*. Finite beings participate in and depend on Being itself, while Being, as the subsistent Being which is God, communicates itself to beings.

Hence, if there is no oblivion of "Being" here, there is an oblivion of the dif-ference which opens up the difference between Being and beings, between *esse* and *ens*, within which St. Thomas thinks. The real matter to be thought, in Heidegger's view, is that dif-ference, which he calls in German *Unter-Schied* (literally: the inter-scission), which grants to Thomas the possibility of thinking in terms of *esse* and *ens*. The matter to be thought is also called by Heidegger *Ereignis*, the Event of Appropriation, the event which sends Being to thought and makes the history of metaphysics possible. *Ereignis* does not mean Being but that which grants Being. We do not say that Being "is" but that "there is/*es gibt*" Being, and the *Ereignis* is the "It" which gives Being to thought. The history of metaphysics is the history of the various ways in which metaphysicians have named Being while leaving the "It" which gives Being unthought. It is the history of diverse dispensations of Being (*Seinsgeschick*) in which Being is sent while the It itself remains behind.

The essential thing from Heidegger's standpoint is not to be taken in by any of these epochal dispensations of Being, not to submit to the metaphysical picture which dominates a given age. The essential thing is to think the sending and not to be taken in by what is sent, to think the giving and not to lose oneself in the gift. All metaphysics makes use of the difference between Being and beings, but metaphysics never thematizes the dif-fering in the difference, that which opens up the difference. Metaphysics thinks the different—Being and beings—but not the dif-ference as such. Plato thinks the difference between εἶδος and individual; Aristotle, between first and second οὐσία; Thomas, between *esse subsistens* and *ens participatum*. But none of these thinkers who stand in the light within which metaphysics occurs thinks the granting of that light, thinks the clearing, the very light process by means of which the ontological difference between Being and beings is illuminated.

The history of metaphysics is the history of competing theories about what Being means, but no metaphysician has undertaken to think this very history as itself what is to be thought, and to think it precisely as the withdrawal of that which is to be thought. To answer Heidegger's critique of metaphysics would at the very least demand an historical acuity, an ability to make the historical "reduction," to use the language of phenomenology, which it is impossible to demand of St. Thomas and impossible to believe that he possessed. Thomas thought Being "naïvely"—from an historical point of view—in the "natural attitude." For St. Thomas thought Being in the terms which were granted to him. His genius was to bring the terms of the Aristotelian tradition which he inherited to a consummating conclusion, one indeed which was so complete as to spell the end of that tradition and to prepare the way for its breakdown and a new *Geschick* (sending, dispensation). Thomas exhausted the possibilities of thinking Christianity in terms of the metaphysics of Plato, Aristotle, and Scholasticism. But his genius was decidedly not to bring this tradition as a whole into question, to question the terms which were handed down to him, to wonder about the sending of Being in the Roman–Latin language he spoke as a *magister*, to wonder whence these terms and categories, this language, this whole metaphysical constellation sprang. From the standpoint of Heidegger, Thomas thinks naïvely within this tradition and leaves the original sending of Being in oblivion.

Seen from this point of view, the argument of Lotz, Rioux, Siewerth, and others that Thomas does indeed think Being in contradistinction from beings, that this is an "existential" metaphysics of *esse* itself, is a dead end; it does not touch Heidegger's point. In fact, it confirms it. For what has above all fallen into oblivion is the primordial Greek experience of ἀλήθεια, the very process by which the world, as an historical configuration of meaning, has been opened up, has come to be manifest. Ἀλήθεια means the emergence into the open, the process by which things are brought into the clear, into the sphere of the un-concealed (ἀ-λήθη). Now, Aquinas is a philosopher, not of ἀλήθεια, but of *actualitas*. He is a philosopher, not of the unconcealment process itself, but of a causal–ontological account of things which, though it itself is made possible by the unconcealment process, lets ἀλήθεια itself fall into oblivion. The early Greeks thought Being in terms of φύσις, which means the simple splendor of appearance, the gentle emergence of things into the light. By the time of Aristotle, φύσις is characterized in terms of ἐνέργεια, which means to set something into the work (ἐν-ἔργον), the way an artist does. Now, an artist is to be thought, not in terms of making and producing, but in terms of disclosing, of bringing something into appearance. But the Romans, the builders of roads and empires, rendered this word as *actualitas*; hence, they conceived Being in terms of acting and action (*agere, actio, actus*), of doing, making, producing. The metaphysics of "actuality" in St. Thomas is a captive of this metaphysical scheme, which is then wedded to the Christian doctrine of creation. Hence, Thomas does not meditate the simple essence of "presencing" (*Anwesen*, coming-into-presence); he maps out the metaphysical dynamics of a thoroughly causal conception of reality. He conceives of Being in terms of maker and made, creator and created. The doctrine of essence and *esse*, far from being the supreme insight into Being, is the final seal on its oblivion. For essence means "that which a thing was (= is supposed) to be" (*quid quod erat esse*), that is, the idea of what is to be made, and existence signifies that the idea has been converted into reality, what was previously mere idea now stands (*sistere*) outside of (*ex*) its causes. Thomistic metaphysics articulates the doctrine of creation in the Roman language of production. It belongs to the escalating oblivion of Being as ἀλήθεια. In fact, it is aligned with the technological conception of Being of the present day, and even bears a relationship to the Nietzschean conception of Being as will.

Hence, all those protestations that Thomas is the philosopher of Being *par excellence* because he thinks Being as act, far from eluding Heidegger's critique, in fact substantiate it. For Thomas, to be is to be in act, and to be in act is to be capable of action and of rendering other beings actual. To the extent that a being is in act, it is causally efficacious. Creatures are capable of producing finite effects; God, infinite effects. *Agere sequitur esse*. Indeed, *agere* is the meaning of *esse*. St. Thomas does not practice a quiet, meditative savoring of the presencing of Being; he has instead reduced presencing to *realitas*, *causalitas*, *actualitas*.

Now, it seems to me that Heidegger is largely right about all this. St. Thomas is a causal thinker, an "aetiologist" rather than an "alethiologist."[1] And if one understands precisely what Heidegger means by oblivion, St. Thomas is part of it, not an exception or an antidote to it. Thomas is not to be excluded from the history of metaphysics as Heidegger conceives it; he is a good example of just what Heidegger means by it. I think that the diverse attempts which have been made to defend St. Thomas against this Heideggerian critique have by and large not come to grips with the radically alethiological character of Heidegger's point of view. And one only makes matters worse by insisting that *esse* is the *act* of Being.

But if Heidegger is "correct"—to turn his own distinction against him—one cannot but wonder if he has told the whole "truth," if that is all there *is* to St. Thomas. For after all St. Thomas is not a Cartesian or post-Cartesian philosopher of the system, not a cold-blooded rationalist, but a man of profound religious piety with a sense of the sacred and of the holy. One suspects that there is another dimension to St. Thomas and perhaps another way out of this Heideggerian critique. But where is one to look for evidence to support such a view? Let us look for the moment—to use a Heideggerian strategy—at the painting of St. Thomas by the fifteenth-century Flemish painter Justus of Ghent which hangs in the Louvre.[2] Our eyes are drawn first to the center of the picture, to the hands of the saint. The right index finger presses the left thumb, as if to say *"primo"*; clearly Thomas is enumerating a point of metaphysical theology. The hands are enlisted in the service of *ratio*, of discursive argumentation. Yet they are delicately poised, and the little finger of the right hand is spaced from the rest of the hand as if it were lifting fine china. The hands belong to a figure which is calmly seated. The pleats of the robe fall gently to his lap; the rolls of the cowl ring peacefully around his neck. The round, soft face is quiet and unperturbed. The eyes are soft, with a composed gaze. The figure is one of perfect tranquillity, complete composure. If the hands are pressed into the service of *ratio*, the whole figure is a model of *intellectus*, of meditative calm. Whatever theological argument is propounded here proceeds from a man of contemplative gifts, one who meditates heavenly things. If there is *ratio* here, it is a *ratio* enveloped by *intellectus*, a *ratio* which knows its place. If this man is a *magister*, he has a look of prayerfulness and contemplative peace.

The painting belongs to the world of St. Thomas. It opens up that world, discloses it, just as, in Heidegger's analysis (*Holz.*[2] 19/163), van Gogh's painting of the shoes reveals the world of the peasant. One can hear the silence in this painting; one can see the meditative calm. The painting discloses a world not of disputatious Scholastic argumentation but of composure, not of *disputatio* but of *pietas*, not of calculativeness but of meditation and *Gelassenheit*. When one hears the words of St. Thomas in the *Summa*, one may miss the silence. But the painting discloses the silence of St. Thomas, which gives the words their meaning.

What I am suggesting then is that the commentators and defenders of St. Thomas have tended to miss the mark in dealing with Heidegger. They have taken St. Thomas at his word and tried to match him against Heidegger word for word, text for text. But they have not noticed, it seems to me, how Heidegger reads great thinkers like Aristotle and Kant. He takes not only their words, but their silence; he meditates not only what they say but what they leave unsaid. He does not ignore the testimony of the great artists. He finds a depth dimension in these thinkers of which the thinkers themselves are to some extent unaware. Now, it seems to me that the metaphysics of St. Thomas likewise deserves this kind of thoughtful interpretation, this kind of hermeneutic wresting loose of its innermost tendencies. In my view, it is superficial to stop at St. Thomas' words, to hear only the clatter of Scholastic argumentation, to pay no heed to the silent religious life of St. Thomas which is left unexpressed in the impressive written corpus he has left behind. I think that Thomas, as much as Kant, as much as Aristotle, needs and deserves a deeper rendering, a more thoughtful appreciation. It is impossible to believe that if Heidegger had undertaken to examine the medieval *Seinsgeschick* in terms of medieval painting and architecture, if he had undertaken to listen to the depth dimension in St. Thomas in the light of medieval art, he would have reached the same conclusions.[3] I am suggesting that the way in which one can meet the Heideggerian critique of St. Thomas is to meet it on its own grounds: not by showing that "existential metaphysics" satisfies everything which is required by the "thought of Being" and eludes the oblivion of Being—for it does not; but rather (and this all the commentators have missed) by showing that in St. Thomas metaphysics itself tends to break down and to pass into a more profound experience of Being—even though the elaborate machinery of St. Thomas' Scholasticism tends to conceal this fact. The thing to do, in the spirit of Heidegger himself, is to bring out into the open, to wrest loose and set free everything Scholastic metaphysics tends by its nature to conceal. Heidegger's critique of St. Thomas can be met by showing that in fact St. Thomas too knows the "step back" out of metaphysics. But this is a step which most Thomistic commentators have not thought to make, for it can be made only by "overcoming" metaphysics.

I shall propose in the pages which follow precisely such a retrieval of St. Thomas. That is to say, I shall undertake to show a more essential tendency in Thomistic metaphysics by which that metaphysics tends of its own momentum to self-destruct and to pass into a more essential experience. A retrieval or deconstruction is, not a destruction or leveling, but a dismantling of the surface apparatus of a thought in order to find its essential nerve, its animating center. But where is the principle of such a deconstruction of St. Thomas to be found? And what is to prevent this interpretation from being a capricious invention, a violent rewriting of St. Thomas in the image of Heidegger? It is no less than Thomas himself who tells us of the need for this deconstruction and for the principle in accord with which it is to be carried out. It is recorded that on the morning of December 6, 1273, shortly after he had finished saying Mass, St. Thomas underwent a transforming mystical experience, after which he fell silent. And on one of the rare moments on which he broke his silence St. Thomas said to his friend and secretary Reginald: "Everything which I have written seems like straw to me compared to what I have seen and what has been revealed to me." These are among the last words which we know St. Thomas to have spoken, and they provide us with an essential hermeneutic principle, a principle of retrieval. They tell us how to read the texts which have been handed down to us. For what has been written must give way to ἀλήθεια—what has been revealed and seen. In the light of the alethiological, the texts appear as straw; that is to say, the texts need to be deconstructed in the light of the experience of Being—of *esse subsistens*—to which they give way.

What the legend of St. Thomas' final days teaches us is that beneath the scaffolding of his Scholastic metaphysics there lies an animating mystical experience. St. Thomas' metaphysics is not the opposite of his mystical life, but a concealed, discursive, representational—one is tempted to say "alienated"—way of expressing it. The metaphysical systems of men like Bonaventure, Thomas, and Meister Eckhart are nothing like the tough-minded, onto-theo-logical structures of the post-Cartesian systems; instead they offer a conceptualization of an essentially mystical view of life. Now, the high irony in all this is that in 1916 Heidegger himself saw this very clearly and warned in ringing terms against thinking that in the Middle Ages Scholasticism and mysticism were opposites (FS[2] 410). Heidegger was at that time intensely interested in medieval thought, and one of his express intentions then was to undertake an interpretation of it precisely in terms of its mystical tradition, especially the mysticism of Meister Eckhart, a subject which I have explored at length on another occasion.[4] But after 1919 Heidegger abandoned these aspirations and

threw away the key with which to unlock medieval Scholastic metaphysics. It is of no little interest to me that Heidegger can find a depth
dimension in Aristotle—who is, I think, a hard-nosed man of reason
who all but invented the principle of causality as a philosophical
principle—but insist that St. Thomas is an onto-theo-logician. And,
of course, the Heideggerians have fallen on Heidegger's breast in this
matter and simply repeat his declarations.

I shall therefore in the final chapter of this study offer a relatively
detailed retrieval of St. Thomas' metaphysics, one which will show,
in my view, that Thomas took *ratio* to be a defective and infirm instrument of whose shortcomings we must continually be aware. I
shall show that in St. Thomas *ratio* tends of its own nature to break
down and to pass into *intellectus*. I shall follow the lead in this regard
of Pierre Rousselot, who has shown in a brilliant and penetrating
analysis in *The Intellectualism of St. Thomas* that intellect for St.
Thomas is only in its more superficial and defective operations a
faculty of discursive argumentation, and that it is on a more radical
level a faculty of mystical—and, ultimately, of beatific—union. It
will become clear in this context that beyond propositional truth,
which is *adequatio*, there is the more profound and more essential
truth of *assimilatio, unio*. At this point Thomas is talking about the
intimacy of mystical union, about the experiential immediacy of face-
to-face vision. All objectivism and representationalism have melted
away. There can be no question here of onto-theo-logic, of what
Heidegger calls "metaphysics." At this point, for St. Thomas, metaphysics is something to be overcome.

This is a conclusion which will not be accepted by every Thomist,
but St. Thomas, it has been pointed out, was not a Thomist. It is a
deconstructive reading of St. Thomas but one which in my mind, far
from doing him violence, actually brings out a deeper tendency within his work which not only extricates him from the Heideggerian
critique—and I know of no other interpretation which does—but is
in fact profoundly faithful to his own deepest intentions, intentions
which, it can be said, were not always clearly before his own eyes.
There is no hubris in saying that the interpreter can understand a
thinker better than the thinker understood himself. For the interpreter has the light afforded by the intervening years.

In the pages which follow, my sights are always set on the matter
to be thought, and not only on the exegesis of texts. My concern is

always with the question of Being and with the way in which Being is to be thought. And it is my view that the only faithful way to think Being is in what I call here an "alethiology of Being," or—to the displeasure of the Heideggerians—an "alethiological metaphysics." I myself think that the objective, discursive, causally minded method of traditional metaphysics discloses to us, not Being itself, but only a creature of our own making. I think that Being is "granted" to us in an experience which we must make every attempt to render faithfully. This is not only explicitly taught by Heidegger. I find it to be implicitly and more obscurely taught by Thomas as well. For when I turn to Thomas I always see the deeper dynamism of the *intellectus*, the *capax dei*, brought out by Rousselot. Intellect can never be satisfied by ratiocination; it wants face-to-face vision, firsthand seeing, union. It seeks to let God be God, to quote Meister Eckhart—who is in my view a more faithful follower of St. Thomas than many Thomists are prepared to admit. And so I find a common wisdom in Heidegger and Thomas on this point. I do not say that mysticism is "thought," as Heidegger means it, or that Thomas Aquinas properly deconstructed turns out to be Heidegger. The mystical unity of *intellectus* and *esse* is worlds removed from the thought of Being in Heidegger's sense. The light in which we see the light of which St. Thomas speaks is not Heidegger's clearing, but it is the only kind of Thomistic alethiology which is possible. I am arguing simply that hitherto all attempts to carry out a confrontation of Heidegger and St. Thomas have failed because they remain lodged on the level of St. Thomas' metaphysics. And I am arguing further that once the depth dimension, the mystical element in St. Thomas' metaphysics, is wrested loose from this metaphysical encasement one finds a Thomas who eludes Heidegger's critique of metaphysics, for whom metaphysics is something to be overcome, a more essential thinker in whom Heidegger would have been compelled to concede that here too—and not just in Eckhart—there is a profound unity of mysticism and thought. The key to St. Thomas lies in the *non possum*. In the *non possum* there lies the most profound possibility of St. Thomas' thought. And, as Heidegger says, possibility is higher than actuality.

The route which I shall follow in developing this argument is as follows. I shall begin with the still untold and unlikely story of Heidegger's earliest beginnings in Scholasticism and South German Catholicism. This is a story which deserves to be told in its own right, as an essential piece of the history of contemporary German philosophy, but it is also essential to my purposes here. For it will be very instructive for us to know what Heidegger saw in Scholasticism, and what he knew about it, and it will help us to understand the full-scale critique which he made of Scholasticism in 1928, and then again in 1943, which will be the subject of the next two chapters. Then I shall undertake a Thomistic defense, first by examining Gilson's thesis concerning "existential metaphysics" and his reading of the history of metaphysics, and then by following up the metaphysics of participation, where we will see how sharply St. Thomas thematizes the ontological difference between *esse subsistens* and *ens participatum*. Next I shall return to the texts of Heidegger to set forth his critique of metaphysics in the fully radical version of his mature years. That will be followed by a treatment of Heidegger's reading of *Anwesen* in the early Greeks and a comparison with Thomistic *esse*. Then, except for a review of the variously futile attempts which have been made in the literature to defend St. Thomas against Heidegger's critique, I will be prepared for the concluding effort at a deconstructive reading of St. Thomas' metaphysics, whose main lines have been sketched here. And with that the argument of the present study will be complete.

NOTES

1. I use the word "alethiology" throughout this study to refer to Heidegger's doctrine of Being as ἀλήθεια. I take alethiology to be the successor of his earlier "phenomenology," a word which ties his later thought too closely to Husserl and to the tradition of transcendental subjectivity, which he takes to be essentially "metaphysical." *The Oxford English Dictionary* defines "alethiology" as the science of truth, and points out that the word is used in this sense in William Hamilton's *Logic*, IV 69. F. W. von Herrmann also speaks of the later Heidegger's "aletheiological conception of truth" as opposed to the "transcendental" conception of truth in *Being and Time* (*Die Selbstinterpretation Martin Heideggers* [Meisenheim: Hain, 1964], pp. 45–46). I follow the OED spelling.

2. This painting is reproduced opposite the title page of the first volume of *St. Thomas Aquinas, 1274–1974: Commemorative Studies*, ed. Armand A. Maurer, c.s.b., 2 vols. (Toronto: Pontifical Institute of Mediaeval Studies, 1974).

3. For example, Kenneth Clark writes of carvings of the kings and queens on the central doors of Chartres Cathedral: "Indeed I believe that the refine-

ment, the look of selfless detachment and the spirituality of these heads is something entirely new in art. Beside them the gods and heroes of ancient Greece look arrogant, soulless and even slightly brutal. I fancy that the faces which look out at us from the past are the truest meaning of an epoch" (*Civilisation* [New York: Harper & Row, 1969], p. 56). And if one is inclined to doubt the importance of art historians for Heidegger, one should see his comments on Wilhelm Vöge in Hans Seigfried, "Martin Heidegger: A Recollection," *Man and World*, 3, No. 1 (February 1970), 4.

4. The present study relies upon the argument of my earlier book *The Mystical Element in Heidegger's Thought* (Athens: Ohio University Press, 1978) that mysticism, though not identical with thought, lies outside the sphere of influence of the principle of sufficient reason and, like thought itself and genuine poetry, is a non-representational, non-metaphysical experience of Being. Mysticism too takes the step back out of metaphysics. In fact, I argue, Meister Eckhart in particular has actually had a formative influence on the development of Heidegger's later work. Now, the case of Meister Eckhart is especially worthy of mention. For not only does Eckhart influence Heidegger, but he himself, as a successor of St. Thomas in the Dominican chair at Paris where he taught a quarter of a century later, is strongly under the influence of "Brother Thomas." Meister Eckhart is a middle term between Heidegger and Aquinas, a point which was first mentioned by Bernhard Welte in "Thomas von Aquin und Heideggers Gedanke von der Seinsgeschichte" (*Zeit und Geheimnis* [Freiburg: Herder, 1975], pp. 181–202), and which I shall exploit in the final chapter of this study.

1

Heidegger's Beginnings and the Project of a Dialogue with Scholasticism

ONE SUMMER DAY IN 1907, when Heidegger was back in his hometown of Messkirch, on vacation from the Jesuit *Gymnasium* in Freiburg which he attended, the young student met with Father Conrad Gröber, who also hailed from Messkirch.[1] Father Gröber knew the Heidegger family well. They were devout Catholics. The father, Friedrich, was sexton in the Church of Saint Martin, a patron of this little but much distinguished *Stadt* in central southern Germany, after whom indeed the young man had been named. The Heidegger family lived in a small but impeccably neat masonry house not more than thirty yards across the courtyard from St. Martin's. Next door was the rectory. Father Gröber and young Martin discussed the youngster's plans. He would be eighteen years old at the end of September and, after graduating from the *Gymnasium*, would enter the seminary. The young man would make an outstanding priest; he was intellectually gifted, very sensitive, and possessed of a strong religious orientation. Father Gröber had a fatherly interest in Martin. People from Messkirch are close. There is a deep bond between the townsmen of this simple place, whose history stretches back seven hundred years. Indeed, if one visits today a charming little restaurant on the main street of the town, in order to partake of a bountiful *Mittagessen*, one will see pictures and paintings of its most distinguished citizenry from over the centuries hanging on its walls. Lately they have hung the pictures of Gröber and Heidegger there too.

Father Gröber and young Martin talked of many things that day
—the difficulties of priestly chastity for a young man, the requirements of health, the responsibility of directing the conscience of simple people, people like themselves, of the soil. They walked through
the tree-lined lane which leads from St. Martin's church, through the
garden doors, and out along the field path (FW 10/32). (Today the
citizens of Messkirch have named this walk after Heidegger.) Their
thoughts turned to theological matters, and the priest stressed to
Heidegger the importance of a sound training in philosophy if one
is to make one's way in theology. Along these lines he had a gift for
Martin. He had brought along this day a copy of an excellent and
trustworthy guide to Aristotle. He explained to the young man the
importance of Pope Leo's encyclical in 1879 (*Aeterni Patris*), which
urged Catholic schools and seminaries to return to the serious pursuit
of philosophy—in particular, that of St. Thomas. And he explained
to him the debt of St. Thomas to Aristotle, and how, at the heart of
the systems of Aristotle and Thomas, there stood "metaphysics,"
which, he said, is the science of first causes. Father Gröber had found
an excellent book on Aristotle's *Metaphysics*, written by Franz Brentano. He explained that, unfortunately, Brentano had left the Church,
but not before writing this fine book.[2] The year Brentano wrote this
book (1862) he was twenty-two years of age and would spend some
months living with the Dominicans. The next year he would enter
the seminary, to be ordained a priest in 1864. The important thing
about Brentano's book, Father Gröber added, is its reliance upon the
great medieval commentators on Aristotle. He pointed to the long
quote from Thomas Aquinas' *Commentary* on Aristotle's *Metaphysics* and the citation of Pico della Mirandola's remark that "Without
Thomas Aristotle is mute."[3] Heidegger took the book gratefully from
his "fatherly friend" and he kept his words in his heart. He would read
this book carefully, he vowed to himself, for it would no doubt be
important for his future studies.

We have no way of knowing, of course, the exact contents of the con-
versation on that day in 1907, but the reconstruction which I have
made of it is faithful to everything we know of Heidegger's beginnings. The book the young man received that day bore him off in
two directions which it was his own peculiar genius to bring together.
It took him back to Aristotle and forward to Husserl, back to the

Greek experience of Being, forward to the phenomenology of experience. That is all well known by now. But what has been overlooked so far is the deeply pious and Catholic beginnings of Heidegger's life, and the "Aristotelian–Scholastic" setting in which he was introduced to philosophy. We cannot forget that Heidegger was initiated into philosophy as a young aspirant to the Catholic priesthood, and that the first "tradition" which he knew was medieval Scholasticism. He came to Aristotle and the problem of Being only through the Scholastics. If Heidegger was to become a critic of Scholasticism, it was only after a period of association with it during which he projected an exciting line of interpretation—one which, had it been carried out, would have represented a breakthrough in Scholastic thought comparable to the initiatives of Maréchal and Rahner. Now, in this study of Heidegger and St. Thomas, the first order of business is to probe this early association with Scholasticism. For not only will this be of interest to the historian of Heidegger's thought, but it will tell us what Heidegger's interests in Scholasticism were, what he knew about it, and why he felt compelled to move beyond it.

"A Fundamentally New Kind
of Treatment of
Medieval Scholasticism"

Heidegger's relationship with Scholasticism was never conventional. And I doubt whether anyone can be justified in calling the Heidegger of these early years—from 1907 to 1916, the year he met Husserl—a "Scholastic" philosopher. He was his own man from the start, independent, self-minded, never one to follow a party line—be it Neo-Scholastic, Neo-Kantian, or phenomenological. Winifred Franzen suggests that the reason he broke off his studies for the priesthood was the "dogmatic ridigity and narrowness" with which priests were trained in Germany in 1909.[4] This suggestion seems very plausible to me, in the light of everything we know about the frame of mind of this young thinker. Rigidity and dogmatism were antipodal to the philosophical spirit which was stirring within him. The young Heidegger did not adopt the standpoint of one of the great masters—Thomas, Scotus, and Suárez are the ones he mentions most—only to expend his energies defending that standpoint from attack from other

quarters in Scholasticism. Nor did he enter into "Scholastic debates"
—about the real distinction of essence and existence, the primacy of
the intellect over the will, God's knowledge vs. His freedom, etc.

Though he showed the greatest respect for the philological work
which was being done by Clemens Bäumker and Martin Grabmann,
and recognized the indispensability of their philological and historical research, this was not the work which interested him: "But with
the mere assembling, registering, and editing of contents, not all the
preconditions for an assessment of the deposit of medieval philosophical thought are fulfilled" (FS² 194). His task was not to edit medieval
manuscripts or to trace the lines of the genesis of medieval thought
from the Greeks through the Arabs to the thirteenth century. Still it
should not go unnoticed that his scholarship in this regard was great
enough to merit him repeated consideration for a post in medieval
philosophy at Marburg and that the appointment which he did in fact
receive there was in part a position in medieval thought.[5]

Heidegger's interests in medieval Scholasticism were neither partisan and dogmatic nor historical and scholarly. What then? The
main task for the young man—and this would be a constant for him
—was the matter itself (*die Sache selbst*), the issues and problems of
philosophy. He wanted "a really *philosophical* assessment of Scholasticism" (FS² 195); he wanted to study medieval philosophy philosophically: "The history of philosophy is not *only* history and it cannot be if it is supposed to belong to the scientific field of philosophy.
The history of philosophy has a different relationship to philosophy
than does, for example, the history of mathematics to mathematics.
And this is not because of the *history* of philosophy but because of
the history of *philosophy*" (FS² 195). Heidegger wanted to solve
philosophical problems and he wanted to seek out in medieval thinkers strategies for attacking issues. That is why the Introduction to his
Habilitationsschrift is entitled "The Necessity of a Consideration of
Scholasticism in Terms of a History of Problems." The idea of a
Problemgeschichte, a history of problems, is of Neo-Kantian vintage,
but it can also be fitted together with Husserl's call in 1911, in *Philosophy as a Strict Science*, which Heidegger will quote many years later:
"The stimulus for investigation must start, not with philosophies, but
with issues and problems" (*die Sachen selbst*) (SD 69/62).

Problemgeschichte is not a narrower kind of history, in which one
follows the particular thread of but one philosophical problem. It is

not historical research at all but philosophical research. It looks to *history* for the solution of *problems*; hence its name. It sees history not merely as a chronological, historical sequence but as a partner in a philosophical dialogue. One can clearly see here how Heidegger's thought begins in a dialogue with, a retrieving (*Wiederholung*) of, the tradition. And the tradition which first presented itself to him was the Aristotelian Scholasticism of the Middle Ages. His thought begins in a dialogue with Scholasticism, and his goal is to unpack its store of philosophical goods (*philosophische Gedankengüter*), to make it hand over (*über-liefern, trans-dare*) its wealth.

Hence, Heidegger's relationship with medieval Scholasticism was quite independent. He himself speaks of his work as "a first attempt at a fundamentally new kind of treatment of medieval Scholasticism, that is, a first attempt at interpreting and evaluating it with the aid of the contents of philosophical problems . . ." (FS² 204). By and large, the Scholastics of the day kept their distance from Heidegger. It was this independence of mind which prevented Josef Geyser, one of the leading Scholastic thinkers in Germany at the time, from taking an interest in the young man while Geyser was on the faculty and Heidegger a student at Freiburg. That task fell to Rickert and Husserl. Martin Grabmann alone took notice of his work on Duns Scotus —the Franciscans ignored it. It was not what they expected; it was not a reverent *expositio* but a dialogue with Scotus from the standpoint of Husserl and modern German logic. Indeed, they must have thought, it was concerned, not with Scotus or the *Grammatica speculativa* at all, but with solving certain problems in philosophical logic. And so true was this that it mattered not a whit to Heidegger's argument that Grabmann later proved that the book was in fact authored by one Thomas of Erfurt, not Scotus himself. It still belonged to the same circle of problems.

The problems which interested the young thinker were those which were being debated by the outstanding philosophers of the day in Germany—by Brentano, Husserl, and the young Lask; by Rickert, his major professor at Freiburg; and by the Marburg Neo-Kantians.[6] They were problems in logic and language and their relationship to reality, problems which suggest more the Anglo-American philosophies of today than either Scholasticism or the mature Heidegger. The problem of Being itself was only implicit at this point and made its presence felt only obliquely. The issue which most concerned him was "meaning" (*Sinn* or *Bedeutung*), its status, locus, and indeed "meaning." The question is posed in virtually every publication between 1912 and 1916. Heidegger argued against all forms of psychologism, a point on which the views of his Neo-Kantian teacher, Heinrich Rickert, his Scholastic *Doktorvater*, Artur Schneider, and Husserl, all converged. He insisted that the problem of the status of logical meaning cannot be solved by purely *logical* considerations, and that such a problem ultimately has a *metaphysical* bearing: logic requires its "true optics," which is metaphysics (FS² 406). Heidegger thus took part in the resurgence of metaphysics which was occurring in Germany in the first two decades of this century after the long epistemological drought called Neo-Kantianism. Heidegger found motives for this rebirth both in Scholasticism, with its characteristic emphasis on the primacy of metaphysics, and in modern thinkers like Emil Lask. Heidegger invoked the Scholastic tradition for help in solving a problem of contemporary relevance, convinced that the resources of Scholasticism—and especially of the sharp-witted Scotus—could be successfully brought to bear in dealing with these problems.

In calling for a strictly philosophical relationship to a past system of thought Heidegger was asking for rather a lot. He demanded an unlikely *coincidentia oppositorum* of both philosophical and historical acumen:

> A purely philosophical endowment and a really fruitful capacity for historical thinking are only rarely combined in one personality. Hence, it is understandable, especially if one takes into account the troublesomeness and protractedness of this pioneering work which is carried out with the most refined critical exactness in libraries and with manuscript collections, that one can reach a really *philosophical* assessment of Scholasticism only in exceptional cases [FS² 194–95].

If Husserl never achieved this integration, it is fair to say that Heidegger himself is not far removed from this ideal. For he has proved himself uniquely capable of this philosophical–historical ambidexterity.

Though the history of philosophy may appear to outsiders as a history of errors, a sequence of opinions in never-ending conflict, it is in fact something far deeper than that. For philosophy is the way in which the living personality comes to grips with the essential problems of existence (FS[2] 195–96). The history of philosophy, there-fore, is not a "development" (*Entwicklung*), a continuous advance in which each subsequent thinker takes the next logical step implied by the work of his predecessors, as in the history of science. It is, rather, an "unfolding" (*Auswicklung*) of certain determinate areas of philosophical investigation (FS[2] 196). The problem of freedom—to illustrate Heidegger's point—keeps getting posed anew in each new historical setting: it has a theological context in the Middle Ages, a Newtonian context for Kant, and a behavioristic context for us today. The horizons of the problem change in each age, and so philo-sophical thought is forced to circle back over to plumb again the same problem. The task for the problem-oriented history of philosophy is to sort out the different horizons, the differing ways in which the problem is posed (*Fragestellung*), in order to see what questions philosophers took themselves to be answering. And in getting at the *Fragestellung* one must be mindful that philosophical questions do not occur in isolation from one another. Any given problem belongs to a total context of problems, to what Heidegger will later call a "hermeneutical situation." It is particularly meaningless, Heidegger thinks, to juxtapose solutions which have been detached from their historical contexts. The result is a superficial doxography of various philosophical views, a catalogue without philosophical merit. Scho-lastic thinkers, Heidegger feels (FS[2] 197n4)—he mentions Grab-mann and also one Charles Sentroul, of whom more later—have been guilty of precisely this.

The task which Heidegger then had to set himself was to discrimi-nate the *Fragestellung* of modern from that of medieval philosophy, for he wanted to bring the results of medieval logic to bear on the problems of contemporary German logic. This he did as follows. In modern philosophy there is a strong sense of "method" which is lack-ing in medieval thought. The modern thinker has a heightened self-consciousness, including a consciousness of the steps which the mind takes as it proceeds. The medieval thinker, on the other hand, is lost in the subject matter itself, delivered over to the contents of thought, oblivious of the intricacies of the thought process itself. This explains the primacy which is given in medieval thought to principles and the universal and the absence of the idiosyncracies of the individual au-thor in the various medieval *Summae*. The medieval thinker is ori-ented toward the transcendent—God and the supersensible world—

and away from the flowing and transient world of the senses and of the "psychic stream" (cf. FS^2 197–99).

One can, of course, question whether the lack of methodic consciousness is all bad, Heidegger mentions. After all, nothing is more unproductive than an exclusive concern with method which spends all its efforts on planning ways to solve problems without ever entering into a solution, something of which medieval philosophy can never be accused. Moreover, the notion of method can be understood in an even deeper way than in the sense of mapping out epistemological strategies. If method means understanding the foundations which makes a certain circle of problems possible, establishing the principles which found an entire context of questions, then medieval philosophy can in no way be accused of lacking a consciousness of method: "The concept of method of this sort appears, however, to be a familiar matter in Scholasticism, at least insofar as it is filled with the genuine spirit of Aristotle. The reference to the treatise on first principles, the whole *Metaphysics* as a science of principles, testifies to this" (FS^2 210). The remark about the "genuine spirit of Aristotle" is important. For the day will come when Heidegger's critique of Scholastic metaphysics will amount to claiming that it has fallen out of a genuine understanding of Aristotle. Then the task will be to return to Aristotle himself, apart from the later Scholastic distortions.

But this brings us precisely to the advantage of Scholastic philosophy. For if it is lacking in a subjective self-consciousness, a self-reflective methodology, Scholasticism gives a certain privileged place to the objective content, the things themselves, the matter to be thought, and by reason of this orientation, it comes into convergence in essential ways with phenomenology:

> But in spite of these metaphysical "deposits" [= the metaphysical realities which belong to the Scholastic viewpoint], which are understandable in view of the total attitude of Scholastic thought and which as such destroy the "phenomenological reduction" or, more precisely, make it impossible, there still lie hidden in the Scholastic mode of thought certain moments of the phenomenological consideration, perhaps the strongest moments of all in it [FS^2 201–202].

Heidegger means, among other things, that the Scholastics possessed a strong sense of the intentionality of consciousness, its direction into real being. One can already see here how Heidegger's dialogue with the Scholastic position will inevitably put him at odds with Husserl: if intentionality means that consciousness is directed into the world, then the reduction is "made impossible." Moreover, Heidegger wanted to emphasize that the Scholastic theories of the soul, of eternal truths, and of the nature of thought, oppose it to every psychologistic interpretation of logic.

Thus, with the problems of modern logic firmly in mind, but with a heightened sense of the unique frame of mind of the medieval thinker, the task before us is to read the Scotist with an eye on what he has to say about problems of current logical interest. One can see how much of a difference existed between Heidegger and even the more progressive Scholastic thinkers of the day. Grabmann[7] and others stood within medieval philosophy and tried to show how it anticipated later developments, and thus contained certain modern elements; Heidegger stood within the contemporary problematic and tried to enter medieval thinkers into the debate. Grabmann was interested in some kind of comparative history; Heidegger was interested in philosophizing. Heidegger knew that Scholasticism and phenomenology were at one in their rejection of psychologism, and this became a focal point for his earliest studies, for it was a principal point of convergence between Aristotelian Scholasticism and Husserl. This, for him, was not an historical comparison but an element in his argument.

I shall devote the rest of this chapter to explaining the concrete investigations which Heidegger carried out between 1912 and 1916 in his efforts to solve these issues in philosophical logic in dialogue with Scholastic thought. I shall begin with his first published article, his early book reviews, and his doctoral dissertation, all of which appeared between 1912 and 1914. Then I shall survey the results of his impressive *Habilitationsschrift*. Finally I shall add a note on his relationship with the theologian Carl Braig.

Scholasticism and Transcendental Philosophy in the Writings of 1912–1914

Heidegger's first steps as a philosopher were taken in the shadows of two strong and competing "-isms": the transcendental philosophy of

"Neo-Kantianism," which reigned supreme in Germany from about 1870 to 1920, and "Neo-Scholasticism," which was localized to Catholic thinkers. As a student at Freiburg—and from 1909 to 1911 a Catholic seminarian—Heidegger was exposed to both influences. I have already mentioned Geyser, who is described in Überweg–Österreich as "the most significant and wide-ranging of the Neo-Thomistic philosophers of the present";[8] and Artur Schneider, his *Doktorvater* and a medievalist, who, among other things, argued against psychologism from a Scholastic standpoint. On the other side, there was the imposing figure of Heinrich Rickert, under whom Heidegger did his most serious work at Freiburg. (Heidegger was officially sponsored for the Ph.D. by Schneider only because of their common confessional affiliation—Catholicism.) As we read these early writings, we see Heidegger struggling to balance the claims of a metaphysical and realistically oriented Scholasticism with the insights of the transcendental standpoint. Although it is a bit aphoristic to say so, one can view *Being and Time* as in a not unimportant way the outcome of this conflict (cf. SZ, § 43a). With the Scholastics, Heidegger rejects the absorption of reality into consciousness (idealism); but with the transcendental thinkers, he rejects naïve realism. And with both movements he rejects psychologism, which had the combined wrath of both Scholasticism and Neo-Kantianism called down upon itself. Heidegger wants to affirm reality while at the same time giving an account of the subjective life in which reality is reached.

The Problem of Reality

In 1912 the youthful philosopher published his first article. Entitled "The Problem of Reality in Modern Philosophy," it appeared in *Philosophisches Jahrbuch der Görresgesellschaft*, a Catholic philosophical journal which until 1950 bore a sketch of St. Augustine on its title page. (Today it is edited by Max Müller under the title *Philosophisches Jahrbuch*.) Though the young author associates himself with Scholastic realism, he does not do so uncritically. Moreover, instead of reciting arguments from one of the Scholastic authors on behalf of realism, he takes up the work of Oswald Külpe, a contemporary thinker then of some importance,[9] whose work he thinks should serve as an impetus to further reflection on the part of the Scholastics: "The Aristotelian–Scholastic philosophy, which has always thought realistically, will not lose sight of this new epistemological movement [= critical realism]; it must be concerned with positive work which furthers it along" (FS² 15/70). The dialogue between Scholasticism and modernity has begun.

The article begins by rejecting the idea that philosophers can get by with "common sense" in dealing with the problem of the external world. Although this suffices for everyday life, philosophy must offer a scientific—that is, epistemological—account of our knowledge of the real world. But if modern epistemology has led us astray, the solution is not to abandon epistemology altogether but to construct a correct one—a realist epistemology. Heidegger points out that the philosophers of the tradition—the Greeks and the philosophers of the Middle Ages—were all realists. Realism was not called into question until Berkeley introduced his famous identification of *esse* and *percipi*. After Berkeley, idealism entrenched itself all the more deeply in Hume and in Kant, finally terminating in "the extravagant idealism of Hegel" (FS² 3/64). Philosophy "parted further and further from reality and from an understanding of the positing and determination of reality" (FS² 3/64–65). Hence, the title of this article: "reality" became a "problem" in philosophy only with the "modern" era. Indeed, it is no accident that the critique of Descartes, who is obviously the source of this tradition, by both Heidegger and the Scholastics follows a similar line of argumentation: viz., that Descartes raised a false problem based on an initially inadequate comprehension of the relationship between man and the world. But in this essay it is Berkeley, not Descartes, whom Heidegger singles out as the turning point. Before Berkeley, philosophy was securely anchored in the real world. But in the modern epoch it has fallen victim to "immanentism" or what Heidegger will call later on simply "subjectivism." And the principal task for modern philosophy, Külpe argues, the way out of the contemporary "crisis," if I may put words into his mouth, is to restore contact between the mind and real being.

Heidegger uses Külpe's expression "the positing [*Setzung*] and determination [*Bestimmung*] of reality." By *Setzung* he means the positing of reality in the sense of affirming its existence; by *Bestimmung*, the determination or characterization of its nature or essence. Kant, for example, allows us to posit the real (*Ding an sich*), but not to determine it, and this position Külpe calls "phenomenalism." Berkeley, on the other hand, denies that we can even posit a real world, and this position Külpe calls "immanentism" or "conscientialism." "Real" in this context means what the Scholastics call *ens reale, ens extra animam*, and what the moderns call "transcendent" as opposed to "immanent" being. Since the word "reality" (*Realität*) has the advantage of having its origin in the Latin word *res*, "thing," both Heidegger and Külpe prefer it to the German word *Wirklichkeit*. "Realism" for Külpe—and this was certainly the case for the Neo-Scholastics as well—is the position which maintains that the mind can both posit and determine reality.

But Heidegger's realism is not unmitigated and unqualified. One can see him searching for some way to take account of the contributions of the cognitive self, and hence of the transcendental standpoint. Thus he agrees in this article with Külpe's claim that it would be a "hasty move" to assert that the contents of perception in the form in which they present themselves to us are objective realities (FS[2] 12/69). Heidegger accepts Külpe's view that the data of sensation are subjective; the "real" world can be ascertained only by the physical sciences, even if the complete determination of the real world is an ideal task which cannot be achieved at any point in time. Thus Heidegger rejects common sense as a final court of appeal, and he rejects the realism of the senses, in favor of a version of scientific realism. In § 43 of *Ideas I* Husserl will present a penetrating critique of this very theory which Heidegger will evidently take to heart. For in the Conclusion to his *Habilitationsschrift* Heidegger will lament that Külpe remained so much under the spell of realism as not to have recognized the necessity of the transcendental standpoint (FS[2] 403n3). This, he thinks, is all the more ironic because, in seeing that the real world is not given to us simply in perception, Külpe was on the verge of seeing the active and creative role which is to be played by consciousness in giving birth to the object of knowledge.

In allowing for some kind of subjective element in his realism, Heidegger moved to the left of most Neo-Scholastics. For Heidegger had a greater sympathy for Kant than they did. Nor did Heidegger reject the Second Volume of the *Logical Investigations*, as Geyser did.[10] Heidegger appears to be unaware that the Louvain Scholastics, under the leadership of Mercier, held a view of perception similar to his own, and that they too sought to dialogue with Kant. (He makes no reference to the work of Pierre Rousselot; nor later on does he mention Maréchal.)

It is important to keep one's balance in describing Heidegger's position at this point. Heidegger wants to take account of the transcendental standpoint. But he remains committed to the affirmation of *reality*: to be is to be real; reality is the opposite of mere appearance. Idealism is not genuine metaphysics, for the idealist never attains true being, the really real world. That is why Heidegger will later speak, in the book on Duns Scotus, of a "breakthrough into true reality and real truth" (FS² 406). One might say that he is trying to reconcile the two different ideas of intentionality which he learned. He wanted to correct the Scholastic theory of intentionality for its lack of a fully developed sense of the subjective life of consciousness; and, at the same time, to modify the idealist tendencies of Husserl. Heidegger's adaptation of Husserl's phenomenology will consist in injecting a realist stream into its veins, even as he required realism to take account of the subjective life. By the time Heidegger met Husserl in 1916 he was already on his way to working out this reconciliation, a reconciliation which originated from his attempt to hold a dialogue with medieval Scholasticism.

The Problem of Kant

The year 1912 marked the appearance not only of Heidegger's first philosophical article, but also of his first book reviews, six of which were published in the Catholic periodical *Literarische Rundschau für das katholische Deutschland* between 1912 and 1914, its final year of publication. The *Rundschau* was edited by Joseph Sauer, a theology professor at Freiburg, and included Carl Braig on its board of consultants. Presumably Braig was instrumental in the appearance of the young graduate student's first published efforts. Four of the reviews are too short to be of much interest, but two of them—one on the logical literature of the day; the other on a book on Kant and Aristotle—are more substantive. He speaks as a Catholic—"we on the Catholic side" (FS² 53)—but, as we have come to expect, his attention is directed to contemporary philosophical problems.

The philosophy of Kant has always been a testing ground for discriminating orthodox from revisionist Scholasticism. Kant had cut the nerve of Catholic intellectualist philosophy and theology by declaring the unknowability of the real, metaphysical world. Kant was the "philosopher of Protestantism," denying reason to make room for faith, waylaying the old realistic metaphysics in order to make room for the claims of the heart and affectivity. The Catholic tradition wanted metaphysical reason to clear the way for faith; it argued for objectively established norms of conduct over the primacy of conscience. In general, it supported the way of the intellect over the way of the will and religious feeling—the Thomistic way over the Augustinian and Franciscan. Heidegger found himself caught up in the middle of this strife, which for him took the form of the conflict between Neo-Scholasticism and Neo-Kantianism. Hence, his review of a book entitled *Aristotle and Kant* by one Charles Sentroul, a student of Mercier's at Louvain, is of special interest to us. The title of this book names the conflicting tendencies Heidegger is struggling to adjudicate at this point in his life.

The Louvain Scholastics were opening a dialogue with Kant, the finest hour of which will be Maréchal's *Le Point de départ de la métaphysique*, published in four volumes between 1922 and 1926—with a fifth volume appearing posthumously in 1947. (I shall have occasion in the concluding chapter of this work to investigate the work of Pierre Rousselot, another Thomist in dialogue with Kant.) Although Heidegger appreciates the direction in which Sentroul is moving, he is not satisfied that Sentroul fully appreciates the strength of Kant's position. Mercier considered Kant the greatest of the modern philosophers and sought to develop a Thomistic theory of knowledge in response to the Kantian critique. Sentroul's book reflects not only Mercier's respect for Kant, but also his undisguised preference for Aristotelian Scholasticism.

In Heidegger's view, Sentroul's book does not simply collect citations from Kant and Aristotle for comparison; rather it gets right to the problems. And that is what gives the book its value. But Heidegger wonders if Sentroul has sufficiently considered the profoundly different intellectual climates (*geistesgeschichtliche Milieu*) of the two thinkers (FS[2] 40–50, 197n4). Here is the characteristic notion of a *Fragestellung*. One simply cannot rake up solutions for comparison; one has to understand the profoundly different character of the question and of the presuppositions of the questions—clearly a "hermeneutic" demand. Sentroul mistakenly thinks that the difference is that Kant presupposes the validity of the sciences, whereas Aristotle presupposes nothing. In fact, Aristotle's thought is laden with metaphysical presuppositions, and so in this sense is even more packed with presuppositions than Kant's is. Aristotle's thought is not presuppositionless; it simply makes different presuppositions. Both Kant and Aristotle assume the possibility of knowledge from the start. But Kant's aims are epistemological; he is interested in the "object of knowledge." And Aristotle's are metaphysical; he is interested in what is (*das Seiende*). Thus Sentroul fails to appreciate the fundamentally differing horizons within which Kant and Aristotle work, the standpoint of being and the standpoint of knowledge. These standpoints differ from one another, but they do not simply contradict one another. (One gets an intimation here of Heidegger's later view that although the great metaphysical systems differ from one another, each has its own justification.) Kant begins with the existence of the science of mathematics and physics and proceeds to show their transcendental conditions of possibility. This is not a dogmatic presupposition, as Sentroul would have it, but the nature of the transcendental method. Kant works from an epistemological standpoint; Aristotle, from that of the psychology of knowledge. And on this point Scholasticism has something to learn from Kant: "Up until now the epistemological attitude has been missing from Aristotelian–Scholastic philosophy" (FS² 53).

The most interesting text in this review, however, is Heidegger's criticism of the correspondence theory of truth. Sentroul concedes the difficulty of erecting a comparison between the thing itself and our thought of the thing (or our judgment about it), but he believes that one can escape this difficulty by distinguishing logical truth from ontological truth. The ontological truth of a thing is the conformity of the thing with what it ought to be (as it is thought by God); logical truth is the conformity of our judgment to its ontological truth. Such a move is a transparent failure for Heidegger, for it simply restates the problem one more time and in new terms. Now, the other term of the *adequatio* is, not the thing, but its ontological truth; yet clearly this solution is revisited by the same objections as those which plagued the first version of the *adequatio* theory.

In connection with this, Heidegger also rejects Sentroul's theory of the copulative "is" as an identity, which is a *real* relationship, a relationship which befits *things* (*res*). He prefers Lotze's theory that the Being (*Sein*) of the copula is "validity" (*Geltung*). *Sein* means *Gelten* for the young Heidegger: to be is to be valid of, to hold good for. Sentroul lacks an adequate theory of the distinction between the ideal and the real, and has no means whatsoever to account for ideal–logical objects, such as mathematical objects. Indeed, he even lapses into a psychologistic interpretation of Kant which stems from Schopenhauer.

One can see the direction in which Heidegger is moving. He wants to erect a transcendental theory which will somehow complement from the subjective side the one-sidedly objectivistic reflections of Scholasticism. Our knowledge of *being* (Scholastic objectivism) must be balanced by an account of the being of knowledge (transcendental theory). Furthermore, the being of knowledge must be safeguarded in its own proper integrity, and not reduced to terms which befit things instead of knowledge. Heidegger's demands are transcendental and are common to the *Logical Investigations* and to Neo-Kantianism. His intention is not to overthrow Scholasticism but to awaken it to the new problems which belong to the hitherto neglected transcendental standpoint. So whatever the shortcoming of Sentroul's book, it at least is a contribution toward opening the dialogue of Scholasticism with Kant: "We on the Catholic side have no surplus of thoroughly scientific studies of Kant which can be taken seriously. Sentroul's book [therefore] represents noteworthy progress . . ." (FS[2] 53).

The Problem of Logic

As we have seen, Heidegger's interests in these early years ultimately centered on the problems of logic, a fact which may appear surprising today but, when more carefully examined, is quite understandable. He was interested in the constellation of problems surrounding the foundations of logic which he no doubt encountered initially in the first volume of the *Logical Investigations*. He disputed the prejudice of the two dominant schools of thought with which he was in contact, Neo-Kantianism and Neo-Scholasticism, that logic was a finished system. The Scholastics had so thoroughly canonized the Aristotelian syllogistic that the study of logic amounted to no more than learning the ancient formulas and such acronyms as *Barbara celarent*. Heidegger saw clearly that formal logic had been considerably expanded by the class calculus of Russell and Whitehead and by the logic of relations, but this was not the essential innovation on the old logic which interested him: "The deeper meaning of the principles remains in darkness. The calculus of judgments, for example, is a calculating with judgments. But logistics does not know the problem of the theory of judgment" (FS² 42). Heidegger is concerned, not with the technical advances made in logic since the latter half of the nineteenth century, but with the questions of the logical theory which arose mainly in connection with the debate over psychologism and the refutation of the psychologistic interpretation of Kant first proposed by Schopenhauer. He is interested not in deductive techniques but in the "essence" of logic. "What is logic?" he asks. "We already stand before a problem whose solution is reserved for the future" (FS² 18). He wanted his Scholastic as well as his Neo-Kantian contemporaries to ask this question again, to raise it anew, and not to settle for old and established ways of thinking about it. That is the thrust of the review entitled "Recent Investigations into Logic" (FS² 17–43), which he published in 1912, as the lead article in the October issue of the *Literarische Rundschau*.

The reader will find this review an excellent introduction to Heidegger's doctoral and *Habilitation* dissertations. Here one sees for the first time that the dominant philosophical problem which preoccupied the young philosopher so many years ago was the problem of the Being of meaning, the status and "realm" of meaning. We shall gradually see that his inquiry into the Being of meaning, its place, as it were, will transform itself into the question of the meaning of Being, the place (*da*) where Being is meant. But in these days Heidegger is arguing for a sharp distinction between the real and the ideal, psychic act and ideal content, the temporal and factual vs. the timeless and the normative. Everything factual belongs to the sphere of Being (*Sein*); every timeless meaning, to the sphere of validity (*Geltung*). Platonism is overcome by seeing that the ideal is not a higher order of reality as opposed to sensible reality, that both the sensible and the supersensible belong to the "real" and are to be contrasted equally with pure logical validity. Heidegger is clearly enmeshed in a tantalizing ontological problem, the problem of the spheres or categories of Being. Does the real differ from the ideal as Being differs from validity? Or are both reality and validity spheres of Being, as long as Being is amply enough understood? Do we say that a meaning is (*ist*)? Or merely that it is valid (*gilt*)? And if the latter, then what *is* validity (*Geltung*)? If the "real" is Being, then what "is" validity? Heidegger will come to regard this whole problematic as a hopelessly muddled dualism in which a bridge can never be built from the real to the ideal, nor any satisfactory account be given of the status of pure logical validity. But at this point he sharply defends the independence and distinctiveness of the sphere of logical meaning, which is a category unto itself, from the sphere of facts. That is why he thinks that the theory of meaning (*Bedeutungslehre*) demands a prior theory of categories (*Kategorienlehre*); logic presupposes ontology. The ontology in question is not the old realistic ontology, but the ontology of the fundamental categories or regions of beings. Being does not mean *ens reale* but the category or types of things which are:

> Kant has created the logic of the categories of Being. To understand this, it must be observed that Being has forfeited its translogical independence, that Being has been reworked into a concept in transcendental logic. This does not mean that objects should be stamped as "pure logical content," but only that objectivity, thingliness as opposed to things, Being as opposed to beings, is a logical value, a form [FS² 24].

One can see in this interesting citation the first signs of the future Kant book, that Kant is doing ontology in the sense of providing the logic of the categories of what is. And one can see too how the idea of Being for Heidegger is from the start allied with the idea of meaning and the diverse spheres of possible kinds of entities. The categories of Being are the diverse spheres of meaning, the diverse ways to be, the logical forms into which existential contents are to be fitted. In this passage one also sees Heidegger distinguish Being and beings for the first time—*das Sein gegenüber dem Seienden*—and this appears as the distinction between the logical sphere in which a being belongs and the being which is. Here Being has become meaning. In *Being and Time*, the issue is meaning as Being, as horizon of manifestness.

From the point of view of Gilsonian and existentialist Thomism, it is not hard to see that Heidegger is flirting here with a philosophy of essence and what Gilson calls "logicism." Heidegger is interested in securing the rights of logical meaning, of a relationship of meaning or essence called "validity," "holding for," a relationship divorced from existence on both the sensible and the supersensible levels. This sphere is somewhat reminiscent of the Avicennian notion of an absolute essence which is neither universal nor particular. And we know that the heir of the Avicennian tradition, the foremost logicist and essentialist philosopher of the High Middle Ages, is Duns Scotus. Hence, it will not be a coincidence that Heidegger will turn to the philosophy of Scotus for a medieval partner in dialogue for the problems of modern German logic. Many questions thus arise. Will Heidegger's maturation in *Being and Time* represent a rejection of this essentialism of which I am speaking, and a turn to existence? Will this bring him closer to the so-called "existential" metaphysics of St. Thomas? Or will the phenomenological mark of meaning and essence be so profoundly stamped upon the problem of *Being and Time* that even there Being will have more to do with essence than with *esse*? Or are such terms as essence and *esse* wholly inappropriate to mediate and interpret Heidegger's problematic?

Other matters are taken up in this review as well. Heidegger raises the question of the status of impersonal and existential judgments, judgments which are particularly problematic because they appear to stand outside the subject–predicate structure of judgment. Such judgments, says Heidegger, show the necessity of separating logic from grammar (FS^2 31–32). In particular he wonders about the logical make-up of a question, an almost prophetic expression of concern. He also devotes some pages to the work of Josef Geyser, who gets a mixed review from the young student. Invoking both an Aristotelian and a transcendental standpoint, Geyser attempts the refutation of psychologism and the establishment of objective logical norms. Heidegger worries that Geyser approaches too closely to Meinong's Platonizing of meaning and criticizes what he has to say about negative judgments (FS^2 22, 34–36). It was perhaps this kind of independence of mind which discouraged the Scholastic philosophers of the day from showing a very great interest in the young man's work.

The Theory of Judgment

In his doctoral dissertation of 1914, Heidegger applies his general theories about logic to the problem of the judgment in particular. The reader who is familiar with recent Thomistic theories about the "existential" judgment will be struck by the singular absence in Heidegger's discussions of any treatment of existence. Heidegger locates the judgment entirely in the sphere of local "validity"—the relationship between "S" and "P" (in the assertion "S is P") is completely ideal; to predicate is to create a relationship in which "P" 'holds of' "S." If anything, Heidegger wants to exclude existence from consideration in the theory of judgment, for existence at this point means what *Being and Time* will call the pure presence-of-hand, or empirical existence, of the existing author of the judgment. The purely logical problem of judgment excludes all reference to psychological existence.

The goal of this study is to root out the "unphilosophy" (FS² 205) of psychologism insofar as it has affected our understanding of the meaning and function of the "judgment" in logic. Although the spell of psychologism as a general theory has been broken by the work of Husserl (FS² 63–64), still one must keep a constant guard to see that this mistaken view does not infiltrate the treatment of specific problems in logic, and especially the problem of the judgment, the all-important "basic element" (*Urelement*) (FS² 64) of logic. Heidegger's program in the dissertation, therefore, will be to make consecutive studies of four "psychologistic" theories of judgment (those of Wilhelm Wundt, Heinrich Meier, Franz Brentano, and Theodor Lipps), each of which Heidegger first presents and then criticizes. In the fifth section he defends his own "purely logical" interpretation of the judgment.

We can get some idea of the character of this study by looking briefly at Heidegger's treatment of the last of these figures, Theodor Lipps (FS² 125–59). Lipps is particularly interesting because his view develops from an undisguised psychologistic posture to a position which he himself describes as "objective idealism," in which he nearly—but not fully, according to Heidegger—extricates himself from psychologism. According to Lipps's view, the laws of thought are the laws of our psychical nature. Logic for him is the "physics of thinking" (FS² 128). A judgment is assigned objective validity when it combines representations in a "necessary" way, but Lipps interprets this necessity in a physicalistic sense. It is a psychic compulsion which forces us to combine ideas in one way (positive judgments) and prevents us from combining them in another way (negative judgments). The necessity is, as in Hume, a "feeling" of necessity (FS² 127–41). In Lipps's later thought two decisive improvements on his theory are introduced. In the first place, he distinguishes between the "content" of the judgment, which he identifies as psychic events (perceptions, images, etc.), and the "object" of the judgments, which is what is "meant" or "thought" in the judgment, and he insists that judgment has to do with the latter. We make judgments, not about our images, but about objects. Secondly, he argues that the "necessity" which belongs to objectively valid judgments originates in the "demand" (*Forderung*) which objects make upon us. Thus we judge that "$7+5=12$" is true because this object demands or calls for our "acknowledgment" (*Anerkennung*). Once the object is thought, this demand is "experienced," and our reaction to this experience is an acknowledgment which constitutes the act of judgment (FS[2] 145). The experience in question is a purely "logical feeling" which has nothing to do with psychical compulsion (FS[2] 141–46).

Heidegger is not satisfied even with Lipps's later position. For Lipps still speaks of the judgment in terms of the act of judging, viz., the act of acknowledging, and of the necessity of experiencing (*erleben*) the logical demand of the object. That is how he is led into the self-contradictory idea of a "logical feeling." Are we to suppose that if the demand which "$7+5=12$" exerts is not experienced this judgment does not hold? Lipps's position has the effect of making logical truth, which ought to be independent of time, dependent upon psychical activities which occur in time; and that is a characteristic of every psychologism. Lipps does not yet take the decisive step out of psychologism (FS[2] 148–59).

If the judgment is to be understood rightly, Heidegger argues in the concluding section of the dissertation, then one must determine the "realm" in which logical entities are to be found, the nature of "logical being." That is the basic defect of psychologism: it does not misunderstand the logical so much as it simply does not understand it at all, for it is always discussing something else (the psychical) (FS[2] 160–61, 165–66). The essence of the logical judgment is found in the self-identical meaning (*Sinn*) which is unaffected by the circumstances in which the judgment is made or by the state of mind of the one who judges. The mode of reality of meaning is the realm of "validity" (*Gelten, Geltensein*), which constitutes the essence of logical being. Validity belongs, not to the psychical, the physical, or the metaphysical realm, but to an irreducible and uniquely "logical" sphere (FS[2] 167–72). The copula, the "is," therefore, plays an important role in the youthful Heidegger's theory of judgment. The "meaning of Being," he says, in the sense of the meaning of the "is," is "to be valid of," "to hold for" (*gelten*) (FS² 178). The structure of the judgment is relational ("x is y" means "of x, y holds," or "y is valid of x"), and the essence of that relation is the purely logical relationship of "holding for." This explains how negative judgments are possible. To say that x is not y is not to annihilate y, because there is no question of a physical relationship, but simply to affirm a negative logical relationship. "To not hold" (*das gilt nicht*) is a mode of validity (*Gelten*) (FS² 183–84).

As Heidegger writes in the doctoral dissertation: "At the same time the question of the 'meaning of Being' [*die Frage nach dem 'Sinn des Seins'*] is thereby settled in the judgment. This Being means, not real existing or some relation of this, but validity [*Gelten*]" (FS² 178). The expression "the question of the meaning of Being" belongs to Heinrich Meier, and it is likely that this is where Heidegger first came across this phrase. But whatever its origin, the essential thing is to see the purely logical, indeed logicist, significance which Heidegger attaches to the expression. This interpretation of the copula sets him at odds from the start with a metaphysics of *esse* and brings him in greater proximity to a philosophy of essence, Hence, if the young Heidegger is to conduct a dialogue with medieval Scholasticism, it is understandable that his partner in dialogue will be, not St. Thomas, but Duns Scotus.

The Being of Meaning:
Scholasticism and Phenomenology
in the "Duns Scotus" Book

The culminating document of the 1912–1916 period, the one in which the dialogue between the contemporary problematic and the Scholastic tradition reaches its most incisive level, is Heidegger's famous "Duns Scotus" book, *The Theory of Categories and of Meaning in Duns Scotus*, his *Habilitation* dissertation at Freiburg in 1915. Heidegger skillfully places the medieval treatise entitled *Grammatica speculativa sive de modis significandi* into a dialogue with Husserl's theory of language in the *Fourth Logical Investigation*. It is not surprising that the work did not occasion much of a response from the Scholastic thinkers of the day, for it very likely had too close a proximity with modern currents of thought for their tastes. But Grabmann at least, who wanted to foster a comparative study of Scholasticism and modern systems—Heidegger, of course, wanted to go further— saw considerable merit in the work:

> Before all, M. Heidegger, in his previously mentioned monograph, *The Theory of Categories and of Meaning in Duns Scotus*, has brought the *Grammatica speculativa*, which he considers a leading work of Scotus', into a modern light; he has brought the course of thought developed in it into intimate contact with the comparable problematic in modern thought and he has clothed the frame of the medieval text with the flesh and blood of living contemporary philosophy. In particular, Heidegger has understood and been able to fit it into the forms of Husserl's philosophy, into the terminology of phenomenology.[11]

The importance of the book for us is the precise way in which it spells out the sphere of Being to which meaning belongs and thus shows us how the theory of meaning (logic) depends upon the theory of the categories of being (ontology, metaphysics). Logic, he says, cannot dispense with its true optics, metaphysics (FS² 406). The question of meaning raises the question of the Being of meaning. The next step, which the young philosopher does not as yet foresee, is to raise the question which is here presupposed, that of the meaning of Being.

The Theory of Categories and the Theory of Meaning

The theory of categories (*Kategorienlehre*) distinguishes the diverse modes of being, the separate spheres of objects (*Gegenstandsgebiete*) (FS² 210), the multiple areas of reality (*Wirklichkeitsbereichen*).[12] Now, one might expect that Heidegger would turn to Aristotle's doctrine of the ten categories for such a theory. But that is precisely what he does not do. For Aristotle's categories are restricted to "natural" reality, to *ens reale*, and thus leave no room for the unique essence of logical being. They do not cover everything which is thinkable (*Denkbar*) (FS² 212). Heidegger finds instead in the Scotist author a wider notion of being, one which includes both real and logical (irreal) being. Hence, the true categories are to be found in the notion of being as that which is most common to all (*ens ut commune omnibus*), the thinkable in the widest possible sense, and the transcendental properties which are convertible with being, specifically the one (*unum*) and the true (*verum*). He singles out these two in particular in order to account for the being of mathematical and logical objects. Needless to say, the Scholastic notion of *ens*, which the young Heidegger studied, primarily signifies, not *esse*, but essence (*objectum, Gegenstand*).

After differentiating the mathematical from the transcendental *unum*, Heidegger takes up a revealing question posed by Scotus (FS² 235–36). If number is the measure of quantity, and if quantity is an accidental feature of material being, then is mathematics not a subspecies of natural science? No, Scotus responds, because the mathematician considers quantity as a "thing existing of itself" (*res per se existens*). Hence, in Scotus' view the mathematician confers an ideal status upon the realm of numbers, and thereby enters them into the world of pure meanings.

The *verum* for Scotus is *ens logicum*, being as known. And since truth resides primarily in the judgment, the status of *ens logicum* is a function of the copula, the "is." But "is" signifies "is valid of," not real being. It establishes a unity of meaning with meaning in a realm which is independent of real existence. That is why Scotus sometimes calls logical being *ens diminutum*, diminished being. To use Husserl's example: real fire burns, but the meaning "fire" is harmless. And that too is why Scotus completely escapes any charge of psychologism. For the soul as a reality is very great indeed; but the being of things in the soul—that is, as known—is diminished. For it is considered to be present only as a meaning.

Now, a place can be found for neither mathematical nor logical being on the map of Aristotle's ten categories. For Aristotle's categories are the regions of real being, whereas "7+5=12" and the copulative "is" belong to another realm altogether, which is the subject matter of a new science, the science of meaning.

If the real and the ideal appear thus far as opposites, the bridge between them is to be found in the linguistic "expression" (*Ausdruck*). For expressions belong to both worlds. As spoken or written signs they are material realities, have a history, and are used in certain places. But of themselves material signs are meaningless (FS² 290). If it is objected that there is some question as to how well a person can actually think without words, Heidegger would reply at this point—in flat contradiction to his later views—that this is a purely empirical question, not a question of essences. A sign derives all the meaning it possesses from the intellect, which endows it with meaning (Husserl's *bedeutungsverleihende Akt*) (FS[2] 299). As Scotus says, "the intellect gives meaning to a sound" (*intellectus rationem voci tribuit*).

This reflection on grammar provides the transition to the doctrine of meaning. For if meaning is embedded in language, in which meaning receives material expression, then there can be a science of grammar which concerns itself, not with the empirical peculiarities of particular natural languages, but with "pure" (or "speculative") grammar. Speculative grammar is the inquiry into the pure forms of meaning which are at work in any language, whatever its empirical idiosyncracies. For no language may combine meanings senselessly. Whether its particular grammar prescribes that an adjective precede or follow the noun, no grammar allows us to combine the adjectival form of meaning with other forms of meaning in a randomly senseless way. No grammar, whatever its empirical oddities, allows us to say what is *meant* when we say in English "the green if and." Husserl had worked out the program of a science whose function would be to generate the rules which disallow senselessness (*Unsinn*), a science he called the theory of meaning, even as logic develops the rules which disallow purely formal nonsense (*Widersinn*) (*Logical Investigations* II, Inv. IV). Husserl is consciously reverting to the old idea of an *a priori* grammar, but he is perhaps unaware of medieval speculative grammar, which Heidegger here brings to the attention of modern German philosophers.

It will not serve our purpose to follow Heidegger through the complicated and sometimes tedious details of the theory of meaning or speculative grammar. Suffice it for the present purpose to point out that general rule which governs this science. In the medieval realist view, the way things are (*modus essendi*) determines the way we think about them (*modus intelligendi*), which in turn determines the way we express ourselves in language (*modus significandi*). In other words, language presupposes meaning, and meaning presupposes the being which is meant. Grammar depends on logic, and logic depends on metaphysics. The form or "active mode" of expressing oneself (*modus significandi activus*) is determined by the content of what is said (*modus significandi passivus*). (The active and passive modes are interpreted by Heidegger as noetic and noematic correlates, respectively.) But things are said in a certain way because we understand them in a certain way (*modus intelligendi activus*), which itself is determined by what is understood as such (*modus intelligendi passivus*). Now, the *modus significandi passivus*, the *modus intelligendi passivus*, and the *modus essendi* are the selfsame thing, viz., reality itself—as known and as expressed. The *modus significandi activus* (the act of expression) and the *modus intelligendi activus* (the act of thinking) are not the same, but different acts which belong to the orders of language and thought, respectively. Heidegger then goes on to consider in turn the eight fundamental forms of meaning, which turn out to be the eight parts of speech of Donatus.

The Importance of the *Habilitationsschrift*

The Scotus book affords us a close-up look at the way Heidegger in fact dealt with medieval Scholasticism. The theory of categories is only implicit in Scotus, Heidegger says. Indeed, he has set it out more clearly and sharply than it was to Scotus himself (FS² 211). But that is only as it should be; for the point is that everything which is said here "belongs to the circle of thought of the philosopher and *this alone is decisive*" (FS² 211). That is why it makes no difference to the problem at issue if the book is written by Scotus himself or by a fourteenth-century Scotist named Thomas of Erfurt, as Grabmann in fact showed was the case. Heidegger wanted to dialogue with the Scholastic tradition, which meant to shake loose its stored-up riches. This is what he meant by the ill-chosen term "destruction" of the Western tradition, an effort which *began* for Heidegger in the dialogue with Scholasticism.

One can also see traces of the Scotus book in the way in which *Being and Time* puts the question of Being. We can never forget that the question of Being was first posed for Heidegger in an Aristotelian–Scholastic setting. For Scotus, being (*ens*) is the "first object of the intellect." It is prior—logically not psychologically—to all other concepts. The intellect knows particular beings inasmuch as they are modes of being itself, its proper object. All this comes through in its own way in the claim which Heidegger makes in *Being and Time* that the "understanding of Being" is the essential structure of Dasein, and that Dasein is endowed with a "pre-ontological understanding of

Being" which enters into the understanding of every particular being. For both Scotus and Heidegger, being is the first thing conceived by the intellect (SZ, § 1, 3/43). Clearly too Heidegger continues in the Scotus book to grapple with the problem of the manifold sense of Being which was first raised for him by Brentano's book. He found this manifold character by exploring the variations between real and logical being in Duns Scotus, and by assigning a primacy to being as truth (*ens verum*), meaning (*Bedeutung*), and validity (*Geltung*) (FS[2] 55).

And this preference affected the very way in which the problem of Being was posed in *Being and Time*. For Being in *Being and Time* is not the *ens reale* of the Scholastics, or merely the *ens logicum* of Duns Scotus. It is closer by far to the notion of *meaning* than it is to mere *reality* (*Vorhandensein, Realität*). It is a transcendental–horizonal structure which allows beings to appear as the beings which they are. In *Being and Time* the notion of *ens logicum* has been transmuted into the "meaning of Being" (*Sinn vom Sein*), a phenomenological, horizonal structure, a structure of the manifestness of things. In *Being and Time* Heidegger settles on the true "place" of meaning, not in the separate realm of an ideal sphere of meaning, but in Dasein itself. The doctrine of categories allows us to find the "place" (*Stelle*) of meaning: "It is more than a popular mode of expression of the logicians to speak of the logical place [*Ort*] of a phenomenon" (FS[2] 212). In *Being and Time* the place (*da*) of the meaning of Being is located, not in an ideal realm, but in the existentialia of Dasein. Only as long as Dasein is is there anything like "meaning" and "truth" (SZ, § 43, 212/255; § 44c, 230/272). It is up to man to be (*zu sein*) the place (*da*) where meaning originates and is founded, the "there" of meaning. In *Being and Time* the theory of categories is replaced with an existential analytic. Meaning no longer enjoys an independent status; it is dependent upon man. Even such expressions as the "clearing" (*Lichtung*) as the place of disclosedness, and the later talk of a "region" (*Gegend*) in the *Discourse on Thinking*, continue this spatially oriented metaphor, this search for the proper sphere of meaning and Being (cf. FS[2] 212–13 and SZ, § 28, 132/170–71).

There is one other matter of interest to us in the *Habilitationsschrift*. In the Conclusion to the book, Heidegger ventures a criticism of Oswald Külpe's critical realism, in which, despite his "reverence" for the recently deceased professor, Heidegger advances the claims of a "transcendental" point of view over and against realism (FS[2] 342n1). He insists on taking into account the life of subjectivity, and he praises Husserl, whose *Ideas I* had appeared since the time of his article on the problem of reality. Referring to §§ 76ff. of *Ideas I*, he says that Husserl's observations "give a decisive and penetrating insight into the 'wealth of consciousness' and dispose of the often-expressed opinion about the emptiness of consciousness in general" (FS[2] 404–405n4). Külpe is criticized for having too one-sided a view of things: though he is right to insist on the reality of the world, and right to say that the world is not the product of the cognitive subject, he has fallen into error by neglecting the essential role which subjectivity has to play. For an object comes to be an object only through the judging subject which in and through the judgment formally determines the object as an object. The judgment does not create the object but the object is not possible without the subject. Objects are always objects for thought; thinking is always a thinking of objects. Thus Heidegger remarks of Külpe's realism:

> If critical realism can be made to take the judgment into account, as a matter of principle, in working out the problem of knowledge, and if, on the other hand, transcendental idealism is able to work into its fundamental position the principle of the material determination of form, there will follow a sublimation [*Aufhebung*] into a higher unity of both these epistemological "directions" which are at present most important and most fruitful [FS[2] 345–46n3].

Heidegger articulates here a position which is virtually the same as his position in *Being and Time* (SZ, § 43a, 207–208/250–52). He begins the attempt, which is also found in his later phenomenology, to surpass both realism and idealism for the sake of a higher standpoint. He retains the full force of the earlier view he had taken over from Scholastic realism, which he found to coincide with Külpe's views: that the world is not the product of a creative human mind. But now this realism has to be accommodated to the transcendental standpoint which points to the correlative subjective acts required in order to let the world emerge. "Experience" is the unity of subject and object, a cooperative product engendered by both. The "material determination of forms" must be counterbalanced by an equally strong sense of the role of subjective acts. There is neither worldless subject nor subjectless thing in itself. Noemata and noetic acts are always correlates. Heidegger is attempting here to unite the two different theories of intentionality he had inherited—from Husserl, on the one hand, and from Scholasticism, on the other.

Medieval Mysticism

It would be a mistake to think that Heidegger saw in medieval thought only a civilization of logicians and metaphysicians. The problem of "the fullness of life" and of the "living spirit," as he called it in those days, was never far from his mind. Even the problems of logic and speculative grammar have their roots in our experience of life (FS[2] 195–96, 296). That indeed is why Heidegger preferred Duns Scotus: "He had found a greater and more refined closeness to real life [*haecceitas*], to its multiplicity and capacity for tension, than any Scholastic before him. At the same time, he knew how to move with the same ease out of the fullness of life into the abstract world of mathematics" (FS[2] 203). Duns Scotus knew at once the univocity of the concept and the equivocity of real being.

One must therefore beware of characterizing medieval thought as a one-sided rationalism. For nothing is farther from the truth. Even an abstract logical and metaphysical doctrine like the theory of analogical predication is no mere schoolroom concept, Heidegger warns us, but rather: "the conceptual expression of the world of experience of medieval man, [a world which is] qualitatively fulfilled, charged with value, and drawn into relationship with the transcendent; it [analogy] is the conceptual expression of the determinate form of inner existence anchored in the transcendent and primordial relationship of the soul to God . . ." (FS[2] 408–409). The theory of analogy or categorical diversity, the medieval experience of the manifold sense of being, gives conceptual expression to the medieval experience of the panorama of being. Medieval man experiences not only the sensible, changing world, but the whole supersensible realm of the soul, angelic life, and the divine being. His world is filled with gods, with what the Scholastics call "separate substances." Medieval philosophy conceptualizes what medieval man experiences, and medieval experience is anchored in a "transcendent and primordial relationship of the soul to God" (FS[2] 409). Medieval man is not immersed in the sensible world, but he sees it always in reference to, and as dependent upon, a higher order of being. Modern man, on the con-

trary, is caught up in the sensible flow, in "insecurity and disorienta-
tion" (FS² 409). Strange words from Heidegger considering the
standpoint from which they are spoken.

It is because Heidegger was interested in medieval man's experience of life that he expresses an interest in medieval mysticism, for he
saw the mystic as one in whom medieval experience reaches its highest pitch. In the Introduction to his *Habilitationsschrift*, Heidegger
says that if one is looking for "what is living in the life of medieval
Scholasticism," then "I consider a philosophical—more precisely, a
phenomenological—elaboration of the mystical, moral–theological,
and ascetic literature of medieval Scholasticism to be especially urgent" (FS² 205). And in the Conclusion he says that "In the medieval world-view Scholasticism and mysticism essentially belong together" (FS² 410). For one expresses on the conceptual level what
the other "lives through." If philosophy is ever detached from life,
he adds, it becomes "impotent"; and if mysticism ever degenerates
into an irrationalist experience, it becomes purposeless (FS² 410).

He expresses a special interest in one medieval mystic in particular,
Meister Eckhart of Hochheim: "I hope to show on another occasion
how, in terms of this [the correlativity of subject and object] and in
connection with the metaphysics of the problem of truth, which we
shall discuss below, *Eckhartian mysticism* first receives its philosophical interpretation and evaluation" (FS² 402n2). I have shown elsewhere and at much fuller length just what the extent and import
of Heidegger's interest in Meister Eckhart were,[13] and I do not intend
to repeat or to summarize my findings here. I want to emphasize only
one point: Heidegger adamantly insists at this stage in his life that
medieval metaphysics will appear to be no more than a hollow shell
if it is detached from its animating spirit, which is expressed in medieval mysticism. The best way to misunderstand medieval thought is
to isolate it from the religious experience by which it was spawned.
Now, this raises the question whether Heidegger's later criticisms of
medieval Scholasticism are mindful of this very admonition. Or has
Heidegger himself become guilty of the very thing which he warns us
against here? This is a matter which can only slowly be unwound
and to which I shall not return until the final chapter.

What is the significance of the fact that Heidegger turns to Meister
Eckhart? Is it of any importance that Meister Eckhart is a Dominican, and that he held the same Dominican chair at Paris as Thomas

himself held some twenty-five years earlier? What are we to make of the frequent references which Eckhart makes to "brother Thomas" and of the high regard in which he obviously held Thomas? Is Eckhart a bridge between Thomas and Heidegger? Again I must wait until the final chapter before I can attempt to answer this question meaningfully.

But now we have a better sense of the "fundamentally new kind of treatment of medieval Scholasticism" of which I spoke at the beginning of this chapter. We can see that it would not be very descriptive of Heidegger's position at this point to call him a "Scholastic" philosopher, any more than it would be to call him a Neo-Kantian. It is clear that Heidegger is already his own man, that he is staking out his own path, the individual path appointed each one of us to travel. But we have learned to see how his thought came to birth in the context of a dialogue with Scholasticism, how Scholasticism was there at the beginning, at the formation of his path of thought. Now, this will prove to be a necessary propaedeutic for understanding Heidegger's critique of Scholasticism in 1927 and thereafter. For it is Heidegger himself who tells us that one ends where one begins, that one's origin is one's future (US 96/10). We cannot forget Heidegger's beginnings; that would be an unpardonable omission in view of Heidegger's own views about time and his belief that all beginnings are great.

APPENDIX:
HEIDEGGER AND THE CATHOLIC THEOLOGY OF CARL BRAIG

No treatment of the origin of Heidegger's thought in the milieu of South German Catholicism can fail to mention Carl Braig. Braig was a paradigm case of the kind of open-ended liberal appropriation of the Catholic tradition for which Heidegger himself appears to have been striving in those days. Braig was no Scholastic, but he was very conversant with Scholasticism and St. Thomas. His own position developed out of a dialogue between Scholasticism and German idealism, represented perhaps more by Schelling than by Hegel. Braig was interested in broadening the horizons of Catholic theology beyond the borders of what Heidegger calls "the dogmatic system of Scholasticism" (SD 82/75). Braig quotes liberally from Aristotle, Plato,

Augustine, Thomas, Scotus, and Suárez, but his Scholastic contemporaries regarded him as a dissident, a friend of German idealism, Leibniz, and Lotze. Braig's obscurity today is matched only by the depth
of Heidegger's regard for him:

> The decisive, and therefore ineffable, influence on my own later
> academic career came from two men who should be expressly men-
> tioned here in memory and gratitude: the one was Karl Braig, pro-
> fessor of systematic theology, and the last in the tradition of the
> speculative school of Tübingen which gave significance and scope
> to Catholic theology through its dialogue with Hegel and Schelling;
> the other was the art-historian Wilhelm Vöge. The impact of each
> lecture by these two teachers lasted through the long semester breaks
> which I always spent at my parents' house in my hometown of
> Messkirch, working uninterruptedly.[14]

In "My Way into Phenomenology" Heidegger mentions Braig's book
Vom Sein in the same breath in which he refers to Brentano's book on
Aristotle and Husserl's *Logical Investigations*. This is rather fast
company—in terms of Heidegger's intellectual biography—for a
book of which few today know more than the title. But of the two
books, Brentano's and Braig's, I find it easier to discern elements of
Heidegger's mature writings in *Vom Sein*, although Brentano's book
receives all the attention today. Of course, one should beware of a
too easy assimilation of Braig to *Being and Time*. I think that his
book had the kind of influence upon Heidegger which one is subject
to at twenty years of age, when one's world is only beginning to take
shape. It is an age of high excitement and deep impressions, when a
teacher can exercise a lasting but not easily analyzable impulse upon
the directions of one's path. Decisive influences are ineffable, indeterminate, obscure. Braig's book is full of motifs and themes which
are so thoroughly transmuted in Heidegger's mature writings that
their original form is no longer recognizable. *Vom Sein* is present in
Sein und Zeit chiefly as an arrow which points the way.

Carl Braig (1853–1923) studied under Johannes Kuhn, one of
the greatest of the Tübingen theologians, and F. X. Linsemann, who
wrote a book on Meister Eckhart.[15] He was ordained a priest in 1878
and taught at Freiburg from 1893 to 1919, serving a term as rector
in 1907. He was noted for his polemics against "modernism," a term
he himself coined, and was a collaborator on the staff of the *Litera-*

rische Rundschau für das katholische Deutschland, in which a number of his articles were published and his books reviewed. He entered into a controversy with a hardline Scholastic, M. Glossner, who wrote a series of articles attacking the whole Tübingen movement from a very dogmatic Scholastic point of view. But of all the Tübingen theologians, Braig was the closest to Scholasticism, particularly to Scotus and St. Thomas.

The Tübingen theologians wanted to mediate between what they considered the one-sidedness of immanentism or pantheism, represented by the German idealist systems, and the one-sidedness of transcendent theism, represented by Scholasticism. They wanted to show how God was both immanent and transcendent, both a creator and immanent in His creation. They wanted too to mediate between naturalism, in which God is reduced to nature (Schelling), and extreme supernaturalism (Scholasticism), according to which in their view the supernatural is something superadded to nature externally by the power of God. For them, grace grows out of nature as from a seed; the supernatural is embedded implicitly in nature. They saw themselves mediating between monism (Hegel) and dualism (Scholasticism) and thereby engendering speculatively the higher truth of both systems.

Braig himself was hardly the "epigone" Glossner took him to be. He was a very independent-minded thinker who chose freely among the Tübingen theses. He does not, so far as I can see, share the enthusiasm of the Tübingers for Schelling's distinction between ground and existence; nor does he deny the ability of the mind to demonstrate the existence of God. In fact, two years after the proclamation of *Aeterni Patris*, he published a study of the proofs for the existence of God according to St. Thomas.[16] But Braig does accept the Tübingen accent on the primacy of self-consciousness and on the identification of spirit as activity. In this he seems to me to borrow more heavily from Fichte than from Schelling or Hegel. The other source which makes its presence felt in Braig is the monadological conception of Being in Leibniz, Herbart, and Lotze. For Braig, Being means activity, the active process of be-ing and acting. There is no lifeless inert being; to be is to be active. The primary instance of the activity of being is self-consciousness, the active life of the ego, which is the paradigm in terms of which all other beings are conceived. And just as each being is active, so it is radically individual, self-identical: an actual, active, individual entity (or monad). All these ideas—from Leibniz and Fichte, from Drey and Kuhn—find their way into a fundamentally orthodox theology which is at home with the language and the arguments of Thomas Aquinas. Braig's biographer, Friedrich Stegmüller, summarized his relationship with Scholasticism well:

> He finds Scholastic philosophy to be in no essential point untrue, but in not unessential points to be incomplete. And just as Scholasticism itself has been eclectic, and just as St. Thomas has reshaped the image of Aristotle in a very independent way, so he wished to expand and improve upon the incompleteness of Scholasticism through Plato, Augustine, and Leibniz. With the help of the Augustinian and Platonic genius, Thomas will then be seen as a genuine student of the true Aristotle. . . .[17]

And in the words of Braig himself, addressed to Glossner: "My advice would be: let us not only study the philosophy *of* St. Thomas; let us also study philosophy *as* St. Thomas does."[18] It should be obvious by now that Braig's approach was very much suited to Heidegger's tastes at this time. Indeed, one suspects that Heidegger's entire approach to Scholasticism was shaped by Braig. Heidegger found in Braig a whole attitude toward Scholasticism, both appreciative and critical, which he himself emulated.

The Foreword to *Vom Sein*[19] begins with a suggestive citation from Bonaventure's *The Mind's Road to God* (5.3–4), in which Bonaventure distinguishes between pure Being (*ipsum esse, esse purissimum*), on the one hand, and particular beings (*entia particularia*) and universals (*et universalia*), on the other. Bonaventure claims that Being is what first enters the intellect, that Being is the first concept the mind conceives, without which nothing else is intelligible. In *Being and Time* Heidegger cites virtually the same notion from St. Thomas (SZ, § 1, 3/43; ST, I–II, 94, 2). For both Heidegger and the medieval thinkers Being is an "a priori," a *prius*, which precedes our understanding of particular beings. Yet despite the priority of the concept of Being, Bonaventure points out an astonishing intellectual blindness (*caecitas intellectus*): "Marvelous then is the blindness of the intellect which does not consider that which is its primary object and without which it can know nothing." The human mind, "intent upon particular and universal beings," ignores Being itself, which it looks upon as darkness and nothingness, even as the eye, intent upon perceiving colors, takes no account of the light which illumines them. Bonaventure says: "when it [the mind] looks upon the light of the highest Being, it seems to see nothing, not understanding that darkness itself is the fullest illumination of the mind. . . ."[20] It does not take much imagination to see what Heidegger could later make of this passage. For the saint is pointing here to our pre-ontological understanding of Being, the forgotten horizon which makes our understanding of beings possible. And the blindness of the intellect suggests Heidegger's oblivion of Being in favor of beings, which even Heidegger himself calls a "blindness toward Being" (*Weg.*[2] 264/241). Though it may be foolish to say that Heidegger learned all this from St. Bonaventure, it is not so foolish to see in this passage a signpost pointing Heidegger in a certain direction.

In the Introduction to the book, Braig argues for the primacy of the science of Being among all sciences in a way not unlike Heidegger's argument for the "ontological priority" of the question of Being (SZ, § 3). Both common sense and the sciences make use of basic concepts which they themselves cannot explain. All concepts make their way back into the one fundamental root which is Being itself (p. 3). Indeed, sometimes the different sciences make assumptions which are inconsistent with one another. Mathematics assumes that space is infinitely divisible, but physics assumes that it is numerable and hence limited: "Thus we are threatened by the danger that the individual sciences will get entangled in contradictions about fundamental presuppositions about the nature of Being in general, contradictions which they will not be able to iron out" (p. 4). There is thus need for a science which treats of the universal nature of Being in general, a science which guides the other sciences in terms of their fundamental presuppositions. Now, Heidegger learned from Husserl that the individual sciences make presuppositions which it is not within their capacity to justify. But he may well have heard for the first time from Carl Braig that the most basic presupposition of all is the concept of Being itself. And on this point, of course, Braig is a good student of the Aristotelian and Scholastic tradition. Hence *Being and Time*, § 3 represents the confluence of Aristotelianism and Husserl, a confluence in which ontology has become radical phenomenology.

Not only is the question of the "pervasive, simple, unified determination of Being that permeates all of its multiple meanings"[21] raised by Brentano's book; but it is also a prominent theme in *Vom Sein*. If this question was "latent" (*sich verbirgt*) in Brentano, it is perfectly explicit in Braig. For the question of the unity of Being in the midst of the multiplicity of beings was the central question of what Braig calls "Eidology":

> The first part of the science of Being as such is called *Eidology*. According to the literal meaning of the word, this term signifies the doctrine of the form of Being. The investigation into the form which is one and the same in all beings is guided by the question "*What is the being [das Seiende] insofar as it is?*" . . . A preliminary answer is given in the observation "Being is what can be predicated of everything which was, is, or will be." But in this sentence Being is taken in several ways, and it does not meet the needs of the questioner [p. 18].

Now, for Braig, what is real is the individual, and so Being in general is an abstraction: "It [= the term Being] designates Being in general—the unknown N which by itself alone signifies nothing, but which can take on all the values of the real predicates of an essential something and does indeed take them on insofar as the thing *is*" (p. 19). The search for Being is the search for an abstract unity which, like a pale shadow (p. 19), reflects the luxuriant diversity of really existing individuals. One gets unity into the concept of Being—and here Braig echoes Scotus and Suárez—only at the cost of diversity. But to occupy oneself with diversity is to fall victim to the intellectual blindness of which Bonaventure spoke.

I think it is fair to say that the young Heidegger was influenced by two theories of εἶδος. The first he met in Husserl's "eidetic phenomenology," the intuition of essences. The second he found in *Vom Sein*, and it consisted in an Eidology of Being. *Being and Time* merges Husserlian and ontological eidetics by making the inquiry into Being possible only as a phenomenological seeing of its unified meaning. But Braig, I should add, does not thematize the "meaning" of Being (*Sinn vom Sein*). Braig is a realist—the subjectivism of which he is accused by Glossner is purely psychological—with nothing but harsh words for Kant. The idea of Being as a horizon of meaning projected by Dasein's understanding, within which beings are set free to appear as beings, is totally foreign to Braig. Braig seeks a unified concept, but not a phenomenological horizon.

But the search for the unified concept of Being does not imply that Being can be defined. Let us listen to a passage from Braig which vis-à-vis Heidegger seems especially prophetic:

> All the attempts to give Being conceptual determinations are defective and contradictory. Being is a "position," "positing," "doing," "energy," "affirmation," "ground of possibility": these and similar definitions mix up the primary characteristic marks [*Erkennungszeichen*] found in beings with the essential character [*Wesensmerkmale*] of Being. Being is a "reposing actuality" in differentiation from happening, from moving actuality: this division creates two groups of Being, but it is not able to exclude the one member of the division (*esse*) from the other (*entia*). Divisions with three or more members suffer a similar breakdown [p. 22].

I have not found a more striking passage in Braig's book than this, or one which more closely approaches Heidegger's "ontological difference," at least in its earlier formulations. Every attempt at a definition ends in failure for it fails to find some defining characteristic of Being which is not a property of beings, or, as Heidegger would later say, which is not being-ness (*Seiendheit*) rather than Being. Braig then goes on to itemize some typical definitions of Being in a sentence which might have been written by Heidegger himself. It is difficult to imagine that this opinion of Braig's, which so closely approximates Heidegger's mature views, did not exert a lifelong influence on the young philosopher, whether consciously or not.

But even if Being cannot be defined, Braig continues, it can nevertheless be "unambiguously asserted" (p. 22), and this by way of differentiating it from non-Being. For Being is the activity of differentiating itself from non-Being. It subsists in a difference (*Unterschied*) from non-Being, on the one hand, in virtue of which the being is rather than is not (*Da-sein*), and over and against others, on the other hand, by which the being is this being rather than that (*Sosein*):

> The activity of Being and of essence, by which the being *is* and remains *what* it is, can, analogously to the conscious activity of thought, which is not able to take a single step forward except in accord with the Principles of Identity and Contradiction, be called

Differentiating [*Unterscheiden*]. Ontologically this means in the sphere of beings: to hold itself over and against Non-being and to assert itself as itself over and against being-other [*Andersein*] [p. 101].

Braig even refers to the second distinction (that between one being and another) as *der ontologische Unterschied* (p. 29). In Braig's difference, the "not" is placed between one being and another, whereas in Heidegger's it is placed between Being and beings. Yet, on the whole, Braig's strategy is not unlike that employed in *What is Metaphysics?* For even if Being eludes definition (*Weg.*[2] 114/105), it is still possible for it to stand out in all clarity—in the clear night of the Nothingness of Anxiety—if we differentiate it from non-Being. But the comparison ends there. For in Braig's view the "Nothing" is a psychological fiction which we have introduced in order to clarify the concept of Being for ourselves, a fiction which we have created by means of logical negation. This position is, of course, so diametrically opposed to *What is Metaphysics?* on this point that one begins to think that Heidegger had it in mind in 1929 as an unnamed target of rebuttal.

Not only is the "Nothing" a psychological fiction for Braig, so is the concept of Being. For only individual things are real. Just as there is no more a Being in general than there is a color in general, "so there is not a pure, general, simply undifferentiated, indifferent, passive Being, a Being without determination, without power, and without effect, a dead Being, [which serves] as the presupposition of beings. Only the *being is*, over and against non-being . . ." (pp. 44–45). And Braig quotes St. Thomas to the same effect, that there is no *esse commune*, except in the intellect (ST, I, 26, 4, c). Braig and St. Thomas do not want to credit a being of reason with real being. For Being in general is an abstraction generated after the fact through a consideration of the common characteristics of God and creatures. Being in general does not *exist* anywhere; it is an abstract concept which names what the things which do exist have in common.

I would hazard the guess that the youthful Heidegger was puzzled and provoked by this state of affairs. He would to some extent agree with Braig in *Being and Time*: "Entities *are*, quite independently of the experience by which they are disclosed, the acquaintance in which they are discovered, and the grasping in which their nature is ascertained. But Being 'is' only in the understanding of those entities to whose Being something like an understanding of Being belongs. Hence Being can be something unconceptualized, but it never completely fails to be understood" (SZ, § 39, 183/228). Being for the author of *Being and Time* belongs to Dasein's understanding of Being, and it is nothing apart from that. But Heidegger could hardly be content with leaving matters at that. For one is then driven to ask: What is Being, what can Being *mean*, if, as Braig would have it, Being is a mere fiction of the intellect, having no more substance than color or sound in general does? What does Being mean if only beings are? In *Being and Time*, Heidegger will hold that even though Being does not exist, as if it were some entity (*Seiendes*), it does enjoy the Being of meaning itself. Being "is" not, in the sense of something existent, but Being "means." Being is the meaning or horizon of understanding within which beings are manifest. Thus instead of being an abstract concept, a vacuous abstraction when separated from concrete beings, as in Braig, Being for Heidegger becomes the meaning-giving horizon, the transcendental *a priori*, which precedes beings and renders them possible in their Being. It is not an abstraction drawn from beings, but an *a priori* which precedes them (GP, § 22c). Now, I am not saying that Heidegger consciously had Braig in mind as he developed his views in *Being and Time*; I am only trying to show how Braig's book could have been "the decisive" influence in those early years.

One other point in Braig's book which deserves mention, though I cannot take the time to develop it here, is the role which the notion of "actuality" (*Wirklichkeit*) plays in his metaphysics. The being is what is actual (*das Seiende ist das Wirkliche*). As something actual, it belongs to a system of causal laws (*Wirkensgesetze*), in which what is actual shows itself to be efficacious and active (*tätig*), at work (*wirkend*). Finally, "actuality" set into action acts for the sake of an end, and this end is the state of complete actuality, total self-actualization or realization (*Verwirklichung*). These three principles are the guideposts of the three divisions of Braig's ontology: eidology, nomology, and teleology. Now, it may be fortuitous, but it is at least very striking, that Heidegger's interpretation of Scholastic metaphysics thematizes precisely this notion of being as the "actual" (*Wirkliche*). This will be a constant in his interpretation of the medieval understanding of Being, and I shall have occasion in the next chapter to examine it with some care.

Finally, I must say that perhaps the most enduring thing which Heidegger took away from reading *Vom Sein* was its *style*. One does not have to read very far into the book to see that the basic terms which the author employs are *Sein* and *Seiendes*. Indeed one often finds these words together in the same sentence (p. 146). The expression "the Being of beings" (*das Sein des Seienden*) occurs more than once. And Braig delights in "*-sein*" endings such as *Was-sein, Dass-sein, Einsein, Andersein, Zahlbarsein, Personsein*, etc. I have even found him using *wesen* in the verbal sense, speaking of "*das 'Wesende' im Seienden*."[22] Similarly, he enjoys using "*Seins-*" prefixes like *Seinsmöglichkeit, Seinsmomente, Seinsordnung*, etc. He will string out long hyphenated phrases such as *das Ihr-was-in-sich-selber-haben* (having your what in itself) and *das Zu-sich-selber-kommenkönnen* (being able to come toward itself). He has a fondness for nominalizing adverbs: *das Wozu, das Woher, das Wozusein*, etc.; and for chiasmus (*das Sein der Wirklichkeit und die Wirklichkeit des Seins*) (p. 40). And so on.

Any reader of Heidegger recognizes these devices, for they are all pushed to their final limits in *Being and Time*. Even though it represents on the whole a much more conventional use of German than *Being and Time*, Braig's book anticipates some of the flavor of Heidegger's treatise. One suspects that Heidegger saw in *Vom Sein* the possibility of a new use of language which would subject the language to a wholly ontological purpose, and wrest from it the ontological structures which it tends to keep concealed. Perhaps Heidegger and his teacher even talked about such things during the "few walks" which he and Braig took together.

I should also point out the importance of the long appendices which appear at the end of each section of *Vom Sein*, of which Heidegger has said: "The larger sections of the book give extensive passages from Aristotle, Thomas Aquinas, and Suárez, always at the end, as well as the etymology of fundamental ontological concepts" (SD 81–82/75). The passages from Thomas Aquinas are the most numerous, although Braig is not a Thomist (he rejects the distinction between essence and *esse*, for example). The appendix to § 4 is perhaps the most interesting to us (p. 20). It contains a lengthy citation from St. Thomas' *De veritate* I, 1—which Heidegger cites on two different occasions in *Being and Time* (SZ, § 4, 14/47; § 44, 214/257) —as well as two passages from Aristotle's *Metaphysics* (IV, 2 and

VI, 2) in which Aristotle says that Being can be said in many ways. Braig entitles this section "On the Manifold Meaning of the Concept of Being" (*Über die mannigfaltige Bedeutung des Seinsbegriffes*). This same appendix then goes on to offer an etymology of the verb "to be" which traces *sein* back to the Sanskrit *as* which he takes to mean well-being. The third person singular *ist* is traced back to *athmen*, to breathe, and hence means life. Together, *as* and *athmen* suggest "restful breathing, uniformly continuing existence" (p. 20, App. II). All this is familiar to the reader of the second chapter of Heidegger's *Introduction to Metaphysics*. Braig offers other etymologies which Heidegger later uses: *ratio* from *ar*, to put in order (cf. SG 167–68); λόγος from λέγω, to cull, collect (p. 105).

Now, it is not to be denied that Braig's book belongs to what Heidegger would later call "onto-theo-logic," that it is in many ways a compendium of the tradition which Heidegger wanted to overcome, and thus served a negative purpose for him. But it seems equally undeniable to me that this book anticipated many of Heidegger's later strategies and that it set his path of thought in a certain direction. In fact, as I said before, I find it easier to understand Heidegger's debt to Braig than to Brentano. Braig seems to me to address himself more clearly to the point in which Heidegger is interested.

But be this as it may, it cannot be denied that Braig belongs, in his own way, to the story of Heidegger and Scholasticism, that he was another figure from Heidegger's Catholic youth who helped to shape the path of thought. Heidegger's initiation into philosophy was clothed in the vestments of Catholicism. Two Catholic priests—Gröber and Braig—took a fatherly interest in him which inspired his academic studies. He breathed the air of Catholicism and Scholasticism, but always freely and independently. He appears never to have conspired with dogmatism and provincialism. The religion of his parents and the philosophy taught by that religion were a tradition which was handed to him, from which he sought to gain strength, never an imperial power over him. He lived in that world for a considerable time—for the whole of his youth, at least. The time would come for him when, in order to be faithful to the chosen path, he had to part company with that world. But when that took place, when Heidegger became a critic of Scholasticism, he would speak, not as an outsider, but as one who had for a time abided in that place.

Heidegger's commitment to the faith of his parents and of his youth appears to have endured until 1916, the year in which he began his work as a *Privatdozent* at Freiburg and the year in which his *Habilitationsschrift* was published, the work which was to begin his wholly new kind of treatment of medieval Scholasticism. During the next two years he would subject his religious and philosophical viewpoint to a fundamental reassessment, and as a result his thought would be set on a new course, one which would effect nothing less than a revolution in contemporary European philosophy. Philosophically this would prove to be a move beyond the questions of pure logic on which he had been nurtured by Husserl and medieval Scholasticism, and religiously it would prove to be a move beyond Catholicism, not to atheism, but to Protestantism. For it was in the concrete life-experience of New Testament Christianity that Heidegger would find his point of departure for the existential analytic.

In January 1919 Heidegger announced in a letter to Engelbert Krebs, a professor of Catholic dogmatic theology at Freiburg and one of his most enthusiastic supporters, that the system of Catholicism was no longer acceptable to him. Heidegger wrote in part:

> The past two years, in which I have taken pains to reach a fundamental clarification of my philosophical standpoint and so have laid aside all specialized scholarly tasks, have led me to results for which, had I any ties beyond philosophical ones, I could not have preserved the freedom of conviction and of what I taught.

> Epistemological insights, extending as far as the theory of historical knowledge, have made the *system* of Catholicism problematic and unacceptable to me—but not Christianity and metaphysics (the latter, to be sure, in a new sense).

> I believe too strongly—perhaps more than those who work officially in this field—to have perceived the values which the Catholic Middle Ages bear within themselves—and we are still far removed from a genuine appreciation of them. My investigations into the phenomenology of religion, which will draw very much on the Middle Ages, should instead bear witness in every discussion that I have not, by reason of the transformation of my fundamental standpoint, been driven to set aside the high assessment and the deep esteem of the Catholic life-world for the vexing and barren polemic of an apostate.

Heidegger goes on to say that he wishes to maintain close contact with Catholic thinkers, and to preserve the friendship of Professor Krebs himself. And then he concludes: "I believe that I have an inner call to philosophy and that by answering it in research and teaching I can do what lies within my powers for the eternal vocation of the inner man—and only for this—and thus justify my existence and the work itself before God."[23]

The first "turn"in Heidegger's thought had taken place; the preparation of *Being and Time* would begin in these lectures on the phenomenology of religion, now in a dialogue, not with Catholic, but with Protestant, theology.[24] Hence, we turn next to the Heidegger of the Marburg years, the author of *Being and Time*, the critic of Scholasticism. This Heidegger is better known, but it has been of no small importance to have recalled the first Heidegger. For it is always important, and indeed a lifelong task, to recall one's beginnings.

NOTES

1. The account which follows is drawn from SD 81–90/74–82; Heidegger's letter to Father Richardson in William Richardson, S.J., *Heidegger: Through Phenomenology to Thought* (The Hague: Nijhoff, 1962), pp. vii–xxiii; and Seigfried's "Martin Heidegger: A Recollection." The best secondary source at present is Thomas J. Sheehan's "Heidegger's Early Years: Fragments for a Philosophical Biography," *Listening*, 12, No. 1 (Winter 1977), 3–20 (repr. in *Heidegger: The Man and the Thinker*, ed. Thomas Sheehan [Chicago: Precedent, 1981], pp. 3–19).

2. For an account of the deeply Catholic character of Brentano's family and his own strong religious orientation, see the essays of Kraus and Stumpf in *The Philosophy of Brentano*, ed. Linda McAlister (Atlantic Highlands, N.J.: Humanities Press, 1976); see also Husserl's remark about Brentano's "priestly gestures" when he attended his lectures in Vienna in 1886–1887, long after Brentano had left the Church (p. 49); and Etienne Gilson's essay (pp. 56–67) which praises Brentano's command of medieval philosophy. Brentano continued all his life to write on the philosophy of St. Thomas and on speculative questions in philosophical theology, despite his departure from the priesthood and the Church. The relationship between Heidegger and Brentano's book on Aristotle has been explored at length by Franco Volpi, *Heidegger e Brentano* (Padua: Cedam-Casa, 1976); see also his "Heideggers Verhältnis zu Brentanos Aristoteles-Interpretation: Die Frage nach dem Sein

des Seienden," *Zeitschrift für philosophische Forschung*, 32, No. 2 (April–June 1978), 254–65. See also David Krell, "On the Manifold Meaning of *Aletheia*: Brentano, Aristotle, Heidegger," *Research in Phenomenology*, 5 (1975), 77–94; Walter Del-Negro, "Von Brentano über Husserl zu Heidegger: Eine vergleichende Betrachtung," *Zeitschrift für philosophische Forschung*, 7, No. 4 (October–December 1953), 571–85.

3. *On the Several Senses of Being*, trans. Rolf George (Berkeley: University of California Press, 1975), pp. 120–21.

4. *Martin Heidegger* (Stuttgart: Metzler, 1976), p. 25.

5. Sheehan, "Heidegger's Early Years," 7–13.

6. Karl Lehmann, "Metaphysik, Transzendentalphilosophie und Phänomenologie in den ersten Schriften Martin Heideggers (1912–1916)," *Philosophisches Jahrbuch*, 71, No. 2 (April 1964), 331–57.

7. See his *Der Gegenwartswert der geschichtlichen Erforschung der mittelalterlichen Philosophie* (Freiburg: Herder, 1913). In an article on Oswald Külpe, Grabmann wrote: "There is great value in such confrontations [of modern philosophy with Scholasticism], both for the assessment of modern philosophy and for the evaluation and expansion of Aristotelian–Scholastic philosophy" ("Der kritische Realismus Oswald Külpes und der Standpunkt der aristotelisch–scholastischen Philosophie," *Philosophisches Jahrbuch der Görresgesellschaft*, 29 [1916], 355).

8. Friedrich Überweg, *Grundriss der Geschichte der Philosophie. IV. Die deutsche Philosophie des XIX. Jahrhunderts und der Gegenwart*, rev. T. K. Österreich (Berlin: Mittler, 1923), p. 623.

9. Aside from Grabmann (see note 7 above) and Heidegger, Külpe's work also attracted the attention of other Catholic thinkers; see, for example, L. Noël, "Les frontières de la logique," *Revue Néo-Scolastique de Philosophie*, 17 (1910), 211–33.

10. See Geyser's book on Husserl: *Neue und alte Wege der Philosophie: Eine Erörterung der Grundlagen der Erkenntnis im Hinblock auf Edmund Husserls Versuch ihrer Neubegründung* (Münster: Schöningh, 1916).

11. *Mittelalterliches Geistesleben: Abhandlungen zur Geschichte der Scholastik und Mystik*, 3 vols. (Munich: Hueber, 1926, 1936, 1956), i 145–46.

12. I have examined the *Habilitationsschrift* in greater detail in "Phenomenology, Mysticism and the 'Grammatica Speculativa': A Study of Heidegger's *Habilitationsschrift*," *Journal of the British Society for Phenomenology*, 5, No. 2 (May 1974), 101–17. The *Habilitationsschrift* was translated by Harold Robbins in 1976 as part of a doctoral dissertation at Loyola University (Chicago) under the direction of Manfred Frings. The *Grammatica speculativa* itself was translated in 1972: Thomas of Erfurt, *Grammatica speculativa*, trans. G. L. Bursill-Hall (London: Longmans, 1972).

13. See my *Mystical Element in Heidegger's Thought*. See also note 23 below.

14. Seigfried, "Martin Heidegger: A Recollection," 4.

15. There is little secondary literature on Braig. See the biographical piece by Friedrich Stegmüller, *Karl Braig (1853–1923)*, an offprint from the *Ober-*

rheinisches Pastoralblatt (54 [1953]), which is to be found in the library at Freiburg University. There is a rather strident and unsympathetic series of articles by one M. Glossner entitled "Die Tübinger katholische Schule, vom spekulativen Standpunkt kritisch beleuchtet," *Jahrbuch für Philosophie und spekulative Theologie*, I: "Drey, der Apologet," 15 (1901), 166–94; II, "Kuhn, der Dogmatiker," 16 (1902), 1–50; III, "Linsemann, der Moralist," ibid., 309–29; IV, "Die Epigonen: Schanz, Braig, Schell," 17 (1903), 2–42 (pp. 18–29 on Braig). See also Glossner's reviews of Braig's *Vom Sein* and *Vom Erkennen* in the same *Jahrbuch*, 13 (1898), 59–64 and 14 (1900), 204–11, respectively. For the exchange which took place between Braig and Glossner, see Carl Braig, "Eine Frage," *Philosophisches Jahrbuch des Görresgesellschaft*, 12 (1899), 59–65; Glossner's reply in *Jahrbuch für Philosophie und spekulative Theologie*, 13 (1899); Braig, "Eine Antwort," *Philosophisches Jahrbuch des Görresgesellschaft*, 12 (1899), 500–504; and Glossner's further reply, "Ein Zweites Wort an Prof. Dr. Braig," *Jahrbuch für Philosophie und spekulative Theologie*, 14 (1900), 248–51. On the Tübingen School in general, see Bernhard Welte, "Beobachtungen zum Systemgedanken in der Tübinger katholischen Schule," *Zeit und Geheimnis*. See also the discussion of Drey in Gerald McCool, *Catholic Theology in the Nineteenth Century* (New York: Seabury, 1977), pp. 67–81; see also pp. 188ff. for an account of the attempt by the nineteenth-century Neo-Thomist Josef Kleutgen to refute the Tübingen school from a Thomistic standpoint. The major study of the Tübingen school is Josef Rupert Geiselmann, *Die katholische Tübinger Schule* (Freiburg: Herder, 1964). See also Geiselmann's *Geist des Christentums und des Katholizismus* (Mainz: Matthias Grünewald-Verlag, 1940). Of interest, too, is Thomas O'Meara, o.p., *Romantic Idealism and Roman Catholicism: Schelling and the Theologians* (Notre Dame, Ind.: University of Notre Dame Press, 1982). For a recent study of Carl Braig, see Franco Volpi, "Alle origini della concezione Heideggeria dell'essere: Il trattato *Vom Sein* di Carl Braig," *Rivista critica di storia della filosofia*, 34 (1980), 183–94.

16. "Die natürliche Gotteserkenntnis nach dem hl. Thomas von Aquin," *Theologische Quartalschrift*, 63 (1881), 511–96.

17. *Karl Braig*, p. 6.

18. "Eine Frage," 65.

19. *Vom Sein: Abriss der Ontologie* (Freiburg: Herder, 1896). All page numbers in parentheses in the body of the text will refer to this volume unless otherwise indicated.

20. Saint Bonaventure, *The Mind's Road to God*, trans. George Boas, Library of Liberal Arts (Indianapolis: Bobbs-Merrill, 1953), pp. 35–36.

21. Richardson, *Heidegger*, pp. x–xi.

22. Quoted by Glossner in *Jahrbuch für Philosophie und spekulative Theologie*, 17 (1903), 21, from Braig's *Die Zukunftsreligion des Unbewussten und das Princip des Subjektivismus* (Freiburg: Herder, 1882), p. iv.

23. This letter is to be found in an article by Bernhard Casper entitled "Martin Heidegger und die Theologische Fakultät Freiburg, 1909–23" in *Kirche am Oberrhein: Beiträge zur Geschichte der Bistümer Konstanz und*

Freiburg, edd. Remigius Bäumer, Karl S. Frank, and Hugo Ott (Freiburg: Herder, 1980). p. 541. Krebs had been entrusted with the philosophical instruction of the theology students at Freiburg and soon after Heidegger's *Habilitation* enlisted his support in this work; in the winter semester of 1916–1917 Heidegger secured an official appointment to teach a course in the area of Catholic philosophy and hence took over Krebs's post. The full text of the letter to Krebs is as follows:

> Sehr verehrter Herr Professor!
>
> Die vergangenen zwei Jahre, in denen ich mich um eine prinzipielle Klärung meiner philosophischen Stellungnahme mühte u. jede wissenschaftliche Sonderaufgabe beiseiteschob, haben mich zu Resultaten geführt, für die ich, in einer ausserphilosophischen Bindung stehend, nicht die Freiheit der Überzeugung und der Lehre gewährleistet haben konnte.
>
> Erkenntnistheoretische Einsichten, übergreifend auf die Theorie geschichtlichen Erkennens haben mir das *System* des Katholizismus problematisch u. unannehmbar gemacht—aber nicht das Christentum und die Metaphysik (diese allerdings in einem neuen Sinne).
>
> Ich glaube zu stark—vielleicht mehr als seine offiziellen Bearbeiter—empfunden zu haben, was das katholische Mittelalter an Werten in sich trägt u. von einer wahrhaften Auswertung sind wir noch weit entfernt. Meine religionsphänomenologischen Untersuchungen, die das m. A. stark heranziehen werden, sollen statt jeder Diskussion Zeugnis davon ablegen, dass ich mich durch eine Umbildung meiner prinzipiellen Standpunktnahme nicht habe dazu treiben lassen, das objektive vornehme Urteil u. die Hochschätzung der katholischen Lebenswelt einer verärgerten u. wüsten Apostatenpolemik hinanzusetzen.
>
> Daher wird mir auch in Zukunft daran liegen, mit katholischen Gelehrten, die Probleme sehen und zugeben u. in andersartige Überzeugungen sich hineinzufühlen imstande sind, in Verbindung zu bleiben.
>
> Es ist mir daher besonders wertvoll—u. ich möchte Ihnen recht herzlich dafür danken—dass ich das Gut Ihrer wertvollen Freundschaft nicht verliere. Meine Frau, die sie erst besucht hat, und ich selbst möchten das ganz besondere Vertrauen zu Ihnen bewahren. Es ist schwer zu leben als Philosoph—die innere Wahrhaftigkeit sich selbst gegenüber u. mit Bezug auf die, für die man Lehrer sein soll, verlangt Opfer u. Verzichte u. Kämpfe, die dem wissenschaftlichen Handwerker immer fremd bleiben.
>
> Ich glaube, den inneren Beruf zur Philosophie zu haben u. durch seine Erfüllung in Forschung u. Lehre für die ewige Bestimmung des inneren Menschen—u. *nur dafür* das in meinen Kräften Stehende zu leisten u. so mein Dasein u. Wirken selbst vor Gott zu rechtfertigen.
>
> Ihr von Herzen dankbarer
>
> MARTIN HEIDEGGER

This article is also of interest to me for it seems to isolate Heidegger's initial point of contact with medieval mysticism and Meister Eckhart. Casper shows (pp. 536–37) that in the winter semester of 1910–1911, Professor Joseph Sauer gave a course on the "History of Medieval Mysticism." We know that Heidegger was close to Sauer, who was the editor of the *Literarische Rundschau,* and Casper claims that Heidegger presented Sauer with a copy of the

Habilitationsschrift containing a handwritten inscription, which has since been stolen from the Freiburg library!

I wish to thank Professor Samuel Ijsseling, Director of the Husserl Archives at Louvain, for bringing this article to my attention.

24. For an account of the dialogue of Heidegger and the Protestant tradition after 1919, see Michael Zimmerman's *Eclipse of the Self: The Development of Heidegger's Concept of Authenticity* (Athens: Ohio University Press, 1981), and "Heidegger and Bultmann: Egoism, Sinfulness, and Inauthenticity," *The Modern Schoolman*, 58, No. 1 (November 1980), 1–20; and Thomas Sheehan's "Heidegger's 'Introduction to the Phenomenology of Religion,' 1920–21," *The Personalist*, 60, No. 3 (July 1979), 312–24.

2

Heidegger's Critique of Scholasticism

By 1927 EVERYTHING HAD CHANGED. The dialogue with Scholasticism had been broken off and the mature author of *Being and Time* had emerged. Indeed, after the appearance of this work, the popular impression grew up that Heidegger was an atheist. His early studies in Scholasticism appeared now to belong to a Catholic background which had simply been thrown over. In reaching his maturity, Heidegger appeared to have rejected not only Scholasticism but Christianity itself. But in fact the popular impression was hastily drawn. The Marburg period—Heidegger's stay at Marburg from 1923 until his call to Freiburg in 1928—was a time of intense dialogue with Marburg theology, with Tillich, Bultmann, and Otto, to name the most prominent. And Heidegger himself did not regard his work as in any way atheistic. On the contrary, in laying a phenomenological–ontological foundation for theology (among other "positive" sciences) *Being and Time*, like every phenomenological inquiry, had merely put the question of God and immortality in brackets. This is seen with perfect clarity in *Phenomenology and Theology*, a lecture which Heidegger gave at the end of the Marburg period (*Weg.*[2] 45ff./3ff.). Heidegger did not come to reject Christianity in the period from 1916 to 1927. Rather, he had moved away from his logical preoccupations to existential ones; that is, he had come to see the foundations of all logical problems in an existential analytic—and he had moved away from a dialogue with Catholic Scholasticism into a dialogue with Luther and Kierkegaard. The detached objectivism of Scholasticism was rejected in favor of concrete existential–phenomenological investigations. This is to say that the problem of Being for Heidegger was no longer the problem of the Being of meaning, clearly the concern of 1912–1916, but the problem of the meaning of Being. Heidegger now argued, in conformity with the transcendental method which is uniquely his own, that the meaning of Being can be investigated only by means of an existential analytic which will work up the implicit understanding of Being embedded in the entirety of Dasein's concrete life. The "doctrine of categories" now became the name for a theory of but one kind of Being, objective presence (*Vorhandensein*), but it left entirely untouched a totally different sphere of Being, and indeed a more radical one, that of the existentialia, which could be searched out only by an existential analytic. Traditional ontology and the logic of categories associated with it understand Being in terms of objective presence, something the tradition takes to be "self-evident." The task which Heidegger set for himself in *Being and Time*, then, was to raise this question anew, putting everything self-evident into question, and to find the clue to the solution of this question in Dasein's own concrete existential life.

And so the Heidegger of 1927 became a critic of Scholasticism, not because he was an atheist, but because he had rejected the intellectualist standpoint common to Scholasticism and the first volume of the *Logical Investigations*. The concern with the "fullness of life" which he found in thinkers like Dilthey, Nietzsche, Augustine, Luther, and Kierkegaard seemed to him to touch deeper grounds than his previous studies in logical theory had. Heidegger was in search of a new λόγος to take the place of all logic and logistics.

But even his critique of Scholasticism would evolve in accord with the dynamics of the "early" and "later" periods. (In the first chapter we examined the genuinely "early" Heidegger.) In 1928 Heidegger gave a series of lectures under the title *Die Grundprobleme der Phänomenologie* (*The Basic Problems of Phenomenology*). Then in the *Nietzsche* lectures of 1943 Heidegger took up the metaphysics of the Scholastic age once again, assessing it from a more distinctly postphenomenological, or what I shall call here "alethiological," standpoint. There are important differences in these critiques and so I shall treat them separately. Let us see now what this thinker, who once attempted a "fundamentally new kind of treatment of medieval Scholasticism" (FS[2] 204), this former partner in dialogue with Scholasticism, now takes to be the basic failing of Scholastic metaphysics.

THE BASIC PROBLEMS OF PHENOMENOLOGY (1928)

Heidegger's thought is by now explicitly given over to raising the question of Being, and the discussion of Scholastic metaphysics occurs in the context of an investigation into four theses on Being, those of Kant, Scholasticism, and the modern epoch, and the copulative "is" of logic. It is interesting to see how all four theses were already at issue for Heidegger in 1912–1916 when he debated the importance of Kant, the dialogue with Scholasticism, the modern problem of "reality," and the idea that Being (*Sein*) means validity (*Gelten*). There is, one suspects, considerably more continuity between the early days of 1912–1916 and the Marburg period than is ordinarily believed.

The basic problem of phenomenology, he says, is the problem of Being, that is, of formulating an explicit concept of Being as the basic *a priori* which lies behind all the factical-positive sciences (GP 14–19/11–15).[1] This means that phenomenology, which is ontology, must learn to think the "ontological difference," the basic differentiation or scission (*Scheidung*), between Being and beings (GP 22/17). As such, ontology is a "transcendental" science which must transcend beings for Being itself. Heidegger here is trying to fuse the classical Aristotelian sense of "transcendental"—as that which transcends all the genera—with the modern sense. For Being is to be met with in Dasein's own transcendental–horizonal understanding of Being. Phenomenology thus names the method of philosophy while ontology names its content. As a method, phenomenology makes use of (*a*) a "reduction" from beings to Being; (*b*) a "construction" which positively projects beings in terms of the kind of Being which is appropriate to them; and (*c*) a "destruction" in which it must deconstruct the average understanding of Being which threatens the present investigation in its effort to be truly radical (GP 28–32/21–23).[2]

Given these presuppositions, all of which are to be found in *Being and Time*, although not in so many words, Heidegger then proceeds to formulate the four theses about Being which the lecture course will investigate: (*a*) Kant's thesis that Being is not a real predicate; (*b*) the medieval thesis that Being is articulated into *essentia* and *existentia*; (*c*) the modern–Cartesian thesis that there are two modes of Being, *res cogitans* and *res extensa*; (*d*) the thesis of logic that Being signifies the copula "is." Each thesis will be deconstructed and turned to account in terms of the more primordial origins which lie hidden within it. Each will be expounded as a kind of "oblivion of Being" in which the true difference between Being and beings is obscured, and the foundation of every investigation into Being in a fundamental ontology of Dasein's understanding of Being is forgotten. That charge is made against all four theses; it applies no less to Scholasticism than to Kant.

Our purposes will not be served by investigating all four theses, but we would do well to pause for a moment to consider briefly Heidegger's account of Kant's thesis, for it is, as he rightly indicates, closely connected with the Scholastic thesis. Kant's thesis, that Being is not a real predicate, occurs within the context of a proof for the existence of God. The key to Kant's position, according to Heidegger, lies in seeing what Kant means by "real." "Real," coming from the Latin *res*, signifies a thing in the sense of the German word *Sachgehalt*, a word which might be translated as "content" or perhaps "substantive content." "Real" therefore signifies some kind of determination of the content of the being. A being is "real" in the measure that it is possessed of some determination or content. (In Scholastic terms, Heidegger is saying that "real" means "essential," pertaining to essence.) When Kant calls God the *ens realissimum*, he is saying that God is the being with the richest content, that being in which no positive determination is lacking. Now, existence, Kant maintains, is not a "real" predicate. That means that existence does not signify anything which belongs to the order of the thing's content or determination. The concept of God is the concept of a being which lacks nothing in terms of content, but which does not, on that account alone, exist. Existence does not signify any addition to the content or determination of a thing; it signifies that a being of such and such content is or exists; it signifies the fact of existing. It means the "positing" (*Setzen*) of such a thing. One cannot deduce existence, therefore, from the idea of a being which lacks no positive perfection in the order of content, in the manner of the ontological argument (GP, §7).

This position offers an interesting parallel to the Scholastic one. For Thomas Aquinas, who likewise rejects the ontological argument, will often say that, although *ens* derives from *esse*, *res* denotes *essentia* (*In I Sent.*, d. 8, 1, 1). Neither *ens* nor *esse* belongs to the order of essence, and *esse* is not a real predicate. Heidegger himself, however, is not fully aware, I think, of the extent of St. Thomas' rejection of the ontological argument. He rightly points out that St. Thomas' objection to the Anselmian argument is not that *esse* does not belong to the order of *essentia*, but rather that we do not know the essence of God. And this implies for Heidegger that the argument fails only because of some kind of contingent failing of the human intellect. Were the human mind able to know the definition of God, Heidegger says of St. Thomas, then one could indeed deduce His existence from His essence. But that is not what Thomas is saying. For Thomas, to know God in some way other than through a nominal and imperfect definition would imply that we were in a position to have an intuitive knowledge of His "essence"—which in fact is a subsistent act of existence (*ipsum esse subsistens*). But that has nothing to do with finding *esse* as one of the predicates in the divine *essentia*. Were we able to behold the divine being, we would not find that *esse* is a predicate; rather, we would behold immediately, in an intuitive vision, the very *esse* of God—in which case we would require no "proof" at all for the existence of God, and certainly not the ontological proof. I do not think that Heidegger appreciates at all the "existential" quality of the Thomistic doctrine of *esse* and the abyss which separates it from the ontological argument.

Kant's thesis is connected with the medieval thesis for, as we have just seen, his *realitas* corresponds to the medieval *essentia*. Hence, his thesis, like so much of modern philosophy, goes back to medieval metaphysics and depends upon the distinction between *essentia* and *existentia* elaborated in medieval ontology. Heidegger speaks of the medieval distinction as the "articulation" of Being into essence and existence. He has in mind here his own "ontological difference" between Being and beings and he is pointing out that the Scholastic distinction falls entirely on one side of his ontological difference. Diagrammatically, this looks as follows:

Heidegger:	Being	beings
Scholastics:	*essentia* & *existentia*	(*hoc ens*)

As Heidegger points out:

> Thus the distinction between realitas—that is, essentia—and exis-
> tentia does not coincide with the ontological difference; it belongs,
> rather, on the side of one member of the ontological difference. This
> means that *neither realitas nor existentia* is a *being*; rather, it is just
> the two of them which make up the structure of Being. The distinc-
> tion between realitas and existentia *articulates* Being more precisely
> in its essential constitution [GP 109/78].

The failure of Scholasticism explicitly to formulate an ontological
difference is ultimately decisive for Heidegger, as we shall see. Instead of the ontological difference, the Scholastics were taken with
showing the theological difference between God and creatures, between the being in whom essence and existence are identical and the
beings in whom they are distinct. The same is true of Kant, who likewise elaborated his thesis on Being in the context of God and took
God to be the being in whom essence and existence are identical.
First philosophy has always been at the same time theology.

Aquinas, Scotus, Suárez

Heidegger expounds the Scholastic thesis by examining the three
principal positions which have been adopted within Scholasticism on
the nature of this distinction.[3] For although all the Scholastics are
agreed upon the identity of essence and existence in God, there are
serious disagreements among them as to the nature of this distinction
in creatures. St. Thomas and the Dominican school defend a real
distinction (*distinctio realis*) between essence and existence; Duns
Scotus and the Franciscan school, a formal distinction (*distinctio
formalis*). Suárez and the Jesuits argue that it is a mere distinction of
reason (*distinctio rationis*). Heidegger notes wryly that since the
Church has adopted the Thomistic position, the Jesuits have had to
fall in line with St. Thomas (GP 113/80).

St. Thomas and the distinctio realis · Heidegger's brief exposition
of St. Thomas is, unfortunately, drawn largely from the commentary
on St. Thomas written by Giles of Rome. Heidegger is prepared to
admit this, arguing, for some odd reason, that Thomas' own position

is so unclear that we are forced to speak of the "Thomistic school" rather than of St. Thomas himself (GP 126/89). Giles created the misunderstanding, which Heidegger simply repeats here, that the distinction between *essentia* and *esse* is a "real" distinction, an expression he himself coined, in the sense of the distinction between two different real things. Now, of course, were this so, both essence and *esse*, as real things, as separate beings, would themselves require principles of essence and existence to explain their own make-up as real things. And so on to infinity. Giles was right, however, and Heidegger too in following him, to argue that if this distinction is not real in some acceptable sense then it would be impossible to explain how the Being of God differs from that of creatures. Later on in the *Basic Problems* Heidegger mentions that essence and existence are not two different things (GP 145–46/104), but he fails to reconcile this with his earlier borrowings from Giles. In any case, it is hardly surprising that, after presenting such a garbled version of St. Thomas' teachings, Heidegger goes on to express a preference for the Suarezian theory. Though Heidegger gives evidence of being familiar with *De ente et essentia*, one is led to ask at this point whether his critique of Scholasticism would have been altered had he been familiar with the existential interpretation of St. Thomas' metaphysics. He prefers the more radically existential nature of Kant's rejection of the ontological argument to his understanding of St. Thomas' position. But what if one could show that St. Thomas rejected the idea that *esse* was a real predicate every bit as roundly as Kant did? Or would this have nothing to do with the essentials of his critique of Scholasticism?

Scotus and the distinctio formalis · Scotus wanted to avoid the error (which Heidegger attributes to St. Thomas) of making essence and existence two different realities. It is true that existence is something real in the thing, not simply a creature of our reason. Yet, while it is real, it is not another reality but a formally different aspect of the selfsame reality which is both essence and existence. Essence and existence are formally different properties of the being, but not different beings or realities. Existence is real, but not a reality (a *res*). It is a formal aspect of the thing, a differentiatable dimension of the concrete reality, which is not the same dimension or modality as essence, even though the two, essence and existence, are but different aspects of the same thing, the concrete being.

Suárez and the distinctio rationis · Heidegger reserves the place of honor in his exposition for the Spanish Jesuit Francisco Suárez (1548–1617), a figure whose pre-eminence for Heidegger is both systematic and historical. Suárez is the bridge between the Middle Ages and the modern world (GP 111–16/79–83). It was through Suárez that the metaphysics of Scholasticism flowed into modern thinkers; his influence is clearly detectable in Descartes, Leibniz, Wolff, Schopenhauer, Kant, and Hegel. Suárez abandoned the format of the *commentarium* employed by the classical Scholastic thinkers and developed instead a strictly philosophical and systematic treatise entitled *Disputationes metaphysicae*. Although it was written in the seventeenth century, it is the first major systematic Scholastic treatise on metaphysics (GP 112/80). St. Thomas' major works, for example, are either commentaries or, when they are systematic, theological treatises. The *Disputationes* is divided into fifty-four tracts. The first twenty-seven treat of *metaphysica generalis* (or *ontologia*); the next twenty-six treat of special beings (*metaphysica specialis*); the fifty-fourth is devoted to beings of reason (*entia rationis*). In general metaphysics Suárez investigates the properties of the abstract concept of being in general. In special metaphysics, he investigates God and creatures, that is, infinite and finite beings. This distinction between general and special metaphysics was imported fully intact by Wolff and made its way to the center of Kant's architectonic —to the distinction between the transcendental analytic and the transcendental dialectic—in the *Critique of Pure Reason*.

Moreover, this Suarezian distinction seems to me to have played a significant role in the formation of Heidegger's own "ontological difference." In his first Kant book, Heidegger attempts to "retrieve" the *Critique of Pure Reason* in terms of Suárez' distinction between general and special metaphysics, and to read the transcendental analytic as an essay in an ontology which founds our knowledge of beings. Moreover, we have already seen that Heidegger was very likely struck by Carl Braig's argument that Being in general is an abstraction with no more claim to reality than color in general. Heidegger has been interested all along in what the Scholastics call *esse* or *ens in communi*, Being in general, and he has insisted all along, in the manner of Suárez, that God is in some sense a particular being treated in a particular science, a science which he calls "positive" because it "posits" a particular being, God (*Weg.*[2] 51–55/8–11). The science of God, theology, cannot provide the answer to the question of Being. But Heidegger could hardly be content to characterize Being in general as a pure abstraction, as Braig and Suárez do, and so he is forced to think Being in a more radical way. The problem with which Heidegger is grappling, the problem of the difference between Being in general (*Sein überhaupt, Sein im Ganzen*) and particular beings, is originally posed in Suárez' distinction between general and special metaphysics.

Suárez holds that the dispute about the distinction between essence and existence has to do with the status of a really existing essence, the "what" (*quidditas*) of an actual being, and with the way in which this is to be distinguished from its actuality (GP 132–39/94–99). It is perfectly obvious, Suárez thinks, that in a merely possible being essence and existence are distinct. The essence of a merely possible being lacks existence and, as such, differs from existence. But if one considers not a merely possible but an actual being, then there can be nothing but a conceptual distinction between them. Pure possibility differs from something actual; but in the actualized essence, essence and existence are the same. For a real thing cannot be real in virtue of something other than itself. Essence and existence cannot be different things, for then we should have not one unified being, but two.

St. Thomas, Heidegger thinks, is arguing from an abstract and deductive standpoint. Thomas starts from the idea of a created being and reasons that in such a being existence has been added to its mere possibility. But Suárez, in Heidegger's view, directs his attention to the concretely existing thing, to the essence in actual existence, and for this reason his procedure is more amenable to phenomenological interpretation. Moreover, Suárez has the authority of Aristotle on this point, citing in this connection a passage from the *Metaphysics* (IV, 2, 1003B26f.) in which Aristotle says that it is the same thing to say "man" or "existent man." In Aristotle, there is no distinction between essence and existence.

Heidegger's suggestion that the Thomistic approach to the dispute is more abstract and intellectualistic, while the Suarezian approach is ordered to the sphere of concrete existence, will particularly rankle the Thomists of the Gilsonian school. For according to Gilson, Suárez is the high priest of modern essentialism, and he is separated by an abyss from the Thomistic doctrine of *esse*. In essentialism existence is systematically eliminated in favor of what can be conceptualized, what can be accommodated to the needs of the intellect. That is why for Suárez—the Gilsonian contends—existence is something of an afterthought which simply gives real status to the essence; it is essence which gives the thing all its content and substance. But I shall have more to say about this in the next chapter.

At the end of his exposition of Suárez, Heidegger introduces a comparison of Suárez with Kant. Neither Suárez nor Kant takes existence to be a real predicate, a "what." Both treat it as that which gives actual status to the essence. But Suárez differs from Kant in that for Suárez existence is something *in re*, in the thing itself, something real (even if it is not really distinct from essence), whereas for Kant existence signifies nothing more than a relationship to our cognitive faculties. For Kant, the difference between a possible thing and a real one is that the real thing has entered into a new relation with the knower, one which it previously had lacked. Thus the actual hundred dollars is perceptible, whereas previously it was only imaginable. Kant's definition of existence was purely "transcendental"— in reference to the cognitive subject—not existential or realistic. Kant does not take existence to be something real, whereas every Scholastic philosopher does. Heidegger's point is well made. And in fact it underlines the importance of reading St. Thomas correctly, for whom *esse*, as the act-of-existence, is far more real a structure than the *existentia* of Suárez. In a text which Heidegger cites (GP 122/87) but does not appreciate, St. Thomas says that *esse* is "the actuality of all things, even of the forms themselves" (ST, I, 4, 1, ad 3). Thus Aquinas has overcome the Kantian thesis on Being in a more radical way than Suárez has. But Heidegger shows no signs of realizing this.[4]

It is clear from § 10 of the *Grundprobleme* that although Heidegger thinks that Suárez' treatment of the distinction between essence and existence is the most plausible (GP 113/80), he does not regard any of these positions as satisfactory. For one thing, he thinks that the dispute is kept alive only because the meaning of the terms of the dispute keeps shifting. The essence which Aquinas takes to be really distinct from existence is a mere possibility (so says Heidegger), while the essence which according to Suárez is identical in reality with existence is a really existing essence. But this confusion points to a more fundamental defect in the Scholastic discussion, a defect which concerns what Husserl would call the "genesis" of these concepts. Thus in the next section of his text Heidegger takes up a critique of the Scholastic thesis on Being from the standpoint of a "genetic phenomenology."

A Phenomenological Genealogy of Essence and Existence

The obscurity which lies at the root of the Scholastic dispute originates, in Heidegger's view, with a failure to interpret the concepts of essence and existence adequately. And for the Heidegger of 1928, who stands in the shadow of Husserl's phenomenology to a much greater extent than is commonly imagined,[5] this means that these concepts have been naïvely taken over without regard to the way in which they originate in experience. On this account, Scholasticism is a species of objectivism; that is, it takes the products of thought to be things in themselves which have somehow entered our world without our cooperation. This, of course, is the trademark of all realism, be it Scholastic or scientific. Heidegger's argument here thus will not be unlike Husserl's "historical reduction" in "The Origin of Geometry," in which Husserl shows how Galileo naïvely took over the structures of Euclidean geometry without regard to their origin in the life-world.[6] That is why Heidegger asks at the beginning of § 11:

> Whence do the concepts of existence and whatness arise, that is, whence do they get the meaning they have as they are used in the discussion of the second thesis to which we have referred? . . . We shall ask what their birth certificate is and whether it is genuine, or whether the genealogy of these basic ontological concepts takes a different course so that at bottom their distinction and their connection have a different basis [GP 140/100].

If we can reach an understanding of the origin of the concepts of essence and existence, we shall then be in a position to clarify their fundamental meaning and to judge their adequacy as an interpretation of the meaning of Being. Just what sort of clarification this analysis brings about we shall see shortly.

In medieval ontology existence is conceived in terms of *actualitas*, a word which, of course, derives from *agere, actum*, and which signifies the action of a human subject. Thus the word *existentia*, though it is "apparently objective" (GP 143/101), in fact makes a concealed reference to Dasein conceived of as a productive agent (*herstellendes Dasein*). The actual is what is brought forth by the action of the active or productive agent. In German, *actualitas* is translated as *Wirklichkeit* (actuality, reality), a word whose root (*wirken*) preserves the sense of acting, making, producing. Thus the modern conception of *Wirklichkeit* (reality) means either the realm of those things which make their presence felt, which act upon the conscious subject (*das auf das Subjekt Einwirkende*) (GP 147/104), or that which belongs within a causal nexus, that which makes an effect on other beings (*das auf anderes sich Auswirkende*) (GP 147/104). But both these senses presuppose the medieval conception of *actualitas* which speaks to the question of how the being comes to be real or actual in the first place. Our task, therefore, Heidegger says, is to show how the "understanding of Being," from which the concept of existence, and with it the concept of essence too, is projected in terms of productivity (*Herstellen*), of the productive comportment of Dasein.[7]

Heidegger carries out this aim by showing how the family of words which signify essence is characterized in varying ways by a reference to the horizon of productivity. Essence and existence then turn out to be two prefitted stones which belong together in a natural unity. The word μορφή, for example, signifies a structure or configuration, not merely in the sense of the spatial shape, but in the phenomenological sense of that which gives rise to the "look" of a thing. From the point of view of perception, the look (εἶδος) is founded on the form (μορφή); a thing looks as it is formed. But in Greek ontology itself, this relationship is reversed. For the form is thought to be impressed upon a thing only in order to bring forth a certain look. That means that the Greeks think of these terms within the framework or horizon not of perception but of making or bringing forth, in terms of what is intended in the making, what is meant to be made by the making (GP 150/106). The model upon which this understanding of Being is based is that of the artisan, the potter, say, who aims to engender a certain form in the clay; the clay then takes on a look which conforms to the exemplar—the anticipated look—which he attempts to copy. The prototype, the exemplar, shows us how the thing is supposed to look before it is actually produced. That is why the expression τὸ τί ἦν εἶναι (*quid quod erat esse*), that which a thing was to be, is used interchangeably with εἶδος (*causa exemplaris*). The εἶδος is that from which the actual thing is descended, its kin, its γένος (*genus*, kind). The members of a genus form a group only because they have a common "descent," belong to the same "family." Hence, the word φύσις belongs to the same sphere of significance. Φύσις (*natura*) means growth, to produce its own kind. The "nature" of a thing is a self-producing essence.

The common thread which runs through all these words is easily detectable. Each signifies some kind of productive attitude on the part of Dasein. Now, to "pro-duce" in German is literally to "put" or "place" something "here" (*her-stellen*): "But *pro*-ducing [*Her*-stellen] means at the same time bringing into the narrower or wider circuit of the accessible, here, to this place, to the there [*in das Da*], so that the produced being *stands for itself* in its own self and, as something *standing for itself*, lies forth and remains discoverable" (GP 152/108). Now, that which primarily lies forth (*vor-liegt*), that which we come across for the most part day to day, is the things of use (*Gebrauchsdinge*), not just tools and implements, but the world with which we work, "house and yard, forest and field" (GP 153/108). This idea is brought out in an interesting way through the observation that the technical term which Aristotle uses for "being," οὐσία, also means in ordinary Greek disposable possessions, property, the goods of one's estate. (In English we hear an echo of this usage when we speak of a "man of substance," meaning a man with many possessions). The Being (*Wesen*) of the beings of daily life is presence-at-hand, being "at-hand," disposable presence. They come "toward" (*an*) us in their presence (*An-wesen*) as things of use.[8]

However, when we think about ancient ontology, what comes to mind is not primarily an ontology of πρᾶξις and of τὰ πράγματα but a "speculative" knowledge of Being. But this knowledge too belongs within the horizon of *Herstellen*, and is achieved by shifting from what is present-at-hand in its disposability (*vorhandenes Verfügbares*) (GP 153/108) to what is simply present, merely present, as something we merely come across (*vor-finden*). By the same token our relationship to what is present shifts from circum-spection (*umsichtigkeit*) to mere on-looking (*an-schauen*). The world is reduced to mere thingness, and the self to the speculative subject. Greek "speculative" philosophy is therefore a derivate, a privative mode of the primal understanding of Being in terms of Dasein's productive comportment.

Greek ontology belongs firmly within the horizon of *Herstellen*, of bringing-forth and producing. Essence and existence, which are the offspring of Greek ontology, likewise belong to the same horizon. However, both the Greek and medieval thinkers are themselves oblivious of the implicit reference of their understanding of Being to the productive comportment of Dasein: "Ancient ontology carries out in a virtually naïve way its interpretation of beings and its working out of the concepts mentioned" (GP 155/110; emphasis deleted). In order to overcome this naïveté, ontology must become "reflective." One is impressed here, and in other places throughout the *Basic Problems*, by the extent to which Heidegger still stands under the influence of Husserl's "transcendental phenomenology." For Heidegger's complaint here is precisely that the ancients do not carry out a "reflective" ontology, by which he means: "reflective in the genuine sense that it seeks to conceive beings with respect to their Being by having regard to Dasein (ψυχή, νοῦς, λόγος)" (GP 155/110; emphasis deleted). Moreover, to the extent to which the ancients do bring in a reference to Dasein, Dasein is itself conceived naïvely and in terms of an everyday understanding of its Being.

One can now see clearly the direction in which Heidegger's argument is moving. The ancient medieval ontology of mere presence-at-hand, or objective presence, is radically incomplete. It thinks the Being of objects but not their reference to Dasein. Hence, the whole of the second thesis about Being becomes questionable: "It is in no way proved and immediately evident that this thesis holds good of every being" (GP 157/111). At best, the thesis appears to have only a restricted validity. Every being is composed of *essentia* and *existentia* only if the proper Being of every being is to be something brought forth, produced. But what if there are other possible modes of Being? What of the Being of Dasein itself, in reference to which things take on the aspect of producibility? Can the Being of Dasein too be constrained within the limits of these categories? The objection which Heidegger makes here has its parallel in Husserl's critique of "reductionism," an error which, naïvely neglecting the Being of consciousness in the constitution of the world, goes on to treat consciousness as one more worldly thing. Thus Heidegger argues that Greek and Scholastic ontology, unmindful of the phenomenological and genealogical origins of their own concepts of *essentia* and *existentia* in Dasein's own productive comportment, go on to treat Dasein itself as one more entity to which these concepts apply in a more or less unexceptional way.

Heidegger's Ontological Difference and the Scholastic Distinction Between Essence and Existence

The final phase of Heidegger's argument in the *Basic Problems* (GP, § 12) consists in a proof of the incompleteness and naïveté of ancient ontology and an argument on behalf of his own "ontological difference," and is carried out by a closer analysis of what he calls the "intentional structure of the productive mode of comportment" (GP 159/112). Heidegger does not simply take over in an unaltered form Husserl's notion of intentionality. Rather he adapts it to, by founding it upon, his own notion of the understanding of Being. To intend is to point at; it is the directionality, the sense of direction (*Richtungssinn*) (GP 159/113), of the so-called directional arrow, that at which the intention aims. Now, for Heidegger this direction and aim are provided by the understanding of Being. To take an example from the sphere of operative intentionality which is developed in *Being and Time*, the famous example of hammering (SZ, § 15, 69/98): we may say that the intentional direction of the hammer (*das "um zu"*) is the construction of something, a cabinet, say. But it is clear that this directionality is provided for only on the basis of Dasein's prior understanding of the Being of the world of tools (*Zeuge*) as a system of references (*Verweisungszusammenhang*) (SZ, § 15, 70/99). In the present case, the case of "producing" (*Herstellen*), Heidegger tells us that the intentional aim is to bring forth a *finished* product. The aim of the making is to bring forth something which is "absolved" from its prior dependence upon the maker, set free, and set on its own, so that the product lives on with a Being of its own even if the producer should cease to be. Hence, Heidegger writes: "The Being which is understood in productive comportment is exactly the being-in-itself of the finished" (GP 160/113; emphasis deleted). Productivity moves within the intentional framework of discharging, dismissing. Here then we find a peculiar kind of transcendence in which the intentional relationship is structured around the breaking up of the relationship or reference of the object (product) to the subject (maker, producer). And clearly it was this unusual characteristic of productive intentionality which led to the naïveté and objectivism which characterize the old ontology, the realistic belief that it had to do with "things-in-themselves." For the being which is brought forth in productive intentionality has the look of the self-sufficient, the independent, the "in-itself."

It can, of course, be objected that the Greeks do not consider the totality of being to be created. For while what Aristotle called artifacts are indeed made, the Greeks thought that nature itself, the cosmos, was eternal and inoriginate. Still, Heidegger responds, in all making we presuppose a material which, as the raw material of the making, is itself not made. It is that "from which" what is made is taken. Thus even the inoriginate belongs within the horizon of production. The very meaning of "matter" springs up within an understanding of Being oriented toward producing. Matter is that from which things are made and that which offers resistance to the production (GP 163–64/116). The horizon of production then seems to have a universal scope and appears to apply to the totality of Being.

Thus the ideas of essence and existence take their origin from the subjective–existential sphere; they have their "birth certificate," to use Kant's expression (GP 140/100), in Dasein's concrete life. But this genetic origin was *forgotten* by the Scholastics, and that is what makes Scholastic "objectivism" possible. Like every objectivism, it is naïveté, forgetfulness (GP 155/110). Producing (*Herstellen*) is that by which something is brought forth so that it may stand there by itself (*für sich steht*) (GP 152/108). But once it is set forth we tend to forget that and how it was put there. We stand back and behold it. On the side of the subject, the practical life which produces is replaced by the theoretical look of the observer. On the side of the object, the being takes on the look of the ready-made, the finished, the in-itself (GP 159–60/113). Being in-itself is really Being which has been "set free" from its subjective origin. Thus even as the origins of geometry were forgotten, and the structures of geometry were taken over as ready-made by Galileo and the practitioners of the new science, so the life-world origin of the ideas of essence and existence dropped out of sight. Essence and existence are then taken to mean objective structures of Being which have nothing to do with the conscious subject out of whose concrete life they are first born.

In the light of this discussion, Heidegger thinks it is abundantly clear why the medieval thinkers found the categories of Greek ontology so amenable to their own theological purposes. For Christian theology interprets the world in the light of the story of creation in Genesis, and creation, even if it is creation *ex nihilo*, "has the general ontological character of producing" (GP 167/118): "Despite its different origins, ancient ontology, in its foundations and basic concepts, was as it were tailor-made to the Christian world view and interpretation of the being as *ens creatum*" (GP 168/118). The ancient ontology was of course "remodeled" when it entered the Christian world and, through Suárez, made its way into the modern world. Yet it is possible to see throughout the entirety of this tradition a single, identifiable understanding of Being in terms of production.

But is this horizon broad enough to encompass the totality of beings? Is there any being which, because of its Being, falls outside its scope? Every reader of *Being and Time* knows the answer to this question. For it is Heidegger's view in 1928 that although essence and existence are adequate categories to articulate the Being of what is present-at-hand, they do not befit the Being of the beings which we ourselves are. For Dasein has neither *essentia* nor *existentia*. Dasein has no *essentia* for it is not a thing (*res*), a whatness (*Washeit*). Dasein is not a thing, but an "I," not a "what" but a "who." One cannot get at the Being of Dasein by naming certain natural properties; none of the categories of things befits us precisely as Dasein. Dasein is not an instance of a universal species (εἶδος), but a uniquely existing individual. Dasein has, not *existentia*, but *Existenz*. *Existenz* has the Kierkegaardian sense of the being which has its Being to be, which takes over its Being as a thrown project for which it itself is responsible. *Existentia* signifies that which, being brought forth, stands outside of its causes (*extra causas sistere*). *Existenz* signifies that which casts itself forth into its possibility for Being (*Seinkönnen*).

There is a being whose Being is articulated into, not *essentia* and *existentia*, but "whoness" or "selfhood" (what is called *Jemeinigkeit* in *Being and Time*) and *Existenz* (or "facticity"). We have, then, two different kinds of articulation of Being, depending on whether we have in mind the Being of Dasein or the Being of what is present-at-hand—as the following diagram indicates:

	Dasein	Non-Dasein
How	Selfhood (*Werheit*)	Essence (*Washeit*)
That	Facticity	Existence

Accordingly, the medieval thesis has a restricted validity. It applies only to the sphere of presence-at-hand, not to Dasein itself. The difficulty with the thesis, therefore, is that it falls prey to what Merleau-Ponty calls the "prejudice of the world." For even though we all understand prephilosophically that man is different from worldly things, nevertheless when ancient and medieval ontology undertake to explicate the Being of Dasein philosophically, they do so in terms of the Being of beings other than Dasein. This ontology is therefore not only incomplete; it is naïve. For in omitting an account of Dasein it does not merely leave some particular being out. Rather it neglects to consider the Being of the being to which the understanding of Being itself belongs. It is only because Dasein itself understands Being in terms of producing and producibility that the categories of essence and existence can arise at all. Not only has Scholasticism omitted a particular being, Dasein; it has omitted the one which is ontically prior, and prior precisely because it is ontological (SZ, § 3).

And that leads us back to the ultimate point which Heidegger has been making all along in this discussion of the Scholastic thesis on Being, but a point which has not been noticeably stressed: the failure of ancient–medieval ontology lies in neglecting to think the ontological difference as such. "The problem of the articulation of Being into *essentia* and *existentia*, formulated Scholastically, is only a more special question touching on the ontological difference generally, that is, the difference between a being and Being" (GP 170/120). That is to say, the articulation of Being into essence and existence is itself dependent upon, and a function of, a more fundamental distinction. For Being will be articulated in different ways depending upon the manner of Being of the being. But that means that we must first learn to see a *being in* its Being, to think the *Being of* the being, before we attempt to articulate the "that" and the "how" of its Being:

"The articulation of Being varies each time with the manner of Being of a being" (GP 170/120). And that insight itself, that the Being of being varies, raises the question of the unity which pervades the evidently multiple meaning of Being, and puts Heidegger in the curious position of maintaining that medieval ontology, despite all its talk about the "analogy" of Being, in fact moved within a univocal horizon of Being as presence-at-hand. Though the Scholastic spoke of the diverse and analogical ways in which Being is predicated of God and creatures, it still took Being to mean presence-at-hand. It made no distinction between *Vorhandensein* and *Dasein*. It is only when we distinguish Being from beings that we see in truth that Being is said in many ways, that every being is a being in virtue of the horizon of Being within which it belongs. And, of course, it was Heidegger's intention to probe these multiple senses of Being further in order to find within them the unified sense of Being in terms of time.[9] Time is the unity which pervades the multiple ways in which Being comes to pass in beings. Ancient and medieval ontology persist in an oblivion of Being precisely because they persist in a single way of understanding Being. They manage only to move about within this single horizon and to articulate what belongs to its constitution while the ultimate horizon of Being itself remains unknown.

Before passing on to the critique of Scholasticism which Heidegger develops in his *Nietzsche* lectures, I should also briefly point out the presence of these same themes in *Being and Time* itself.[10] For according to Heidegger the *Basic Problems* is supposed to be a "new reworking of Division III" (GP 1n1/1n1) of this work. In *Being and Time*, medieval ontology was to be discussed in Division II of the projected Second Half. There Heidegger intended to show how medieval ontology had been taken over by, and incorporated within, Descartes' *cogito sum* (SZ, § 8). Though Descartes undertook a radical critique of all our epistemological presuppositions, his thought remains ontologically naïve. Though he establishes the *cogito* as his *fundamentum inconcussum*, he neglects to question the Being of the *sum*. Instead he simply takes over the ontology of the medievals. As a being (*ens*), the *cogito* is *ens creatum*, and the idea of God which is implanted in the *cogito* is the idea of an *ens increatum*. Ontologically, his thought moves within the horizon of the medieval understanding of Being in terms of *Herstellen*:

But createdness in the widest sense of the producedness [*Hergestellt-heit*] of something is an essential structural moment of the ancient concept of Being. The apparently new beginning of philosophizing reveals itself as the planting of a fateful prejudice, on the basis of which latter times omit a thematic, ontological analytic of the "mind" which would be guided by the question of Being as also a critical confrontation with the inherited ancient ontology [SZ, § 6, 24–25/70].

The source of this prejudice on Descartes' part is his familiarity with Suárez, whose *Metaphysical Disputations* turned on the distinction between the metaphysics of finite and infinite being: "In its Scholastic mold, Greek ontology makes the essential transition via the *Disputationes metaphysicae* of Suárez into the 'metaphysics' and 'transcendental' philosophy of the modern period; it still determines the foundations and goals of Hegel's *Logic*" (SZ, § 6, 22/67). Heidegger's discussion of Scholasticism in the *Basic Problems* thus fills out for us what is only fleetingly alluded to in *Being and Time* itself. This work belongs firmly within the framework of *Being and Time* and tells us what the author of that classic treatise, and sometime student of Scholasticism only a little over a decade earlier, has to say about the understanding of Being which is to be found in Scholastic metaphysics.

THE *Nietzsche* LECTURES (1941)

If the critique of Scholasticism which is worked out in the *Basic Problems* belongs to the standpoint of *Being and Time*, the discussion of Scholasticism in "Metaphysics as the History of Being" (N II, 399–420/1–19) moves decidedly within the framework of the "later" standpoint. It is of no small importance to us to follow this discussion. For not only does it tell us something about how Heidegger's position has progressed in the intervening years, but it also carries his critique of Scholasticism forward to an even more radical level. In these pages, Heidegger looks on medieval ontology in terms of the "history of Being" and, from that standpoint, finds a great distance between Greek and medieval ontology. In *Being and Time* the Scholastics are thought to have furthered (*weiterführen*) the problematic of ancient ontology, despite the dogmatic formulation which they gave to their thought (SZ, § 6, 22/67). But in the later writings the Greeks and the medievals are thought to be separated by an abyss. The medieval translation of the basic words of Greek thought represents a fateful covering over of the original Greek experience (Holz.² 371/56–57). Now the medievals are thought to belong to the wake of Plato and Aristotle, who themselves are but echoes of a great beginning in the early Greeks. The history of metaphysics is a continual falling out from the first Greek encounter with Being, a falling out which received a decisive push from the Scholastic doctrine of Being.

Plato and Aristotle: 'Iδέα and 'Ενέργεια

The distinction between essence and existence is an essential part of the formation of the history of Being. The expression "history of Being," to those who are not already familiar with the later Heidegger, must seem to be quite odd. Heidegger does not speak of the history of philosophy, of thought, or of man, because he does not want to suggest that this history is the doing of man:

> The history of Being is neither the history of man and mankind nor the history of the human relationship to beings and Being. The history of Being is Being itself and only this. Yet because Being lays claim to the essence of man for the foundation of its truth in beings, man remains drawn into the history of Being, but always only with respect to the way in which he takes his essence from the relation of Being to himself and, according to this relation, takes over his essence, loses it, gives it over, surrenders it, founds it, or squanders it [N II 489].

This history is Being itself, and it involves man only insofar as man is required by Being in order to bring about its self-disclosure. For the Heidegger of the later period metaphysics is no longer a name for the authentic uncovering of Being—as it was in the Kant book and in *What is Metaphysics?*—but a name for that kind of thinking from which Being in its truth has withdrawn. What is disclosed in metaphysics, what comes to presence in metaphysics, is a sequence of formations of Beings, epochal shapes of Being in which we experience, not Being itself, but what Heidegger calls the "Beingness"

(*Seiendheit*) of beings, features and names of Being which are drawn from one region of beings or another—will, mind, matter, spirit, etc. The history of metaphysics is, therefore, not the history of human speculation about Being, but the history of Being's progressive concealment of its truth by means of its revelation of itself through these various metaphysical faces.

The dominant metaphysical look which Being has in the modern world is that of "actuality" (*Wirklichkeit*), a word which suggests that which is real (*wirklich*), not merely mental. But having a root, as we have seen, in the word *wirken*, this word suggests a connection with working, making, producing. Now, the predominantly modern sense of "actuality" (*Wirklichkeit*) is causal: that is real which acts or is capable of acting on another. The real world is the spatio-temporal–causal world. As a translation of the Latin *existentia*, *Wirklichkeit* refers to the fact "that" a thing is. This in turn is distinguished from "what" a thing is, which is a mere "possibility." For the Heidegger of 1941 this metaphysical distinction between essence and existence, is not just one more metaphysical theory; it is a prescription and delineation of the essence of metaphysics:

> Being is divided into whatness and thatness. The history of metaphysics begins with this distinction and its preparation. Metaphysics includes the distinction in the structure of the truth about beings as a whole. Thus the beginning of metaphysics is revealed as an event that consists in a determination of Being, in the sense of the appearance of the division into whatness and thatness [N II 401/2–3].

The task which Heidegger sets for himself in this essay is to go back to the origin of this distinction which is taken everywhere to be self-evident (*selbstverständlich*). The question of the origin of this distinction is one which metaphysics itself cannot raise, for metaphysics moves *within* the distinction and is made possible by it. Thus the attempt to inquire about its origin is an essay in overcoming metaphysics. This origin is "concealed" from it, or "expressed in the Greek manner: forgotten" (N II 402/3). This oblivion means "the self-concealing of the origin of Being divided into whatness and thatness in favor of Being which opens up [*lichtet*] beings as beings and remains unquestioned as *Being*" (N II 402/3–4). Being itself remains unthought in favor of the Being (= Beingness, *Seiendheit*) which is divided into essence and existence. But this oblivion is, not human forgetting, but rather a withdrawal on the part of Being, "an event in the history of Being" (N II 402/4).[11]

The "genealogy" which Heidegger offers us in the *Nietzsche* lectures, therefore, differs in a fundamental way from the genealogy found in the *Grundprobleme*. For the origin of essence and existence is traced back, not to a way in which Dasein projects the Being of beings, not to Dasein's projective understanding of Being (*Verstehen, Konstruction*), but to the primal beginnings of Western thought among the Greeks. Essence and existence are fundamental concepts which have been handed over to us by the tradition, and spring from the first disclosure of Being among the Greeks. The history of the West begins with the self-disclosure of Being to the early Greeks, a disclosure which is given its highest expression in the Greek words ἀλήθεια and φύσις. Φύσις signifies the upsurge of beings into Being, the emerging of Being in and through beings; it signifies Being as emergent process, as rising up, as upsurge (*Aufgehung*) (VA 269/ 112). Ἀλήθεια signifies the "light" dimension of the emergence process, and means the emergence of Being into presence (*Anwesen*), into the clearing (*Lichtung*), the process of opening up an open space, a space of manifestness in which beings are disclosed as what they are. This primal disclosure of Being as a kind of limpid self-revelation is bestowed upon the early Greeks, the Greeks before Plato and Aristotle, those thinkers who are greater "thinkers" than Plato and Aristotle because they are not yet "philosophers" (WdP 52–53).

The primal disclosure of Being as pure presencing which is granted to the early Greeks soon passes over into a certain "congealment" of presencing in the form of permanent presence: "In the beginning of its history, Being opens itself out as emerging [φύσις] and unconcealment [ἀλήθεια]. From there it reaches the formulation of presentness [*Anwesenheit*] and permanence [*Beständigkeit*] in the sense of enduring [*Verweilen*], οὐσία" (N II 403/4). The fluid, emergent process of φύσις is congealed into a kind of permanence and static presence. The verbally thought "coming to presence" (*An-wesen*) hardens into the more rigid nominative present-ness (*Anwesen-heit*). The fluctuation between presence and absence is consolidated in rigid presence. The Being of a thing, as a lingering between the absence from which it emerges and to which it returns, becomes a predominantly present presence which tries to expel all absence. Presencing in absence strives to become presencing without absence, a theme which is announced with particular clarity in Heidegger's provocative interpretation of the Anaximander fragment, which I shall examine below (Chapter 6). The fluctuating coming to be and passing away is resisted; the being attempts to maintain itself in Being, and the process of un-concealment gives way to something permanently present. And this is the fateful (*seinsgeschichtlich*) meaning of the word οὐσία, the name for Being which is spoken by Aristotle.

How then does Aristotle understand what is present (*das Anwesende*) in its presence (*Anwesen*)? "What becomes present shows itself to Aristotle's thinking as that which stands in a permanence having come to a stand, or lies present having been brought to its place" (N II 403/4). The being for Aristotle is that which lies forth in its presence (*das Vorliegende*), what is brought to a standing rest (*das Beständige*). This rest is, not a mere cessation, but a completion in the literal sense of the German *Voll-endung*, being brought to a fullness, to a full ending, which explains Heidegger's interpretation of the Aristotelian terms ὑποκείμενον, lying forth, and ἐντελέχεια, fulfillment. He gives the example of a house:

> The house standing there is *set out* in unconcealment in that it is set forth in its outward appearance and stands in this appearance. Standing, it rests, rests in the "out" of its setting out. The resting of what is produced is not nothing, but rather gathering. It has gathered into itself all the movements of the production of the house. . . . The house there *is* as ἔργον. "Work" means what is completely at rest in the rest of outward appearance—standing, lying in it—what is completely at rest in presencing in unconcealment [N II 404/5].

The house is thought, not in terms of a "thing" in the sense of a substance, as οὐσία was later translated, but in terms of manifestness, unconcealment. Heidegger interprets the Aristotelian work not in the sense of making but in the sense of setting a thing out into the exposure (*Ausstellung*) of being manifest. Heidegger wants to read ἐνέργεια in "alethiological" terms: "Thought in the Greek manner, the work is not work in the sense of the accomplishment of a strenuous making. . . . It is a work in the sense of that which is placed in the unconcealment of its outward appearance and endures thus standing or lying." And again: "Ἔργον now characterizes the manner of presencing. Presence, οὐσία, thus means ἐνέργεια, to presence as work (presence understood verbally) in the work of workness" (N II 404/ 5). For Heidegger, therefore, Aristotle is not the father of the four causes, not the tough-minded philosopher of natural causality which we today associate with his name (VA 15–20/289–94), but an alethiological thinker who speaks, not of how things are made, but of how they rise up into manifestness.[12]

But even granted this rather bold interpretation of Aristotle, what does it tell us about the bifurcation of presencing into essence and existence? To answer this question, Heidegger has recourse to Aristotle's distinction between first and second οὐσία. Οὐσία in the primary sense (that which comes to presence in the primary sense) is the "this," the singular, e.g., this man. But what is present in a secondary sense is the outward look, e.g., the individual man stands in the outward appearance (εἶδος) of a man. This is the distinction between the existing individual and what the individual is, in other words between that it is (*existentia*) and what it is (*essentia*). But this is a distinction which originates in Being as presence, for presence can signify alternately either the singular thing which is present (*das Anwesende*) or the look which it has as it is exposed to view.

In Aristotle, *existentia* predominates over *essentia*. For Aristotle assigned the primacy to the τόδε τι, the particular thing. It was Plato who took the outward look, the εἶδος, ἰδέα, as what is truly present. Both Plato and Aristotle take Being to mean the permanent presencing of οὐσία. But Aristotle emphasizes the singular thing; and Plato, the κοινόν, the universal look. In staying with the concrete and singular, Aristotle is truly more Greek than Plato: "However, to say that Aristotle is more truly Greek in his thinking than Plato in the way described does not mean that he again comes closer to the primordial thinking of Being. Between ἐνέργεια and the primordial essence of Being [ἀλήθεια–φύσις] stands the ἰδέα" (N II 409/10).

As a result of the labors of Plato and Aristotle, the foundational concepts for all subsequent metaphysics—essence and existence—are worked out in principle. The subsequent history of metaphysics consists in the working out of the possible interrelations between these ideas. All later metaphysics moves within the interplay of these two concepts.

Heidegger mentions that within the metaphysical tradition of Being as *Anwesenheit* and οὐσία, ἐνέργεια takes precedence over εἶδος, existence over essence (N II 410/10). Here is a recognition on his part of the "primacy of existence"; but it evidently does not affect his thinking about essence and existence. No matter which principle is taken to be primary, both remain captive of a tradition in which Being as φύσις and ἀλήθεια is contracted to Being as permanent presence. Even the existential revolution in Thomistic metaphysics, it would seem, makes no change in principle in the kind of Being which this metaphysical tradition has in mind. Even if all the claims of the Thomists are true, Thomism would represent some kind of completion and perfection of its particular tradition of Being as *Anwesenheit*, but it does not, in Heidegger's view, succeed in escaping that tradition. The oblivion of Being persists no matter whether essence or existence is given primacy. Even where existence is taken to be prior, Heidegger insists, existence itself merits no further comment (N II 411/11). Existence is the positing of something by which it is recognized as actual. Its meaning is self-evident and it warrants no further consideration. But can this be seriously maintained about the metaphysics of *esse* in St. Thomas? Still, even if this is not true of St. Thomas, is not Thomistic metaphysics fixed within the tradition of Being as permanent presence? These are the questions which must occupy us as we proceed with this study. But for the moment we must continue to examine Heidegger's critique.

From Ἐνέργεια to *Actualitas*

The next step in Heidegger's interpretation of the history of metaphysics, a history which can be told entirely in terms of the distinction between whatness and thatness, is the examination of the medieval Scholastic phase. In this stage ἐνέργεια is translated as *actualitas*. As with all translations, Heidegger does not take this to be an innocent linguistic convention, but a fateful historical event. On the face of it, the word *ex-sistentia* is an apt choice which appears to preserve the impact of ἐνέργεια. Literally, it means to stand (*sisto, sistere*, a cognate of *sto, stare*) outside of (*ex*). Hence, the word literally translates the Greek ἔκστασις. Accordingly, it suggests an alethiological sense: that which stands out in the light of the day. Heidegger writes: "*Ex-sistere speculo* means for Cicero to step out of the cave. One might suspect here a deeper relation of *existentia* as stepping out and forward to coming forward to presence and unconcealment. Then

the Latin word *existentia* would preserve an essential Greek content."
But our hopes are dashed: "That is not the case. Similarly, *actualitas*
no longer preserves the essence of ἐνέργεια. The literal translation is
misleading. In truth it brings precisely another displacement to the
word of Being, a displacement of another type of humanity to the
whole of beings, one which comes about in virtue of the closure of
Being" (N II 411–12/12).

An essential change of meaning sets in with this translation, and
not merely a change of meaning in a particular word. Rather an entirely new epoch of Being comes about in which the meaning of Being and the relationship between Being and man undergoes a profound modification. In the end, to understand this claim, one would
have to examine Heidegger's conception of language, according to
which it is not so much man who speaks but language itself speaking
in and through him, or, alternately put, in which human speaking is
more a response to a word addressed to man by Being (see Chapter
5, below). *Existentia* is not a human choice but a movement on the
part of Being.

What, then, happens with the advent of *actualitas* and *existentia*?

> In the beginning of metaphysics, the being as ἔργον is what comes to
> presence in its being produced. Now ἔργον becomes the *opus* of the
> *operari*, the *factum* of the *facere*, the *actus* of the *agere*. The ἔργον
> is no longer what is freed in the openness of presencing, but rather
> what is effected in working, what is accomplished in action. The es-
> sence of the "work" is no longer "workness" in the sense of distinc-
> tive presencing in the open, but rather the "reality" of a real thing
> which rules in working and is fitted into the procedure of working
> [N II 412/12].

In other words, *existentia* and *actualitas* strip ἐνέργεια of its alethiological sense. Even if the primordial essence of presencing (*der an-
fängliche Wesen des Anwesen*) (N II 409/10) had congealed in the
Platonic and Aristotelian conception of οὐσία, it nonetheless had re-
tained an *alethiological* content. It still meant the realm of the open,
the manifest, the sphere of self-presenting. But in the medieval *actualitas* Being is now understood in terms of making and being made,
of causal work. Ἔργον comes to mean *opus*, *factum*. This is con-
firmed by the Scholastic interpretation of the derivation of the word
ex-sistere. This word signifies that a thing stands outside of its causes,

that it is real or actual in the sense of being really made and finished. Thus the cabinet which the carpenter is thinking about making is an essence, a possibility, until it is actually made, in which case it "exists" outside the carpenter's mind in the real world. To be is to be actual (*wirklich*), that is, to be brought forth (*pro-ductum*) outside of one's cause (*pro-ducens*). All the world, the totality of beings, is divided between the being which makes (*ens infinitum, creator*) and the being which is made (*ens finitum, creatum*). The understanding of Being which governs medieval metaphysics belongs to the metaphysics of making. Not only has original presencing hardened into permanent presence; but it has lost its original quality of self-showing manifestness and been turned into what is present as a product, what is objectively present, not what is self-showing but what is made and manufactured.

In the *Basic Problems*, Christian creationism was said to fit hand in glove with the categories of Greek ontology which were oriented toward the horizon of making and producing. But now that interpretation has been revoked, and we are asked to read Plato and Aristotle in an alethiological manner. Hence, Heidegger looks elsewhere for a companion to the medieval dispensation of Being. This he finds in Rome: "But in order to realize sufficiently even merely historically the scope of this transition, the Roman character must be understood in the full wealth of its historical developments . . ." (N II 412/12). The metaphysics of making which comes about in the Christian Middle Ages is assisted into birth by the Roman language. Rome is a world civilization of action (*actus, agere, actus, actualitas*): the conquerors of the world, the imperial power. And it is also the world civilization of making, of productive work, of the builders of roads and bridges. The shadow of this imperial–productive civilization reaches across the Christian Middle Ages and into the modern world. Hence, the text cited above continues: "so that it includes the political imperial element of Rome, the Christian element of the Roman Church, and the Romantic element as well." Thus the medieval Christian conception of Being in terms of making and what is made is articulated in a language which belongs to the people of making and doing. The "Roman Church" is not just an historical appellation. It points to an inner harmony between Christian metaphysics and the metaphysics of making, which come together in the conception of Being as *Wirklichkeit*. Our tradition then is more Roman than Greek;

we are determined more by the builders of empires and roads than by those who let things be present in their presence.

In the transition from ἐνέργεια to *actualitas*, the primordial essence of Being experienced by the Greeks is covered over: "the primordial Greek essential character of Being is once and for all misunderstood and made inaccessible by the Roman interpretation of Being" (N II 415/14).

An essential feature of this interpretation of Being as actuality is the predominance of the principle of causality. But the Greek conception of presence is not without relationship to this development. For, after all, the metaphysical epochs are all transformations of the fullness of *Anwesen* itself (*die Wandlungsfülle des Seins*) (SD 7/8), so that even the extreme covering over (*Verdeckung*) of Being as presence which takes place as technology is itself a mode of presence. In the Greek conception ἰδέα is connected with ἀγαθόν, which has the role of cause, αἰτία, of the coming-to-be of a thing in accord with its ἰδέα. Αἰτία then comes to predominate over ἀρχή so that in Aristotle the two tend to coalesce. At that point Being comes to mean that which is responsible for, effects, or brings about the constant (*das Beständige*).

This is all brought out very clearly in the Scholastic conception of God. The more what is present endures in its permanence, the more actual it is. But God cannot be lacking in Being. And since Being means permanence, God is the most enduring, most fully actual being, the *actus purus*. His Being is self-persisting; He owes His presence to nothing other than Himself. But this self-persisting being (*für sich Bestehendes*) is the *summum ens* and as such the *summum bonum*, which makes Him the cause of causes. Plato, Aristotle, and the Scholastics all agreed that among the causes the end is the highest cause: *causalitas causae finalis est prima*. As the highest cause, God endows (*er-wirkt*) what is real (*Wirkliche*) with its persistence (*Beständigkeit*). The original Greek experience of Being then is covered over by the categories of actuality (*Wirklichkeit*), causality (*Wirken*), and persistent presence. Even presence itself—the divine *omnipraesentia*—is defined in terms of causality. Thus St. Thomas says that God is present to everything in virtue of being its cause (ST, I, 8, 3).

Both *actualitas* and *existentia* have a causal meaning in Scholastic metaphysics. *Ex-sistentia* means that which stands outside of. But the crucial point is to determine that in reference to which it is "outside."

Though for Aristotle the being stands outside speech and thought, the Scholastics think the being as standing outside its causes. Suárez says that existence is that by which "something is constituted outside its causes" (*quo . . . aliqua constituitur extra causas suas*) (N II 418/17), that by which a thing "is posited outside of the state of possibility" (*ponitur extra statum possibilitatis*) (N II 419/18). The being is set free from its cause and made to stand on its own. This we have already seen from the *Basic Problems* lectures.

The meaning of Being is determined in terms of *Wirken*, effecting, and the manifold ways for beings to be are all modes of effecting, derivatives of effecting: "Being presences [*west*] as effecting in the unified–manifold sense according to which the being is: the effecting, but also the effected and also the effecting–effected and the effective. The being thus determined in terms of effecting is real [*wirk-lich*]" (N II 420/18–19). We who have taken the time to examine Heidegger's relationship to Carl Braig can only wonder how much this characterization of Being in the Middle Ages is determined by *Vom Sein*. But that is a "merely historical" (*historisch*) question. Our ultimate concern is with the legitimacy and aptness of this interpretation of medieval metaphysics, especially as it applies to the metaphysics of *esse*.

Let us then briefly survey the result of this inquiry into the history of Being. Being is experienced among the early Greeks in terms of a primordial presencing (*Anwesen*) which takes shape in the words φύσις, λόγος, and ἀλήθεια. The first beginning (*Anfang*) passes over into the beginning (*Begin*) of metaphysics in Plato and Aristotle, in which original presence congeals into οὐσία, permanent presence. In this congealment both ἀγαθόν and αἴτιον are allowed to emerge. But even though original presencing has hardened into οὐσία in Plato and Aristotle, these thinkers retain at least an "echo of the great origin of Greek philosophy" (*Weg.*[2] 300/268) and so οὐσία retains a vestige of an alethiological meaning. But in the transition to the Scholastics one hears only a "much weaker, much-harder-to-find echo" in which the original sense of presencing has been covered over in terms of *Wirklichkeit* and causality, effecting and what is effected. This is what takes place in the movement from φύσις to ἐνέργεια to *actualitas*.

Nor is this the end of the story, for Heidegger has always insisted upon the continuity of the missions of Being. Even if they do not re-

duce to a necessary progress in the manner of Hegel, still there is a
unity and cohesiveness to the manner of their movement (SD 55–
56/52). The medieval epoch prepares the way for the withdrawal
of Being in the modern epoch (= ἐποχή): "The essential origin of
Being as making possible and as causing dominates throughout the
future history of Being. Making possible, causing, accounting for,
are determined in advance as gathering in virtue of the One as what
is uniquely unifying" (N II 420/19). The modern conception of
"nature" (natura, Natur) as a spatio-causal system, as the "real"
world in the sense of what produces real effects, is rooted in medieval
creationism, in creationistic metaphysics.[13] Heidegger is thus suggesting that the metaphysics of modern technology, the Ge-stell, is
not so far removed from the causa prima and creator-God of the Scholastics. When the Church took on Bruno and Galileo at the time of
the birth of modern physics, this had to be for Heidegger a merely in-
house controversy which took place within the parameters of an understanding of Being in terms of causality and actuality.

THE CHANGING PERSPECTIVE OF HEIDEGGER'S CRITIQUE

There are two significant differences between Heidegger's treatment
of Scholastic metaphysics in the Basic Problems and in the Nietzsche
lectures. (a) To begin with, Heidegger sees a much greater distance
between the Greeks and the Scholastics in 1941 than he did in 1928.
He has a stronger sense of the primordiality of the Greeks, and he regards the medieval dispensation of Being as a fateful concealment of
the original Greek experience. In the Basic Problems the medieval
thinkers are thought to be the continuation of Greek ontology; in the
Nietzsche lectures they are a distortion of it. In 1928 the Greeks mean
primarily Plato and Aristotle—no special importance appears to
be placed yet on Parmenides, Heraclitus, and Anaximander. These
thinkers are taken to have projected the meaning of Being in terms
of making and producing (Herstellen), which is said to have been
tailor-made to the needs of the creationist metaphysics of the Middle
Ages. But in 1941 Plato and Aristotle are read in primarily alethiological terms. In this reading, ἰδέα and ἐνέργεια occupy something of
a halfway house between the primordial experience of presencing as
φύσις and ἀλήθεια and λόγος in the early Greeks and the hardened,

congealed understanding of presence in Scholasticism, in which the measure of Being is the permanence and steadfastness of a being's hold on Being. Thus, if we listen carefully to ἐνέργεια, and do not translate it *actualitas*, we shall hear the Greek experience of setting a thing out into manifestness in the form of the work. But *actualitas* speaks only of making and producing effects. Thus the main features of Heidegger's "history of Being" are much more sharply carved in 1941 and, because of that, he sees a much sharper division between the various epochs of Western history. His historical sensitivities are keener, and the early Greeks are now taken to be the "great origin" of the West, an origin which antedates the "beginning" (*Beginn*) of metaphysics in Plato and Aristotle. (In *Being and Time*, the great beginnings were taken to be identical with Plato and Aristotle—SZ, § 1). In 1941 he sees the Scholastics as constituting the crucial bridge to the modern metaphysics of "actuality" (*Wirklichkeit*) which represents a still greater removal from the original Greek experience of Being. Scholasticism is viewed as transitional to modern technology, whereas Plato and Aristotle are the last echo of the primordial origin of Western thought.

(*b*) The strong sense of history which Heidegger displays in 1941 is itself the result of his conviction, first developed in the late '30s, that the history of the West is the history of Being itself. I have already adverted to this in my introductory remarks to the *Nietzsche* lectures above; I must add here, however, that this shift constitutes a critique of the earlier position. Hence, Heidegger writes: "But this destruction [which is carried out in *Being and Time*], like 'phenomenology' and all hermeneutical transcendental questions, has not yet been thought in terms of the history of Being" (N II 415/15). In 1941 the medieval Scholastic conception of Being is understood as an address which is sent to medieval thought by Being itself. The greatness of a thinker like Thomas Aquinas is that he has heard what Being addresses to him, and says what is contained in this address. But in 1928 Heidegger held rather a different view. He took the Scholastic conception of Being to be a projection of Being in terms of a certain horizon of understanding—and this is why the view is in the broad sense "transcendental." And his criticism is that this projection is carried out naïvely, that while it is drawn from Dasein and its way to be, the unique way to be of man lies in oblivion. Hence, the categories of medieval metaphysics are too narrow; they suffice to explain things but not to explain the Being of man, that is, of Dasein, itself. Scholasticism is lacking in an appreciation of the Being of *Existenz*, despite all its talk of *essentia* and *existentia*. Now, this is rather a different criticism from that put forward in 1941. In *Basic Problems* the criticism is not that these categories are too narrow—that they apply only to things and not to Dasein—but that they are a degenerate form of the original experience of presencing, that they do not suffice for an understanding either of man or of things. They represent a falling away from original essence of presencing to be found in the early Greeks. In 1928 the criticism is not that medieval ontology is all that wrong-headed, but that it is objectivistic, thing-oriented, naïve, oblivious of the transcendental, projective role which Dasein plays in giving meaning to things and of the unique mode of Being of Dasein itself. Hence, it was in no position to lay claim to a universal ontology; it had succeeded only in working up a more or less adequate regional ontology. It lacked a fundamental ontology of Dasein's founding mode of Being and it was therefore unable to say what Being in general means. Although Heidegger does not bring this out explicitly in *Basic Problems*, §§ 10–12, it is obvious that any conception of Being in general which is put forth in medieval ontology would have to miss thematizing the transcendental clue of time —because it never secured its bearing by an analysis of Dasein's way to be as temporality. Scholastic metaphysics falls victim to the prejudice of the world.

But the critique of 1941 is more radical. *Essentia* and *existentia* are not said to have a limited validity, in the sphere of things; they are taken to be "masks" or coverings (*Verbergungen*) (N II 415/14) which conceal the early Greek experience of Being. They do not capture the fluctuating essence of presencing as rising up and falling back, as a lingering in the juncture between presence and absence. Rather they turn what is present (*das Anwesende*) into a permanent thing, *substantia*, which abides permanently (*das Beständige*), a thing which is put forth and made to last by a lasting maker. The thing which presences has become a piece of durable goods, made to last.

It is to a large extent futile to argue against the "transcendental" critique which Heidegger launches against Scholasticism, inasmuch as he himself abdicated that position and, to my knowledge, does not repeat this criticism elsewhere. Moreover, the possibility of articulating Scholasticism from a transcendental standpoint has been widely experimented with today. In fact, as I noted in the first chapter, the work of Maréchal at Louvain was already underway in 1928, but Heidegger either does not know about it or for some reason chooses to pay it no mind, perhaps regarding it as immaterial to his present purposes. Rahner, Lotz, and Coreth have all attempted to develop a transcendental Thomism which goes back not only to Kant but specifically to *Being and Time*. They have tried to root St. Thomas' notion of *esse* in an inherent dynamism of the intellect. In a brief but quite illuminating study of Heidegger's "existential philosophy," written in 1940, Karl Rahner argues, in keeping with Heidegger, for the importance of taking up the question of Being from a transcendental standpoint. Being cannot be gotten at "head on," he says; an access to Being through the human subject must first be established. For Being is not a being, not just something lying about which we can grasp:

> As the a priori and necessary universal propositions show, the notion of being pre-exists, underlying every individual cognition. There is no way of defining it by appealing to such and such a characteristic of some particular being; we have to go all the way back to that initial notion that the human mind possesses of it; in other words, we must go back to man himself: the inquiring subject becomes the subject of the inquiry. Now the return to the subject is precisely the essence of a transcendental approach.[14]

And in his *Metaphysics* Coreth argues that the point of departure for metaphysics is the question of Being. Coreth takes into account the necessity of a fundamental ontology, the idea of hermeneutic of Dasein, and the importance of the pre-ontological understanding of Being.[15] Though I do not want to decide the issue here, and in spite of the fact that a really complete study of this question has yet to be done, it would seem that it is possible for Scholasticism to meet Heidegger's charge of transcendental naïveté, and that Transcendental Thomism is a considerable step forward in this direction.[16]

I shall therefore not pursue the transcendental criticism of Scholasticism any further in this study.[17] Instead I shall turn my attention to another point around which the essence of Heidegger's genuine critique of Scholasticism as a species of *Seinsvergessenheit* seems to me to turn. Heidegger always regarded the Scholastic conception of Being as articulated in terms of making and production, *Herstellen*. In his view, *esse* means to be actual, *wirk-lich*, and so belongs within the horizon of effecting, *wirken*. As such it is a falling away from the primordial Greek experience of presencing. Following up this point will lead me into the central issue: the relationship between the metaphysics of *esse* and the attempt on Heidegger's part to think Being in terms of the historical movement of Being through the West. This will lead me straight to the question of the *Ereignis* and *esse*.

But for the moment the problem is to be posed as follows. Heidegger takes Scholasticism to have fallen short of a genuine conception of Being as such, to be in oblivion of the genuine meaning of Being, and to have thought Being solely in terms of producing (*Herstellen*) and actuality (*Wirklichkeit*). In Scholasticism there is a genuine conception, not of Being, but of beingness (*Seiendheit*). The Scholastic thinker, or at least the students of St. Thomas, on the other hand, resolutely insist that the only genuine conception of Being as Being, the only conception which does not reduce Being to some ontic property, is to be found in the metaphysics of *esse*. Everywhere else there is the oblivion of Being, of *esse*; everywhere else there is only some variation of essentialism. These are competing claims which I must now try to adjudicate.

NOTES

1. For an excellent overview of the argument of the *Basic Problems*, see John Sallis, "Radical Phenomenology and Fundamental Ontology," *Research in Phenomenology*, 6 (1976), 139–50.

2. I have examined Heidegger's conception of phenomenology in the *Basic Problems* in my "The Question of Being and Transcendental Phenomenology: Heidegger's Relationship to Husserl," ibid., 7 (1977), 84–105.

3. Before taking up these three positions Heidegger adds an observation (GP 126–28/90–91) which, in the light of my previous study *The Mystical Element in Heidegger's Thought*, deserves comment. We are inclined to think, Heidegger says, that these controversies are so many exercises in Scholastic hairsplitting. In fact, a knowledge of the issues at work here is essential for understanding matters of the highest importance, matters such as the history of modern philosophy, Protestant theology, and medieval mysticism, in particular, the mysticism of Meister Eckhart. In medieval mysticism God is taken as "the authentic essential Being" (*das eigentliche Wesen*) who must be understood in His essentiality (*Wesenheit*). Here one of the principles of the articulation of Being—*essentia*—itself becomes a being of the highest order.

Heidegger is referring to Meister Eckhart's notion of the divine Godhead (*Gottheit, divinitas*) beyond God (*Gott, deus*), a "superessential" region or core of God which every name or property we ascribe to God fails to grasp. It is the region which Eckhart calls alternately the divine "abyss" (*Abgrund*), the divine "wasteland" (*Wüste*), or even the divine "nothing" (*Nichts*). He concludes with a sentiment which exactly parallels a remark in *Der Satz vom Grund* (SG 71) : "The mysticism of the Middle Ages, more exactly expressed, mystical theology, is not mystical in our sense, in the bad sense, but rather it can be conceived in a wholly eminent sense" (GP 128/91).

4. On this point, see Cornelio Fabro, "The Transcendentality of *Ens–Esse* and the Ground of Metaphysics," *International Philosophical Quarterly*, 6, No. 3 (September 1966), 389–427.

5. This point is argued in the study mentioned in note 2.

6. In *The Crisis of European Sciences and Transcendental Phenomenology: An Introduction to Phenomenological Philosophy*, trans. David Carr, Northwestern University Studies in Phenomenology and Existential Philosophy (Evanston, Ill.: Northwestern University Press, 1970), Appendix VI, pp. 353–78.

7. We cannot forget that for Carl Braig the acting subject was the paradigm case of all Being, which was itself to be understood in terms of *Wirklichkeit* and *actualitas*. See above, chap. 1, appendix.

8. At this point Heidegger seems to have collapsed the distinction between *Vor-handen-sein* and *Zu-handen-sein*, making the former do duty for both senses by exploiting the *hand* in *Vorhandensein*.

9. Of course, Scholastic thinkers, like Johannes Lotz (see chap. 7 below), respond that Heidegger's conception of Being is time-bound and hence in this sense univocal.

10. It often goes unnoticed that of the first seven footnotes in *Being and Time* three refer to Aristotle and two to St. Thomas.

11. Heidegger means that the oblivion of Being is, in fact, the self-withdrawal or self-concealment of Being itself, for which no human being is to be held responsible. To be sure. But insofar as it remains the task of thought to think this withdrawal as a withdrawal, to stand in this oblivion and take cognizance of it (SD 32/30), is there not a responsibility failing which we can speak of human omission?

12. This is a good example of Heidegger's attempt to read Greek philosophy phenomenologically or alethiologically, to read off the experiential value of original Greek words. Heidegger said he could not help seeing a phenomenological meaning in the words of the Greeks, for he always took them to be speaking of the things themselves and of the manner of their rising up into presence. This is an illustration of what is meant (cf. SD 86/78).

13. This recalls the thesis of Harvey Cox in *The Secular City* (New York: Macmillan, 1965), except that Heidegger takes no account at all of the Judaic character of making, which is central to Cox's thesis.

14. Karl Rahner, "The Concept of Existential Philosophy in Heidegger," trans. A. Tallon, *Philosophy Today*, 13, No. 2 (Summer 1969), 126–37.

15. Ed. and trans. Joseph Donceel (New York: Herder & Herder, 1968; repr. New York: Seabury, 1972). See also my "Fundamental Ontology and the Ontological Difference in Coreth's *Metaphysics*," *Proceedings of the American Catholic Philosophical Association*, 51 (1977), 28–35.

16. I should like at a later time to address this question in a more detailed way, particularly in terms of a study of the work of Emerich Coreth. In the meantime I look forward with great anticipation to the appearance of Thomas Sheehan's study of Karl Rahner forthcoming from Ohio University Press.

17. Let me only repeat here what I wrote on a previous occasion on this question: "Scholastic theory is naive, according to Heidegger, because it believes it attains an objective being-in-itself whereas in fact every objective structure is a projection of subjective life. This is a transcendental criticism of scholasticism which stems from a Cartesian standpoint that is radically at odds with scholastic realism. The scholastic philosopher who reads Heidegger's critique might want to direct our attention to the doctrine of analogy. For there scholastic philosophy achieves a critical–reflective awareness of the origin and applicability of the terms which it uses. It would be pointed out that the scholastic philosopher is aware that his determination of God as a maker must ultimately be based upon a direct knowledge of human making, which is what we know directly and properly about making. But, it would be argued, human making is then subjected to an analogical transfer by which it is predicated of God only '*eminentiore modo*.' The scholastic philosopher is not naive because he knows that whatever is affirmed of God is also denied of Him, inasmuch as everything predicated of God has its epistemological origin in the sensible world.

"But Heidegger's argument cuts deeper than any theory of analogical predication. For one thing, his argument is that every theoretical object comes back to the existential subject from which it derives its meaning. It asserts therefore the primacy of the practical and the derivative character of all theoretical objects, a thesis which is incompatible with the primacy of the speculative among medieval intellectualists. But more importantly Heidegger's (and Husserl's) 'genetic phenomenology' denies the whole idea of objective being-in-itself and so of realism—scholastic, scientific or whatever. Being for Heidegger is always Being as it enters into Dasein's understanding of Being. There is Being, Heidegger says, only insofar as it is understood by Dasein (SZ, 212/255). Being is always thought in terms of a horizon which is projected by Dasein. The ultimate conclusion to which *Being and Time* builds up is that the meaning of Being is time, that is, Being is projected upon time inasmuch as temporality constitutes the Being of Dasein. Thus Heidegger's claim is far more radical than any theory of analogy. The theory of analogical predication does not escape Heidegger's charge of naiveté, for this theory allows us to believe that we attain being-in-itself, even if such being is only imperfectly grasped. But it is only because the genetic origins of such being-in-itself have been forgotten, in Heidegger's view, that we entertain such an illusion. The scholastic who wishes to respond to Heidegger's critique has to come to grips with the whole premise of transcendental philosophy.

"This is not to say that scholasticism is incompatible with every form of transcendental philosophy, as is testified to by the emergence of 'transcendental Thomism' in the 20th century in the writings of Maréchal and his followers. Here the attempt is made to relate St. Thomas's metaphysics to 'the regress to the subject,' i.e., to relate the Thomistic doctrine of Being to the Being of the subject which understands Being. Thus Emerich Coreth looks with favor upon Heidegger's project of a 'fundamental ontology.' He attempts in his *Metaphysics* an exposition of Thomistic metaphysics which thematizes the idea of the 'question of Being' and of the Being of the questioner. He makes use of Heidegger's idea of a preontological understanding of Being which Dasein 'always already' (*immer schon*) possesses. The task of metaphysics, says Coreth, is to make this implicit understanding of Being explicit. Such a metaphysics must in the end depart in a fundamental way from Husserl and Heidegger, but it belongs to the circle of problems raised by the early Heidegger's critique of scholasticism and it represents, I believe, a fruitful line of interpretation of St. Thomas" ("The Problem of Being in Heidegger and the Scholastics," *The Thomist*, 41, No. 1 [January 1977], 79–81).

3

Gilson's Critique of Metaphysics:
The Oblivion of Being
as "Essentialism"

HAVING EXAMINED HEIDEGGER'S CRITIQUE of Scholastic metaphysics as the oblivion of Being, I now turn to the counter-thesis which is to be found in Thomism, and especially in Gilson's interpretation of the history of metaphysics. For there is a provocative symmetry between the claims of Heidegger and of Gilson. Just as Heidegger wants to think beyond beings to their very Being, so Gilson sees in Thomas the only genuinely "existential" metaphysics, that is, the only one to attain *esse* itself. And like Heidegger Gilson undertakes to defend this thesis historically, by a concrete hermeneutic of the history of Western metaphysics which is guided beforehand by an understanding of what Being means. Each thinker presents extensive historical investigations which show how the great metaphysicians in the Western tradition have each in his own way "contracted" (*beschränkt*) (N II 409/10) Being by turning it into some kind of essence (Gilson) or by making some property of beings do service for Being itself (Heidegger). And although Gilson is primarily known as a distinguished historian of philosophy, and Heidegger is regarded as an eminent philosopher in his own right, it can hardly be denied by anyone familiar with their writings that both thinkers fulfill in their own persons what Heidegger wrote in his *Habilitationsschrift*: "A purely philosophical endowment and a really fruitful capacity for historical thinking are only rarely combined in one personality" (FS² 194).

I might mention that I have chosen Gilson to begin the defense of St. Thomas against Heidegger precisely because of the extraordinary symmetry of his and Heidegger's claims and because of the historical method both employed. I have also chosen Gilson because of his relative unfamiliarity with Heidegger's writings; hence, I cannot be accused of answering Heidegger with a Heideggerianized Thomism. To my knowledge no one accuses Gilson of being a Heideggerian.[1] It is for this reason that I do not as yet mention Gustav Siewerth, whose work I shall examine in Chapter 7. For although Siewerth also argues that the history of metaphysics is a destiny of oblivion from which Thomas Aquinas is a salient exception, it is difficult to know where Siewerth's Thomas begins and his Heidegger ends. What I want for the moment is a "pure" Thomism; I shall examine the "Heidegger school" of Thomists at the end of this study.

It is in Gilson's articulation of Thomism that one finds the most stirring defense of the authenticity of St. Thomas' understanding of Being. One comes away from a reading of *Being and Some Philosophers*[2] with the feeling that Heidegger's charges against the metaphysics of *actus* (EM 14/14) are based upon his failure to appreciate the uniquely existential structure of Thomistic metaphysics. It appears that one can meet Heidegger's critique by showing that Thomas does not belong to the tradition of Suárez, Wolff, and Hegel, and that Heidegger himself, whose own beginnings, as we saw in Chapter 1, were in a thoroughly "essentialistic" version of Scholasticism, has mistakenly written Thomism off as another instance of Scholastic essentialism. Thomas alone has appreciated the uniquely "existential" quality of Being. Thomas alone understands Being in terms of the active upsurge of the being into Be-ing (*esse*). Outside of Thomism, Gilson shows, metaphysics is nihilism because, having set its sights on intelligible natures, on the "whatness" of Being, it takes existence (*esse*), which is no "what," to be nothing at all (p. 67). Outside of Thomism, the understanding of God as pure Being, pure *esse*, lies in "complete oblivion" (p. 112). After St. Thomas, the existential quality of Being is "forgotten" (p. 118).

The question which Gilson's work ultimately provokes is whether pointing out the existential character of Being in St. Thomas is enough to answer what Heidegger calls the oblivion of Being. Are Gilsonian "essentialism" and the oblivion of Being in Heidegger's sense the same? Or is existential metaphysics but one more version of the oblivion of Being? To answer this question, I shall need to undertake in the subsequent chapters a closer examination of the texts of

Heidegger and St. Thomas. For this question is a central problem of the present study.

GILSON'S FOUR THESES ON BEING

Being and Some Philosophers represents something of a "destruction" of the history of metaphysics from the point of view of St. Thomas. It is a philosophical history, a book which takes the *history* of philosophy as the history of *philosophy*, as a problem-history (*Problemgeschichte*), just as the young Heidegger insisted. I should say, however, before I take up the four theses on Being which Gilson proposes, that the history of metaphysics for Gilson is the history of human speculation about Being, and in no wise the history of Being itself (where "of" is to be understood as a subjective genitive) (*Weg.*[2] 313/ 194). Gilson does not take the history of metaphysics to be the way Being sends itself to human thought. If the metaphysics of Plato or Aristotle leaves something to be desired, Gilson would say, this is to be laid at the door of Plato and Aristotle themselves, not to a withdrawal of Being. Nor does he attempt to "deconstruct" or "retrieve" the past history of metaphysics in order to wrest loose from it the truth which has been withdrawn from it. His goal is critical: to establish the truth of an existential metaphysics by setting forth the error of essentialism as its foil. Gilson has a straightforward idea of history which has nothing to do with Heidegger's extraordinary idea of the "history of Being," which in fact for Heidegger is Being itself.

According to Gilson there have been four fundamental metaphysical traditions. In the first, which is fathered by Plato, Being is understood as the self-identical (αὐτὸ καθ᾽ αὐτό). The second tradition, which is headed by Aristotle, takes Being to mean substance (οὐσία). The third thesis is represented by Avicenna, whose dissident Aristotelianism gave rise to the first formulation of the distinction between essence and existence, but one in which essence was given primacy over existence. Finally it was reserved to Thomas Aquinas himself to propound an interpretation of Being precisely *as Being*, as the very act of existing, and thus to fulfill the definition of metaphysics which was set forth by Aristotle: that metaphysics is the science of Being as Being and not of a particular region or part of Being. In the first three theses, Gilson has, from the Heideggerian point of view, isolated out certain basic, global determinations of Being in which "ontic" properties are made to do service for Being itself. These are so many kinds of Being-ness (*Seiendheit*), so many ontic generalizations about Being. But Heidegger would certainly dispute the privileged place reserved for St. Thomas. Heidegger would insist that, as a fourth possibility *within* metaphysics, existential metaphysics remain metaphysics, that is, an oblivion of Being.

The common defect which Gilson finds in each of the first three traditions is their refusal to come to grips with the act of existing and their predilection for an intelligible nature of one sort or another. Metaphysical interpretations of Being outside of Thomism fall prey to conceptualism, an obsessive need for intelligible and definable natures. The existential order resists conceptualization, however, and cannot, at the risk of absurdity, be turned into an essence. In existence the intellect meets the other, the irreducible act which animates the forms and structures which the intellect so dearly loves:

> For, indeed, the cognition of being entails an all-too-real difficulty, which is intrinsic to its very nature. When confronted with an element of reality for which no conceptual representation is available, human understanding feels bound, if not always to reduce it into nothingness, at least to bracket it, so that everything may proceed as though that element did not exist. It is unpleasant for philosophy to admit that it flows from a source which, *qua* source, will never become an object of abstract representation [p. 214].

This is a fairly heady and rather novel point of view for a Thomist, one which seems to admit something of a Dionysian element into the Apollonian throneroom of Thomism. We cannot, in the strict sense of the word, "conceive" existence, in Gilson's view. It cannot be abstractly represented. One is reminded, of course, of Heidegger's critique of "representational thought" (*vorstellendes Denken*), in which he says that Being cannot be "re-presented" as an object to a subject, but can only be experienced directly in its immediacy. Gilson and Heidegger agree that Being cannot be conceptually and abstractly represented and that the history of metaphysics is largely at fault for precisely this. But is it possible that even if one moves beyond conceptual thinking in Gilson's sense, one still remains caught up in representational thinking in Heidegger's sense? That, I think, is what Heidegger would maintain. But this remains to be seen.

Plato and Aristotle

The first major thesis on Being was enunciated by Plato but it was prepared for by Parmenides, whom Gilson sees, not at all as a poet who surpasses the philosophers (WdP 52–53), but, in the standard way, as a "*pre*-Socratic" (pp. 8–10). In Parmenides existence is eliminated by being so absorbed into Being that there is no difference between Being and existence. Now, by existence Gilson means here the order of real, actual, given, experienced entities, the whole sphere of multiple and changing beings. This sphere is done away with by Parmenides in favor of an abstractly conceivable "Being" which is one, self-identical, and unchanging. Here for the first time—but not the last—in the history of metaphysics, the givenness of existence is subjugated to the requirements of thought. Hence, the paradox of Parmenides' position: what "is" does not exist, and what exists "is" not.

And on this central point, Plato is the "heir and continuator" of Parmenides (p. 10). For Plato, the "really real" (ὄντως ὄν) is the selfsame. Being means selfhood. A character in a Dickens novel is real, not because it is actual, but because it is a reproducible, self-identical unity for thought. The forms, which are the entities which truly are, do not become other, do not change. Though individuals may lose justice and become unjust, justice itself is always justice. Individuals thus do not possess true οὐσία (essence, reality). The breakdown in the Platonic theory for Gilson has to do with articulating the being of unity. For "if we look at unity for the root of being, the being of unity is no more conceivable than the unity of being" (p. 18). That is, if unity accounts for being (= the εἶδος, οὐσία), how are we to account for unity itself? Does it have being? Not if it is unity, for then it would be composed of unity and being. By the same token, if being is self-identity, then it too would be composed of being and unity, which, if it is self-identical, it cannot be. The resolution of these paradoxes, formulated by Plato himself in the *Parmenides*, is to be found in a move which Plato could not bring himself to make: namely, saying that unity is beyond being. Thus being, since it is lower than unity, can participate in it and be compounded with it. And unity, since it is beyond being, is absolutely one, unmixed with being, a non-being. This is the doctrine of Plotinus, who represents a mystical extreme which Plato himself dared not adopt (p. 24).

Let me now briefly contrast Gilson's critique of Plato with Heidegger's. Heidegger criticizes the stability and congealing of οὐσία, its permanent presence, rather than its self-identity. Gilson's argument is that in Plato Being has been reduced to one of its properties, unity, a property with which abstract thought is at home. Heidegger is concerned with the solidification of φύσις, with the freezing of the emergence process into something stably present. Gilson objects to what has become of the act-of-existence, the *esse* of concrete beings, for the sake of abstract *ens*, while Heidegger has his eye on the presencing process. Still, both complain that in Plato Being has become something less than it is.[3]

If οὐσία means selfhood in Plato, according to Gilson, it has a different meaning in Aristotle, where οὐσία means ἐνέργεια: "If we follow Aristotle thus far, we are entering with him a world entirely different from that of Plato: a concretely real and wholly dynamic world, in which being no longer is selfhood, but energy and efficacy" (p. 44). To be is to be an act, to exercise the activity of being. Whatever οὐσία means for Aristotle, it means something active. (In Heidegger's view, as we have seen, this is a fateful Romanizing of the Greek experience of Being.) The next question is whether ἐνέργεια means existence. Gilson holds that it is a hasty assumption to think that it does. For although Aristotle is talking about concrete existing things, it does not follow that he has a philosophy of existence (p. 44). In fact, according to Gilson, Aristotle is ultimately unfaithful to his own intentions and lapses back into a philosophy of essence.

Ἐνέργεια in Aristotle means form (μορφή), not existence. What ἐνέργεια makes actual, what it gives actuality to, is matter (ὕλη). The actuality of οὐσία is actually to be structured in such and such a way, actually to take such and such a form. To be (εἶναι) for Aristotle is to be οὐσία, real being, and οὐσία primarily means to have form. The act in the actuality (ἐνέργεια) of οὐσία is the act of forming, of giving form. Thus Gilson writes:

> Obviously, if there is in a substance anything that is act, it is not the matter, it is the form. The form then is the very act whereby a substance is what it is, and, if a being is primarily or, as Aristotle himself says, almost exclusively *what* it is, each being is primarily and almost exclusively its form. The distinctive character of a truly Aristotelian metaphysics of being . . . lies in the fact that it knows of no act superior to form, not even existence. There is nothing above

being; in being, there is nothing above the form, and this means that the form of a given being is an act of which there is no act [p. 47].

And, in obvious reference to St. Thomas, Gilson adds: "If anyone posits above the form an act of that act, he may well use the technical terminology of Aristotle, but on this point at least he is not an Aristotelian." Thus, from Gilson's point of view, it is a mistake to take Aristotle to be the author of the principle of existence in metaphysics. For Aristotle, ἐνέργεια is form, and there can be no ἐνέργεια of that ἐνέργεια, no actuality of that act, no actuality which actualizes form, making *it* to be.

What then has become of existence? To begin with, we should recall with Joseph Owens that Aristotle did not have a language which expressed a distinction between *essentia* and *existentia*.[4] In Greek there is but the one word for "to be," εἶναι, and no separate word for "to exist." Οὐσία, which comes off the participial form οὖσα (= *ens*), is a feminine nominal form. Hence, for many centuries οὐσία was translated as *essentia*, for *esse* : *ens* : *essentia* :: εἶναι : οὖσα : οὐσία. Οὐσία and *essentia* then meant that which is in being, that which a concrete being is. But when the Latin language introduced a distinction between *essentia* and *existentia*, an opposition grew up which cannot be expressed or thought in Greek. (And this is as clear an example as one could wish of what Heidegger means when he says that it is language, not individual men, which speaks!) The notion that "Being is composed of essence and existence" belongs to another age and another language and cannot be expressed in Greek.

What are we to conclude from this? Suárez, and, with him, Heidegger, conclude that in Aristotle there is simply no difference between essence and existence: a man and an existing man are one and the same. Ἐνέργεια includes existence. But Gilson and Owens think that in Aristotle existence is "overlooked" (p. 46). Once we answer the question of whether something is, then the really serious business of philosophy begins, which is of telling what its οὐσία is, what its substantial nature is. Aristotle takes the question of existence for granted; it is not philosophically interesting to him because he does not believe the world ever came into existence. Existence is never formalized into a philosophical principle for him. Once the contingent question is settled as to whether or not there *are* men or states or works of art— in general, a fairly simple matter to decide—then the serious matter of determining their οὐσία begins. Philosophy begins where existence leaves off.

On the Gilson reading, therefore, Aristotle tends to slip back into Platonism, that is, into taking οὐσία to mean *what* a thing is; and that means that Aristotle gives primacy to the universal, to the κοινόν— quite in violation of his own stated orientation. The acid test of this claim for Gilson is Aristotle's views on the relationship between the individual and the species. Gilson writes: "On the one hand, Aristotle knows that *this* man alone, not *man*, is real; on the other hand, he decides that what is real in this man is *what* any man is; how could his *this* and his *what* ever be reconciled?" (p. 48). What interests Aristotle about the individual is, not his individuality, but his generic quality, his species-being. Aristotle finds the truest being of the individual in his *form* (μορφή). The contradiction is most manifest in Aristotle's explanation of individuality. The principle of individuation is matter, which is that which is lowest in a thing, so low, indeed, that of itself it does not exist. Hence, the reality of what is supremely real—the τόδε τι—is explained by what is lowest of all: ὕλη. What Aristotle lacked is a principle of existence to explain the individuality of the individual, a supreme act which actualizes even form, an act belonging to the individual and constituting him in his individuality—as in Thomas Aquinas (SCG, II, 81). But, instead, Aristotle's thought is a philosophy of existents without existence (p. 50). It rapidly passes by the question of existence to direct its attention to *what* exists, to *that which* is found in existence. And on this point he remains Plato's pupil and a friend of the forms, *magis amicus Platonis.*

Gilson's analysis of Aristotle contrasts sharply with Heidegger's, for although Gilson finds no principle of existence in Aristotle, Heidegger finds the distinction between essence and existence already announced in Greek philosophy in the distinction between ἰδέα and ἐνέργεια. But for Gilson the distinction between these two terms collapses and ἐνέργεια reduces to ἰδέα. Ἐνέργεια means μορφή, and it answers the question about *what* the being is, not whether it is— which flatly contradicts Heidegger's interpretation (cf. N II 406–407/7–8). Aristotle does not escape the sphere of influence of the Platonic predilection for the question of *what* something is; whether it is is a preliminary item which is easily disposed of. Aristotle's ἐνέργεια is still a captive of Plato's ἰδέα.

Moreover, and this is at least as important as the first point, Heidegger understands ἐνέργεια as a mode of presencing, not in terms of causality: "Thought in the Greek manner, the work is not work in the sense of accomplishment of a strenuous making. It is also not result and effect. It is a work in the sense of that which is placed in the unconcealment of its outward appearance and endures thus standing or lying" (N II 404/5). Heidegger finds something deeper in Aristotle than a philosophy of causality; he sees ἐνέργεια as something more than a causal account of things. He claims to hear in these Greek words the original sounds of the first and greater Greek thinkers, Anaximander, Heraclitus, and Parmenides. This is not simply a matter of preferring "Presocratic philosophy" to the philosophy of the "Golden Age." It has to do with what was once called Heidegger's "phenomenology" and is now a matter of the "thoughtful" experience of things, a "meditative" thinking in which we let things emerge and rise up in their own presence, an "alethiology." But such a framework is entirely alien to Gilson, and it never enters his considerations. He does not read Parmenides this way, and still less Aristotle. This difference makes all the difference, and it even reduces me to wondering whether I am simply arguing at cross purposes in comparing these two philosophers—Gilson and Heidegger—in the first place. Do they think and work on such entirely different planes that no comparison is possible?

From Avicenna to Hegel

I cannot follow Gilson's entire argument in detail here, but I should like to devote some time to a discussion of his third thesis since it touches upon the fateful importance of Suárez in mediating essentialism to the modern world, a point with which I think Heidegger is in agreement. It explains too how the identification of Being with Nothing in Hegel's *Logic* is possible, which for both Gilson and Heidegger is an unfortunate emptying of the meaning of Being.

For Gilson the pre-eminence which Aquinas has in the history of metaphysics is due to the inspiration which his metaphysics received from the Christian doctrine of creation. Greek and medieval thinkers are separated by an abyss by this teaching—a point which, we have seen, Heidegger would accept, although with rather different consequences. In Gilson's view, the Greeks found it necessary to give an account of how the world took on the *form* which it has, but they never raised the question of how the world came to *be* in the first place. The case of Averroës and Avicenna is therefore very telling in this regard. In Averroës, a ferociously loyal Aristotelian, Aristotelian-ism came face to face with the problem of existence; the result was that Averroës denied that creation was anything more than a benevo-lent lie told by theologians to instill in the untutored a sense of de-pendence upon God (p. 52). Avicenna wished to remain faithful to his religion and so it was he who introduced for the first time into Western metaphysics the principle of existence. A created substance, said Avicenna, must, in order to be created, have had existence su-peradded to it. For a substance of itself is merely possible, not actual. Existence "happens to" the substance and is an accidental addition to it. Thus, contrary to Heidegger's claim, the distinction between es-sence and existence is not to be traced to the opposition between Aris-totle's ἐνέργεια and Plato's ἰδέα, but to Aristotle's distinction between οὐσία and συμβεβηκός, "substance and accident." Moreover, once existence is made a problem, οὐσία means no longer actuality but possibility. *What* a thing is is what it is able to be. Heidegger makes no mention at all of this Arabic interlude, yet for Gilson the whole debate about essence and existence reaches a turning point here. Averroës could not locate existence within the ten categories and so concluded it was nothing other than οὐσία itself. Avicenna insisted on the uniqueness of existence, but he treated it as a category of ac-cidental being, with the result that existence is subordinated to οὐσία.

With the advent of Avicenna, οὐσία and *essentia* cease to mean real being and begin to signify possibility. Avicenna emphasizes "es-sence" and treats existence as something external to it, something which happens to it to make it actual. In order to pass from possibility to actuality something necessary is required. And this is the role played by God, who, as necessary being—and hence as lacking an essence—actualizes the possibles in a necessary process (pp. 74–82). Although Avicenna's necessitarianism was alien to the Christian world, theologians like Duns Scotus endorsed his doctrine of es-sence while rooting the process of creation in the supremely free will of God. But Scotus too thinks of existence as an accident of essence, something which happens to it, completing it, giving it full determi-nation. When an essence achieves actuality, nothing is added to it; it merely shifts into the mode of actuality (pp. 84–96).

In Suárez, the metaphysics of essence is carried one step farther. Scotus took existence to be at least some kind of appendage of essence, something which added to its full complement. But in Suárez existence is reduced entirely to essence, and the distinction between essence and existence becomes merely a distinction of reason. Metaphysics is then determined as the science of the concept of being, and being is said to mean possible being, *habens essentiam*. (That is why, we recall, the young Heidegger, enamored of logic and mathematics, preferred Suárez and Scotus.) To be is to be an object of thought; non-being signifies a lack of essence. But "real being" can be either actual or possible. This, in Gilson's view, represents the triumph of essence (pp. 96–105). The analysis contrasts sharply with Heidegger's. For Heidegger Suárez is the most concretely oriented of the Scholastics because, in denying the distinction between essence and existence, he took the concretely existing being as a theme. But for Gilson, in denying the distinction between essence and existence, Suárez reduces existence to essence, turns existence into a mere name for essence, and thereby divests philosophy of its true subject matter, the act-of-existence (*esse*).

However they may disagree about the merits of Suárez, Gilson and Heidegger are in full agreement about the extent of his influence: Suárez is the bridge to the modern world. In the fifth chapter of *Being and Some Philosophers* Gilson provides us with an insightful account of the fate of "existence" in the modern period, an account which bears an interesting similarity to Heidegger's critique of the history of metaphysics.

Descartes, who had read Suárez, absorbed his ideas about essence and the deducibility of existence from essence. Indeed, the unchallenged supremacy of essence in the seventeenth century is vividly testified to by the whole Rationalist movement. It is only in the philosophy of essence, of the concept, that the ontological argument can flourish. For the argument holds that real existence, the order of actual being, can be wrung out of concepts, that concepts can give birth to being. But concepts give rise only to other concepts, and if being is taken to be deducible in the seventeenth century, it is because being has become a concept, like the properties of the triangle. Rationalism is a philosophy of being without existence. Gilson writes:

> The God Essence of the Middle Ages is everywhere carried shoulder high, and every philosopher of note pays him unrestricted homage.

As to that other God of Whom it had been said that He was not a
God whose essence entailed existence, but a God in Whom what in
finite beings is called essence, *is to exist*, He now seems to lie in a
state of complete oblivion. . . . The times are now ripe for some
systematic science of "being qua being," as completely free from
existence as being itself actually is.

And then Suarez begot Wolff [p. 112].

Wolffian rationalism subscribes to the division of metaphysics into
general and special metaphysics which was delineated by Suárez.
Being is defined as that which is able to exist (*existere potest*), and
existence as a "complement of possibility," a formula which recalls
Avicenna and Scotus. Wolffianism was rightly criticized by Kant,
Gilson thinks, and both he and Heidegger reject it outright. Wolffianism is the paradigm case of onto-theo-logic. Being becomes in
Wolff the object of a science of its most general properties, onto-
logic; and beings are explained causally in terms of the highest being,
the *ens realissimum* of theo-logic. Both Gilson and Heidegger reject
the excesses of Wolffianism: Gilson, because existence has been excluded; Heidegger, because Being has been displaced in favor of beings, their properties and causes (pp. 113–19; ID 125–58). And
neither Gilson nor Heidegger is satisfied with Kant's thesis about being, even though it was designed to curb the pretenses of Wolff. Gilson sees empiricism as a sign of health, a protest that existence must
always be given, that essences give birth only to essences. Kant took
up Hume's charge by arguing that existence is not a real predicate, a
claim Heidegger has carefully studied (GP, §§ 7–9; *Weg.*[2] 445ff.).
On the face of it, Kant made progress by refusing to conceive existence as an essence. But what, then, is existence for Kant? What is
added to a thing when I say that it exists? In effect, Kant says, nothing. All that has changed is my relationship to it. The change is in
me; I bring myself into a new relationship to it. I have shifted, as
Husserl might say, to the "thetic" mode. Existence for Kant is just the
positing mode of a subject. This view has its roots all the way back in
Avicenna, where Being means primarily essence, and existence is
some kind of modification of essence, some change in mode. Hence,
while Kant and Aquinas both reject the ontological argument, Kant
is light years from saying what Aquinas does: that existence is a non-
conceptualizable act in the being itself (pp. 124–32). Heidegger's
dissatisfaction with Kant is similar. In Kant's thesis the only thing

which is real is the *res* itself, and Being is forgotten. Being has become nothing more than the relation of the thing to human subjectivity. Gilson's criticism of Kant is that Kant does not admit that existence is a real principle, an enlivening act intrinsic to the being; Heidegger's criticism is that Being has become the posit of a subject, a mere relationship to a subject.

And so, with Heidegger, Gilson holds that the history of (bad) metaphysics—which has been a sustained attempt to drive existence out of Being—culminates in Hegel (pp. 132–34). Hegel is the high priest of the concept and essentialism, not because he subscribes to Wolffian rationalism, but because he attempts to animate concepts with a dialectical life. In keeping with Scotus, Suárez, and Wolff, he holds that Being is the most general, poorest, and most vacuous concept. But, with the magic wand of dialectics, this concept passes into its opposite (non-being) and emerges as "becoming," the first concrete universal. Gilson writes:

> Hegel's absolute idealism is a thorough overhauling of ancient essentialism, and it appears as so triumphant a one that it buries itself under its own trophies. Logic has eaten up the whole of reality. After raising a helpless protest in the doctrine of Hume, existence had attempted at least to hide somewhere in the critical idealism of Kant. It had made itself so inconspicuous that it could reasonably hope to be there to stay. But now the brand new essence of Hegel has not only explained it *a priori*; it has explained it away. In the centuries-old process of "essence versus existence," essence has at last won its case; which means, of course, that the process of "existence versus essence" is about to begin again, and this time, owing to the complete victory of Hegel, if it is to be fought at all, it will have to be fought out to a finish [pp. 141–42].

The reference is to Kierkegaard, who speaks on behalf of existence. Religion has always sided with existence (Avicenna against Averroës, St. Bernard against Abelard, Pascal against Descartes). Kierkegaard siezed upon the raw evidence that philosophy wants to eliminate existence. It wanted to turn Christianity into a doctrine, whereas the whole point is to *be* a Christian. If Wolff wanted an ontology without existence, Kierkegaard wanted existence without ontology. He argued that Hegel tried to inject existence into logic, but succeeded only in logicizing existence, which is the fate of all philosophy. Existence disappears under objective thought. Kierkegaard did not want to make the same mistake; he did not want to reintroduce existence into philosophy. The very idea of an "existential philosophy" is a monstrosity to him. This was the protest of religious existence against all philosophy. Since philosophy will have nothing to do with existence, Kierkegaard argued, existence must have nothing to do with philosophy (pp. 142–53).

Given the state into which metaphysics had drifted, given the total domination of essentialism, Kierkegaard's protest was understandable. But his existentialism is no more than the inverse coin of essentialism. Being (*ens*) without essence is no more to be preferred than Being without existence. Absurdism is no more a solution than rationalism. What is needed is an integrated philosophy of essence and existence, in which Being primarily signifies existence without eliminating essence, in which Being means "that which *is*" (to inflect the old formula slightly differently).

Heidegger would have sympathy with these views. He too sees Hegel as a consummation in which the essential drift of modern metaphysics toward subjectivism is absolutized. And he too finds no solution in the complete inversion of metaphysics—which for him is to be found in Nietzsche. Anti-metaphysics is as much as ever still metaphysics. Moreover, he was critical of Kierkegaard, whom he regarded a "religious author" who remained a captive of Hegel's ontological categories, and not a "thinker" in the special sense he gives to that word (*Holz.*[2] 230–94; WD 129–213). Like Gilson, Heidegger thinks that Kierkegaard shared the ontological assumptions of modern metaphysics, and simply formulated an anti-metaphysical reaction against it.

St. Thomas' Thesis on Being

The one place in the history of metaphysics where existence assumes its rightful place of supremacy over essence, without, as in Kierkegaard, expelling essence from philosophy altogether, is in the existential metaphysics of Thomas Aquinas. Here alone is a genuine philosophy of Being as *esse*, in which not substance, not unity, not form is allowed to displace existence from its primacy within the understanding of Being. Here alone is a genuine philosophy of Being as Being in which Being is not reduced to something other, and so less, than it is. And though this metaphysics has a certain Aristotelian point of departure, it soon severs its Aristotelian moorings and enters into a wholly different world, a world from which all Greek philosophy is in principle barred. Gilson develops the originality and uniqueness of St. Thomas' metaphysics of *esse* by sharply contradistinguishing it from the Greek metaphysics of Aristotle, a metaphysics which for Gilson is rarely more than a "physics" in the classical sense. His interpretation of Aristotle, therefore, flatly contradicts Heidegger's, which, had he examined it carefully, would have left Gilson totally nonplused.

Like the later Heidegger, but for entirely different reasons, Gilson thinks that the philosophies of the Greeks and of the Christians are separated by an abyss, even when they may seem to use the same formulas. They belong to different worlds, different dispensations of Being, Heidegger would say. But the difference between them in his view is not that Aristotle is a non-causal phenomenologist of "presencing" and St. Thomas a metaphysician of "productivity," as Heidegger holds, but that Aristotle's thoroughly causal thought never succeeds in attaining the genuinely metaphysical understanding of causality to be found in St. Thomas. It is Aristotle and not St. Thomas who remains a captive of the metaphysics of "making," if making (*facere*) is distinguished from creating (*creare*), a point which we shall see Johannes Lotz attempt to exploit.[5] Focused as it is upon changing material Being, and not upon Being as such, Aristotle's metaphysics is something less than metaphysics, not yet metaphysics, and certainly not, as for Heidegger, more than metaphysics. For Heidegger Aristotle meditates the essence of φύσις; for Gilson Aristotle is a "physicist" whose thought must make way for the truly metaphysical attainments of St. Thomas.

The difficulty with Aristotle's philosophy, as Gilson sees it, lies in the limitations of his doctrine of the "four causes." For Aristotle could speak only of a moving cause, not a truly efficient cause. The Aristotelian agent which induces form into matter does no more than to effect a change in pre-existent matter, to change its state. But in St. Thomas the agent cause is a true cause of Being, not merely of motion or change. To change the form of a thing, to gain or acquire form, is, in virtue of St. Thomas' metaphysical principle that Being follows upon form (*esse consequitur formam*), to produce a modification in Being itself. But in St. Thomas the *causa prima* is a *causa agens*, a supremely creative being which draws Being out of non-Being. This can only be a stumbling block and a scandal to the physicist Aristotle. It never entered Aristotle's mind that matter, that "out of which" things are made, could itself be made. Aristotle is forced into the awkward position of having defined metaphysics as a science of true being—οὐσία—and of having at the same time to include the untrue being of matter (ὕλη) among his four irreducible causes. When he wants to speak of Being as Being, he is forced to admit into the discussion that whose Being is so low that it cannot be of itself and is itself excluded from the highest beings.

But if Aristotle's theories of the *causa agens*, the *causa finalis*, and the *causa materialis* are deficient, his greatest shortcoming—and that which lies at the root of the entire problematic—involves the *causa formalis*. For the four causes hang together, and a mistake about one is a mistake about them all. For Aristotle, the supreme act of the being, that which makes the being to be a being, its ἐνέργεια, is form, μορφή; but that is precisely where Thomas departs from Aristotle:

> But Thomas Aquinas could not posit existence (*esse*) as the act of a substance itself actualized by its form, without making a decision which, with respect to the metaphysics of Aristotle, was nothing less than a revolution. He had precisely to achieve the dissociation of the two notions of form and act. This is precisely what he has done and what probably remains, even today, the greatest contribution ever made by any single man to the science of being. Supreme in their own order, substantial forms remain the prime acts of their substances, but, though there be no form of the form, there is an act of the form. In other words, the form is such an act as still remains in potency to another act, namely existence [p. 174].

Here is the animating intuition of Gilson's interpretation of Thomas Aquinas. St. Thomas has found his way into a region of Being from which Aristotle—and every Greek philosopher—was barred. St. Thomas discovered an act, an ἐνέργεια, which is the very upsurge of beings into Being, their very act of Being. Here more than anywhere else, the students of St. Thomas are convinced, Aquinas refutes Heidegger's charge of the forgetfulness of Being. Aquinas has answered Heidegger's call to think; he has recalled what remained in oblivion throughout antiquity: that the being is, that the being is a being in virtue of a rising up and emerging into Being which is the very act of

Be-ing. It is in the Greeks before Thomas and in the moderns after Thomas that this existential act is devalued. It is in Greek substantialism and modern essentialism that the existential act is transmuted into form and essence and a thinkable whatness. But Aquinas himself has had the persistence and endurance to stay within the element of Being, to think Being purely in its own terms. Thomas takes Being as Being, in the purity of the act by which the being rises up into Being, and he resists the temptation of the particular sciences to turn Being into an essence.

Both Gilson and Heidegger are in agreement about the fact that the Christian (and Judaic and Moslem) belief in creation is the pivotal point in medieval thought. For Heidegger this religious belief commits medieval man to the metaphysics of making, to a causal explaining of one being by another. But in Gilson's view, the Greeks remained captive of a necessary world. Aristotle's κόσμος had no beginning in time and no author in terms of Being. The world always was and will be, and though individuals come to be and pass away, the species which they instantiate remain forever, as does the matter out of which they come and into which they pass away. There can be no creation, no real innovation, no genuine individuality—rather as with Zarathustra's soothsayer, for whom all is the same, all has been. But for the existential metaphysics of St. Thomas, not only does the world admit of novelty, but it itself is the greatest and most radical novelty of all. Moreover, this creative process is the work of a supremely free creator who can intervene in history at any moment. It is to this world that the spiritual autobiography of the "individual" soul of an Augustine belongs. Indeed, Heidegger himself has told us that he has learned to think the facticity of human existence from his meditations on the Scriptures.[6] His historical orientation is the gift of the Christian tradition, not of the Greek. The personal historicity of Dasein is in no small part due to Heidegger's exposure to Protestant theology during the Marburg years. If Heidegger learned to think Being in terms of time, he learned this, not from the Greeks, who at best moved implicitly within this domain, but from the Christian tradition, in which time and history became thematic.

The doctrine of creation does not confine St. Thomas' metaphysics to the horizon of "making" but brings it face to face with the upsurge of Being as such. Indeed Heidegger himself found the old formula of Christian metaphysics *ex nihilo ens qua ens fit* to be a useful expression to articulate his own experience (*Weg.*[2] 120/110)—as long, that is, as it is understood alethiologically and not causally. But this causal formula contains an intuition of the sheer act of Being, the simple upsurge of the being into Being vis-à-vis nothingness. The demiurge, the original chaos, μορφή, pre-existent exemplars—these are all Greek inventions and they belong to the metaphysics of making and forming. But the metaphysics of *esse* is an unknown god to the Greeks, and to the Greek and Latin Fathers who remain subject to the Greek tradition. With it one enters the horizons of Judaeo-Christianity in which the world is contingent, in which the being has Being only as a gift. To think Being as *esse* is to shatter the conceptual horizons of Hellenism.

GILSON AND HEIDEGGER

After the first appearance of *L'Etre et l'essence*—the French ancestor of *Being and Some Philosophers*, a slightly different book written in English—Gilson was asked how he would fit Heidegger into the scheme of things developed in his book. The question is to us an obvious one, for Heidegger would seem to have eminently distinguished himself as thinker who does *not* reduce Being to essence or entity. In response to this question Gilson added an appendix to the second edition of *L'Etre et l'essence* in which he takes up Heidegger's attempt to overcome metaphysics from the standpoint of the Thomistic metaphysics of *esse*, and these remarks will serve as an excellent conclusion to the present chapter.[7]

One is struck from the start by Gilson's respect for Heidegger. He is hesitant to make any final pronouncements about Heidegger, partly because he says he is not at home in the German language, but chiefly, one suspects, because he wants to avoid facile objections against a thinker of this magnitude. He is impressed with Heidegger's sustained attempt to think Being and to avoid replacing it with an unworthy substitute. Heidegger, he writes, "introduces one more case in which the philosopher decides to evade the limits of the being [*l'étant–das Seiende*], that is to say, the essentiality of essence, in order to engage himself courageously on the desert path of being."[8] Heidegger is not one more essentialist for Gilson and so he hesitates to put him anywhere on the map which he has drawn in the preceding pages; Hei-

degger is one of those thinkers who want to think Being itself. Gilson
simply would like to assure Heidegger that the path of thought is not
as lonely as Heidegger insists: "One would like to know how to tell
Martin Heidegger how many unknown companions he has on the
path where one sometimes says that he believes himself to be alone."[9]

But Gilson will have none of Heidegger's insistence that metaphysics itself, all metaphysics, belongs in an oblivion of Being, for he
thinks that Heidegger's critical arrows land only on bad metaphysics,
onto-theo-logical metaphysics. Thus for Gilson the real point of contention with Heidegger is not essentialism, for Heidegger is not an
essentialist, but metaphysics, for Thomas Aquinas is not an onto-
theo-logician. Gilson writes: "The root of philosophy is no longer to
be looked for in philosophy, and if metaphysics is the summit of
philosophy, it is necessary to look for this root outside of metaphysics.
This is the catastrophic moment of his doctrine."[10] Gilson argues this
point as follows. Even if, in actual historical fact, metaphysics has
indeed tended to be no more than an onto-theo-logic, this is not
what metaphysics must in principle mean. Heidegger rejects all possible metaphysics on the basis of all existing metaphysical doctrines.
But even if every existing metaphysical theory were defective, this
would not rule out the possibility of the appearance of a genuine metaphysics in the future, or even in the past, if Heidegger had missed it.
However, I think that Gilson is misled about this. Heidegger expressly
states that his account of the history of metaphysics is not an historical "report" (N II 399/1), but a probing of the "essence" of metaphysics in terms of the *Seinsgeschick* which animates it (WdP 40–
41). Metaphysics is essentially, not just factually, a withdrawal of
Being in which it is impossible to think Being as such without aban-
doning its very structure as metaphysics. But Gilson makes no mention of the *Seinsgeschick*. He also argues from the very idea of "first
philosophy" that it cannot, by definition, be outstripped:

> the notion of surpassing a first philosophy scarcely makes any sense.
> If it is necessary to surpass the metaphysics of the being as a being,
> this simply means that the latter is not first philosophy; let us re-
> place it then with a new philosophy which is truly first, that of
> Heidegger, for example, but we will not have surpassed metaphysics.
> By definition, and inasmuch as it is first philosophy, metaphysics
> is a knowledge which cannot be surpassed.[11]

But once again, what is first in philosophy for Heidegger—and meta-physics is certainly that—is not first in thought (*Weg.*[2] 367/209). For Heidegger *first* philosophy must always be first *philosophy*, which is metaphysics. But Gilson does not address himself to the entirely different kind of thinking, the transformation of thinking, for which Heidegger calls, the meditative thinking which overcomes all philos-ophy, first or last.

In Gilson's view, the metaphysics of St. Thomas is neither an onto-theology nor an ousiology, but a philosophy of *esse*, Being (*Sein*, εἶναι). Though St. Thomas accepts the Aristotelian formula that metaphysics is the science of the being as such (τὸ ὄν ᾗ ὄν), he is driven by this formula beyond the being to its very Being. For to de-termine the being as such (*ens qua ens*) is to understand the being in terms of its to-be, its act of existing (*esse*). *Esse* is the act in virtue of which the being (*ens*) emerges into Being. Nor is St. Thomas' thought a theo-logic in Heidegger's sense, for God as St. Thomas con-ceives Him is not some *ens realissimum*. Indeed, as we shall see in the next chapter, God is not an *ens* at all for St. Thomas, in the strict sense, but *ipsum esse subsistens*, the pure subsistent act-of-being it-self. St. Thomas' metaphysics does not terminate in a first being causing other beings, but in pure Being itself whose Being is com-municated by participation to created beings. It is a metaphysics of *esse* throughout, not of *ens*.

Now, it would seem to make no sense at all to speak of a forgetful-ness of Being in connection with St. Thomas if one bears in mind the existential quality of Thomistic metaphysics stressed by Gilson. If the oblivion of Being means taking Being thoughtlessly for granted, taking the being itself without ever thematizing its Being, then Tho-mism is a paradigm case of a philosophy in which Being has been re-called (*Denken an das Sein*), in which a thought of Being (*Seins-denken*) takes place. No one has shown more clearly than Gilson that in other metaphysical theories the act of being is overlooked, denied, or reduced to some kind of appendage to essence. In these philos-ophies Being is "taken for granted" as too obvious, simple, and self-evident a matter to warrant further consideration. All one's attention is directed in these philosophies to *what* the being is, without paying any special heed to the fact that what is does indeed *exist*. Gilson and other contemporary students of St. Thomas have thematized this aspect of Aquinas' work so vividly and clearly that the charge that in St. Thomas Being has fallen into oblivion seems patently ill-founded.

But the question which is raised by Gilson's study is whether this "existential" metaphysics is enough to overcome what *Heidegger* means by the oblivion of Being, or whether it merely amounts to an existential version of *Seinsvergessenheit*. Even if in Thomism *esse* regains its authority over *essentia*, even if we have in St. Thomas an existential and not an essentialist metaphysics, is this not simply, from the perspective of Heidegger, a reversal which takes place entirely within metaphysics without ever stepping back out of metaphysics as an oblivion of Being? We must never forget the radically alethiological and phenomenological character of Heidegger's thought. What Heidegger means by Being is φύσις and ἀλήθεια, the emergent process of rising up into unconcealment. But Gilson and the Thomists think in terms of *ens reale*, of what Heidegger calls in *Being and Time* "reality" (*Realität*), real Being, presence-at-hand (*Vorhandensein*). Even if Gilson has thematized the very *act* of Being, for Heidegger this would not amount to more than a stress on one principle of objective Being (*Vorhandensein*) over another. Indeed it is a stress on a uniquely Roman notion—*agere, actus, actio*—in which the original Greek experience of ἀλήθεια has badly deteriorated into a concept of Being in terms of efficiency and productivity.

We must constantly bear in mind the radically historical and alethiological structure of Heidegger's notion of Being and of the oblivion of Being, and we must be wary of rushing blindly into straightforward comparisons between Heidegger and Thomas, Gilson, or any Thomistic commentator. I do not in fact believe that any Heideggerian would be moved by the "existential" metaphysics of St. Thomas because he would take *esse* to be an objectivistic and ahistorical notion; that is, he would take it to be phenomenologically and historically naïve. Thomas' metaphysics may indeed thematize Being as *actus*, but it does not thematize the very light process in virtue of which Being as *actus* is bestowed upon medieval man. Thomas is carried along by the medieval dispensation of Being, drawn in by its pull (*Ent-zug*), without being mindful of the power which pulls, the historical giver and taker of meaning (cf. SG 143–47). It is Being as ἀλήθεια which Heidegger thinks has fallen into oblivion. And ἀλήθεια belongs to a phenomenological–historical kind of thinking which would be altogether impossible for a thirteenth-century man.

But all this needs to be developed more carefully, and it is too soon to draw anything but tentative conclusions from the analysis up to this point. For now I must go back to the works of Aquinas and Heidegger, and probe more deeply into how each of these thinkers understands Being. Only then shall I be in a position to say with surety whether from Heidegger's side the notion of an oblivion of Being befits the metaphysics of *esse* and how a response can be made to this critique on behalf of St. Thomas. Hence in Chapter 4 we shall listen more carefully to St. Thomas' own words about Being, and in Chapter 5 I shall attempt again a more decisive confrontation of the metaphysics of *esse* with the thought of Being.

NOTES

1. William Barrett's criticism of Gilson is to a different point. See his *Irrational Man: A Study in Existential Philosophy* (Garden City, N.Y.: Doubleday Anchor, 1962), pp. 106–107.

2. 2nd ed. (Toronto: Pontifical Institute of Mediaeval Studies, 1952). All page references in parentheses in this chapter are to this volume unless otherwise noted.

3. I might also add in this connection that Heidegger does not at all see in the "selfsame" (τὸ αὐτό) the dead end which Gilson finds there. For Heidegger does not take Plato to be the authentic heir of Parmenides. On the contrary, he shows in *Identity and Difference* that in the expression τὸ αὐτό we can hear the word of Parmenides not about the abstract identity of a thing with itself— as it has become in Plato—but about the "belonging together" (*zusammengehören*) of Being and thought, the reciprocal unity of being and man. But this difference springs from the irreconcilable difference between Gilson and Heidegger on the sort of thinker that Parmenides is.

4. *The Doctrine of Being in the Aristotelian* METAPHYSICS: *A Study of the Greek Background of Mediaeval Thought*, 3rd rev. ed. (Toronto: Pontifical Institute of Mediaeval Studies, 1978), pp. 137–54.

5. See below, in chap. 7, the section "Being and *Ipsum Esse Subsistens*."

6. Otto Pöggeler, *Der Denkweg Martin Heideggers* (Pfullingen: Neske, 1963), pp. 36ff.

7. (Paris: Vrin, 1962), pp. 365–77.

8. Ibid., p. 377.

9. Ibid.

10. Ibid., p. 373.

11. Ibid., p. 369.

4

Esse and the Metaphysics of Participation in Thomas Aquinas

IN THIS CHAPTER I want to present the metaphysics of St. Thomas in the light of the renewed image of St. Thomas which has emerged in the last forty years of Thomistic research. In particular I want to set forth a presentation of St. Thomas as the philosopher of *esse*—and so of Being—*par excellence* in whom the manifest Aristotelian influences have been subsumed into a more profound metaphysics of participation, the end result of which is, as W. Norris Clarke says, neither Christian Platonism nor Neo-Aristotelianism but Thomism itself.[1] These two joint themes—the primacy of *esse* and the depth structure of Platonic participation—will together enable us to sharpen our grasp of St. Thomas' thesis on Being. We shall see that Thomas is first and foremost a philosopher of Being and of the difference between Being itself and the beings which participate in Being. And we shall see more clearly than ever why Thomists like Emerich Coreth can write: "No thinker of the past has been more clearly aware of the ontological difference than Thomas Aquinas, nobody has more clearly distinguished between beings (*ens*) and being (*esse*), or interpreted beings more consistently in the light of being."[2]

Then in Chapter 5 we shall turn back to the texts of Heidegger to test further whether this new presentation of St. Thomas does indeed constitute a rejoinder to Heidegger's critique of Scholastic metaphysics as an oblivion of Being.

Esse AND SPIRITUAL SUBSTANCES

Gilson contends that the discovery of *esse* as an explicit and central principle of metaphysics by St. Thomas was occasioned by Thomas' attempt to come to grips with the Christian belief in creation. I should like to develop this important insight into St. Thomas by taking up the specific case of Aquinas' treatment of spiritual substances, in which, it seems to me, the problem of existence was visited upon him with particular insistence. I think that Thomas might have been tempted to leave existence out—that is to say, not to thematize *esse* as a distinct principle—had it not been for the problem of the "separate substances" or what as a Christian believer he called "angels." The problem was to explain the difference between God and angels. Why were angels regarded as greater than men but less than God? How can the angelic nature be purely spiritual and yet imperfect? How can the angel be a pure spirit and yet created? The explanation which was current in St. Thomas' day, and which enjoyed the prestige and authority of St. Augustine himself, was put forward by the Franciscans. They located the finitude of the angels in an ethereal or spiritual matter, which lacked the mass and resistance of ordinary, earthly matter. Angels are not material the way men are, but neither are they absolutely pure spirit the way God is. This explanation has the effect of positing a potency in angels which differentiates them from God, who is pure act. It identifies potentiality with materiality in the broadest sense and makes of matter the universal characteristic of anything created. Because potentiality had been identified in terms of materiality, the potentiality for existence itself was missed, and the confrontation with existence did not take place.

But for St. Thomas the Franciscan view flatly contradicted the Scriptures, which speak of angels as pure spirits. And the notion of a "spiritual matter" must undoubtedly have seemed too odd and ambiguous a conception for a thinker as rigorously clearheaded as St. Thomas. To say that angels are pure spirits is to say that they are pure forms, and for Aristotle this means that they are pure act, the highest and most perfect form of Being, the self-thinking thought, the θεός. But then what would remain of the finitude and createdness of angelic beings? Now, we know that St. Thomas' Aristotelianism, such as it was, was mediated to him by a close reading of Avicenna, and that he was deeply impressed by the revolutionary, if ultimately erratic, distinction which Avicenna had opened up between substance and existence. And so St. Thomas saw another way to explain how separate substances are both pure forms and still creatures. He found a new composition of act and potency which had nothing to do with matter. Angels, he would argue, are composed of form and *esse*. Potentiality is not identical with materiality, for even form itself is a potentiality for existence itself. This means that God Himself is free of form, for He is free of potentiality. The angelic being is free of matter but not of potentiality, while human nature, even though it belongs to the order of intellectual substances, is not free even of materiality. Thus St. Thomas carries to completion the revolution begun by Avicenna, as Gilson has conclusively shown.

The composition of form and *esse* in the angelic being was a constant teaching of St. Thomas'. His theological career began with a short treatise, written sometime around his thirtieth year, entitled *On Being and Essence* (*De ente et essentia*) in which he already defends this view: "In this, therefore, the essence of composite substances and of simple substances differ, since the essence of a composite substance is not the form alone but includes both form and matter, whereas the essence of a simple substance is the form alone" (*De ente* iv/53). Inasmuch as they are simple substances, angels are pure forms without matter. Yet though they are pure forms, they are not pure act, for they are not in every way simple substances, but forms to which *esse* has been superadded. That is indeed how they are distinguished from God, in whom essence and *esse* are identical. Hence, angels are totally dependent for their *esse* upon God:

> It is therefore necessary that everything whose act of existing is other than its nature have its act of existing from another. And because everything which exists through another is reduced to that which exists through itself, as to a first cause, there must be something which causes all things to exist, inasmuch as it is subsistent existence alone. Otherwise we would proceed to infinity in causes. . . .
>
> It is evident, therefore, that an intelligence is a form and an act of existing, and that it has its act of existing from the First Being which is existence only . . . [*De ente* iv/55–56].

In arguing that God is subsistent *esse*, pure *esse*, *esse* only, and angels pure forms which have received *esse*, Thomas makes a definitive break with Aristotle and passes into a new sphere. Thomas is the author of the wholly un-Aristotelian thought of an act which is not a form, of an act which actualizes form itself, an act of the very being of a thing: "Likewise, because the quiddity of an intelligence is, as has been said, the intelligence itself, its quiddity or essence, therefore, is itself that which is; and its act of existing, received from God, is that by which it subsists in the nature of things" (*De ente* iv/56).

THE TRANSFORMATION OF ARISTOTLE

One of the most significant achievements of the contemporary understanding of St. Thomas is the recognition of the extent to which Thomas differs with Aristotle and has definitively left the Greek world behind. To a large extent Thomas speaks the language of Aristotle, but he uses this language to articulate the metaphysics of a believer who takes the world to be created, the soul to be personally immortal, and God to be lovingly concerned from all eternity about each individual person. For Heidegger, St. Thomas speaks a medieval Latin translation of the Aristotelian language in which a fateful deterioration of Greek experience took place. But for his recent commentators, Thomas has transformed the sense of Aristotle's words by allowing these words to assume a radically existential sense which was unknown to Aristotle himself. But the new meaning which Aristotle's words assume under Thomas' pen is largely an "operative" rather than a "thematic" topic for him, to use Eugen Fink's distinction. That is to say, it is a transformation which he carried out in practice without explicitly thematizing it as an issue. Still he does advert to the difference between the composition of matter and form (a strictly Aristotelian distinction) and that of substance and *esse* (his own innovation) in the *Summa Contra Gentiles* (II, 54). He points out that in the latter composition, potency is not matter alone but matter and form together (or form alone), and that act is the act not of matter alone but of matter and form together (or of form alone). He points out too that in the composition of substance and *esse*, form is a potential principle and hence there is an act even of the form itself.

But let me add here something which Thomas himself does not make explicit and which is brought out in a penetrating and lucid way by the study of W. Norris Clarke to which I have just referred. By transposing the language of potency and act to the order of Being, and thus extending them beyond the order of changing, sensible substance, Thomas has shattered the Greek predilection for limit, definition, structure, form. In Aristotle μορφή is the principle which gives structure and determination. The infinite, the indefinite, is a negative principle for the Greeks, and as such it must be brought into subordination to a higher principle of order. Form must rule over chaos; ὕλη must take on μορφή. But as Father Clarke points out, everything changes in the Neoplatonic doctrine of emanation from the One:

> In this perspective all the intelligible essences below the One now appear as limited and hence imperfect participations of this supremely perfect and absolutely simple first principle, which somehow embraces within itself the perfection of all the lower determinate essences but is none of them in particular. The One, therefore, must be above all particular intelligible determinations of essence, and can be described only as a supreme indetermination or infinity, not of defect but of excess. Forced to invent a new terminology, Plotinus for the first time in Western thought uses the old Greek word for the infinite, *apeiron*, to express this radically new content of indetermination as identified with the plenitude of perfection of an unparticipated source compared to the limited participations below it.[3]

Because of his Neoplatonic heritage, St. Thomas was thus able to distinguish two kinds of infinity. On the one hand, there is a material infinity, which is always potential and imperfect, just as Aristotle said. This refers to the infinite divisibility of *extenda continua*, the infinite series of numbers, the infinite kinds of actuality which matter can take on—the infinity, in short, which is never actual. Such infinity is perfected when it is rendered definite, finite; it was this alone which the Greeks knew. But the Neoplatonists had opened the eyes of the Christian believers to a new infinity, an infinity of perfection in which to be finite meant to share partially, to possess imperfectly. Now, for St. Thomas *esse*, which is beyond form, is beyond the finitude of form. Hence, St. Thomas teaches an infinite being itself, being infinitely, without limit or restriction. In the order of *esse* as opposed to form, it is the actual principle which is infinite while the potential principle gives limit or determination. Thus angels, whose *esse* is received into (pure) form, are not infinite. Form, which gives actuality and perfection for Aristotle, restricts and contains *esse*, and thus limits actuality and perfection for St. Thomas. He writes:

> it is clear that the first being, who is God, is infinite act possessing within himself the total plenitude of being not restricted to any

generic or specific nature. And so his very existence must not be one
that enters some nature that is not its own existence, because it
would thus be limited to that nature. . . . Consequently, everything
existing after the first being, inasmuch as it is not its own existence,
receives existence in something by which the existence itself is restricted . . . [*De spir. creat.*, 1, c/AR 66].

In Aristotle, the actual principle determines matter and saves it from
being unformed; in Thomas, the potential principle determines and
restricts the being in its very be-ing. As Father Clarke so conclusively
shows, potency does not limit act in Aristotle, act limits potency. The
limitation of act by potency is a Thomistic breakthrough.

I should also point out that St. Thomas' discovery of a potency for
being itself, and therefore his discovery of an act of being, have re-
sulted in another important transformation of Aristotle's principles.
In Aristotle, where potency and act always have to do with change in
the material order, the potential principle can precede the actual in
time and can stand about, in a sense, awaiting actualization. The
potential principle is matter, the "second matter" of bronze, say,
which awaits the hand of the artist who will shape it into the form of
Apollo. Or it is the "first matter" of fruit which will soon become the
substance of the animal which is about to ingest it. But it would make
no sense at all in Thomistic metaphysics to speak of essence as pre-
existing *esse*—by the very nature of the case. For how can an essence
pre-exist the very principle by which it exists in the first place? St.
Thomas writes:

Since existence [*esse*] is attributed to the quiddity [essence], not only
the existence [*esse*] but the very quiddity are said to be created, since
it is nothing before having existence [*esse*], except perhaps in the
Creator's intellect, where it is not a creature but the creative essence itself. . . . At the same time as He gives existence [*esse*], God
makes that which receives existence [*esse*], so He has no need of
causing from pre-existing things [*De pot.*, 3, 3, ad 2 et ad 17/AR
74–75].

It is a serious mistake, but not an uncommon one, to think that essence somehow floats about awaiting actualization by existence. Essence is a potentiality, for St. Thomas, not because it exists in one
way now while being able to take on a new form later—although this
is what potentiality meant for Aristotle—but because it is a principle

of receiving and limiting *esse*. To be potential in this case means to be able to *be*, not to be *formed*. Essence signifies the capacity to exist in such and such a way, to be able to be so much and no more. Of itself it is not; and when it is conjoined with the actual principle it "is" only so much, and no more. The only thing which does pre-exist is the divine idea of the possible creature, but this can hardly be identified with the thing's essence. For the divine idea is identical with the divine being itself—whatever is in God is God, as Meister Eckhart liked to say—while essence is an intrinsic, constitutive principle of the creature itself. Indeed, in view of the wholly transformed sense which Thomas has given to this word, Aquinas could have entirely dropped all talk of "potency" here and spoken simply of a limiting principle. Indeed, we shall see below that there is a certain tendency in St. Thomas to shift his language out of the Aristotelian framework and to begin to think in other terms altogether.

Ens IS TAKEN FROM *Esse*

The confrontation of Heidegger with Thomas Aquinas is confused by a certain linguistic asymmetry in their respective vocabularies of Being. Heidegger's thought turns on the well-known distinction between "Being" (*Sein*) and beings (*Seienden*). *Das Sein* is a verbal, neuter noun constructed from the nominalization of the infinitive *sein*, to be. Hence, it signifies Being in the most unrestricted, infinitival sense (EM 42–48/45–52). *Ein Seiendes*, a being, and *das Seiende*, the being, are taken from the present participle *seiend*, and so refer to that which is in being, either definitely (*ein Seiendes*) or indefinitely (*das Seiende*). Now, like German, and unlike English, the Latin language has a convention of forming verbal nouns out of infinitives. Thus from a strictly linguistic standpoint, one would formulate Heidegger's "ontological difference" in Latin as the difference between *esse* and *ens*. The difficulty with this suggestion is obviously that this is a distinction of which St. Thomas does not appear to make use. We are accustomed to think that the operative distinction for him is between *esse* and *forma, substantia, quid est*, or any of the various names for essence. Now, we have seen *essentia* originally meant something like "that which is," having been constructed from the infinitive *esse*, just as οὐσία was constructed from εἶναι. But after Avicenna, *essentia* came to mean, not the concrete being itself, but only a part of that being, the essential, possible part. In Thomas himself, it became an intrinsic co-principle of the concrete being along with *esse*. Thus in St. Thomas *esse* and *essentia* are thought of as co-principles of *ens*. In the language of Heidegger, *das Seiende* (= *ens*) is composed of *Sein* (= *esse*) and *Wassein* (= *essentia*). Thus from a strictly linguistic standpoint, Thomistic metaphysics appears very much caught up in Heidegger's notion of the "oblivion of Being." For its focus is on the being (*ens*) and not on Being itself. It is a science of *ens qua ens*, τὸ ὄν ᾗ ὄν, *das Seiende als das Seiende*. It has subordinated Being (*Sein*) to the being (*Seiendes*). Even if Thomistic metaphysics declares the primacy of *esse* over *essentia*, still this is a primacy within the framework of *ens*. For *esse* and *essentia* are subordinate to *ens* as principles are to what is to be explained by the principles, as *explicans* to *explicandum*.

The attention of Thomistic metaphysics appears to be on *ens*.[4] The τέλος of introducing the notion of *esse* is to account for *ens*, for *ens* is seemingly the subject matter, the *Sache*, of metaphysics. It would appear in this light that Thomistic "existentialism" is a misnomer, not because it has nothing to do with Jean-Paul Sartre, but because Thomistic metaphysics is oriented more toward *ens* than toward *esse*. Even if Thomas and Suárez are at odds as to the relative relationship of *esse* and *essentia*, they seem to agree that metaphysics is a science of *ens* and that these principles are subordinate to *ens*. Just as Aristotle's metaphysics is an "*ousiology*,"[5] a philosophy of οὐσία, not of μορφή, for μορφή is meant to account for οὐσία, so Thomistic metaphysics is "ontology," a philosophy of *ens*, not of *esse*. If *esse* enjoys a primacy over *essentia*, it does not enjoy the same primacy over *ens*.

If the foregoing account of St. Thomas' metaphysics were the final word on his thought, there would be little doubt about the validity of the charge of *Seinsvergessenheit*. But I do not believe that this version of St. Thomas' teaching is faithful to his deepest insights, or even to all the pertinent texts, although it is supported by a literal reading of certain texts and by a certain popular acceptance. I want now to show the shortcomings of this interpretation of St. Thomas and the far greater proximity of Thomas to Heidegger's "ontological difference" than the standard version of strict observance Thomism would suggest.

To begin with, I think that, far from holding that *esse* is subordinate to *ens* as a principle is subordinate to its *explicandum*, St. Thomas actually holds the opposite view. For he frequently points out that *ens* takes its meaning from *esse*, that *ens* is a participle which derives from the infinitive. Hence, *ens* signifies a limitation upon *esse*, a limited, participated share in what *esse* is in infinite perfection. Thus he writes that if an entity is called "thing" (*res*), we have essence primarily in mind—which is Avicenna's position: ". . . Whereas the name 'being' [*ens* or what is] is imposed from the very act of existence itself [*ipsum esse*]" (*In I Sent.*, d. 8, 1, 1/AR 44). To say *ens* is to signify the act of being in virtue of which the *ens* is an *ens*. Thus *ens* always means *ens-in-esse*, the being in its be-ing, its act of existing, the Being of beings. To think *ens qua ens*, being as being, is to think being in terms of *esse*, Being. For Thomas Aquinas, then, a philosophy of being, *ens*, ontology, must become a philosophy of *esse*, "einaiology," were it possible to coin such a word.

The interesting test case of St. Thomas' genuine teaching on this matter is the designation of God. It is clear that for Thomas the highest and most proper designation of God is expressed in terms of *esse* rather than of *ens*. God is most properly referred to as *ipsum esse subsistens*, subsistent Being itself, rather than as *primum ens*, an expression which he uses, to be sure (ST, I, 3, 4, c), but which is not the most appropriate possible expression.[6] If God is an *ens*—the very word suggests the participial, participatory mode—He is an *ens* in which there is only *esse*. In other words, *ens* would in this case give way entirely to *esse*, the participated to the unparticipated fullness. It says more about God to say *esse* than to say *ens*. In the creature, on the other hand, in whom *esse* and essence are distinct, it is more appropriate to speak of *ens*, that is to say, the participation in or having of *esse*: *ens significat habens esse*. The word *ens* is taken from *esse* (*imponitur ab esse*) (cf. *In IV Met.*, lect. 2, no. 558), even as creatures are derived from God. We call a creature a being on the basis of its *esse*. But with God the distinction between *ens* and *esse* does not hold; God is His own *esse*. And so we ought not to use a word which is derived from *esse*; we ought to say *esse* itself, *ipsum esse subsistens*, which is indeed the truly fundamental expression in Thomas' vocabulary of Being. We designate a creature in terms of *esse* by calling it an *ens*; we designate the creator as *esse* itself.

That is why St. Thomas writes in his commentary on the *Book of*

Causes that God is beyond *ens,* not because, as the Neoplatonists taught, the good is beyond being, but because He is *esse* itself:

> But in the opinion of the Platonists the first cause is beyond being [*ens*] insofar as the essence of goodness and unity exceeds even separate being itself, as we have said above. But the truth of the matter is that the first cause is beyond being [*supra ens*] inasmuch as He is infinite *esse* itself. But *ens* means that which participates in *esse* to a finite degree, and this is proportioned to our intellect whose object is "that which is," as it is said in the Third Book [of Aristotle's] *De anima* (429B10ff.). Whence that alone is able to be understood by our intellect which has a quiddity which participates in *esse.* But the quiddity of God is *esse* itself, whence He is beyond understanding [*In De causis,* lect. 6, no. 175].

St. Thomas here distinguishes Being and beings, *ipsum esse* and finite *entia,* with all possible sharpness. Both essence and *ens* are clearly subordinate to the focal conception of *ipsum esse infinitum* in such a way that the *ens* is a finite mode of *esse,* the extent of its finitude being measured by its essence. The text is immensely suggestive too for it opens up the sense in which God, as beyond being (*supra ens*), is not any being, and hence is a kind of non-being. This does not mean anything of a Neoplatonic sort but, more in the Heideggerian spirit, that which is not any being, the Being which is other than and concealed by beings. And this in turn opens up a mystical dimension in St. Thomas' thought, for the being which is not a being but Being itself exceeds the capacity of our intellect (*supra intellectum*), which is at home only with beings (*quidditas participans esse*) and cannot comprehend Being itself. All this brings St. Thomas' metaphysics far closer to Heidegger's thought of Being than the standard act–potency Thomism would have dared to admit. But I must not run ahead of my argument. These are all matters which need to be developed with greater care and precision.

THE PARTICIPATION OF BEING

Now, what may have seemed at first a purely linguistic point, that *ens* is taken from *esse,* that *esse* has a grammatical and verbal priority over *ens*, actually carries us into the heart of a doctrine which in the last forty years of Thomistic research has emerged as the central teaching of St. Thomas' metaphysics: that is, the doctrine of the participation in Being. We have already seen that St. Thomas is not merely a Neo-Aristotelian carrying Aristotle to the next decimal point by discovering an "application" of the doctrine of act and potency to the level of Being rather than merely restricting it to the sphere of change. In fact, Thomas has switched from an Aristotelian to a Platonic paradigm in which the Aristotelian differentiation of the lower from the higher in terms of the composite and the simple substance has been replaced with a Neoplatonic distinction between an original, unlimited fullness and its finite, imperfect shares. Stated in its most general terms, this doctrine means that every being is a being (*ens*) in virtue of its participation in Being itself (*ipsum esse*). Such a formulation of St. Thomas' views is clearly more favorable to bringing his thought into relationship with Heidegger's distinction between Being and beings and indeed appears to constitute, at first glance at least, a response to Heidegger's critique of Scholasticism. Coming to grips with this teaching of St. Thomas', therefore, is of the utmost importance for the present study.

I take as my point of departure for this discussion the second lesson of St. Thomas' *Commentary on the "De hebdomadibus" of Boethius*.[7] In this work Boethius distinguishes between *quod est*, that which is, and *esse*, being, and he says that the *quod est* participates in *esse* in order to exist, but that *esse* does not participate in anything beyond itself. St. Thomas illustrates this distinction by comparing *esse* with running (*currere*) and that which is or *ens* with the runner (*currens*): "For running and being [*esse*] signify in the abstract, as also does whiteness; but that which is, that is, a being [*ens*] and a runner [*currens*], signify in the concrete, as also does white" (*In Boet. De hebd.*, lect. 2, no. 22/AR 51). *Esse* differs from *ens* as a pure perfection does from the concrete subject which participates in the perfection. Thomas then enumerates three differences between *esse* and *ens*. In the first place, "*Esse* itself is not signified as the subject of being, as indeed running is not signified as the subject of the run; whence as we are not able to say that running itself runs, so we are not able to say that *esse* itself is." Then he adds: "Thus we are able to say that being [*ens*], or that which is, is, inasmuch as it participates in the act of being [*actus essendi*]" (*In Boet. De hebd.*, lect. 2, no. 23/AR 51). It is not proper to say that *esse* is, but only that the being is. (This is a precaution which Heidegger too was careful to take, sometimes distinguishing *west* from *ist* and restricting the latter to the being, or more often using *es gibt*, "there is," Being.) The being, the concrete thing, is, according to St. Thomas, only by participating in the act of being (*actus essendi* = *esse*), which is not itself a being.

The second difference is taken from the very idea of participation. To participate, St. Thomas says, is to "grasp a part" (*partem capere*); that means, the participating subject receives the perfection in a partial or particular way. There are three such cases. A logical inferior participates in the universal, as Socrates participates in humanity or as "man" participates in "animality." There is more to man or animality than is to be found in Socrates or humanity. Secondly, matter participates in form, inasmuch as matter can only imperfectly take on the perfection of the form. But neither of these modes befits being (*esse*) because *esse* is neither a universal nor a form. Hence, Thomas writes: "But that which is, or being [*ens*], although it is something most common, is nevertheless said most concretely. And therefore it participates in being [*esse*] itself, not in the way the more common is participated in by the less common, but in the way the concrete participates in the abstract" (*In Boet. De hebd.*, lect. 2, no. 24/AR 52). *Esse*, the in-finitival noun, is "indeterminate" (*In Boet. De hebd.*, lect. 2, no. 20), something which of itself is not contracted to any particular being or mode of being. The concrete being (*ens*) is a determinate, finitized instance of *esse* and hence is in a particular way what *esse* is without restriction.

The third and final difference which St. Thomas mentions is that *esse* itself is a "pure" perfection, that is, nothing extraneous is added to it or admitted with it, which is not the case with the concrete thing. Thus pure humanity is humanity only, but a concrete man is not only human but also tall, white, seated, etc. What else is found in the concrete *ens* other than *esse*? Clearly, essence. The being, *ens*, is an admixture of *esse* and *essentia*, a concrescence of *quid* and *est*, and not *esse purum*, pure and subsisting *esse*. The concrete thing is a participation in pure *esse* by receiving *esse* in admixture with, or restricted by, essence. But *esse* in its unparticipated state is pure *esse*, and only *esse*.

In the next section St. Thomas applies this doctrine of participa-

tion to the important question of the simple substances which I discussed above. Pure forms—angelic natures and (were there such)
Platonic forms—have only a partial share in *esse*, despite the purity
with which they have form:

> Nevertheless because any form is determinative of being itself,
> none of them is being itself, but is something having being [*habens
> esse*].

> It will be manifest that the subsistent immaterial form itself, since
> it is something determined to a species, is not common being itself,
> but participates in it [*In Boet. De hebd.*, lect. 2, no. 34].

No form can be pure *esse*. For form is a contraction of *esse* to a certain modality of *esse*, something which participates in *esse* within
the limits which the form itself allows. Consequently that alone is
truly simple which does not participate in *esse* at all but is subsistent
esse itself. Such a being alone is truly a "simple substance" for in Him
that which is (*ens*) and *esse* are the same. He is only *esse*: "But this
simple and sublime unity is God Himself" (*In Boet. De hebd.*, lect. 2,
no. 35).

The doctrine of participation comes to play an ever more prominent role in St. Thomas' later and most mature writings. As he begins
to develop his own most distinctive contribution to the history of
metaphysics, the doctrine of *esse*, his language starts to lose some of
its rigorous Aristotelianism and he begins to adopt the Neoplatonic
discourse of participation. Vis-à-vis Heidegger, this means that, not
only does ἐνέργεια not mean existence in Aristotle, but when the great
philosophy of existence of St. Thomas does appear, it invokes at a
critical point the Platonic language of ἰδέα and μέθεξις—a move
which Heidegger appears to have missed entirely.

Let us hear this new discourse of St. Thomas, beginning with a
classic passage from the opening pages of the *Summa theologica*, in
which Thomas is presenting proofs that in God essence and *esse* are
the same:

> Thirdly, because, just as that which has fire, but is not itself fire, is
> on fire by participation; so that which has *esse* but is not *esse* is a
> being by participation. But God is His own essence, as shown above.

If, therefore, He is not His own *esse*, He will be, not essential, but participated, being. He will not therefore be the first being—which is absurd [ST, 1, 3, 4, c].

Just as in the old physics fire is thought to be heat itself in which all other hot things participate—and hence functions as an excellent Platonic paradigm—so God is thought to be *esse* itself in virtue of which all other beings exist. God cannot receive *esse* any more than fire can receive heat or the form of justice can receive justice. As the form of justice is subsistent justice itself, so God subsists in His own *esse*. And as hot things come to be hot but are not heat itself (fire), so every being (*ens*) comes to share *esse*. The created thing is given *esse*, is lent *esse*, shares *esse*, but God alone subsists as *esse*. The *entia* which we encounter in the world, and among which we ourselves are numbered, point to an unreceived *esse* itself, an *esse* which subsists through itself. The panorama of Being in Thomistic metaphysics is the community of *esse* which is constituted, on the one hand, by subsistent *esse* itself and, on the other, by the *entia* to which *esse* is communicated. Thus, because it is a science of *ens*, as Aristotle's definition would have it, Thomistic metaphysics must become the science of *esse*. It is, therefore, properly named, not "ontology," the λόγος of τὸ ὄν, but—were it possible to say so—"einaiology," the λόγος of εἶναι itself. Moreover, as the science of *esse* itself, it is the science of God as subsistent *esse*—not as if this were a science different from the science of *esse*. It cannot be maintained that in St. Thomas there is a patchwork "onto-theo-logy," a composite of mutually reinforcing "-ologies," such as Heidegger depicts. This kind of criticism befits Suárez and Wolff but it has nothing to do with St. Thomas' authentic teaching, with the seamless garment of the inquiry into *esse*. There is but a single science, of *esse* itself—in its unreceived and subsistent perfection (*esse per essentiam*) and in its received and participated reflections (*esse per participationem*). We have here no onto-theo-logy but the unity of an "einaiology."

At this crucial juncture in his thought, Thomas speaks not of Aristotelian ἐνέργεια but of the Platonic ἰδέα, of *esse per essentiam*, *esse essentialiter*. There is a being whose ἰδέα is *esse* itself. St. Thomas is emphatically saying, *not* that *esse* is a form—one will not to my knowledge find such a text in St. Thomas—but that in God *essentia*, ἰδέα, gives way to and passes over into *esse*. The essence (ἰδέα) of this being is *esse*; this being is *esse essentialiter*. Thus two questions later in the *Summa* Thomas writes:

> Plato held the existence of separate forms of all things, and that individuals were denominated by them as participating in the separate ideas; for instance, that Socrates is called man according to the separate idea of man. Now, just as he laid down separate ideas of man and horse which he called "man itself" and "horse itself," so likewise he laid down separate ideas of being [*ens*] and *one*, and these he called being itself and the one itself, and by participation in these everything was called *being* or *one*.

Now, Thomas thinks that Plato is half-right:

> Although this opinion appears to be unreasonable in affirming separate ideas of natural things subsisting of themselves—as Aristotle argues in many ways—still, it is absolutely true that there is first something which is essentially being and essentially good, which we call God, as appears from what is shown above [ST, I, 6, 4, c].

We see here clearly how Thomas has appropriated Plato's thought for his own "existential" (in the sense of *esse*) purposes. He is by no means a Neoplatonist; he will have none of Plato's doctrine of the subsistence of the forms of natural species. The only subsistent forms for him are the immaterial substances (angels), each of which is purely and subsistently its own form. As to what Plato called forms, none of these subsists, except Being, and Being is, not a form, but *esse*. Thomas has appropriated, not the content of Platonic participation, but the structural relationship of the ἰδέα or εἶδος to the concrete thing which participates in that idea. But he transposes that structure of *per essentiam* and *per participationem* wholly out of the sphere of form and essence and into the sphere of *esse*. And if he calls God *ens per essentiam*, as he does indeed, he means that God is *esse purum*, neither *ens* nor *essentia* but subsistent *esse*.

It is also important to see in the above text both that Thomas does not play Aristotle off against Plato, and that he takes them to be in agreement on the question of the good and being. But, of course, the position he is defending is not *both* Plato's and Aristotle's, but *neither* Plato's nor Aristotle's. For the notion of subsistent *esse* never crossed the mind of any Greek philosopher. Thomas means that, just as he has formulated his doctrine in a Platonic way, by speaking of *ens per essentiam* and *ens per participationem,* so he can also formulate his views in an Aristotelian way, by speaking of act and potency. He writes in the *Commentary on Aristotle's Physics*: "Everything which participates in something is composed of something participating and something participated, and the one participating is in potency to the thing participated" (*In Phys. XIII*, lect. 21, no. 1153). The creature which participates in *esse* is a composite of two principles, of the subject which receives and of the perfection which is received. Now, this obviously can be given an Aristotelian formulation in terms of intrinsic co-principles, that is, of act and potency. Thus Thomas writes in the *Summa*:

> It must be said that everything participated is compared to the thing participating as its act. . . . But participated *esse* is limited to the capacity of the thing participating. Whence God alone, who is His own *esse*, is pure and infinite act. Now in intellectual substances there is a composition of act and potency, not indeed of matter and form, but of form and participated *esse* [ST, I, 75, 5, ad 4].

Here the language of Plato is brought into conformity with the language of Aristotle. If God is pure unparticipated *esse, esse per essentiam, esse* according to His very ἰδέα, then God is pure act. And if creatures are beings by participation, if they have received *esse* in a limited way, then that means that creatures are composed of potency and act.

Of course, the reconciliation which Thomas carries out here is possible only because he stands on a higher ground than either Plato or Aristotle. He effects an *Aufhebung* of the two only because his thought moves wholly within the element of Being, that is, of *esse*, a sphere which neither Plato nor Aristotle ever entered. Judging for myself I think that Thomas does not really need the language or conceptual framework of Aristotle at all, and that, having passed through an Aristotelian understanding of change and motion, he would have done better to have adopted his own vocabulary to speak of Being itself. Act and potency are terms which belong originally to the sphere of making and sensible being, and they need to be overhauled thoroughly in order to become suitable for Thomas' higher metaphysical purposes. These purposes would be better served by speaking of participated and unparticipated *esse* rather than of act and potency. His thought is more forcefully articulated in terms of subsistent *esse* and participated *entia*. Frankly, I do not think that even the highly Avicennian word *essentia* belongs to his true vocabulary or serves his truest purposes. The word *essentia* inevitably suggests the Suarezian misinterpretation and tends to make of existence an afterthought, an appendix, an *additio*, as Gilson has shown so convincingly. Emerich Coreth has an interesting passage in his *Metaphysics* which brings this point out very well:

> For the Suarezian, existence is nothing but the factual state of existing, of being posited, of being real, as contrasted with mere possibility. Such existence has no content, no positive determination, no grade of perfection in being. All of this is contributed only by the essence or quiddity. . . . Hence even before it exists, while it is in the state of mere possibility, the existent is already fully determined, it has only to be transferred from the state of possibility into the state of actuality. The essence is not merely, as for the Thomists, an empty structural principle of that which this existent is, but the concrete positive determination of all that which it is. Whereas the Thomists claim that the whole positive content, the degree of perfection in being, derives from being as the principle of positivity, the Suarezians attribute it to the essence, to which existence only adds the state of actuality or of reality.[8]

In St. Thomas' thought the only role of essence is to put a limit on the positive upsurge of Being (*esse*), to contain it within certain borders, to circumscribe it. A thing is perfect for Thomas insofar as it is (*esse*), not insofar as it is not (*essentia*). *Essentia* is a positive word for a negative structure, a perfective term for a principle of imperfection, an active word for a receptive principle.[9]

There is a simpler and deeper vocabulary of Being in Thomas Aquinas than is provided by the words *actus, potentia,* and *essentia*. The really operative vocabulary in St. Thomas' metaphysics is the distinction between *esse* and *ens*, between unparticipated *esse, ipsum esse per se subsistens,* and the participating *ens*, the *ens* which is an *ens* only inasmuch as it is *habens esse*. Thomas' thought moves in a sphere which is closer to Heidegger's ontological difference, which is best expressed by that difference, and whose true intent is not served by the traditional formulas. That is why Max Müller writes: "the fundamental opposition in Thomas himself was always that between *esse* and *ens, ens quod* and *ens quo*, and . . . it is only in

Thomism that the difference between existence and essence overtook the importance of the former, outshone it, and even darkened it."[10] The traditional formulations of Thomistic metaphysics—that it is a philosophy of *ens*, and that *ens* is composed of *essentia* and *esse* (or worse still, of *existentia*)—cover over the truly animating insight which St. Thomas has into the distinction between *esse* and *ens* and lend credence to the charge of *Seinsvergessenheit* which Heidegger makes. But a more thoughtful reconstruction of St. Thomas' thought, one aided in part by Heidegger's formulation of an ontological difference between Being and beings, forcefully underlines the inadequacy of all such formulations of Thomas' authentic teaching.

In recommending this more extreme and streamlined vocabulary of Being, I am conscious, of course, that Thomas Aquinas himself often enough expresses himself in the more conventional way, and that he uses the language of *actus*, *potentia*, and *essentia* on nearly every page of his writings. But I am invoking the right of the interpreter to interpret a thinker in the light of the ages, in the light of the clarity which the intervening years bring to the text, a light in which the merely external elements of his thought fade and the truly vital elements remain fresh and alive. The interpreter can indeed understand the thinker more perfectly than the thinker understood himself, as all hermeneutics maintains, not because the interpreter is a better thinker than the thinker himself, but because he has the advantage afforded by the intervening years. He has the light of time to shine on the texts, to see the texts in their enduring significance, and to sort out what belongs merely to the idiosyncrasies of the age and the setting of the thinker.

The construal I have made of St. Thomas' metaphysics is not artificially imposed upon him; it arises from the true dynamics of his thought as it has been thematized by the extensive and profound research of his best commentators in the past forty years.[11] And when the results of this research are brought together, when the primacy of *esse* first articulated by Gilson is seen together with the doctrine of participation studied by Geiger, Fabro, and others, and when both these interpretations are seen in the light of Heidegger's ontological difference between Being and beings, there can be no doubt about where St. Thomas stands on the matter of Being. For Thomas is, above all, intent on thinking Being and not merely beings. Thomas too takes the being in its Being. More clearly than anywhere else in the history of metaphysics, one will find in Thomas Aquinas the most explicit awareness of the distinction between Being and beings. And if that is so, one wonders what the notion of a *Seinsvergessenheit* can possibly have to do with Thomas Aquinas.

THE BEING OF GOD AND THE BEING OF CREATURES

I should like to conclude this discussion of the metaphysics of participation in St. Thomas by taking up two important refinements of his position which will at once serve to make his views clearer and to define them more sharply in relation to Heidegger's. In the first place, I want to show that even though creatures participate in Being, and God is Being, the Being of God and the Being of creatures are not to be confused. And, secondly, I want to show that for St. Thomas, even though God is distinct from creatures, God is not a being, not even a "highest being."

(1) Let me begin the consideration of the first point with the following text of St. Thomas:

> Things differ, therefore, by reason of their different natures receiving *esse* diversely in proportion to each nature. Now, the divine *esse* is possessed by no other nature but is itself the very nature or essence of God. And so if the divine *esse* could be identified with the *esse* of all things, all things would coalesce together into the absolute unity of one single being [SCG, I, 26/129; AR 55].

Even though St. Thomas holds that creatures participate in *esse*, and that God is pure, subsistent *esse*, he does not want to suggest that the participation of creatures in God's Being means that God is the Being of creatures. Thomas rejects a kind of Parmenidean pantheism in which all things are one by having the very *esse* of God. He also rejects a strictly Platonic participation in which creatures, by participating in the *esse* of God, would be different from God as mere shadows and reflections of God, images in which *esse* does not properly inhere, pale copies of true *esse*. St. Thomas had a robust sense of the intrinsic being, the genuine reality, of each individual being or *ens*. This came to him in part from his Aristotelian realism and in part from Christianity, in which the reality of the individual and of the natural world are part of the common faith.

It might be, then, that Thomas' doctrine of participation means no more than that creatures participate in *esse commune, esse in communi*, Being in general. Each creature has a partial share in Being in general; each is a partial expression of the infinite diversity of which Being in general is capable. Now, it is true that this is sometimes what Thomas means. When he says in the *Commentary on the De hebdomadibus of Boethius* that we may not say that Being (*esse*) is, but only that beings are, he is referring to *esse commune*, not to the subsistent *esse* of God (*In Boet. De hebd.*, lect. 2, no. 23). But that ultimately is not a very satisfying way to speak, because for Thomas *esse in communi* is an abstraction. There "is" no *esse in communi*. *Esse commune* is what the things which are have in common, but it is not something which "is" in its own right. *Esse commune* is a universal constructed by the mind in the light of actual beings (*entia*) and posterior to them. It is something in which beings participate not in a real or a metaphysical way, but only in a logical way.

The real sense which participation must have, then, is the participation of creatures in the *esse* of God, from whom their *esse* is causally derived. Otherwise participation is no more than a way the mind has of conceiving being. But how can the creature participate in God's *esse* without being part of God, as the very word participation suggests? Thomas writes: "It must be said that the first act is the universal principle of all acts, because it is infinite, 'precontaining all things in itself' virtually, as Dionysius says. Whence it is participated in by things, not in terms of a part, but according to a certain diffusion of its processions" (ST, I, 75, 5, ad 1). The creature which participates in God does not have a part of God's *esse*. Rather, the Being of the creature represents a certain diffusion of God's Being. What is this diffusion?

Hence from the First Being, existent and good by essence, everything can be called "good" and a "being" inasmuch as it participates in that First Being by way of a certain likening [*assimilatio*]. . . . Therefore everything is called good by the divine goodness as by the first exemplar, efficient and final Source of all goodness. Nevertheless everything is called "good" by reason of the likeness of God's goodness inhering in it, which is formally its own goodness, whereby

it is denominated good. And so of all things there is one goodness
and yet many goodnesses [ST, I, 6, 4, c].

The creature participates in God because the creature is a likeness
(*similitudo*) of God. But it is a genuine being in its own right, because
the similitude which it has of the divine being inheres intrinsically in
it (*sibi inhaerens*). The created *esse* formally belongs to the creature.
But it originates in God, who is at once the source of all *esse* (*principium*) and the exemplar of all *esse*, the being which is *esse*, purely,
subsistently, perfectly, "with the whole power of being" (*tota virtus
essendi*) (ST, I, 4, 2, c). The beings which God creates are like Him;
they are similitudes of Him, not in the sense of shadowy imitations,
but in the sense of being intrinsically but imperfectly what He is intrinsically but perfectly.

It is clear then that one cannot separate the doctrine of participation from the principle of causality. Participation has a causal sense.
Participated *esse* depends upon unparticipated *esse* as an effect does
upon its cause:

> Everything existing in any way comes from God. For whatever is
> found in anything by participation has as its necessary cause that to
> which it essentially belongs, just as iron is made hot by fire. Now, it
> was previously shown . . . that God is essentially self-subsisting *esse*.
> . . . And so with the exception of God all beings are not their own
> *esse* but participate in *esse*. And so it is necessary that all things dif-
> ferentiated by the diverse participation in being, so that they are
> more or less perfect, are caused by one first being who most per-
> fectly has being [ST, I, 44, 1, c].

Wherever there exists a series of perfections such that all the members of the series have the perfection according to a greater or lesser
extent, but one being possesses that perfection subsistently, then the
other members of the series are related to that one being as effects are
to a cause. The model which suggested itself to Thomas, as we have
seen, is that of the relation of heat itself to the things which are more
or less hot. Fire, one of the four natural substances, is heat itself and
as such it is the cause of the heat in other things. He does not say that
things are hot by hotness, which would be a strictly Platonic hypos-
tasizing of abstract heat, but that they are hot by fire which is a con-

cretely subsistent heat. And that is how God is conceived. He is Being itself, not in the abstract, like *esse commune*, or like a Platonic form of Being, but as the being which is Being by its very essence.[12]

I can now clarify the difference between the relationship between pure *esse* and the concrete *ens* in Thomas Aquinas and the relationship between Being and beings in Heidegger. For Heidegger's *Sein* is anything but subsistent: Being never "is" (*west*) without beings (*Weg.*[2] 306/354). If *ipsum esse subsistens* were related to *esse participata* in Aquinas the way in which *Sein selbst* is related to *Seienden* in Heidegger, then either Heidegger would have hypostasized Being, which he has not, or Aquinas would be a pantheist, which he is not. If Being is taken as something subsistent, then in Heidegger's eyes we would have made the error of reducing presence itself (*Anwesen*) to something present (*Anwesendes*). Insofar as Heidegger's *Sein* is not subsistent, we are inclined to relate it to *esse commune*, as in fact many Thomistic commentators do.[13] But *esse commune* is an abstraction and clearly belongs to what Heidegger would call "being-ness," *Seiendheit*, a representation of a Being generated out of a generalization of beings. We find ourselves here face to face with the ἀπορία which, as I have shown in Chapter 1, the young Heidegger must have encountered. On the one hand, he knew from Aristotle and Carl Braig that Being is nothing existent; on the other, he was convinced that Being is more than a mere abstraction. Heidegger attempts to resolve this dilemma with a Being which is neither the subsistent Being of St. Thomas nor a mere abstraction like *esse commune*. What Being does indeed mean in a positive sense for Heidegger will, I hope, become clearer as this study progresses.

And because Being is always the Being of beings, Being is not the cause of beings in Heidegger. It does not subsist apart from beings and hence it does not bring them forth into Being as a cause produces effects which are distinct from itself. Rather Being comes to pass in and through and as beings. Beings are not the effect of Being in Heidegger; they are its manifestation, as well as its concealment. This is a point of great importance for understanding the difference between Thomas and Heidegger and it is one to which I shall have occasion to return below (Chapter 7) in examining the work of Johannes Lotz, who thematizes the relationship between Thomas and Heidegger in terms of "subsistent Being and Being itself."

(2) The second point which needs to be clarified about St. Thomas' conception of subsistent Being vis-à-vis Heidegger has to do with Heidegger's insistence that in metaphysics God is a being, a highest being, no doubt, but a being nonetheless. Heidegger often remarks that metaphysics is content to terminate its considerations with a first cause, a first being among beings, a causal ground of other beings, and so to fall short of Being itself. Now, it is clear that when Thomas speaks of God as *ipsum esse subsistens* he does not have in mind a being, a particular *ens*, an individual entity. Recall that splendid text from the *Commentary on the Liber De causis* which was cited above: "But the truth of the matter is that the first cause is beyond being [*supra ens*] inasmuch as He is infinite *esse* itself. But *ens* means that which participates in *esse* to a finite degree ..." (*In De causis*, lect. 6, no. 175). God is not a being, for this implies finitude, the contraction of *esse* to a determinate mode, limitation. God is, not an *ens*, but *esse subsistens*.

This can be made clear by a consideration of Thomas' views on "individuals" and the "principle of individuation." For Thomas individuality is a mark of limitation. An individual is a being which has been individuated within a more universal whole. The material individual—a man, say—has been individuated within the natural species man, so that he participates or shares in a limited way in the essence of the species. Even spiritual substances are individuals inasmuch as these substances, despite the fact that they are subsistent forms, remain confined to the mode of being circumscribed by their forms (*De spir. creat.*, 8, ad 4/AR 90–91). Now, in these terms it makes no sense to speak of God as an individual for He is in no way limited or contracted within a particular defined mode of Being. Individuality implies restriction and God is unrestricted Being, the whole power of Being.

But there is a possible sense in which one could speak of God as an individual: "But individuality cannot belong to God insofar as matter is the principle of individuation, but only inasmuch as it implies incommunicability" (ST, I, 29, 3, ad 4). Individuality not only implies that something has been individuated and hence limited; it also implies incommunicability of Being. Humanity is not an individual because it is something which can be communicated among numerous individuals. But the divine *esse* is uniquely God's own. Other beings do not exist with the *esse* of God, as I have just shown. Of course,

God's Being can be communicated after the manner of a certain like-ness or diffusion, but, properly speaking, the *esse* of God and the *esse* of creatures are different. Creatures are within their own limits what God is infinitely. But creatures are not God. Now, God and creatures do not differ as one being and another do. For the creature is distinct from God as the likeness is distinct from the original, as the par-ticipated from the unparticipated. There is no simple "ontical" dif-ference between God and creatures, but an ontological difference, although it is not, for the reasons which I have here enumerated, an ontological difference which is in every sense like Heidegger's.

The conception of a subsistent Being, of Being itself subsisting through itself, does not fit into Heidegger's categories, for it is not what he means by Being (*Sein*), being-ness (*Seiendheit*), or beings (*Seienden*). But while Thomas has undoubtedly conceived the onto-logical difference in his own terms, there appears to be no reason to think that he has somehow or other fallen into oblivion about this difference. On the contrary, what I have said here suggests that his entire thought turns on this distinction. It is time now to turn back to Heidegger once again to test this interpretation more carefully.

NOTES

1. "The Limitation of Act by Potency: Aristotelianism or Neoplatonism?" *The New Scholasticism*, 26, No. 2 (April 1952), 193. For an overview of the developments in Thomistic research in this century, see Helen James John, s.n.d., *The Thomist Spectrum* (New York: Fordham University Press, 1966).

2. *Metaphysics*, p. 29. See also my "Fundamental Ontology and the Onto-logical Difference in Coreth's *Metaphysics*."

3. "Limitation of Act by Potency," 186. See also his similar study "The Meaning of Participation in St. Thomas," *Proceedings of the American Catho-lic Philosophical Association*, 26 (1952), 147–57.

4. Welte, "Thomas von Aquin und Heideggers Gedanke von der Seinsge-schichte," *Zeit und Geheimnis*, pp. 209–10.

5. Werner Marx, *Einführung in Aristoteles Theorie vom Seienden* (Frei-burg: Rombach, 1972), Part 2, "Die Ousiologie," pp. 30ff.

6. Johannes Baptist Lotz, *Martin Heidegger und Thomas von Aquin: Mensch, Zeit, Sein* (Freiburg: Herder, 1975), pp. 196–97, argues a similar point, but the opusculum *De natura generis* 1, which he uses to support his argument, seems to me to be far less explicit than the text from *In De causis*, lect. 6, cited below.

7. I. T. Eschmann, O.P., writes of this text: "In this work the basic text is the third of Boethius' Tractates whose correct title reads as follows: *Quomodo substantiae in eo quod sint bona sint, cum non sint substantialia bona.* . . . It is of no slight importance for the knowledge of Thomistic metaphysics and is indeed the starting-point for any study of the Thomistic notion of *participation* and of the distinction between 'quod est' and 'esse' " ("A Catalogue of St. Thomas's Works," in Etienne Gilson, *The Christian Philosophy of St. Thomas Aquinas*, trans. L. K. Shook, C.S.B. (New York: Random House, 1956), p. 406.

8. Pp. 81–82.

9. This point has been established with great clarity by William Carlo in his *The Ultimate Reducibility of Essence to Existence in Existential Metaphysics* (The Hague: Nijhoff, 1966). See also his "The Role of Essence in Existential Metaphysics: A Reappraisal," *International Philosophical Quarterly*, 2, No. 4 (December 1962), 557–90.

10. *Existenzphilosophie im geistigen Leben der Gegenwart*, 3rd ed. (Heidelberg: Kerle, 1964), p. 166. I shall examine Müller's interpretation of Heidegger and Thomas with some care in chap. 7.

11. See John, *Thomist Spectrum*, pp. 55ff. for a review of the discovery of the doctrine of participation in contemporary Thomistic research.

12. See the controversy concerning the meaningfulness of Thomas' claim that God is Being itself in Anthony Kenny, *The Five Ways: Saint Thomas Aquinas' Proofs of God's Existence* (New York: Schocken, 1969), pp. 82–95, and the response by Stephen Theron: *"Esse," The New Scholasticism*, 53, No. 2 (Spring 1979), 206–20.

13. See chap. 7 below and in particular my discussion of the studies of Lotz and Rioux.

5

Heidegger's Dif-ference and the *Esse–Ens* Distinction in St. Thomas

IN THE PREVIOUS CHAPTER I attempted to radicalize the existential element in St. Thomas' thought, that is, to bring out the full force of the primacy of *esse* and of the difference between *esse* and *ens* in Thomistic metaphysics. My task now is to probe the fully radical element in Heidegger's overcoming of metaphysics. I argued in the preceding chapter on behalf of St. Thomas not only that the distinction between Being and beings is to be found in his thought, but that his entire metaphysics can be seen to turn upon it, as soon as one gets beyond a certain superficial presentation of his work. Now I must turn to a more searching examination of the theme of the difference in Heidegger to see if what I have set forth in Chapter 4 does indeed support the claim that Thomas is a salient exception to the history of *Seinsvergessenheit*. This inquiry will be conducted in terms of four themes: (*a*) Heidegger's notion of "dif-ference" (*Austrag*); (*b*) the linguistic character of the dif-ference; (*c*) the "event of appropriation" (*Ereignis*); and (*d*) dif-ference and the oblivion of Being.[1]

THE "DIF-FERENCE" (*Austrag*)

In Heidegger's view man moves about continually within the distinction (*Unterscheidung*) between beings and Being: "We stand in the distinction between beings and Being. This distinction sustains the relationship to Being and the relationship to beings. It rules over us without our paying it heed" (N II 207). Our attention for the most part is drawn to what is disclosed or opened up by this distinction, while the distinction itself remains unthought. This is true no less of metaphysics than of common sense. For metaphysics is concerned with what constitutes the being as such (τò ὄν ἧ ὄν), which is why metaphysics bears the name ontology. Yet this distinction is the unknown root from which metaphysics springs, the soil which nourishes its roots. Heidegger says of this distinction:

> The distinction [*Unterscheidung*] is more suitably named by the word "difference" [*Differenz*], by which it is indicated that beings and Being somehow are carried outside of one another [*aus-einander-getragen*], separated and yet related to one another. . . . The distinction as a difference [*Differenz*] means that a dif-ference [*Austrag*] exists between Being and beings. Whence and how it comes to such a dif-ference is not said. Let difference be for the moment only named as the occasion and impulse for the question into this difference [N II 209].

Dif-ference (*Austrag*)[2] names what is differing in the difference (*Differenz*), the way in which Being and beings are borne or carried outside of one another yet at the same time borne toward one another. The dif-ference is thus somehow deeper than the more straightforward ontological difference, or, better, is the depth dimension in it. Every metaphysics offers us some version or another of the difference (*Differenz*) but no metaphysics manages to think the differing itself. This distinction between the difference of which every metaphysics is aware and the depth dimension within it, the differing (*Austrag*), is a refinement which Heidegger introduces into his doctrine of the ontological difference, and it casts the argument which I have been pursuing on behalf of St. Thomas in a new light. For it raises the suggestion that although St. Thomas' metaphysics does indeed invoke the ontological difference between *esse* and *ens*, it nonetheless leaves unthought the dif-fering itself in this difference. This, in my view, is precisely what Heidegger would claim were he presented with the argument put forward in Chapter 4.

It should, of course, be stated again that Heidegger is not pointing an accusing finger at Thomas Aquinas individually or personally. For the dif-ference is not a distinction which has been introduced by human thought, by an "act of differentiating" (N II 209). And by this Heidegger does not merely mean to say that this distinction is "real" rather than just "rational" (*distinctio rationis*). He also means to say that this distinction is not based upon human nature, that human nature is based upon it. Man comes to be insofar as he enters into this distinction, into the open space which is cleared by the difference between Being and beings. Hence, what is dif-fering in the difference is the doing not of man, but of Being itself, which in opening up this difference recedes immediately behind it. Hence, the oblivion is not that Thomas has "forgotten" something, but that the dif-fering itself has withdrawn from what is opened up in the difference.

Although Heidegger does not discuss how the dif-fering is the concealed origin of the difference of which St. Thomas' metaphysics makes use, he does discuss its foundational role in the metaphysics of Hegel in the essay entitled "The Onto-theo-logical Constitution of Metaphysics." Hegel is a more appropriate paradigm of metaphysical thought from Heidegger's point of view. For, like Heidegger himself, Hegel was significantly occupied with the history of thought, of metaphysics itself. But while the metaphysical Hegel wanted to raise up the whole history of metaphysics in a consummating *Aufhebung*, Heidegger wants to make the humble "step back" into the difference between Being and beings (ID 116/50). By means of this step back (*Schritt-zurück*) Heidegger wants to engage in a confrontation (*Gegenüber*) with what is thought. Thus the step back will carry us back from Hegel's metaphysics to the source which makes his metaphysics possible. This is the move from the thought to the unthought, and the unthought is precisely the difference as such. What is unthought is at the same time what is to be thought (*das Zudenkende*), and what is to be thought is precisely the oblivion into which the difference has withdrawn.

We see now how much more complicated the expression "ontological difference" has become. In the first instance, this expression means metaphysics itself: "The difference [*Differenz*] between beings and Being is the area within which metaphysics, Western thinking in the totality of its essence, can be what it is" (ID 117/51). Metaphysics takes place in and as this difference. Metaphysics is possible only as a distinction between beings and Being. But the task of thought is to go one step farther than metaphysics: "Consequently, the step back moves out of metaphysics into the essence of metaphysics" (ID 117/51). The step back moves from a naïve acceptance of the difference between Being and beings to the origin of that difference, to that which makes the difference possible. Hence, Heidegger says it attains the "essence" (*Wesen*) of metaphysics, in the verbal sense of its originative rising up.

The paradigm case of metaphysics which Heidegger singled out for examination in this essay is the Hegelian *Science of Logic*. This book is so called not merely because it deals with Being as "thought," but more importantly because it determines Being as "ground" (*Grund*), which is a translation of the Latin *ratio*, which itself translates the Greek λόγος.[3] As such, the *Logic* "thinks the ground-giving unity of what is most general" (Being in general); it also seeks out the highest ground. Thus, metaphysics for Hegel is a search for grounds (logic) in the highest ground (theo-logic) and in the most general ground (onto-logic). All metaphysics, as this paradigm case makes plain, understands Being in terms of ground and beings in terms of the grounded, and it thinks the difference between Being and beings as the difference between ground and grounded. God Himself, therefore, enters metaphysics as the highest ground, the first cause, the *causa prima* and *ultima ratio* of beings (ID 127/60).

The "onto-theo-logical" nature of metaphysics lies in its conception of the difference between Being and beings. And the question of the origin of metaphysics has to do with the deeper source of this difference. For Being and beings both appear only in virtue of this difference, something which itself can be made plain only if we take a step back from the difference, a step back which brings the difference near and thus enables us to encounter it face to face (*das Gegenüber*). The next three paragraphs of this text (ID 132–33/64–65; cf. US 25–26/202–203), in which Heidegger effects this face-to-face encounter with the difference, are the most difficult but also the most suggestive in the essay. Being is always the Being of beings, that is, Being passes over into beings; it is transitive, in transition (*übergehend*): "Being 'is' [*west*] here in the mode of a going-over [*Übergang*] to beings." Inasmuch as it is the Being of beings, Being gives itself over to beings, comes to pass in and as beings, discloses itself, reveals itself, "un-conceals" itself in beings. Being "is" (*west*) as the process of "coming-over" (*Überkommnis*). Beings, on the other hand, are not already there, pre-existing Being, waiting for Being to come. Rather, beings themselves appear only in and through this coming-over: "Being comes over into, comes unconcealingly over, that which arrives [*an-kunft*] as something unconcealed only through such a coming-over." Thus, the coming-over of Being into beings is at the same time the coming-on (*an-kommen*) the scene of beings. Beings arrive in appearance only in the coming-over of Being. And just as the coming-over of Being is the revelation of beings, so the arrival of beings is the concealment of Being. The unconcealment of beings is the concealment of Being. I offer the following diagram:

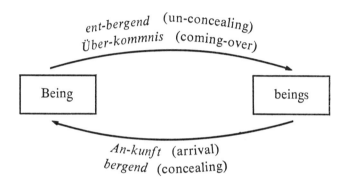

This twofold process—it is, of course, but a single process—is called by Heidegger the *Unter-Schied*, literally, the scission between Being and beings, or, in the Stambaugh translation, the "differentiating." In this *Unter-Schied*, the coming-over (*Überkommnis*) and the arrival (*Ankunft*) "are borne away from and toward one another" (*auseinander-zueinander-tragen*), that is, kept apart while bearing in on each other. This *auseinander-zueinander-tragen* Heidegger calls the *Aus-trag*, which appears in this text almost as a shorthand version of the longer phrase. Now, *aus-tragen* is the literal translation of the Latin *dif-ferre, dif-ferens*, to carry away from, to bear outside of.[4] Hence, the *Austrag* is the dif-fering in the difference between Being and beings, that which makes the difference between them, that which opens up the difference, holding them apart and sending them to one another in the appropriate manner, so that Being revealingly conceals itself in beings. The *Unter-Schied* (differentiating) is, thus, "the revealing–concealing dif-fering" (*der entbergende–bergende Austrag*). To come back to the diagram:

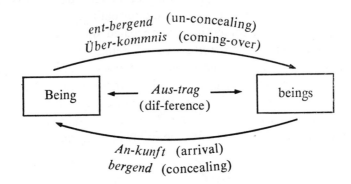

The "step back" for Heidegger is in a sense constituted of two steps. First, there is the step back from beings to Being, the step back which establishes the difference (*Differenz*) which belongs to metaphysics. Then there is the truly radical step back, from the difference within which metaphysics moves to the *Austrag*, the dif-ference which makes the metaphysical difference possible. Metaphysics thinks the difference between Being and beings; it understands beings in terms of some idea of Being. But it does not gain access to the origin of this difference, that which makes the difference, that which opens it up as the kind of difference which it is. To return to the case of Hegel: to understand Hegel's metaphysics is to understand how the difference between Being and beings has been cleared and opened up in his thought. It is to understand "the respective stamp of the difference between Being and beings to which a respective interpretation of beings as such corresponds" (ID 135/67). The character of metaphysics is measured by the character of its understanding of the difference (*Differenz*), which itself is a function of the way in which the dif-ference (*Austrag*) opens up the difference. The *Austrag*, then, is the hidden source of metaphysics:

> The only thing which matters for our task is an insight into a possibility of thinking of the difference as the dif-ference [*Differenz als Austrag*] so as to clarify to what extent the onto-theo-logical con-

stitution of metaphysics has its essential origin in the dif-ference [*Austrag*] which begins the history of metaphysics, governs all its epochs, and yet everywhere remains concealed as dif-ference, and remains thus forgotten in an oblivion which escapes even itself [ID 136/68].

Hence, in the case of Hegel, Being comes over into beings as the ground, and beings arrive in Being as the grounded. Beings in turn—and this is the completion of the circle—are themselves grounds and causes. The dif-ference not only holds Being and beings apart as ground and grounded; it also holds them together so that, while Being grounds beings, beings in turn ground Being. The coming-over and the arrival (coming-in) mutually determine one another and thus constitute a circle, "the circling of Being and beings around each other" (ID 138/69), as the above diagram illustrates. The onto-theo-logical nature of metaphysics originates out of an understanding of Being as ground and of beings as either grounded (creatures) or ground (God). And this understanding of Being and beings is governed by the way the dif-ference breaks open the difference.

It is furthermore possible to understand how God makes His entrance into metaphysics, for this too is determined by the manner in which the dif-ference gives rise to the metaphysical difference of ground and grounded. God enters the frame of reference of metaphysics as *causa sui*, and to this god, Heidegger says in an oft-quoted remark, "Man can neither pray nor sacrifice"; "man can neither fall to his knees in awe nor play music and dance before [him]" (ID 140/72). Hence, the "god-less" thought, which excludes the God of metaphysics, is closer to the really divine God (*der göttliche Gott*) than onto-theo-logic would like to admit. Presumably, in another dispensation of the dif-ference (*Geschick . . . des Austrags*) (ID 141/72), God could appear in His true divinity. But this is governed (*waltet*) by the dif-ference itself, and it is not clear that God Himself has anything to say in the matter; in the Judaeo-Christian understanding of God's appearance in history, of course, the coming of God is God's own doing.

Now, none of what has been set forth here about metaphysics can be comprehended within metaphysics, for we have entered the very region from which metaphysics itself originates. And the words of metaphysics are no longer able to express what this thinking has accomplished:

> That which bears such a name [*Austrag*] refers our thinking into the region for which the guiding words of metaphysics—Being and beings, ground and grounded—no longer suffice. For what these words name, what the manner of thinking which is guided by them represents, originates as that which differs by virtue of the difference [*Differenz*], the origin of which can no longer be thought within the scope of metaphysics [ID 139–40/71].

With the notion of the dif-ference, I have penetrated further into the heart of Heidegger's thought than is permitted by any discussion of the "ontological difference" (WG 26/27) between Being and beings. And it is fast becoming clear that any defense of Thomistic metaphysics on the grounds that it recognizes the ontological difference between *esse* and *ens* must necessarily prove to be inadequate. It is indeed true that in St. Thomas there is a "transcendence" beyond beings (*entia*) to Being itself (*ipsum esse*). Indeed, one can identify in St. Thomas the very structure of "coming-over" and "arrival" of which Heidegger speaks. *Esse* comes over to the being and lets it be, renders it present, actual, real—establishing it, in other words, *in rerum natura*. The being (*ens*), for its part, arrives in *esse*, comes to be as something having *esse*. What else is the "participational" structure of Being in St. Thomas but the "circling around one another" of *esse* in *ens* and *ens* in *esse,* as the following diagram illustrates?

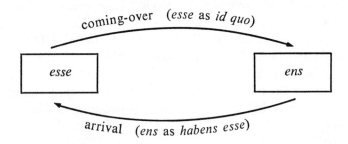

The being (*ens*) comes into Being (*esse*) in the coming-over of *esse* to the *ens*. *Esse*, on the other hand, comes over to the being (*ens*) by communicating itself to the *ens*. Now, this articulation of the *esse–ens* relationship has to do with *esse* understood as *esse commune*, and this, as we have seen, is for St. Thomas a merely logical relationship. But the same kind of circling holds true when *esse* means God. Then the circle becomes a *similitudo*-process, the process of *exitus* and *reditus*:

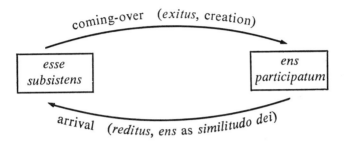

In the first movement, God communicates, not His own *esse*, but the likeness of His *esse*, so that there is, as St. Thomas says, a kind of "diffusion" of the divine Being, not in the sense that it is broken up and spread around, but in the sense that its likeness is reproduced everywhere. This is the *exitus* of God into the world, of *esse subsistens* into the *ens creatum*. In the second movement, creatures arrive in the likeness of God; they come into Being as analogical, participated likenesses of Being itself. Their very being is to be analogically like God.

But if there is a difference (*Differenz*) in Thomas' metaphysics, if there is a coming-over and an arrival, a differentiating of Being and beings, this is no more than is to be expected of a metaphysics; it is what constitutes the nature of metaphysics. But what is clearly lacking in St. Thomas is any doctrine, or doctrinal analogue to, the dif-ference in the sense of the *Austrag*, the setting outside of one another of *esse* and *ens*. Thomas' thought moves wholly within the horizon of *esse* and *ens*, and there is nothing more ultimate in his thought. There is no act, no perfection, more perfect than *esse* (*De pot.*, 7, 2, ad 9), and so there can be no more ultimate framework for Thomas than the distinction between *esse subsistens* and *ens participatum*. Now, from Heidegger's point of view, St. Thomas moves within the horizon of this difference without questioning the source from which this difference opens up, without questioning the dif-ference itself, the "between" (ID 132/65) in the distinction between *esse* and *ens*.

The oblivion of Being is not an oblivion of Being, for all meta-physics understands Being and does so in terms of presencing. It is an oblivion of the dif-ference between Being and beings, the dif-ference which makes possible the "ontological difference" of which all metaphysics makes use. That is why Heidegger later wrote in his marginalia to *Holzwege* that it is not enough to think in terms of "Being"; one must think instead of terms of dif-ference (*Unter-Schied*). "The distinction [*Unter-Schied*] is infinitely different from all Being [*Sein*], which remains the Being *of* beings. Consequently, it remains inappropriate to name the distinction still with 'Being'— be it with or without a 'y' [*Sein* or *Seyn*]" (*Holz.*[2] 364, note d). As long as one construes the charge against the metaphysics of *esse* as an oblivion of Being, it is all but ludicrous. But as soon as one sees that the real concern (*Sache*) in Heidegger's thought is the dif-ference itself, one can more readily see what his criticism is.

It can be rejoined from the Thomistic side that such a demand is in principle meaningless. For if in thinking *esse*, whether as the *esse* of every *ens* or as subsistent *esse* itself, Thomas has succeeded in thinking Being itself (*Sein selbst*), then the call to think that which is somehow deeper or beyond Being is in principle to be rejected. But this response underlines precisely that point in St. Thomas which Hei-degger would regard as an essential "oblivion" (*Vergessenheit*). For the dif-ference in Heidegger's thought is an historical–alethiological structure, that is, a process of clearing (*Lichtung*) and of dispensa-tion (*Geschick*) which makes the Western historical tradition possi-ble: "In the dif-ference [*Austrag*] there prevails a clearing [*Lichtung*] of what veils and closes itself off . . ." (ID 133/65). In the dif-ference there is a granting of the historical horizon within which any given metaphysics takes place. It is the origin of every metaphysical epoch. In opening up the difference which prevails at any given time, the dif-ference determines the whole horizon of manifestness, the whole shape of appearance in a given epoch. Now, I have said that the basic structure of appearance for St. Thomas, the very horizon of Being for him, is the difference between *esse subsistens* and *ens par-ticipatum*. But from Heidegger's standpoint, this articulation, this giving shape to Being in terms of subsistent and participated, is itself granted by the dif-ference, a way the dif-ference has opened up the metaphysical difference between Being and beings. It is a gift of the "it gives" in which the it itself (*das "Es"*) remains unthought. St. Thomas has taken the first step, from beings to Being, but he has not taken the second step which is required in order for thought to advance to a face-to-face confrontation with the difference between Being and beings. But I shall have more to say of this below, in my discussion of the "Event" (*Ereignis*).

Let me turn for the moment to another matter raised by Heidegger's notion of the circling around one another of Being and beings. In Heidegger's view, as we have seen, the coming-over of Being into beings is responded to by a rebound effect on the part of beings. Thus, while Being gives itself to beings as their ground, the being itself which is so grounded can become a ground. "The being as such, the arrival concealing itself in unconcealment, is the grounded; [but] so grounded and so effected, it in turn grounds in its own way" (ID 136–37/68). Heidegger means that one of the beings which comes to be within the horizon of ground and grounded is assigned the privilege of first ground, *causa prima*, and made the ground of other beings. Yet we saw, at the end of Chapter 4, the wholly improbable character of speaking of *ipsum esse subsistens* in St. Thomas as a first being. The doctrine of *esse subsistens* in St. Thomas is no more a "theo"-logic in Heidegger's sense than it is an "onto"-logic. Thomas does not take God to be an individual being, and he shows precious little interest in *esse commune*. The doctrine of *esse*, properly understood, has nothing to do with a science of the *primum ens* or of *esse commune*. It is more radical than the rationalist ontologies of the seventeenth and eighteenth centuries.[5] The one point in Heidegger's notion of "onto-theo-logic" which does befit St. Thomas' metaphysics, however, is that the doctrine of *esse* is a "-logic," a science of Being in the causal sense. Thomas consented to enclose his experience of *esse* within the borders of a *scientia*, a *Wissenschaft*. Though he knows that there are matters higher than *scientia*, such as faith itself, mystical and finally beatific union, he is nonetheless content to confine his experience within the concepts and propositions of a science, without insisting that the meaning of *esse* is destroyed by the very scientific mode of expression. And one is left to wonder about the possibility of a non-metaphysical appropriation of Being as *esse*, of a non-metaphysical element in St. Thomas' metaphysics. This is a matter I shall discuss at length in the concluding chapter of this study.

Dif-ference and the Essence of Language

The sense in which the *esse–ens* distinction in St. Thomas remains in "oblivion" from Heidegger's point of view is further brought out when the profoundly "linguistic" character of the dif-ference in Heidegger's thought is considered. St. Thomas remains "oblivious" of the truly radical role which is played by language vis-à-vis Being, and, like every philosopher in the tradition, is innocent of the encompassing importance of language in bringing beings to appearance, in letting them be in their Being. Heidegger's radical critique of metaphysics is at the same time a radical critique of the traditional Western conception of language. His overcoming of metaphysics is at the same time a breakthrough to a new relationship to language, a relationship which it is idle to seek in St. Thomas. St. Thomas' thought takes place entirely within a traditional conception of language, and for this reason the distinction which he thematizes between *esse* and *ens* is light years removed from the dif-ference in Heidegger's thought, which takes place essentially at the point at which language opens up the metaphysical difference. In other words, the dif-fering in the dif-ference which belongs to all metaphysics, including the metaphysics of St. Thomas, is an essentially linguistic event. We are indeed under the obligation, from St. Thomas' point of view, to find exact and appropriate language to discuss the distinction between *esse* and *ens*. But St. Thomas does not see this distinction as itself a bestowal of language, a gift of the historical movement of the "it gives" which at once gives the thinker the sphere of openness within which this distinction is manifest, the historical moment in which to say it, and the language in which it comes to birth. St. Thomas takes pains to give his language the precision which befits a *scientia*, but he never meditates the essence of language in the same radical way as Heidegger does. Let me try to work this out with greater detail.

The traditional metaphysical conception of language—which, as we saw in the first chapter, Heidegger himself once vigorously defended—turns on the distinction between meaning (*Bedeutung*) as something interior and expression (*Ausdruck*) as something exterior. The word is an external sign of a meaning which has been constituted interiorly, in the mind. This essentially Aristotelian conception of language dominated all subsequent theories of language, no matter how much new "information" was later acquired about language. In this view, language is primarily taken as communication. Since language does not play a role in the formation of meaning, it is assigned the role of communicating meanings which are already constituted.[6] Heidegger rejects this dualist theory and insists that language gives birth to meaning, or, better, to the appearance of what appears. Language is not primarily communication but the way in which things emerge into presence. Nor is language primarily something which man does, as if it were man who brings things into presence. Language is, rather, the doing of Being in man, in human speech.

This radically new conception of language, along with its bearing on his notion of the dif-ference, is brought together by Heidegger in an essay which bears the simple name "Language," and in which he claims that, properly speaking, it is not man who speaks, but language itself. Of course, men do speak, but their speech comes as a response to a more primordial address which issues from Being—or "language"—itself. Speaking is not man's representation of Being; rather, language is Being's own way of coming to words in human speech. This is illustrated, Heidegger thinks, in "A Winter Evening," a poem by Georg Trakl, which is an instance of "pure" speech (US 16/194). The poem speaks of a snowy evening in which travelers come upon a warmly lit house at vespers time, finding a table invitingly set for the evening meal. But the poet's words—vesper bells, snowfall, etc.—do not represent objects: "No. This naming does not hand out titles; it does not apply terms [*Wörter*], but it calls into the word [*ruft ins Wort*]. The naming calls. Calling brings closer what it calls" (US 21/198). Naming is, not the labeling of things, but the summoning up of their presence, an invoking which brings them near, that is, present (*anwesend*). Calling calls up presence: "The call does indeed call. Thus, it brings the presence of what was previously uncalled into a nearness" (US 21/198). It calls to the realm of the absent, summoning it into presence. Hence, it does not represent beings but lets them emerge into presence, lets them be in their Being. Language is not representative, but manifestative. This is what Heidegger means by λέγειν in *Being and Time*, § 7c, and it is what language means if we understand it in accordance with the original essence of λόγος.

What does language summon into presence? This question brings us closer to the dif-ference, for language summons both "thing" and "world." The poem names the winter evening *sky*, the snowy *ground*, the weary *mortal* travelers, a vesper bell tolling for the *divine*. In other words, it names the things which make up Heidegger's well known "fourfold" (*Geviert*). Each thing is what it is within the constellation of the fourfold which is the world. The poem, therefore, names at one and the same time the way in which things give birth to the world and the way in which world makes it possible for things to be things. It bids things come to world and world to things. These two, world and things, belong together. Each penetrates the other. They cross over to one another and so "traverse a middle" which is their "intimacy" (*Innigkeit*) with one another: "The middle of the two is intimacy—in Latin, *inter*. The corresponding German is *unter-*. The intimacy of world and thing is not a fusion. Intimacy obtains only where the intimate—world and thing—divides itself cleanly and remains separated. In the midst of the two, in the between of world and thing, in their *inter*, division [*Schied*] prevails" (US 24/ 202). The open space between world and thing which binds them together and keeps them apart is called the *Unter-Schied*, an otherwise normal word in German for "distinction" or "difference."[7] The *Unter-Schied* is the "between" which opens up the difference between Being and beings, which opens up the ontological difference.

Hence, *Unter-Schied* must be thought in terms of *Aus-trag*: "The intimacy of the *Unter-Schied* is the unifying element of the διαφορά, the carrying out which carries through [*des durchtragenden Austrags*]. The *Unter-Schied* carries out world in its worlding and carries out things in their thinging. Thus carrying them out, it carries them toward one another" (US 25/202). *Aus-trag* is the literal translation of the Greek διαφορά (cf. VA 221/71), which means to carry outside. Διαφορά is preserved in English only in some technical terms. In medicine a diaphoretic is a drug which induces perspiration, because in Greek διαφόρησις means perspiration, that is, the carrying off via perspiration. In mathematics "diaphoric" means having to do with differences, as in "diaphoric functions," which are functions of the difference of variables (as the law of inverse proportions). The Greek verb διαφορεῖν, to carry outside of, is translated into Latin by *dif-ferre*, as I observed above. The German *aus-tragen* attempts to render it literally with a Germanic root, as the English difference (and the German *Differenz*) derive from the Latin root. *Unter-Schied*, on the other hand, is related to the Latin *inter-cidere*, to cut asunder, to divide, to cut through. In *Identity and Difference*, *Austrag* means, as I have already noted, the mutual carrying outside of one another and bearing in on one another of Being and beings. Here, in the essay "Language," it means in a parallel way the carrying of "world" (Being) and "thing" (beings) outside of one another while also bearing them in on one another so as to open up the whole field of presence, the presence of what is present (*das Anwesen des Anwesenden*). The *Unter-Schied* names the event (*Ereignis*) of this carrying-out (*Austrag*). It is the event in which the "dimension" is opened up, in which both world and thing are allotted their proper places: "Its allotment of them first opens up the separateness and towardness of world and thing. Such an opening up is the way in which the *Unter-Schied* here spans the two. The *Unter-Schied*, as the middle for world and things, metes out the measure of their presence" (US 25–26/203).

But what does all this have to do with the essence of language? The poet does not name the *Unter-Schied* as such, in its own proper nature, but rather calls it by its poetic name ("pain" as the rending or rift [*Riss*] between Being and beings). The speaking of the poet is meant to summon up world and thing in the intimacy with which they belong together. The poetic speech lets the difference between world and thing come into presence. Hence, the dif-ference itself (*Unter-Schied*, *Austrag*) requires language. The difference between world and thing emerges from the dif-ference itself which is essentially linguistic. It is the *Unter-Schied* which does the "bidding" which we experience in the poet's words: "In stilling world and things into their own, the *Unter-Schied* calls world and thing into the middle of their intimacy. The *Unter-Schied* is the bidder" (US 29/207). The dif-ference (*Unter-Schied*, *Austrag*) is at once both what calls thing and world and that into which they are called. It is that which calls inasmuch as it is the silent source—here the "stillness"—from which thing and world emerge. Then, when this call is taken up into human language, when man hears this address, thing and world and so the intimacy and dif-ference in which they subsist come into words. The dif-ference stirs human talk to name world and thing. But the original call of the dif-ference, since it precedes human talk, is itself silent. The original and silent call of the dif-ference, which Heidegger calls the "peal of stillness," is the speaking not of man but of language itself. Language speaks: that means the original dif-ference calls out to human talk to let world and thing be in their intimacy and dif-ference:

> *Language speaks as the peal of stillness.* Stillness stills by the carrying out of world and thing in their presence. The carrying out [*Austrag*] of world and thing in the manner of stilling is the appropriative taking place [*Ereignis*] of the *Unter-Schied*. Language, the peal of stillness, is while the *Unter-Schied* takes place. Language comes to presence as the taking place or occurring of the *Unter-Schied* of world and things [US 30/207].

Language is nothing human; on the contrary, man is something linguistic, given to speech. Man belongs to the essence of language by being required by language for language to come to words: "the *coming-to-presence* [*Wesen*] of language as the peal of stillness *needs* and *uses* [*braucht*] the speaking of mortals in order to sound as the peal of stillness for the hearing of mortals. Only insofar as men belong within the peal of stillness are mortals able to speak in *their own* way in sounds" (US 30/208). Mortals are needed by the essence of the dif-ference in order to bring the intimacy and separation of Being and beings, world and things, into words. The speaking of man is, not the "expression" of something interior, but the response of man to a call which is addressed to him by the dif-ference. The speaking of language itself, on the other hand, is the appropriation of mortal speech by the dif-ference itself (US 31/209). Language speaks by bidding men; men speak by heeding the bidding.

The dif-ference (*Unter-Schied, Austrag*) is by its nature for Heidegger a linguistic event, not in the sense that it happens *in* language but in the sense that it is the happening *of* language. The disclosure of beings occurs in virtue of the opening which is cleared for them by the dif-ference itself. Beings appear in the opening which the dif-ference opens up. But this opening is cleared by language. The dif-ference prompts the speech of mortals within which the distinction between Being and beings is brought to words. Thus it is Heidegger's view that the structure of appearance is governed by the structure of language. Language not merely "expresses" the world; it gives it shape. The shape of appearance in a given age is always linguistic. It comes to birth within a certain kind of linguistic formation. The Greek and the Latin, the French and the German worlds are quite literally worlds which are formed by these languages. Each language "sings" the world in its own way, as Merleau-Ponty adds. Its particular constellation of vowels and consonants, of inflections and accents, gives the world a peculiar flavor and sense.[8] The destiny of Being which is bestowed on each epoch is a function of the linguistic structure in which it is articulated. Here in a sense is Heidegger's "structuralism," a structuralism which roots the structure of discourse in Being itself, in the Event which sends itself, which gives "presence" to each linguistic community. The dif-ference itself, as a pre-linguistic structure, opens up the shape of appearance in a given age by addressing a call to that age, the response to which constitutes its language.

Now, let me bring these reflections to bear on Thomas Aquinas. The metaphysics of St. Thomas is contained in Latin. On its simplest level this implies, as every worthy scholar has always known, that it is only *in* the Latin of St. Thomas that his authentic teachings are adequately contained. But on a deeper level, and this is what Heidegger is getting at, it means that the metaphysics of St. Thomas is contained *by* his Latin language, that it is a function of what the structuralists would call his "discourse," the system of rules and the range of meanings which inhere in medieval Latin. Now, we have seen that for Heidegger St. Thomas speaks a language which is both Roman and ecclesiastical, both imperial and curial. For Heidegger Latin is the language of the Romans, and the Romans are associated by him with the will-to-power and even with Machiavelli's *Prince* (N II 221). And in the *Basic Problems*, we saw, Heidegger identifies this language as the language of "making" (*facere, Herstellen*). Hence, from Heidegger's point of view, Thomistic metaphysics is "fallen" into its language; that is, Thomas speaks in Latin but he never experiences that from which his language derives, and by that I do not mean Greek. I mean that Thomas does not experience his language as the response to a primal address. In the same way as in the previous section I said that Thomas distinguishes *esse* and *ens*, but not that which grants that distinction, so here I must say that Thomas thinks *in* the Latin language without thinking that which bestows that language. He does not see the particular ontology which is embedded in Latin to be just that, a particular way in which "language itself speaks," a particular way in which Being sends itself and indeed, more importantly, withdraws under the guise of "making."

St. Thomas himself does not at all attach the importance to language which Heidegger does. I do not mean to suggest, of course, that he does not think that language is important. On the contrary, it is of the utmost importance, according to St. Thomas, to be careful in the use of language. He himself is a master of technical precision. He uses words with a painstaking exactitude. And though his Latin is the typically unadorned prose of a thirteenth-century *magister*, there is even at times a beauty in the simplicity and limpidness of his formulations. One marvels, too, at the simple beauty of his hymns and prayers, compositions which suggest another side to the character of St. Thomas, one which I hope to probe more fully in the final chapter of this study. There is nothing to fault in the rich and marvelous commentary which Père Chenu makes on St. Thomas' language.[9] Yet none of this addresses itself to the point which Heidegger is making in his essays on language. For the truth is that for St. Thomas language is always a human instrument, and the perfection of language is always to be as supple an instrument as possible, whether in the adorning of ideas in poetry, or in the precise scientific communication of them. For St. Thomas, language is especially a tool which is to be hewed to the demands of *scientia*, as is evident in his attempts to purge his own language of all metaphor and poetic license, of unnecessary imagery, and of everything subjective.

The idea never entered St. Thomas' mind that language opens up the field of presence in which we dwell, that language shapes and structures the whole understanding of Being which is at work in a given age. He lacked an historical consciousness in general and thus he lacked as well a consciousness of the historicality of language. He did not thematize the medieval Latin spoken in the thirteenth-century universities, and so he never understood it to be a stage in the history of the address of language to man. Language was good or bad, precise or imprecise, and that is unaffected by history. He took Plato's use of metaphor and allegory to be a defect, and Aristotle's more technical language to be a mark of superiority. But this is not an historical is-

sue. He attaches no importance to the historical shift from Greek to
Latin. Imprecise Greek (that of the early Greeks, Plato) is inferior
to the precise Latin of the "moderns." But imprecise Latin is inferior to exact Greek. Language is something over which men can
and should have mastery, and by which they should never allow themselves to be beguiled. He is light years removed from Heidegger's
plea for an "experience" of language, that we submit ourselves to it,
that we listen to *its* speaking and to what *it* has to say. He would be
at a loss for words had he heard these of Heidegger: "To reflect on
language, thus, demands that we enter into the speaking of language
in order to take up our stay with language, i.e., within *its* speaking,
not within our own. Only in that way do we arrive at the region within
which it may happen—or also fail to happen—that language will call
to us from there and grant us its nature. We leave the speaking to
language" (US 12/190–91). He would have been nonplused at the
suggestion that his entire metaphysics, the whole disclosure of Being
in terms of *esse* and *ens*, is a function of the way the dif-ference si-
lently addresses mortal speech.

Thus no matter how vigorously the Thomists defend the precision
of St. Thomas' language or the inventiveness of what Gilson calls his
vocabulary of Being, St. Thomas' understanding of language is separated by an abyss from Heidegger's. And this is an integral part of
Heidegger's notion of the *Seinsvergessenheit* into which medieval
thought has fallen. St. Thomas, like other medieval men, indeed like
every philosopher of the tradition, understands language as an activity of men, to be mastered and perfected like any other craft, not
as a response to the address of Being. Language is viewed by him in
terms of man, not in terms of Being. The silent peal of Being remains
unheard, in oblivion. He does not hear the address of Being in the
words of men. He does not see the hand of Being in the words of the
metaphysicians.[10]

It may be objected that even if St. Thomas himself has not thematized the relationship of language and Being, this relationship was not
unknown to Scholasticism as a whole, which witnessed the "speculative grammar" movement in the thirteenth and fourteenth centuries.
These medieval grammarians are the closest analogues one will find
in the Middle Ages to the modern structuralists, for like the structuralists, they understood the isomorphism of the structure of Being
and the structure of language. Indeed, that is why Heidegger's own

interest in medieval speculative grammar is so telling for understanding his development. For it was here that he first saw the connection between Being and the word; it was here that he first saw how an entire metaphysics is embedded in the structure of language.

Perhaps then the oblivion of language and of its "speaking" applies to St. Thomas, but it cannot be assigned to Scholasticism as a whole. Did not the speculative grammarians point out the relationship between the grammatical distinction between *substantivum* and *adjectivum* and the metaphysical categories of *substantia* and *accidentia*? Is not Heidegger's own penetrating exposition of the *De modis significandi* in the *Habilitationsschrift* an eloquent commentary on the Scholastic appreciation of the way in which language brings Being into words?

Heidegger would hold that this is so only in a very limited sense. For the Scholastic grammarian was as "fallen" into medieval metaphysics as any metaphysician was. He too took grammar to be the reflection and "expression" of thought, even as thought was taken to be the reflection and "adequation" of Being. That indeed was the main thesis of the *De modis significandi* and precisely what was signified by the "principle of the material determination of every form." The medieval grammarian takes grammar to be the reflection of metaphysics, the stamp which metaphysics leaves on language. To put it somewhat cryptically: he holds that language is metaphysical, not that metaphysics is linguistic. He does not see that medieval metaphysics itself is a function of the form of discourse in which it is embedded, that it is a function of the particular linguistic constellation called Latin. He thinks that language reflects Being, not that it "calls it up," "bids it come to presence."

Moreover, the medieval grammarian takes the form of meaning which he articulates to be an eternal structure which itself reflects the eternal truths of metaphysics. He is oblivious of the historical character of all linguistic formation. He does not see the grammar which he develops to be time-bound, one which articulates a "Latin" understanding of Being. On the contrary, he strives against precisely such an interpretation and argues that he has indeed to do with eternal formations and unchanging rules which govern all languages. He provides us with a universal, *a priori* grammar. When Heidegger said in § 7 of *Being and Time* that not only was the vocabulary of Being lacking but also its grammar, when he spoke of the necessity of liberating language from grammar, he was, as we have seen, directing these remarks precisely against the predominance of a logical theory of grammar which we find in Aristotle, in the medieval grammarians, and in Husserl's *Fourth Investigation*. Thus the tradition of speculative grammarians in the Middle Ages does not testify to an awareness on the medievals' part to the way in which Being is shaped by language. It is, rather, an institutionalizing of the categories of a particular metaphysics. The medieval grammarian is not liberated from medieval metaphysics by his reflections on logic; he is all the more fallen into it. He does not seek out the first beginnings of metaphysical language among the Greeks, or hear a more primal word being spoken in the technical terms of metaphysics. Despite his systematic reflection on language, he remains a captive to the metaphysics of his day. He does not hear the original, silent dif-ference bidding the medieval thinker to give words to the metaphysical difference. The dif-ference as such entirely escapes his theory of grammar; his grammar belongs entirely within the field which is opened up by the dif-ference, but the dif-ference itself remains unknown to him.

The Event of Appropriation (*Ereignis*)

The Archimedean point of every fundamental Heideggerian theme— *Austrag, Unter-Schied, Sage, Sprache, Geviert, Geschick,* etc.—is found in the word *Ereignis*, which the English translators have rendered as "event of appropriation."[11] The *Ereignis* is the dif-fering in the dif-ference, that whose harmony (*Einklang*) with dif-ference (*Austrag*) (ID 84/21–22) yields the metaphysical difference between Being and beings, between *esse* and *ens*. *Ereignis* is the original saying (*Sage*) in language in virtue of which language itself speaks (*Ereignis der Sprache*), in virtue of which the language of the Romans is handed down to the schoolmen of the thirteenth century to become the language which Thomas himself speaks. The *Ereignis* is the primal sending in the *Geschick* (dispensation) and the ringing in the ring-dance of the four. If ever there were a temptation to allow Heidegger's language to sediment and to be systematized around a single "term"—and then of course everything would be lost: the whole path of thinking, of relentless questioning, and of pushing forward—it is presented by the word *Ereignis*. Heidegger himself notes in the marginalia to the *Letter on Humanism*: "Since 1936 *Ereignis* [has been] the guide word [*Leitwort*] of my thought" (*Weg.*[2] 316, note a). If ever there were an "answer" to the question of Being —and, of course, there can be no "closing" of this question with any final formulation, no matter how alluring—it is *Ereignis*. The *Ereignis* is the "and" in *Being "and" Time*; it is the meaning of Being in terms of time, and of time in terms of Being. It is the "It" which "gives" when we say "there is/it gives Being" (*es gibt das Sein*).

Hence, any confrontation of Heidegger and Aquinas must in the end be a confrontation of *esse* and *Ereignis*. And again we see that there is nothing in St. Thomas' metaphysics to answer to this depth dimension in Heidegger. There is no better example of the radically historical nature of Heidegger's thought; St. Thomas' thinking, on the other hand, is largely ahistorical. If St. Thomas thinks the being (*ens*) in terms of its very Being (*ipsum esse*), he does not think the very giving of Being itself, the very process which yields and grants (*gibt*) Being. Even if it be conceded that Thomas is the first among metaphysicians, as Gilson claims, he does not think the very granting of metaphysics and the sending of its history. All this becomes clear upon confronting the metaphysics of *esse* with Heidegger's lecture "Time and Being" to which I now turn.[12] After this analysis is complete, I shall be in a position, in the final section of this chapter, to reach a decision about the "oblivion of Being."

There is a Platonic, even Neoplatonic, ring to Heidegger's project in "Time and Being," a ring which Heidegger himself notices (GP 399/282), for the project is to go beyond Being to that which grants Being and to go beyond time to that which grants time. The upshot of the lecture is to show that the *Ereignis* grants Being in terms of time and time in terms of Being. For Being and time belong together. Being has always meant presence (*Anwesen*) in Western thought. But presencing or presence refers us to the "present" (*Gegenwart*) in the temporal sense, that which is neither past nor future, and this clearly belongs to the horizon of time. Time, on the other hand, means that which passes away. But the more it passes away, the more it remains. Hence, time means the constancy of what passes away. But to be constant is to be constantly present. And presence means Being. Thus, the middle term by which Heidegger passes from Being to time and from time to Being is "presence." But there is no dialectical relationship between Being and time, for it is not Heidegger's intention to resolve the mutual interplay of Being and time into some higher concept which unites the two in their higher truth. He is intent not on sublimation (*Aufhebung*), as we have seen, but on "stepping back" (ID 115/49). He wants to think each in terms of something deeper, behind and beneath them, which somehow issues in Being and time, allowing us to say "there is/it gives Being," "there is/it gives time." He wants to determine the "*It*" which "gives" Being and time.

If Being means presence, then the distinction between Being and beings is the distinction between letting-presence (*Anwesenlassen*) and what is present (*Anwesendes*): "Letting-presence shows its character in bringing into unconcealment. To let-presence means to unconceal, to bring into openness. In unconcealing a giving prevails, the giving which gives presencing, that is, Being, in *letting*-presence" (SD 5/5). Letting-presence means bestowing presence, granting presence, and that means bringing something into the open, the realm of the unconcealed. Thus the expression "there is/it gives Being" means: it grants presence, presence is bestowed. Now, we must be very careful, and Heidegger warns us about this point, not to interpret "granting" (*Geben*) in terms of making and causing (SD 5/5, 50–51/47). This admonition is especially pertinent to us, for we have seen the profoundly causal character of the metaphysics of St. Thomas. Subsistent being itself is the cause of those things which participate in Being, and metaphysical thinking is a search for grounds (*Ergründen*). Indeed, we shall see in Chapter 7 that the main thrust of Johannes Lotz's thesis on Aquinas and Heidegger centers in the confrontation of *Ereignis* and *creatio*, even though *creare* is a pre-eminent kind of causality. And so Heidegger's warning is well taken. "Granting" (*Geben*) is not making but letting-be-seen. In Aquinas Being is not thought as un-concealing, the bestowal of presence, but—unlike in Heidegger—in terms of giving actuality, effecting actual status.

In Heidegger's view, Thomas belongs to the long history in which Being is thought as presence, a tradition which commences in the earliest beginnings of Western philosophy in the early Greeks themselves. Indeed, the interpretation of Being as presence is the defining characteristic of Western philosophy. But among the early Greeks presencing was thought with a kind of primal simplicity and undistorted originality which is untouched by the later "metaphysical" determinations of presence in terms of unchanging and changing, eternal and temporal, cause and effect, subject and object. Presencing "hardens" (*verhärtet*) into the doctrine of οὐσία in Plato and *Aristotle*, as we have seen. And in Thomas Aquinas himself, where presence is determined as *actus*, it is thoroughly subjected to the categories of causality and making (SD 56/52). After Thomas, presence is determined as *res cogitans* and *res extensa* and as reason and will; finally, in its most extreme concealment in modern technology, Being as presence becomes the standing stock (*Bestand*) of stuff to be calculated and manipulated (SD 7/7). In the whole history of metaphysics the early Greeks stand closest to the primal giving of presence itself, but even they, though they have received the gift of presence, do not think the giving itself which is at work in presence. The giving withdraws in favor of the gift which is given. And so Thomas, like every metaphysician after the early Greeks, stands in a twofold oblivion: of the primal sense of presencing (disclosed in the fundamental words of the early Greeks) and of the historical giving process itself which grants to each age its apportioned sense of Being. Hence, the giving of presence to Thomas, and to every metaphysical thinker, is a "sending." I "send" a gift or another person to take my place while I myself remain behind. Sending is a giving in which the source of the sending withdraws behind the gift. The giving of Being as presence is a sending (*Schicken*), and this sending is what is at work in the history (*Geschichte*) of Being. The "It" which gives holds itself back. And in Greek holding back means ἐποχή. An "epoch" of Being is thus a self-concealing sending (*ein sich selber verbergendes Schicken*). The task of thinking is to "de-construct" (*ab-bauen*) or dismantle this accumulated structure of self-concealments, to find the original giving which gives presence, the original sending which sends Being as presence.

Perhaps then it is time which gives Being, for the sending of Being is clearly historical. What then is time? This question is answered in the present essay in terms of the notion of "reaching" (*Erreichen*), which the English translator also renders as "extending" and "giving." Presence is reached or extended to us in the present (*Gegenwart*). But not only then. For presence means more than the present; it is upon us just as really in the mode of absence. The presence of what is present no more (*nicht mehr Gegenwart*) is "having-been" (*Gewesen*). In the having-been, presence is extended as what has been all along. And presence is extended to us also in the absence of what is not-yet. For the not-yet, thought more carefully, is that which

is coming toward us, the "future." In the having-been and the coming-toward us (*Auf-uns-kommen, Zu-kunft*), presence is extended
or reached out to us. Presence is encountered in the present and outside it. The future or the coming-toward us reaches over or extends a
presence to us, but not the presence of the present, for it is precisely
not present, but rather the presence of the having-been. In plainer
terms, the future delivers over to us possibilities which have been all
along but have never become present (actual, in the present, *in der
Gegenwart*). On the other hand, having-been reaches over or extends what has been all along to the future. There is, then, a mutual
interplay and exchange by which each, by imparting its own presence
to the other, gives rise to the present. The present then is not the now
but the space which has been opened up between the having-been and
the future; it is rife with the presence of what has been and is coming
toward us. Hence, the notion of time–space: "Time–space is the name
for the openness which opens up in the mutual self-extending of fu-
tural approach, having been, and present" (SD 14–15/14). Time–
space is a clearing (*sich lichten*), an openness (*Offene*), which is
cleared and opened up by the mutual reaching over and extending of
presence, each to the other. Time clears a temporally structured
opening; an opening for presence is made by time. Time is the unity
of the threefold crossing over of presence, the mutual interplay, which
is called by Heidegger the fourth dimension or "the near." All "nearing" involves distancing. In bringing the three dimensions toward one
another, it also holds them apart. In holding the having-been open, it
refuses its arrival in the present. A thing remains as having-been as
long as it is not present. By the same token, nearing holds the future
open only by holding back or detaining what is coming. A thing is
coming toward us only as long as it is not present. It is the near which
gives time, for it holds the time–space open by preserving what is re-
fused in the having-been and by preserving what is withheld in the
arrival of the future. Clearly then time is given as much as Being. We
have found the giving of Being in sending, and now we encounter the
giving of time in the extending or reaching over of presence. It is not
time which gives Being, for both Being and time are given.

But if time and Being are given, from what source are they granted?
What is the "It" which "gives" time and Being? "In the sending of
Being, the extending of time, there becomes manifest a dedication
[*Zueignen*], a delivering over [*Übereignen*] into what is their own

[*Eigenes*], namely, of Being as presence and of time as the realm of the open" (SD 20/19). Being is sent into its own as presence, and time into its own as the temporal clearing, by the process of *Zu-eignen*, appropriating. This process is called *Ereignis*, event of appropriation: "What determines both, time and Being, in their own, that is, in their belonging together, we shall call *Ereignis*, the event of appropriation" (SD 20/19). Notice that Heidegger says that the *Ereignis* not only delivers Being and time into their own nature, but also delivers them over to one another. It is the *Ereignis* which holds (*hält*) the two *Sachen*, time and Being, together in the unity of a single state-of-affairs (*Sachverhalt*).

And so this lecture is brought to full term by naming the "It" which gives. But we must be on guard against thinking that we have thereby named something existent, some new present entity (*etwas Anwesendes*) hitherto not met with in ordinary experience. The lecture has nothing to do with "asserting" the "existence" of some entity or other. It summons up the experience of the primal originating of the presencing-process, of the primal emergence of what is present into presence. These sentences do not come as "propositions" in response to the question "What is the *Ereignis*?" Furthermore, we should be on guard against thinking that we have now attained the latest and best determination of Being, that hitherto Being was named ἰδέα, ἐνέργεια, *actualitas*, etc., but in these days by Heidegger as *Ereignis*. *Ereignis* is not a name for Being precisely because Being is what is sent by *Ereignis*. *Ereignis* itself is, not a destining or dispensation (*Geschick, Schickung*) of Being, but the source or origin of every dispensation. With the turn into the *Ereignis*, thinking escapes the gradually escalating concealment, the chain of epochal transformations, of Being and enters into the source from which they arise.

Let me now return to St. Thomas. It is clear from this reading of "Time and Being" that Thomas necessarily belongs to the history of metaphysics, within the tradition of Being as presence, and that he does not, from the point of view of this lecture, succeed in thinking the *Ereignis* itself from which this tradition takes it source. It would be too much to ask of Thomas that he have the kind of historical acuity which the thought of Being as event requires. As Max Müller writes, had Thomas come at the beginning of the Western tradition, or at its end, he might have been led to think this tradition as a tradition, as an historical sending.[13] But there is nothing eschatological in the Thomistic conception of *esse*, no thinking on its term and move-ment. Instead, as a "medieval" man, as one who belongs squarely in the middle of the tradition, in the midst of things (*im mitten des Sei-enden*) (WG 106–109), the "historical reduction" is impossible for him. Instead of thinking the tradition as a tradition, he remains em-bedded in it, advancing it no doubt, shifting it away from a necessi-tarian to an existentially contingent conception of presence, but nonetheless always in such a way as to remain part of the history of metaphysics. He does not think the *Ereignis* itself, yet he remains with-in the clearing which the *Ereignis* has opened up in and through his own metaphysics. The tradition delivers over to him the possibilities which inhere in Aristotelian and Platonic metaphysics, in the writing of the Fathers, and ultimately in the writings of the sacred authors. These possibilities cross over into the future so as to come toward him and open up that dimension within which takes place the great synthe-sis of Plato and Aristotle, of Greek philosophy and Christian dogma, of reason and faith which defines his thought. The day and the hour of the understanding of Being in terms of *esse subsistens* and *ens par-ticipatum* are made possible, from Heidegger's point of view, by the way in which the possibilities which inhere in the Western tradition cross over and open up the field of presence, the dimension within which St. Thomas' metaphysics takes place. Thirteenth-century Eu-rope is built in its most essential lines not by the architects of its great cathedrals, not by the popes and kings who drew the lines of ecclesi-astical and political force across its map, but rather by the way in which presencing reaches across and back again, reaching out to medieval man who, being so approached (*der Mensch, der von An-wesenheit Angegangene*) (SD 12/12), is drawn into the tradition in the way which is apportioned to him.

It is hardly conceivable that St. Thomas would have possessed this kind of radical historical appreciation of the Western tradition. The history of Being itself has withheld from Thomas an historical con-sciousness.[14] I do not mean to say, of course, that Thomas does not have an idea of history at all. As a Christian, he was convinced of the importance of the history of salvation, and it would be a fruitful proj-ect to comb his commentaries on the Scriptures in particular to learn more of what he thought about such matters. I mean rather that Thomas does not conceive *esse* as an historical presencing, a giving and apportioning of itself in time. Being in its perfection and plenitude transcends time for him, because it is removed from all potency and change. From the point of view of St. Thomas, and we shall see this clearly in Chapter 7 of the present study, to affirm the historicality of Being, of Being as *Ereignis*, is a failure to reach Being in its purity and perfection; it is to limit one's horizons to this world.

But the question is not yet adequately posed. For on this level we are merely debating two competing metaphysical theories of "Being," two different kinds of metaphysics—an ahistorical metaphysics, such as we find in most traditional metaphysicians, and an historical metaphysics, such as we find in Hegel. But the issue is not whether one understands Being to be historical or not. The issue is to see that all metaphysical thought arises from a withdrawal, that every account of "Being" has a deeper source. From Heidegger's point of view, Thomas is a captive of his times even in being its greatest spokesman. Thomas thinks upon Being as it is granted in the thirteenth century—and his greatness is found precisely in the depth and scope with which he articulates this gift—but not upon the granting process itself. He thinks within the clearing which has been opened up for him, but not upon the clearing as such. He does not thematize the self-giving of Being and the self-reaching of time or the It which gives. He does not meditate upon precisely that which withdraws behind every historical sending; rather, he remains caught up in the sweep of historical sendings. Thomas thinks Being as it is given in the medieval epoch—and he outstrips all his contemporaries in the process—but not upon its epochal character. The "participation in Being" is the way in which Being cleared itself for Thomas. This is the final word for Thomas but not for Being itself, or, better, for the It which gives. For this mode of presencing, of bringing presence to words, will be transformed into another coming. The medieval sending already harbors within itself the makings of the modern world, as indeed Gilson himself has shown so decisively in his first works on Descartes. It is not the medieval world view, or the modern, or some synthesis of the two in the manner of an *Aufhebung*, which contains the truth of Being. Only the step back into the giving itself from which arise the various shapes and configurations of Being, be they historical or ahistorical, provides an access to what is to be thought from Heidegger's point of view.

More than anything else, it is the notion of the *Ereignis* which separates Heidegger from St. Thomas. And if we fully appreciate the abyss which divides these two thinkers on this point, then we shall see why Heidegger and his followers are so singularly unmoved by all the protests made on behalf of the metaphysics of *esse* against the charge of the oblivion of Being. For no matter how forcefully one asserts that *esse* is active upsurge, and I do not deny that this is a fundamental and enduring insight of St. Thomas, one has not gotten beyond square one in dealing with what Heidegger calls the oblivion of Being. For by this, Heidegger means that the Being of metaphysics, the Being which is given to be thought in metaphysics, is the gift of a more primordial source. And this means that the metaphysics of *esse* is the gift of an historical sending, of "time–space," of *Austrag, Sprache, Ereignis*. It remains within the confines of what is given and thus in oblivion of the giving which, quite unknown to metaphysics, is at work in all metaphysics.

Put in the language of phenomenology: Heidegger thinks that Thomas remains in the "natural attitude" about the historical giving of Being, and that he does not make the historical "reduction." Thomas accepts his tradition "naïvely" without questioning whence it springs. He takes over the understanding of Being as objective presence first put forward by Plato and Aristotle and mediated to him by his Arab sources. And although he creatively adapts this tradition to his own needs, although he is an important innovator within this tradition, he does not put the tradition itself into question; he does not think the tradition as a tradition. Thomas thinks Being within the historical terms which have been granted to him without thinking that historical granting itself. He thinks within the tradition without thinking the tradition as precisely what is to be thought, that is, as a Being-process in which Being is withdrawn precisely insofar as it gives itself. It never occurs to Thomas to put into question the Latin language with which he speaks as a *magister*, a language which is handed down to him by the Romans and which harbors within itself a particular vocabulary and grammar of Being. He never puts the causal and ontological mode of discourse into question. He does not question the self-evident determination of Being as what is "objectively there." In short, Thomas is caught up in the historical sweep of the "it gives" without experiencing the giving itself which is at work in Scholasticism, without experiencing Scholasticism as a constellation of meaning which itself has been made possible on deeper—alethiological—grounds. Thomas stands within the clearing without thinking the clearing as such.

The follower of St. Thomas might object at this point that not every age of Being is equally an oblivion, not every period of thought is equally an "epoch" of withdrawal. For even though the "It" which gives remained behind, Being as presence was bestowed upon the early Greek thinkers with a primal and undistorted originality. And if such a gift has been granted to the early Greeks, who were no more historically minded than St. Thomas, why not for Thomas too? Why cannot Thomas have a status somewhat like Parmenides who thought Being in its truth as presencing, even though the "It" which "gives" was concealed from him (SD 8/8)? There are, I think, important differences between the primal bestowal of Being as presence in the early Greeks and the metaphysics of *esse*, many of which are already apparent, but this is a question of sufficient importance to warrant a separate treatment in Chapter 6. But the question also points to an ambiguity in the meaning of the "oblivion of Being" which I want to examine more carefully. Hence, I want to conclude this chapter, the argument of which is central to the present study, with a careful scrutiny of just what Heidegger means by the "oblivion of Being."

Dif-ference and Oblivion

The oblivion of Being is an oblivion, not of Being, but of the difference between Being and beings (ID 116/50).[15] And in terms of what Heidegger means by oblivion, I cannot rightly say that Thomas has managed to evade it. Thomas has not awakened from this oblivion, recalled what has fallen into neglect in it. Still, it is not completely obvious yet what it means to "awaken" from the oblivion of which Heidegger speaks. There is an ambiguity in Heidegger's formulations which is yet to be rooted out. It is not clear what it would mean for anyone, including Heidegger himself, to be awakened from the oblivion of which he speaks.

If the history of metaphysics is constituted by its oblivion of Being, then presumably the thinker who has escaped this oblivion has in some way escaped from the history of metaphysics itself. In some way he attains what is called in the "Seminar" on "Time and Being" "the end of the history of Being" (SD 44–45/40–42). The incessant withdrawal of the "it gives" behind its historical grantings is at the same time the bestowal of Being as presence upon the great metaphysical ages of Plato, St. Thomas, and Hegel. The greatness of these thinkers lies in the profound and comprehensive way in which they bring to words what has been bestowed upon their age. But the "oblivion" which envelops them is their unmindfulness of the *Ereignis*, the "it gives" itself. If that is so, then the thinker who has thought through to the granting of the "it gives" has in some way managed to escape the constant ebb and flow, the giving and withdrawing, of the various destinings of Being to man. He has, therefore, acquired a standpoint in which he is no longer affected by the withdrawal. For such a thinker, the history of Being, as a history of withdrawal and oblivion, is at an end. This is to say, not that for him historical time ceases to flow, but rather that the withdrawal which is at work in each and every historical dispensation of Being no longer holds him captive. It is not that the development of metaphysics in historical time is over but only that the spell of metaphysics is broken.

But what does it mean to break the spell of metaphysics? We must not get the idea, the "Seminar" warns, that this means that the "preceding oblivion of Being would thus be overcome [*aufgehoben*] and negated [*getilgt*]" (SD 31/29). When we think through to the withdrawal of Being (= dif-ference), we do not thereby obliterate the oblivion and replace it with total disclosure. On the contrary, the oblivion of Being, inasmuch as this means the *withdrawal* of Being, is essential to Being insofar as it is the condition of every possible granting of unconcealment. Hence the "awakening" (*Erwachen*) to this oblivion must be such as to preserve this very oblivion. It is, on the one hand,

> an awakening which must be understood as a recollection of something which has never been thought—but, on the other, as this awakening, it is, not an extinguishing of the oblivion of Being, but the placing of oneself in it and the standing within it. Thus the awakening from the oblivion of Being to the oblivion of Being is the awakening into *Ereignis*. The oblivion of Being can first be experienced as such in the thinking on Being itself, on *Ereignis* [SD 32/30].

One does not extinguish the preceding oblivion of Being; one comes to stand in it (*stehen in ihr*), to set oneself up within it (*sichstellen in sie*). That is why the "Seminar" speaks of awakening *from* oblivion *to* oblivion. The overcoming of metaphysics is the awakening *to* the oblivion *as* an oblivion. It is the experience of metaphysics precisely as an oblivion, as a withdrawal. With this awakening the withdrawal of Being (more precisely, of that which gives Being) does not cease; thinking becomes attentive to it as a withdrawal. The withdrawal is experienced as such. We do not obliterate this movement; we come to stand in it, to be awake and alert to it. One thinks of a religious analogy: the sinner who achieves self-consciousness does not eliminate the sin, but comes rather to stand in it, to be awakened to it.[16]

Now we can see what is meant by the "end" of the history of Being. The history of Being as a concealment of the primordial giving and sending of Being is over *as* a concealment: "the history of Being is at an end for thinking *in* the *Ereignis*, that is, for the thinking which enters into the *Ereignis*—in that Being, which lies in sending—is no longer what is to be thought explicitly. Thinking stands in and before That which has sent the various forms of epochal Being" (SD 44/41). If metaphysics means the concealment of that which withdraws, and which by withdrawing grants the history of Being, then the turn into the *Ereignis* is "the end of this withdrawal's history." The withdrawal does not cease, but the *concealment* of that withdrawal, the withdrawal *as* a withdrawal, ends: "But now this concealment does not conceal itself. Rather the attention of thinking is concerned with it" (SD 44/41). Does this mean that thinking enters into a timeless now, a motionless ahistorical source of history? Not at all. Thinking enters instead into the movement of the *Ereignis* itself, the movement which is most appropriate to it, viz., the movement of withdrawal. The "movement" (*Bewegtheit*, κίνησις) (*Weg.*[2] 239ff./ 221ff.) is withdrawal and concealment (κρύπτεσθαι) (VA 270/113) —to fuse Aristotle, Heraclitus, and Heidegger into a single sentence.

Hence, Heidegger does not want to say that the history of metaphysics in objective time will come to a close: "This means that the history of Being as what is to be thought is at an end for the thinking which enters the *Ereignis*—even if metaphysics should continue to exist, something which we cannot determine" (SD 45/41–45). The history of metaphysical formations, of epochal structures of Being as presence, may well persist, but for the thinker who has thought through to the *Ereignis* itself the spell of metaphysics is broken; the withdrawal is exposed as such and thereby loses its power to entrap. That is why it is added in the "Seminar": "In this sense, one cannot say that the destinies are 'stopped' with the entry of thinking into the *Ereignis*. But one must nevertheless consider whether one can still speak in such a way about Being and the history of Being after the entry, if the history of Being is understood as the history of the destinies in which *Ereignis* conceals itself" (SD 54/50).

One thing which emerges with great clarity from the above discussion, even though this is not often noticed, is that the expression "oblivion of Being" (*Seinsvergessenheit*) is extremely ambiguous.[17] And this ambiguity goes beyond the fact that what stands in oblivion is not Being, precisely, but *Ereignis*. It is not merely the fact that it is impossible to name the dif-ference by speaking in terms of Being and beings (*Holz.*[2] 364, note d). There is a dangerous ambiguity in the word "oblivion" (*Vergessenheit*) itself. For the expression means either the withdrawal of the *Ereignis* or the hiddenness of this withdrawal from thought. It means either withdrawal *simpliciter* or the withdrawal of that withdrawal, oblivion *simpliciter* or the oblivion of that oblivion, concealment *simpliciter* or the concealment of that concealment. Sometimes oblivion means the withdrawal of Being itself. Now, oblivion as withdrawal is ineradicable, for it belongs to the very structure of the sending and reaching of the *Ereignis* that *Ereignis* itself remain behind. The *Ereignis* itself is not something which is sent; it is not a being or the Being of beings. It is that which bestows Being and in so doing remains withdrawn, in oblivion. It is that withdrawal which makes possible the history of the West, the history of the granting of Being as presence from *Anaximander* to the present age. Were *that* oblivion to be overcome, history would cease, and beings and Being would melt into a totally self-disclosed self-giving of the *Ereignis* in which all time, history, finitude, and distinction would volatilize. And that is essentially unthinkable on Heideggerian terms. Hence, there can be no overcoming *that* oblivion—the oblivion which is withdrawal itself.

The "awakening" from the oblivion of Being has to do rather with the second sense of this word, the oblivion of the oblivion, the concealment of the withdrawal. That is why the minutes to the "Seminar" speak of awakening *from* oblivion (in this second sense, as oblivion of the withdrawal) *to* oblivion (in the first sense, as sheer withdrawal).

The oblivion to which we are awakened is the ineradicable withdrawal of the *Ereignis* itself, which belongs to its very structure. The oblivion from which we are awakened is the concealment of the withdrawal *as* a withdrawal. Oblivion in the second sense can be overcome, but not in the first. Withdrawal belongs to the very essence of the *Ereignis*, but thought can be awakened from its oblivion *of* this withdrawal. Oblivion in the second sense is metaphysics, and metaphysics can be overcome—not eliminated but recognized for what it is. Its spell can be broken.

One can then determine where the element of human "responsibility" enters into Heidegger's thought. It has not always been possible to overcome metaphysics, to spot the withdrawal *as* a withdrawal. For as long as thought was caught up within the sweep of the tradition and what it passed along, *in medias res*, the thinker was inevitably drawn along with it. But now, in these days, we live *in extremis*, in the extreme radicalization of this withdrawal, at the "end" of philosophy, when the tradition of withdrawal and concealment has reached its deepest and most ominous stage. Now, in this very moment of extreme danger, the saving is most palpable for those who would submit themselves to the discipline of "thought" and who would lay aside the pretention of rationality.[18] Awakening from oblivion in this sense can be carried out. If men would be thought-ful enough, attentive enough to the movement of withdrawal whose vibrations we all can feel, whose soft reverberations we all can hear if we lend an ear, then the awakening from oblivion to oblivion would take place. The primal withdrawal of Being itself is something over which no man has any influence, for which he has no responsibility. But the oblivion of this concealment can be escaped. It lies within the pale of man's responsibility, that is, of his responsive-ness, to awaken to the movement of this withdrawal and to think this withdrawal as a withdrawal. If we make the turn into the *Ereignis* (*Einkehren in das Ereignis*), the withdrawal of the *Ereignis* is not removed; we come rather to stand in it, to attend to it. And this is a possibility for thought itself.

Now, it is also Heidegger's view that once this turn into the *Ereignis* is made, a new beginning will become possible. This turn on the part of thought will set free (*auslöst*) the possibility that "another destiny" (*Geschick*) will commence (*Holz.*[2] 336/25). A new history of sendings (which will at the same time be a history of withdrawal) will be set loose, and we shall be granted an experience of Being comparable to that of the early Greek thinkers. Then we too shall be the recipients of the gift and grace of presencing in its primal splendor. But there is no exact coincidence between the dispensations of Being (*Seinsgeschick*) and historical ages (K 39/39). Even though the withdrawal of the *Ereignis* has been thought through, the concrete history of metaphysics and of technology may persist. The new dawn is uncertain. One can only think and wait. Thinking the dispensations of Being is in no way predicting the future history of the West. Thinking is not fortune-telling.

Now, it is clearly unreasonable to think that St. Thomas Aquinas would have held the kind of position which I have described here. This is a thoroughly "historical"—I do not say "historicist"—position of which no medieval man was capable, by reason of his very historical situation. It requires that one undertake the historical reduction in which the thinker experiences the tendency of an age as a giving which withdraws, a particular historical granting in which the "it gives" itself is withdrawn. This kind of overcoming of oblivion is not to be found even in the early Greek thinkers. Even they failed to think the "it gives": "The latter withdraws in favor of the gift which it gives. The gift is thought and conceptualized from then on exclusively as Being with regard to beings" (SD 8/8). Every attempt to think Being from Anaximander to Husserl has understood Being in terms of "presence" (*Anwesen*) without attending to that which lets presence be (*Anwesen-lassen*). That is why Heidegger is reported to have responded to an alleged proposal by Maritain that Heidegger and Aquinas shared many fundamental insights, that he (Heidegger) would need to be shown the texts, because he could not conceive that a thinker who belonged to a destiny of Being so far removed from the present could have experienced *Ereignis*.[19]

The most one can hope for in the case of St. Thomas is, not that he would have made the turn into the *Ereignis*, but that he would have been granted an experience of Being as presencing, *Anwesen*, which would share some of the same radiance which was granted the early Greeks. The gift of *Anwesen* which was bestowed upon the early Greek thinkers was of a primal and pristine quality, even if these thinkers themselves remained in oblivion of the "it gives" itself. After the early Greek thinkers, the primal sense of *Anwesen* congealed into "permanent presentness" (*stetige Anwesenheit*) in Plato and Aristotle. Instead of experiencing its rising up, lingering, and sinking away, Western metaphysicians identified Being as that which clings steadfastly to actuality.

And so the question I am posing comes down to this: Does the Thomistic experience of *esse* possess the pristine quality of the experience of the early Greeks? Do the categories of φύσις, λόγος, and ἀλήθεια at all befit *esse*? Or does *esse* remain captive to the tradition of Being as οὐσία in the widest sense, that is, as that which permanently endures, which persists without lapse or lack? If one could show the proximity of Thomas to the early Greeks, then one would have demonstrated indeed that Thomas himself, like Anaximander, Parmenides, and Heraclitus, though remaining in oblivion of the *Ereignis*, would nevertheless be the privileged recipient of a gift of presence as primal emergence-into-presence. It is clear that Thomas was innocent of the "history of Being." But was he, like the early Greeks, a recipient of a favored experience of presencing?

My answer to this question will be given in two parts. In the first place, I shall show in the next chapter, on the basis of a study of the early Greek experience of Being as Heidegger interprets it, that one cannot plausibly interpret *esse* in these terms, at least if one takes the texts of St. Thomas as they were evidently intended to be taken. But then I hope to show, in the concluding chapter of this study, that there is "depth" dimension in St. Thomas, as I like to think, a layer of meaning beneath the *evident* sense of his words which can be found if one probes for the more profound intentions and motives which are at work in his thought sometimes even in ways which are unknown to Thomas himself. I shall try to show in this final chapter that there is a more primal experience of Being in St. Thomas which can and does indeed possess an "alethiological" character. This structure in St. Thomas' thought is found only by a deconstruction of Thomism as a metaphysics which makes plain its more primordially mystical inspiration. And since I have shown on another occasion the kinship between the experiences of the mystic and the thinker I shall have shown, in this chapter, that there is another, a non-metaphysical dimension, to the philosophy of *esse*, one indeed to which most philosophers are systematically blind. At that point, and only at that point, will it be possible, I think, to bring the experiences of Heidegger and Thomas Aquinas into a kind of harmony.

NOTES

1. The argument presented in this chapter is a development of my study "Heidegger's 'Dif-ference' and the Distinction Between *Esse* and *Ens* in Thomas Aquinas," *International Philosophical Quarterly*, 20, No. 2 (June 1980), 161–81.

2. The actual etymology of the word *Austrag* is discussed in the following section on language and dif-ference. I have chosen to render *Austrag* as dif-ference and *Differenz* as difference.

3. See my *Mystical Element in Heidegger's Thought*, pp. 73–80, for a discussion of these translations.

4. I shall have more to say about the Greek origin of this word in the next section on language and dif-ference.

5. This has been shown not only by Gilson but, from a Heideggerian perspective, by Gustav Siewerth in *Das Schicksal der Metaphysik vom Thomas zu Heidegger* (Einsiedeln: Johannes Verlag, 1959).

6. Merleau-Ponty gives an almost satirical account of the traditional theory as a twofold process: speaking is first thinking, then externalizing; hearing is first listening, then decoding. See *The Phenomenology of Perception*, trans. Colin Smith (New York: Humanities Press, 1962), pp. 177–79.

7. I leave the word *Unterschied* untranslated because I have already preempted "dif-ference"—which Hofstadter justifiably uses—for *Austrag*. One would need a neologism to capture it otherwise—like "inter-scission." Elsewhere I have translated it as "distinction."

8. Merleau-Ponty, *Phenomenology of Perception*, p. 187.

9. M. D. Chenu, *Toward Understanding St. Thomas*, trans. A. M. Landry and D. Hughes (Chicago: Regnery, 1964), pp. 100–25.

10. One might want to point out, from the Thomistic side, that St. Thomas, as indeed all medieval theologians generally, recognized the Son as the *Logos* and *verbum*, and so was not lacking in a conception of language as something which is more than human. Indeed it is precisely this which leads Max Müller to speak of the "presence of Being as *Logos* and *verbum* in all beings . . ." in St. Thomas' thought (*Existenzphilosophie*, p. 244). However, if one examines this view more carefully, as I have done in connection with Meister Eckhart, one finds that it moves within the traditional metaphysical distinctions which Heidegger wants to overcome, viz., those between the eternal and the temporal, the uncreated and the created, the inner meaning and the outer expression, etc. See my *Mystical Element in Heidegger's Thought*, pp. 166–72 and 224–25.

11. For an excellent account of *Ereignis*, see J. L. Mehta, *Martin Heidegger: The Way and the Vision* (Honolulu: The University Press of Hawaii, 1976), pp. 430–44.

12. For a discussion of "Time and Being" which is pertinent to the present analysis, see my "Time and Being in Heidegger," *The Modern Schoolman*, 50, No. 4 (May 1973), 325–49.

13. *Existenzphilosophie*, pp. 240, 242.

14. In *Being and Time* Heidegger writes, "Only because it is 'historic' in the first place can an age lack the discipline of history" (SZ, § 6, 20/42). Although Heidegger is using here his argument from "deficient modes" (the fact that we lack something proves that it belongs to us), this text can also be constructed to mean: the lack of historical consciousness is itself an historical characteristic of an age.

15. I am indebted to my correspondence with Professor Thomas J. Sheehan for sharpening my appreciation for the texts from the "Seminar" on "Time and Being" which are treated here.

16. Or a Socratic analogy: Socrates does not eliminate the ignorance but he comes to stand in it and to be alert to it.

17. Johannes Lotz has also pointed this out in *Martin Heidegger und Thomas von Aquin*, pp. 26, 45–46. He distinguishes *Seinsvergessenheit* from *Seinsverborgenheit*.

18. This is the remarkable argument of "Die Kehre" in *Die Technik und die Kehre*. In the recognition of the *"Gestell"* as *Gestell*, as the withdrawal of Being, there is already the "saving." In this recognition there is a flash of truth (*Blitzen*) in the midst of the dark night of technology. In the withdrawal, we see what is withdrawn. The difficulty with Thomas Aquinas, then, is that his times were not altogether dark enough, rather the way one cannot yet see the stars in the late afternoon because it is not yet dark enough! That is why Heidegger wrote of the "clear night of the Nothing" (*Weg.*[2] 114/105).

19. Hans A. Fischer-Barnicol, "Spiegelungen—Vermittlungen," in *Erinnerung an Martin Heidegger*, ed. Günther Neske (Pfullingen: Neske, 1977), pp. 99–103. See also the anecdote recorded by Helmut Franz ("Das Denken Heideggers und die Theologie," in *Heidegger*, ed. Otto Pöggeler [Cologne: Kiepenheuer & Witsch, 1969], p. 193): when Heidegger was asked whether or not Luther might not be excepted from the charge of *Seinsvergessenheit*, he responded by pointing out how many times he had been asked the same thing about Thomas Aquinas by Catholics.

6

Presencing (*Anwesen*) and the Meaning of *Esse*

IN THE PRECEDING CHAPTER, I indicated that St. Thomas was entirely innocent of the *Ereignis*, of the "it gives" which makes the sending of the various epochs of metaphysics possible. But I also pointed out that this is no less true of the early Greek thinkers who, though they enjoyed the gift of a privileged sending of Being as presence, nonetheless remained in oblivion of the "it gives" itself (SD 8/8). The greatness of these thinkers does not consist in their having "overcome" metaphysics, in the sense of having thought through the epochal sendings of Being to the primal *Ereignis*. Their greatness is, rather, to have thought *before* metaphysics, to have stood at the beginning of the tradition before it became metaphysical. Anaximander, Parmenides, and Heraclitus were not *yet* philosophers or metaphysicians, and because of this they were all the greater *thinkers* (WdP 52–53). Their thinking preceded the congealing of Being into εἶδος and οὐσία in the so-called "Golden Age" of Greek philosophy. Hence, the anomaly of describing these men as "Presocratic" (Diels), "pre-Platonic" (Nietzsche), or "pre-Aristotelian" (Hegel) (*Holz.*[2] 321–24/13–15), as if they took their measure from Socrates, Plato, or Aristotle and are to be estimated by the degree to which they prepare for and approximate those thinkers. Parmenides' poem is not a defective stylistic mode which must be distinguished from its "strictly logical contents." On the contrary, these thinkers, whom philosophy considers to be semi-philosophic and still encumbered by the old myths, are in fact non-metaphysical thinkers who were not yet victimized by Western *ratio*. Their thinking is still close to the source, primal, freshly bestowed upon Western man, like the new-fallen snow outside the cabin in Todtnauberg. They experience Being thought-fully, poetically, and they bring it to words in the memorable terms φύσις, λόγος, ἀλήθεια, and μοῖρα.

Hence, even if a thinker remains in oblivion of the *Ereignis*, even if he does not think the giving itself, still it may be that the gift of presence has been bestowed upon him in a primal and original (*an-fänglich*) way. And so the question is whether there might not be in Thomas' doctrine of *esse* something of this same pristine essence of Being as presencing. Thomas is altogether innocent of the *Ereignis*, of the historical dif-ference (*Aus-trag*) which opens up for each metaphysical age the way in which it understands Being. But that does not rule out the possibility that in thinking Being as *esse* Thomas too, like the early Greek thinkers, is the recipient of a primordial ex-perience of Being. Now, we have already seen that in Heidegger's view the medieval Scholastic experience of Being as *actualitas* is a corruption of the early Greek notion of Being. But I should like now, in this chapter, to examine this early Greek experience more care-fully and to hold it up against the renewed and more vital reading of *esse* which I pursued in Chapter 4 and of which I think Heidegger was essentially unaware. Is there anything of the quality of φύσις, λόγος, and ἀλήθεια in the Thomistic *esse*? Or, put otherwise, is any-thing of the gift of Being as presencing which was granted to the Ionians and Eleatics to be found also in the thirteenth-century Do-minican *magister* at Paris?

To answer this question I shall examine in turn the sayings of Anaximander, Heraclitus, and Parmenides to which Heidegger has devoted so much attention over the years, and then take up a con-frontation of the experience of presencing which Heidegger finds there with the Thomistic doctrine of *esse*.

ANAXIMANDER

Before I turn to the Anaximander fragment, I want first to mention what Heidegger calls the "eschatology of Being," for this expression underlines the importance which he attaches to the study of the early Greeks. In Heidegger's view, we today live in the ἔσχατον, that is, at that end-point, that outermost extreme into which the history of the decline of Being has run its course.[1] And that means that we live in-between two beginnings: the first, creative, originary beginning which took place in the early Greeks, and that "other" or "new" beginning which is hoped for, anticipated (*vor-laufen*), and thought forth to (*vor-denken*). We today live in the eschatology, in the ending of the first great beginning, in the ever-growing night which is the evening-land called the "West" (*Abendland*). We seek not literally to repeat the first beginning, which would be "vain and absurd" (*Weg.*[2] 369/ 210), but to find in what the early Greeks thought a renewal of our own history in a way which is uniquely proper to us.

By means of eschatological thinking we latecomers (*wir die Spät-linge*) are enabled to hear in what came first, the early Greek experi-ence of Being, what is yet to come. By means of it, we think on the two ends of the history of Being and seek the new beginning in the old. For this early Greek experience is far more primordial than the present age of technology: "But what if that which is early outdis-tanced everything late, if the very earliest far surpassed the very lat-est?" (*Holz.*[2] 327/18). Hence, this early Greek experience must come again, at the end of the present history of Being, and thereby set free a new dispensation, a new beginning, precisely at the point at which the old dispensation takes its leave: "What then occurred in the dawn of our dispensation [*Geschick*] would then come, as what once oc-curred, at the last [ἔσχατον], that is, at the departure of the long-hidden dispensation of Being" (*Holz.*[2] 327/18). The eschatology of Being is precisely this gathering up (λόγος) of the history of Being into its present term (ἔσχατον) in such a way as to enable this tradi-tion to pass over into a new beginning:[2]

> The Being of beings is gathered [λέγεσθαι, λόγος] in the ultimacy of its dispensation. The essence of Being up to the present time disap-pears, its truth still veiled. The history of Being is gathered in this departure. The gathering in this departure as the gathering [λόγος] at the outermost point [ἔσχατον] of its essence up to the present time is the eschatology of Being [*Holz.*[2] 327/18].

Hence, if we think eschatologically we shall learn to hear in what is earliest what may come latest. But the first step is to listen to the early thinkers on their own terms.

Eschatological thinking is possible only now, for us latecomers, who live in that extreme and final consummation of the oblivion of

Being where metaphysics has spun itself out in all its potentialities, at that precise point where the danger is greatest, even while the saving power is at hand. Where the extreme danger of the *Ge-stell* is most intense, Being turns itself around, the oblivion is reversed, and the new beginning is commenced (*Holz.*[2] 373/58).[3]

Now, the effort which I am making in the present chapter is also eschatological, even though it concerns a thinker—Thomas Aquinas —who stands at neither end (*terminus*, ἔσχατον) of the tradition, but precisely, as a "medieval," in the middle. For we want to think this medieval man eschatologically, that is, we want to see whether and to what extent the beginnings have left their traces on his thought. To what extent do the words of the earliest Greek thinkers find an echo in the metaphysics of *esse*? To what extent does *esse* say φύσις, λόγος, ἀλήθεια? And, therefore, to what extent does *esse* point beyond the present age of *Technik*?

Having said that much, let me turn now to Heidegger's interpretation of the Anaximander fragment. Anaximander says: "But that from which things rise also gives rise to their passing away, according to what is necessary; for things render justice and pay penalty to one another for their injustice according to the ordinance of time" (*Holz.*[2] 329/20). Heidegger singles out for consideration the words γένεσις and φθορά, generation and corruption, coming-to-be and passing away. But these words must be thought alethiologically, in terms of "luminous rising and decline" (*lichtendes Auf- und Untergehen*) (*Holz.*[2] 342/30). Hence, they signify rising up into and passing out of manifestness, coming forward into unconcealment and departure back into concealment. Γένεσις and φθορά refer to the arrival and departure into presencing which "lingers for a while" (*ver-weilt*) in the open. We say in English that someone "whiles away the time"; it is this verbal use of the conjunction "while" which Heidegger intends with the verb *verweilt*, to linger for a while, to make a passing appearance, to gain a temporary respite within the γένεσις–φθορά process. Whiling is the transition (*Übergang*) from arrival (*Hervorkommen*) to the departure from (*Hinweggehen*) presencing. Whiling is a stay in the open, a transitory interlude in the realm of the unconcealed. It is a stay in presence inserted in the midst of absence, a temporary overcoming of absence, a presence in the midst of absence. It can be graphically represented thusly:[4]

ἀ-λήθεια *Un-verborgenheit* *An-wesen*	*Verweilen* (lingering for a while) transition (*Übergang*) (*Gegenwart*)	
	departure	arrival
	(*Hinweggehen*)	(*Hervorkommen*)
λήθη *Verborgenheit* *Ab-wesen*	past (*Gewesen*)	future (*Zukommen*)

Here is the very process of ἀ-λήθεια, of *An-wesen*, of rising up into and passing out of the unconcealed, and one begins to see here how far removed the alethiological conception of Being is from St. Thomas' realistic, objectivistic conception.

Now, the fragment also speaks of injustice, ἀδικία, the lack of δίκη. What, then, is δίκη? Heidegger translates it as joining or juncture (*Fuge*); hence for him ἀδικία refers to a state in which things are out of joint, disjoined, uncoordinated. And what is this joining except the juncture in which the lingering of whiling takes place?

> The while occurs essentially as the transitional arrival in departure; the while comes to presence between approach and withdrawal. Between this twofold absence the presencing of all that lingers occurs. In this "between" whatever lingers awhile is joined; this "between" is the juncture in accordance with which whatever lingers is joined, from its emergence here to its departure away from here. . . . Presencing comes about in such a juncture. What is present emerges by approaching and passes away by departing; it does both at the same time, indeed because it lingers. The "while" occurs essentially in the juncture [*Holz.*[2] 335/41–42].

The juncture is the space which is cleared on the one end by rising up and on the other end by passing away and within which what is present emerges into presence. What, then, is the lack of δίκη of which Anaximander speaks:

Whatever lingers awhile becomes present as it lingers in the juncture which arranges presencing jointly between a twofold absence. Still, as what is present, whatever lingers awhile—and only it—can stay the length of its while. What has arrived may even insist upon its while solely to remain more present, in the sense of perduring. That which lingers perseveres in its presencing. In this way it extricates itself from its transitory while. It strikes the willful pose of persistence, no longer concerning itself with whatever else is present. It stiffens [*versteift sich*]—as if this were the way to linger—and aims solely for continuance and subsistence [*Holz.*[2] 355/42].

One sees in this passage how, in Heidegger's view, the original presencing process (*Anwesen*), experienced in a primordial way by the early Greek thinkers, hardens, stiffens, and congeals into the "permanent presence" (*ständige Anwesenheit*) of later Greek philosophy (εἶδος and οὐσία in Plato and Aristotle), and then into the *substantia* of the Middle Ages and into the *Gegenständlichkeit* of modern representational thinking (EM 148/162). In its later formulations, presencing congeals more and more into a stable stuff until finally, in the modern epoch, it becomes a stuff at the disposal of technological man. The being which is out of joint is the being which resists the emerging–departing structure, which persists in a way which Heidegger does not hesitate to call "haughty" (*Holz.*[2] 359/45–46) and "willful" (*Holz.*[2] 355/42). Injustice is the persistence which resists the all-embracing rule of δίκη. Δίκη is the rule which would contain this disorder, which would subdue the stubbornness of that which wants to persist inordinately.

But whence does this order originate? What is its source? For the answer to this question Heidegger turns to the preceding phrase κατὰ τὰ χρεών, "according to necessity," with which, along with John Burnet, Heidegger considers the original fragment to begin. The word κατά suggests the way in which something lower comes from something higher (*Holz.*[2] 363/49), in particular the way in which the lower, beings (τὰ ἐόντα), come into Being (ἐόν). Χρεών thus is the Being of beings, the presence of what is present. For χρεών enjoins order and the respect of considerateness of one being for another. Χρεών, which grants to beings their manner of arrival, names the matter to be thought, which is the Being of beings. And that means that the word χρεών names the distinction between Being and beings (*Holz.*[2] 364, note b), that is, the distinction between presence and what is present. Nonetheless even here, in Anaximander, this difference is not named as such: "Although the two parties to the distinction, what is present and presencing, reveal themselves, they do not do so *as* distinguished" (*Holz.*² 364–65/50–51). The difference as a difference is forgotten: "The essence of presencing, and with it the distinction [*Unter-Schied*] between presencing and what is present, remains forgotten. The oblivion of Being is oblivion of the distinction between Being and beings" (*Holz.*² 364/50). To the word *Unterschied* in this text Heidegger adds the note which I cited in Chapter 5: "The distinction [*Unter-Schied*] is infinitely different from all Being [*Sein*], which remains the Being *of* beings. Consequently, it remains inappropriate to name the distinction still with 'Being'—be it with or without a 'y' [*Sein* or *Seyn*]" (*Holz.*² 364, note d). This note brings the passage into line with the essays of the '50s, in which the *Unterschied* or *Austrag*, as we saw in the preceding chapter, is taken to be the deeper source of the Being-beings distinction. *Unter-Schied* is precisely what remains missing, not only from metaphysics, but even from the early Greek thinkers. That is why Heidegger writes in another note on the same page: "In the shining [*Scheinen*] of presencing, what is present appears [*erscheint*], comes forth. [But] the shining [itself] never appears! [*Das Scheinen erscheint nie!*]" (*Holz.*² 364, note c). The early Greek thinkers experienced Being as presencing, and in a pristine way, and they experienced beings as what is present, but they never succeeded in naming—or it was never granted to them to name—the very opening up of the difference as a difference between presencing and what is present. And it is this difference which constitutes the highest matter to be thought. Xρεών does not name the distinction as such, but the distinction has left its "trace" on this early word: "we may surmise that the distinction has been illuminated more in that early word about Being than in recent ones; yet at no time has the distinction been designated as such" (*Holz.*² 365/51).

How then are we to translate χρεών? Heidegger settles on the German word *Brauch*, usage. Proper use means delivering a thing into its proper destination, bringing it into its own way to be (cf. WD 114/187). It means dispensing presencing to what is present. Usage (*Brauch*) refers to that which gives, the reaching over of presence to that which is present. It names the *Aus-trag*, the *Unter-Schied*, the "It" which gives Being as presence, the *Ereignis*. The *Ereignis* thus leaves its trace in the words of Anaximander, and we who engage in eschatological thinking, who undertake to hear what is said in the first dawn of the Evening-land, must learn to follow its tracks. For, as Heidegger says, "This trace quickly vanishes in the destiny of Being which unfolds in world history as Western metaphysics" (*Holz.*² 369/ 54). If we hear Anaximander's words eschatologically, we shall hear instead of the standard translation this new but really very old saying: "along the lines of usage: for they let order and thereby also considerateness belong to one another in the surmounting of disorder" (*Holz.*² 372/57).

HERACLITUS

I have consistently maintained throughout this study that it is the alethiological dimension of Heidegger's work which separates him from St. Thomas and all traditional Scholasticism in a decisive way. And so it is particularly urgent for my purposes to follow Heidegger's reflections on the ancient word ἀλήθεια. This he does in connection with Heraclitus, who, far from being "obscure," is for Heidegger the philosopher of the open clearing (*Lichtung*). I shall examine first Heidegger's remarks on Heraclitus contained in the essay "'Αλήθεια," and then his 1944 essay entitled "Λόγος."

The essay "'Αλήθεια" comments on Fragment 16, in which the word ἀλήθεια does not appear: "How can one hide oneself before that which never sets?" On the face of it the fragment states, in the form of a rhetorical question, that a man cannot hide before the light. That is why Clement of Alexandria very plausibly read it to say, How can a sinner hide before an all-knowing God? But the thinker always runs the risk of thought and so of the less plausible interpretation (VA 261/106). The fragment ends with the word λάθοι, which means hiding, remaining concealed. The Greeks always understood Being in terms of what is hidden and unhidden, concealed and unconcealed, which is a "fundamental trait of presencing itself" (*Anwesen*) (VA 262/106). This is not an etymological issue, Heidegger says, but a question of how "the presencing of what is present comes to language only in shining, self-manifesting, lying before, arising, bringing itself before, and in assuming an outward appearance" (VA 262/107). Hence, even if the etymology of ἀλήθεια is otherwise than Heidegger describes it, it is nonetheless true that the Greeks thought of truth in terms of light and darkness, shining and appearing—in a word, un-concealment. The verb λανθάνω, "I remain concealed," refers not just to human behavior but also to "the basic trait of every response to what is present or absent" (VA 265/109).

The fragment speaks of "the never setting" (τὸ μὴ δυνόν ποτε). Δύω means to submerge, to go under, to be lost in. It refers to a "setting" of the sun, which means its going into concealment. Stated affirma-tively, the fragment speaks of the ever-rising, which is what is signi-fied by the word φύσις, rising up into unconcealment, or what Hei-degger here calls "upsurgence" (Auf-gehung) (VA 269/112). But φύσις is not one-sidedly self-revelatory, for Heraclitus says that "φύσις loves to hide" (φύσις κρύπτεσθαι φιλεῖ). Thus φύσις signifies both ris-ing up and self-concealment. Self-revealing loves self-concealing. But what is concealed is also thereby sheltered and preserved. The love of self-revealing and self-concealing for one another is that each preserves the other. Self-concealing is possible only as a restraining of self-revealing, which it protects from being exhausted. And self-revealing is possible only as a rising up out of concealment. But does not the fragment speak of the never-setting, of a rising up which is not restrained? Not for Heidegger, for whom the never-setting means that which never falls prey to concealment, that which never is lost in concealment, but is always emerging from it (VA 272/114).

Does the fragment mean that the ever-rising sees and notices every-thing, so that nothing can be hidden from it? But the fragments say nothing about seeing and noticing. It means that no one, neither gods nor men, can remain concealed, not because anyone sees them, "but because—and only because—each comes to presence" (VA 277/119). Why single out gods and men? Because their relation to the clearing (φύσις = Lichtung) belongs to the very essence of the clear-ing, which needs and requires gods and men for the place of its mani-festness: "Gods and men are not only lighted by a light . . . so that they can never hide themselves from it in darkness; they are luminous in their essence. They are alight [erlichtet]; they are appropriated into the event of lighting and never concealed" (VA 278/121). Thus Heidegger has effected a rather different reading of the fragment. Clement understood Heraclitus to be saying that a sinner cannot hide from the eyes of God. But in Heidegger's view, a view which may even have been hidden from Heraclitus himself, Heraclitus refers to the way in which men and gods are required to complete the clearing (*das Lichten zu vollbringen*). They are never concealed from the clearing, but always appropriated by it.

Why then does Heraclitus ask a question which so obviously requires an affirmative answer? Because Heraclitus is *appealing* to mortals to heed that which speaks to them from this clearing: "Mortals are irrevocably bound to the revealing–concealing gathering which lights everything present in its presencing. But they turn from the lighting, and turn only toward what is present, which is what immediately concerns them in their everyday commerce with each other" (VA 281/122). The mistake of mortals, against which Heraclitus warns, is to turn from the clearing as such and to allow themselves to be taken up by what appears within the clearing, to turn away from presence in favor of what is present. And in so doing mortals fall away from their most proper dignity: "For they have no inkling of what they have been entrusted with: presencing, which in its lighting first allows what is present to come to appearance. Λόγος, in whose lighting they come and go, remains concealed from them and forgotten" (VA 281/122). That is why Heraclitus has spoken the words which we read in this fragment. For mortals could emerge from their oblivion "if only they would ask: how could anyone whose essence belongs to the lighting ever withdraw from receiving and protecting the lighting?" (VA 281/122). This last citation from Heidegger could well serve as his translation of Fragment 16.

Heidegger's interpretation of Heraclitus is centered not only on Fragment 16 but also on the Heraclitean notion of λόγος which, it is well known, he translates as "gathering together." A trace of this original meaning is found in the English "col-lect" and in the German *legen*, to lay, and *lesen*, to cull or gather. Now, I do not want to analyze Heidegger's reading of λόγος in detail here; I want simply to bring it into line with what he has said about χρεών in Anaximander and about ἀλήθεια. The text which he comments on is translated as follows: "When you have listened not to me but to the λόγος, it is wise within the same λόγος to say: *one* is all." The one (ἕν) is the unifying principle which gathers and assembles everything present. That means that λόγος, the one, lets what is present be present, that it releases it into unconcealment. In a pregnant paragraph, Heidegger writes: "The laying which gathers assembles in itself all sending by bringing things and letting them lie before us, keeping each absent and present being in its place and on its way; and by its assembling it secures everything in the totality. Thus each can be joined [*sich fügen*] and sent into its own" (VA 222/72). Thus the λόγος does not refer to some kind of systematic principle which imposes a unity of order upon things in the manner of Hegel's *Vernunft*, of Spinozistic necessity, or of Newtonian determinism. It refers instead to the principle (ἀρχή) which governs over the dispensing of presence which in the Anaximander essay was called χρεών, the source of the juncture between presence and absence. If it does not grant a systematic order, it does govern over the ἀδικία and so prevents one being from persisting unduly in Being and expelling all others. The λόγος is what gathers things together into the juncture, which selects things for appearance in the juncture and holds back the disjoined. As such it is what sends each thing into its appointed place and lets it come to presence in its due and apportioned time. That is why in the Parmenides essay Heidegger will call it μοῖρα, destiny.

Heraclitus also referred to the λόγος as lightning (*Blitz*). Now, Heraclitus is one of those founding geniuses in whom the birth of the West came to pass, for the Western tradition was born when Being became thought-worthy. But the word λόγος names Being as "that which gathers all present beings into presencing and lets them lie before us in it." To which Heidegger adds: "But this lightning-flash of Being remains forgotten. And this oblivion remains hidden, in its turn, because the conception of λόγος is forthwith transformed" (VA 227/76). This means that in the flash of lightning which took place in Heraclitus the distinction between Being and beings, the distinction *as* a distinction, was momentarily lit up, and then, just as suddenly as it was illuminated, fell again into darkness. The Greeks experienced λόγος but they never thought it, and that includes Heraclitus (VA 228/77). They allowed Being to come into language as the difference between Being and beings but they did not name that difference as the essence of language. Instead, when they turned to language as a theme, they spoke in terms of the φωνὴ σημαντική, the meaning (*Bedeutung*) which receives verbal expression (*Ausdruck*), and this determines our thinking about language even today: "Once, however, in the beginning of Western thinking, the essence of language flashed in the light of Being—once, when Heraclitus thought the λόγος as his guiding word, so as to think in this word the Being of beings. But the lightning vanished abruptly. No one held onto its streak of light and the nearness of what it illuminated" (VA 229/78).

PARMENIDES

The final figure in the trilogy of early Greek thinkers who interest Heidegger most is Parmenides. Heidegger is especially interested in interpreting Parmenides' words ἐόν and μοῖρα, and the connection between them. In so doing, Heidegger formulates his views in a way which comes quite close to the 1962 lecture "Time and Being."

In Fragment 8 (of Diels–Kranz), Parmenides uses the word ἐόν, the participle which corresponds to the Latin *ens*, the German *seiend*, and the English being. The importance of the participial form, Heidegger holds, is that it refers at once to Being and beings, which he calls here the "duality" (*Zwiefalt*) or, more literally, the "twofold." It is this duality which is intimated in such expressions as the being "in" its Being and the Being "of" beings (VA 239–40/86). Parmenides intimates this duality, but he does not state it as such. Hence, it fell into oblivion shortly after him and was replaced with the distinction between the highest being and other beings. What then is it which Parmenides first hints at but which afterward is forgotten?

Parmenides says that Being and thinking are the same (τὸ αὐτό), which is to be interpreted as the "belonging together" of Being and thought, the "gathering" of thought to Being in order to let the duality come to pass. But thinking (νοεῖν) is grounded in and comes to presence from gathering (λέγειν) (VA 243/89). Parmenides uses the word πεφατισμένον, "something uttered," which has the root φάναι, whose meaning is documented in the word φάσμα, the shining of the stars and the moon, their way of coming forward into presence. Ἐόν thus calls for a gathering of λέγειν and νοεῖν to itself inasmuch as λέγειν and νοεῖν complete the gathering of what is present into presence.

Τὸ αὐτό, the same, is not an empty identity; it refers to the unfolding (*Ent-faltung*) of the two-fold (*Zwei-falt*). The twofold is the opening up of the difference between presencing and what is present, the bringing forward into view of this duality. The unfolding of the twofold is the revealing of the Being in its Being, the illumination of what is present in its presence. And so it is also called ἀλήθεια. Thinking belongs to Being, not because it too is one more being, but because it is required for the completion in which Being is brought to its fullness. The unfolding requires both λέγειν and νοεῖν. Now, Parmenides says that μοῖρα binds ἐόν to be whole and immovable. Heidegger translates μοῖρα as the "apportioning" (*Zuteilung*), which signifies for him the dispensation of presence to what is present (*die Schickung des Anwesen als Anwesen von Anwesendem*) (VA 251–52/97). At this point, it is clear that μοῖρα joins hands with χρεών from the Anaximander fragment, which oversees the juncture in which presence and absence are joined. And it also bears the name of the "dispensation of Being" (*Seinsgeschick*), in the sense that it gives Being through the unfolding of the difference between presence and what is present. It gives the shining (*Scheinen, Anwesen*) in which what is present (*Erscheinung, Anwesendes*) appears. But it is only presence and what is present which are manifest. The duality between them, the difference which opens out into these two, which unfolds in them, remains behind, concealed. Hence, the source of the unfolding itself remains in λήθη. Μοῖρα is a sending which remains behind what is sent, the sending which sends the difference between presencing and what is present. Thus, μοῖρα names the "it gives" which gives Being as presence and thereby sets into motion the history of metaphysics.

It remains now only to mention δόξα, the opinions of mortals. In the standard rendering, δόξα refers to those who believe in change and becoming, that which in Parmenides' view involves non-being. For Heidegger δόξα refers to the realm of what is accepted at first blush, to the most superficially evident. It thus means the realm of the unfold*ed*, what is present (ἐόντα), the sphere in which there is a mere naming of this or that and the profusion of thoughtless terms (*Wörter*). Ordinary opinion knows presencing too, but not in the way of the thought which is gathered to ἐόν; rather, it knows presencing "as well as" (τε . . . καί) non-presencing, which it mixes indiscriminately together with presencing. Opinion is concerned with what shines in the light and is brightly colored (φανόν), but it pays no heed to the light itself which emanates from the duality which is gathered in the true word (*Wort, Wörte*) (VA 253–55/99–100). Indeed, this fall into δόξα is itself occasioned by μοῖρα, inasmuch as it sends what is present into presence while remaining behind. Hence, just as φύσις in Heraclitus loves to hide, so in Parmenides the origin of the twofold is necessarily concealed.

One can see running through these essays on the early Greeks the common thread of what I have called Heidegger's "alethiology." Χρεών, φύσις, λόγος, ἀλήθεια, μοῖρα: the same but not identical. Each names in its own way the presencing process, the process by which things emerge into the unconcealed, rising up out of and falling back into concealment. The Anaximander essay is the most detailed: the rising up and falling back occurs with the juncture in which presence is joined and fitted. In the ἀλήθεια essay the juncture is called the open clearing, the space which is cleared for the emergence of what is present. And in the λόγος study the juncture is called the place in which the λόγος gathers things together, "keeping each absent and present being in its place" (VA 222/72). And that is why it can be called μοῖρα, which is the fate which apportions to each thing its manner and due measure of presence. In each case Heidegger speaks in terms of what is manifest or kept hidden, in the light or recessed in darkness, revealed or concealed. This alethiological interpretation of the Greeks is at once made possible by and is the rightful heir of what once was called "phenomenology," a term which Heidegger finally decided belonged to the tradition of transcendental subjectivity. Alethiology is a more radical, non-subjectivist way of savoring the being in its Being, of allowing it to emerge on its own and from out of its own resources. And it is light years removed from any realistic or causal interpretation of Being put forward by metaphysical thought.

Anwesen AND *Esse*: A CONFRONTATION

Let me now return to the metaphysics of *esse* to take up again the thematic concern of this study, the confrontation of the conception of Being in Heidegger and St. Thomas. And let me now ask, in the light of this reading of Heidegger, whether it is possible to understand the metaphysics of St. Thomas within the framework of Heideggerian alethiology.

For myself, I find it difficult to imagine that in the texts of St. Thomas as they have been handed down to us in their own historical actuality there is to be found a philosophy of ἀλήθεια. I say this because St. Thomas' metaphysics seems to me to be in the first place "realistic," and in the second place "causal," and on both these accounts, therefore, at odds with alethiological thought. Let me examine each of these points in turn.

To begin with, *esse* for Aquinas means that act by which a thing comes to be "real" rather than "present," in the original Greek sense of shining and appearing, revealing and concealing. In virtue of its *esse*, a thing becomes *ens reale, ens extra animam*. It comes to stand outside its causes and outside the mind of the one who knows it. Being as *esse* means Being as the act which brings the being forth "in the nature of things" (*in rerum natura*), as something actual. And even if it is objected that *ens* is a truly transcendental notion in St. Thomas, encompassing every mode of Being (not just real Being), it is clear that in Thomas' realism *ens reale* is the primary meaning of Being in reference to which every other mode is determined. *Esse* grants actuality, reality. *Esse* refers to what Kant would have called Being "in itself" (*an sich*), not in the sense that Thomas is in any way involved in a phenomenal–noumenal distinction, but in the sense that he claims to speak of Being as it is "independent" of thought, and hence of all revelation and concealment. Matter and form are "objective" features of natural beings; the highest principles of morality are universal and necessary, drawn from an objectively determined human nature, etc. St. Thomas' thought is through and through a philosophy of objective being. From the standpoint of *Being and Time, esse* means *Vorhandensein*, objective presence, being objectively there. In St. Thomas the original Greek notion of presencing as the shining in which all appearances shine, as a rising up into appearance, into manifestness, has declined into an understanding of Being as "objective presence," the presence of what is mutely there, as a sound in an empty room is thought to be "there" in naïve realism and common sense. *Esse* is not a phenomenon in the Heideggerian sense, but an abstraction, a distillate which is contrived by imagining the world as it would be without Dasein (cf. SZ, § 69b)

But St. Thomas' metaphysics is not only a philosophy of *realitas*—and not ἀλήθεια; it is also a philosophy of *actualitas*—and not ἀλήθεια. The Thomists have always thought that St. Thomas' notion of *esse* as *actualitas omnium rerum* (ST, I, 4, 1, ad 3), and in particular of God as *actus purus*, emancipates St. Thomas once and for all from any possible charge of *Seinsvergessenheit*. Yet in fact, from Heidegger's point of view (EM 14/14), it only testifies to it all the more decisively.[5]

The translation of ἐνέργεια into *actualitas* is fateful: "Meanwhile an epoch of Being soon comes in which ἐνέργεια is translated as *actualitas*. The Greek is shut away, and to the present day the word appears only in Roman type. *Actualitas* becomes *Wirklichkeit*, reality becomes *Objektivität*. . . . The decisive turn in the destiny of Being as ἐνέργεια lies in the transition to *actualitas*" (*Holz.*² 371/56–57). Now, I have already examined Heidegger's interpretation of *actualitas* in Chapter 2 of the present study. But I want to return to it here in order to underline all the more forcefully the abyss which separates the original Greek meaning of ἀλήθεια and the notion of *esse*. In particular I want to make use of Jean Beaufret's penetrating exposition of Heidegger's view in his *Dialogue with Heidegger*, a work which was partly inspired by the seminar at Thor in which he participated.

Beaufret writes:

> The Thomistic interpretation of the being in its Being as *actus essendi* or as *actualitas* does not at all correspond to the phenomenological sobriety of the experience of Being as presence. It corresponds instead to a metaphysical attempt to speak of the being as a creature homologously to the creator, in whom *esse* is *actus* itself, indeed *actus purus*, the creation being in its turn *unica actio solius Dei*.⁶

The Greeks wanted to "save the appearances" phenomenologically, but St. Thomas wanted to "save creation" metaphysically.⁷ Hence, St. Thomas takes the being, not in its very Being—that is, in its quiet emergence into manifestness—but in its character as something *created*. We do not find in St. Thomas an account of *ens qua ens*, for *ens* is always and from the start *ens creatum*, and the *esse entium* is conceived in terms of *actus, agere, actualitas*. However strange it may seem to Thomistic ears, St. Thomas' is a metaphysics of power, not really as far removed from the will-to-power as Thomists like to think.⁸ It conceives of Being in terms of power, efficiency, action, force, making. The Greeks do not take the carpenter as an "efficient cause" but as τὸ ποιοῦν, as an artist who brings something to the light of day. He does not manufacture something; he shows us something. Greek thought is epiphanic; Thomistic thought is causal.⁹ Operating under the invisible influence of the Roman language, St. Thomas translates the phenomenology of presencing into a metaphysical dynamics, a system of limited and unlimited acts and actualities, of finite and infinite causes. *Actualitas* is the measure of *causalitas*, as *causalitas* is the sign of *actualitas*. God and creatures differ as acts, powers, potencies. *Esse* is what a thing *does*, Gilson says, and Beaufret regards this as a telling, if unwitting, concession of Heidegger's point.[10] Being is not simple presencing but action, activity, efficiency, work. The whole doctrine of essence and *esse*, far from giving us access to the ontological difference, amounts to no more than a "paraphrase of creation."[11] God is the being who does not stand in need of being created, who is *a se, per se subsistens*, uncreated and uncreatable, as Meister Eckhart would have said. But beings—creatures —have *esse receptum et participatum*. Their *esse* is given to them, bestowed; they are (*sistere*) by being set outside of (*ex*) mere possibility. To ex-sist means to stand outside of one's causes. The whole conception of Being here is in terms of producing, and Being is divided into the spheres of the unproducible producer and his products. The doctrine of *esse*, arising on the horizon of creation, gives us access, not to the simple splendor of presencing, but to a world of metaphysical production.

The metaphysics of *actualitas* is basically at odds with the meditative savoring of the original sense of Being as presencing. Of course, *esse* too is a mode of presencing—*adesse*—but it no longer contains the original essence of presencing; it is a modification and derivate, turned over to the categories of causality, actuality, and reality. In terms of the historical actuality of his texts, St. Thomas' thought is caught up in metaphysical objectivism. But whether or not this is the final word about St. Thomas, whether or not, behind the historical actuality of what is said, there lies the possibility of what is unsaid— that I leave for discussion in the final chapter of the present study.

The preceding discussion might lead me to advance the supposition that I have been pursuing the wrong point all along. Perhaps I ought not to have suggested that Being as original presencing is comparable to Thomistic *esse*, but rather to Thomistic *verum*, for it is here after all that St. Thomas speaks of Being as *truth*. It is here that one can see the intrinsically *relational* structure between Being and the mind which is not explicit in the notion of *esse* and which is essential to

Heidegger's idea of ἀλήθεια. Transcendental *verum*, ontological truth, signifies that to be is to be true, that *verum* and *esse* are convertible. Is this not the proper analogate in Thomas' thought to the original meaning of presencing?

However, if we turn to *De veritate*, I, 1, the celebrated text in which St. Thomas sketches his theory of truth, we see how radically Being-as-truth is subordinated to objective Being.[12] In St. Thomas' view, truth is the name we give to Being when Being enters into relation with intellect. For Heidegger, Being in itself (*Vorhandensein*) is the name we give to the unconcealed (ἀλήθεια) when we try to prescind from mortal speaking and thinking. Truth, in Heidegger's view, is not a property of Being; Being is a property of truth (*Holz.*[2] 349/ 37). Thomas attempts to stand outside of the relationship between Being and intellect and to speak of the various relationships into which Being subsequently enters. And from that perspective, *ens* becomes *verum* when it enters into relation with intellect. Prior to entering this relationship, it is *ens simpliciter*.

It is instructive, in this connection, to follow up the three ways in which truth may be defined for St. Thomas in this text: "In one way, in terms of that which precedes the notion of truth and in which truth is founded. And this is how St. Augustine defines it in the *Soliloquies*, 'truth is that which is.' " Here we see the objectivism of St. Thomas. Being "is" not truth; being is the foundation of truth. Being is prior to truth. Augustine names not truth itself but the foundation in reality for truth. It is reality (*res, Realität*) (cf. SZ, § 44) which has the primacy. Truth comes by a certain addition to being. He continues: "And in another way it is defined in terms of that which formally perfects the notion of truth. And this is what Isaac says, that 'truth is the adequation of the thing and the intellect.' " Properly speaking, truth is the propositional adequation or rectitude of the intellect with reality. Hence truth, properly speaking, belongs to judgment. Now, it is well known that in Heidegger's view propositional truth is founded upon the prior manifestness of what is. It is important to understand, however, that for Heidegger propositional truth is founded, not on the *un*manifest, mute *ens reale* which is the *fundamentum in re* for Thomas Aquinas, but on manifest Being, Being as it rises up and shows itself so as to make it possible to have something to judge about. The Heideggerian sphere of pre-predicative manifestness is radically different from the Thomistic *ens* *reale* which precedes predicative truth (cf. WG (18–24/19–25).

The most interesting of the three definitions from a Heideggerian standpoint is the third: "And in the third way truth is defined according to the effect which follows upon it. And this is how Hilary defines it: 'truth is manifestative and declarative being.' And St. Augustine says in *On the True Religion*, 'Truth is that by which that which is is shown forth.' " Truth is Being which shows itself, which manifests itself. But the critical point is that Thomas takes this to be the effect which is consequent upon truth (*effectum consequentem*). Thus we see a movement in St. Thomas' theory from objective being in itself to propositional truth, and from propositional truth to manifestation. And just as propositional truth is founded on objective Being, so manifestness is founded on propositional truth, for the being is manifest only to the extent that it has been made known in the proposition. Now, if one were to hierarchize these three definitions from a Heideggerian perspective, one would have to reverse the order completely. For the primordial and founding sense of truth in Heidegger is ἀλήθεια (or perhaps in Latin *manifestatio, ostensio*): Being which declares and manifests itself. Upon this is founded propositional truth in which thought disengages itself from the event of unconcealment by standing back and looking on at the aspect (εἶδος) which Being shows and to which thought conforms itself. Finally, there is the abstract conception of a Being in itself which stands there, independent of mortals. Indeed, this attempt to speak of Being as it is prior to its relationship with intellect is an impossibility for Heidegger; it is an attempt to occupy the position of the *res* itself, to speak from the standpoint of the thing itself, from which standpoint there is no thought at all.

The notion of *verum* belongs irremediably to the objective standpoint and does not approach the primordial Greek experience of Being as presencing, as rising up into presence. In the transcendental conception of *verum*, Heraclitus' λόγος means the logic of propositions, the rational assertion, and it has lost the original sense of "gathering." Even when St. Thomas says that *esse* is light (*In lib. De causis*, VI, lect. 6, no. 168), he does not mean that Being is ἀλήθεια. For even there, *esse* retains its objective sense, and light is but one of the names for Being, a property of Being. Manifestness has become an effect of Being; that for Heidegger can only be a decline from the original Greek experience.

Heidegger says that after the early Greeks the notion of presencing "hardens" (*Holz.*[2] 368/54) and "stiffens" (*Holz.*[2] 355/42) so that the fluctuating essence of Being announced in Anaximander is lost in favor of a permanent and perduring reality. Being falls into an ἀδικία in which one being, in inconsiderateness of the rest, persists and perseveres at the expense of other beings, refusing to relinquish its hold on Being. After the early Greeks, Being becomes "permanent presence" (*ständige Anwesenheit*) (EM 148/162), persistent, perduring Being. From οὐσία we pass on to the *substantia* of the Middle Ages. And if there were an "echo" at least of original presencing in Aristotelian οὐσία (*Weg.*[2] 300/268), in the medieval period that echo is even more effectively silenced (EM 148/162). The question I must ask now is whether St. Thomas does indeed endorse the idea of permanent presence.

There would appear to be no arguing the matter. St. Thomas holds that only substances truly are and that accidents have being merely attributed to them (*Quod.* IX, 3, c). Substance endures whereas accidents come and go. However, I must proceed with some caution here. To begin with, Thomas does not deny Being of accidents. He is arguing that we do not say that "tall" is, but that the man is, and that the being of tall is found "in" the being of the man. For accidents, to be is to be "in." Moreover, it is a question not primarily of time and eternity, transience and permanence, but of the dependent and the independent. He does not discriminate substance from accidents as the perduring from the changing but as the independent from the dependent. Some accidents, indeed, are far more permanent in Being than some substances. The intellect, for example, as a faculty of the soul is as incorruptible as the soul itself and hence enjoys a considerably greater permanence than the substance of something corruptible—wood, say. Heidegger makes the same point in support of Aristotle (*Weg.*[2] 269/244–45), when Aristotle says that the four elements, being substances, are eternal.

And for Aquinas what is true of substance is also true of God. It is important to understand that Thomas defines God not in terms of eternity but in terms of self-subsistence. Created substances subsist (*ens per se*), but they have *esse* from another (*ab alio*), by being created by God. God, on the other hand, does not "have" *esse*. He is *esse*; He subsists in His *esse*. Hence, St. Thomas' celebrated formula:

God is *esse* itself subsisting through itself (*ipsum esse per se subsistens*). This is not to say that God is not eternal, and hence permanent presence itself; it means that eternity is something which follows upon God's description in terms of *esse*. Eternity is something we know of God by knowing that God is subsistent *esse*. It has been argued by Gilson that Augustine and other Christian philosophers in the Middle Ages gave a much greater primacy to God's eternity in formulating a philosophical notion of God than Aquinas did. Be that as it may, it is at least certain that Aquinas himself thought of God more in terms of the autonomy of His act of Being than in terms of His permanence.

Now, the point I want to make is that there is a more dynamic quality to what Thomas means by *esse* than Heidegger is prepared to admit. Gerard Phelan writes:

Things which "have being" are not "just there" (*Dasein*) like lumps of static essence, inert, immovable, unprogressive and unchanging. The act of existence (*esse*) is not a state, it is an act, the act of all acts, and therefore, must be understood as act and not as any static, and definable object of conception. *Esse* is dynamic impulse, energy, act—the first, the most persistent and enduring of all dynamisms, all energies, all acts.[13]

It is, of course, perfectly true, as I have already argued, that insofar as the "dynamic" quality of this "act" has a causal sense, it belongs to what Heidegger would consider a "fallen" conception of Being. But what I am maintaining here is that there is some trace of φύσις still preserved and still detectable in Thomistic *esse*. For *esse* is indeed an upsurge (*Aufgehung*), a rising into Being, an overcoming of nothingness, an active coming (*An-kommen*) or arrival (*Ankunft*) into Being, albeit one which takes place in the sphere of objective thought. But if it is possible to prescind from the objective–causal setting of this insight into Being, one can see here a much more genuine echo of original φύσις than Heidegger likes to admit. For St. Thomas, the being is not a brute fact, a simple stuff, but something which exercises Being, which rises up into Being. For Thomas, Being is not a given which requires no further consideration, but rather an achievement, an accomplishment which is continuously being carried out. *Esse* refers not to the *fact* that something is real, but to the upsurge in virtue of which there is something real at all. To be is to be *ex nihilo*; it is the power by which a thing is continually sustained and held out of non-Being, by which it rises up out of non-Being. Now, it must be insisted that all these formulations of Thomistic doctrine are bound by the pervasive qualification that in each case St. Thomas has in mind a rising up into objective presence, into *ens reale*. *Esse* decidedly does not mean φύσις insofar as φύσις means ἀλήθεια, insofar as φύσις means rising up into unconcealment. But *esse*, I would say, is an objectivistic correlate of φύσις, an upsurge and rising up into Being, thought within the domain of objective thought, of a mute being in itself, prior to all phenomenality. It is perfectly true that this is not Being as ἀλήθεια; but it cannot be one-sidedly labeled a philosophy of permanent presence without further ado. There is a vestige here of original φύσις.[14]

Heraclitus said that φύσις loves to hide, which means for Heidegger that every granting of presence is accomplished at the expense of a holding back. The "It" which grants presence remains behind its gift; the sender remains behind what is sent. The ἀλήθεια process for Heidegger is a process of ἀ-λήθη, where the hyphen serves to bring out that the emergence and rising up of presence take place out of an ineradicable core of concealment, of λήθη. Presence is an interlude in absence, a temporary overcoming of absence. Concealment is inscribed in the heart of un-concealment.

Hence, the last question I want to ask in carrying out this confrontation of *Anwesen* and *esse* is whether the metaphysics of *esse* is a philosophy of total presence which excludes all absence and concealment. And I think that this question must be answered in the affirmative. Let me begin with St. Thomas' notion of God as the fullness of Being, the complete perfection of *esse*. As the fullness of being (*plenitudo esse*), God is also the fullness of truth and intelligibility. God is subsistent intelligibility and subsistent intellectuality and hence subsistent truth. He is an unlimited act of knowing united perfectly to an unlimitedly perfect being. He is light through and through; there can be no talk of absence in God. As *ipsum esse per se subsistens*, God is pure and perfect presence, a perfect upsurge into Being (not in the sense that He is generated, but in the sense that *esse* is act) in which there is no prior, concomitant, or subsequent concealment. He is φύσις without κρύπτεσθαι, a total and instantaneous

overcoming of concealment which *abolishes* concealment. Concealment is simply expelled from the *esse* of God; it does not remain as
an ineradicable core from which God continually emerges, which He
continually overcomes. It appears that Jacob Böhme held such a view
of God, that God somehow overcomes a lower nature, a darker and
unintelligible side. But such an idea is foreign to the metaphysics of
esse.

I do not mean to suggest, of course, that the *esse* of God is totally
knowable by us or by anyone other than God. It is absolutely knowable in itself, *quoad se,* as regards itself, but not to us, *quoad nos.*
There is darkness in God, an unknown depth, unprobable mysteries,
inscrutable designs, etc. But all this is to be attributed to the weakness
of our intellect (*debilitas intellectus*). It is not that there is a negativity inscribed in God's very Being, but rather that our minds are
simply not able to probe the unknown depths of God. So true is this,
indeed, that Karl Rahner has recently shown how this obtains even in
the case of the beatific vision.[15] Heidegger, on the other hand, re-
peatedly insists that the oblivion of Being is no human error, but a
withdrawal on the part of Being. Φύσις loves to hide. That means,
φύσις is self-concealment, even as it is self-revelation. But the Being
of God for Aquinas is unlimitedly knowable and "declarative of
itself."

With the created being, the situation is, of course, somewhat altered. The created being, as we have seen, has only *esse participatum*;
it is granted only a partial share (*partem capere*) of *esse.* Hence, there
is a negativity, an unintelligibility, which is essential to every created
being. Its being is a continued arising out of nothingnesses, *ex nihilo.*
Nothingness, which is totally foreign to the Being of God, is the horizon of creatures. The creature comes to be out of nothing, and as
long as it is, it is suspended over and held out of non-being by the
power of God, and then it falls back into nothingness. Even in those
special cases (the human soul and the angelic nature) where *esse* is
sustained forever, the being remains continually exposed to non-
being, because it is always dependent upon the power of God who
could, were He so minded, simply withdraw *esse* from the essence of
such beings, even if their essence as incorruptible nature demands
esse. The Being of creatures is finite and permeated with negativity.
Indeed, one is inclined to think, from a Thomistic standpoint, that
Heidegger's "alethiology," as I have called it, has to do with created

beings, not with God. Viewed Scholastically, it is in a sense a philosophy of created or finite Being.

Yet even here I must make a distinction. To the extent that it is, the creature is wholly intelligible. It is simply not the whole of intelligibility. Its being is wholly transparent to the infinite intelligence of God, even if it is not infinite intelligibility itself. The limit of its intelligibility is at the same time the limit of its being. There is nothing in it which is unintelligible. But its finite intelligibility is a pointer in the direction of infinite and subsistent intelligibility. Created beings are not a scandal, not a mockery of the intelligibility of Being. They are simply limitedly intelligible and point beyond themselves to their unlimited source. Their own Being, which is circumscribed by non-being, is a limited share in the autonomous and subsistent Being who is entirely untouched by non-being.

Now, one can at best find only a trace of the ἀλήθεια process here. For inasmuch as every created being is a participation in the unlimited Being of God, a partial grasp of that of which God is the perfection, then to that extent the creature is a revelation and manifestion of the Being of God. But with the emergence of every creature, something essential remains concealed. Every creature is an expression of the divine Being which leaves something unexpressed. The manifold and variegated sphere of beings is but an imperfect and perspectival expression of the divine bounty. Each creature singly, and all creatures collectively, are concealments of the Being of God. Being gives itself in beings, Thomas could say, but Being itself remains behind in its hidden truth. In the coming-over (*Ankunft*) of Being into beings, Being itself remains behind, hidden, concealed. The creature is the sphere of un-concealment; the creator is its concealed depths.

But all this takes place within the horizon of total presence and perfect intelligibility. The concealed depth of the divine Being is not the abyss of λήθη but a plenum of intelligibility, the fullness of truth and light. The darkness of the divine depths, of the subsistent Being which remains concealed, is due to the infirmity of our intellect, which is like the eyes of the owl at noon. It fails to see, not because of the absence of light, but because of its excess.

On almost any accounting, then, the metaphysics of *esse* is separated from the early Greek experience of presencing in a fundamental way. *Esse* means *realitas* and *actualitas*, not ἀλήθεια. *Verum*, which is convertible with *esse*, is conceived within an objectivistic framework; in the philosophy of *verum*, manifestness is but the "effect" of truth. And even to the extent that *esse* has something of the quality of the "upsurge" (*Aufgehung*) of φύσις, this remains an objectivistic and not an alethiological notion. Finally, the metaphysics of *esse* is a philosophy of total presence from which all absence and concealment are expelled. The early Greek experience of *Anwesen*, of the simple emergence of things into the light, differs fundamentally from St. Thomas' metaphysics of actuality and science of first causes.

And so the "review" of Heidegger's critique of Scholasticism, first set forth in Chapter 2, is now complete. After presenting the revitalized version of Thomistic metaphysics which has been developed in the twentieth century, I determined in Chapter 5 that the metaphysics of *esse*, even so presented, does not think the *Ereignis* which gives Being as *esse* to medieval metaphysics, or the *Austrag* which opens up the distinction between *esse* and *ens* in medieval thought. And in the present chapter I inquired whether, despite its innocence of the *Ereignis*, the metaphysics of *esse* might not have been granted a privileged experience of Being as presencing. Now that I have examined as carefully as space permits what this early Greek experience was, and have held it up against the metaphysics of St. Thomas, it has become clear that on this account, too, the philosophy of *esse* remains a victim of what Heidegger (more or less adequately) calls the oblivion of Being.

There appears to be no way out. One takes a stand either with Thomas and against Heidegger or with Heidegger and against Thomas. But one cannot maintain that Thomas is somehow an exception to what Heidegger objects to in Western metaphysics, that he somehow eludes Heidegger's criticisms, that he falls outside the scope of what Heidegger criticizes. For that is manifestly not so. The case of St. Thomas is clearly included within the range of what Heidegger calls the metaphysical oblivion of Being, the failure to think Being itself and on its own terms. One cannot subscribe to Heidegger's *Seinsdenken* and hold too that it is practiced by St. Thomas. One cannot accept Heidegger's criteria and think that Thomas meets them. One must stand with either one or the other. The competing claims are forever at odds with each other.

But perhaps I have been too hasty. Perhaps there is a way to relate these thinkers other than those which I have considered in the past two chapters of this study. Perhaps there is a deeper harmony between them, a concealed way in which they stand together, which has eluded me up to now. Hence, I must turn now to a discussion of the literature on Thomas and Heidegger in the hope of finding some deeper connection and with the aim of testing the results which I have thus far achieved against the opinions I find there.

NOTES

1. Hence the ἔσχατον is *"das Ende der Philosophie,"* that terminal point—which may last indefinitely—in which metaphysics reaches its completion *(Vollendung)*; cf. SD 63/57.

2. For other commentary on the expression "eschatology of Being," see Pöggeler, *Der Denkweg Martin Heideggers*, p. 197; Werner Marx, *Heidegger and the Tradition*, trans. Theodore Kisiel and Murray Greene (Evanston, Ill.: Northwestern University Press, 1971), pp. 165–66; Thomas Langan, *The Meaning of Heidegger* (New York: Columbia University Press, 1961), pp. 146–51.

3. The dynamics of the "reversal" is at work in the eschatology of Being. The ἔσχατον is the danger of the *Gestell* which harbors within it the saving dawn; cf. *"Die Kehre"* in K 37ff./36ff.

4. This diagram represents something of a Heideggerian equivalent of the well-known Husserlian diagram of the flow of inner time consciousness.

5. Cf. Thomas J. Sheehan, "Notes on a 'Lovers' Quarrel': Heidegger and Aquinas," *Listening*, 9, Nos. 1–2 (Winter–Spring 1974), 140.

6. *Dialogue avec Heidegger*, 3 vols. (Paris: Editions de Minuit, 1973), I 139. See also Martin Heidegger, *Vier Seminare*, trans. Curd Ochwadt (Frankfurt: Klostermann, 1977), pp. 47–50, Seminar in Thor, September 5. Beaufret attended this seminar, and the minutes are suggestive of the argument in his book.

7. Beaufret, *Dialogue avec Heidegger*, I 14.

8. Ibid., 143–44.

9. Ibid., 126.

10. Ibid., 137.

11. Ibid., II 209.

12. See my "Problem of Being in Heidegger and the Scholastics," 86–89.

13. "The Existentialism of St. Thomas," *Proceedings of the American Catholic Philosophical Association*, 21 (1946), 35.

14. See my "Problem of Being in Heidegger and the Scholastics," 85.

15. "Thomas Aquinas on the Incomprehensibility of God," *The Journal of Religion*, 58 (Supplement 1978), S107–25.

7

Approaches to
Heidegger and Thomas:
A Survey of the Literature

I SHOULD LIKE TO FIND OUT if there is in Thomas a dimension of his metaphysics of *esse* which eludes Heidegger's critique of metaphysics, a dimension which shows that St. Thomas does not stand in the oblivion of Being, as Heidegger conceives it. Now, it has been my contention that if one appreciates the radicality of Heidegger's critique, and if one understands St. Thomas in his own historical actuality, then Heidegger's critique of metaphysics holds true even of St. Thomas. But the competing claims of Heidegger and of the followers of St. Thomas to a unique access to the meaning of Being have generated a large and sometimes impressive (though at times partisan[1]) series of studies which it behooves me now to examine. For I want to test the thesis which I have developed, that even St. Thomas belongs to the oblivion as Heidegger conceives it, against those interpreters of St. Thomas' work who find in his metaphysics of *esse* an authentic "thought of Being" in Heideggerian terms.

At the end of the perusal of the literature, it will be clear that the argument I have developed thus far remains unshaken, that the usual strategies for defending St. Thomas against the charge of *Seinsvergessenheit* ultimately fail. This result will lead me into the next and concluding chapter in this study. There I shall try to show that the only possible route for relating the enduring insights of St. Thomas to Heidegger's thought of Being which is at once faithful to the greatness of St. Thomas and which does not fail to come to grips with the full force of Heidegger's "overcoming" of metaphysics lies in a "deconstruction" of Thomistic metaphysics which addresses itself to what I have called the mystical element in St. Thomas' metaphysics.

I have chosen to examine four principal interpretations of Heidegger and Aquinas. I begin with perhaps the most basic position, and one of the most well known, that of Johannes Lotz, who argues that by reason of his conception of *esse subsistens* Thomas not only has attained the thought of Being itself but has in fact advanced to a more radical level than Heidegger himself has. That it seems to me is the first and most fundamental claim which I would expect any follower of St. Thomas to make who is confronted with Heidegger's critique of metaphysics. Bertrand Rioux, without disagreeing with Lotz, introduces into the discussion St. Thomas' conception of the transcendental *verum*, arguing that in Thomas there is an understanding of Being as truth and of truth in terms of Being, precisely as Heidegger insists. John Deely, the author of the only book-length study of this question in English prior to the present work, argues a related point: that it is not in *esse reale* but in the Thomistic *esse intentionale* that one finds the bridge between Thomas and Heidegger. The advantage of both Rioux's and Deely's approach is to have taken into account the radically phenomenological or, as I prefer, alethiological character of Heidegger's conception of Being. Finally I examine the positions which are developed by Max Müller and Gustav Siewerth, who are, in my view, the closest thinkers to Heidegger himself. I shall try to show how Müller makes the most provocative and suggestive recommendation for understanding the relationship between Heidegger and Aquinas, one which I nonetheless cannot accept without further ado. For although Müller appears to affirm the necessity of "deconstructing" St. Thomas, he gives us no reason to believe that this is anything more than a capricious invention of Heideggerian hermeneutics. Hence, the need for my concluding chapter.

Being and *Ipsum Esse Subsistens*

I turn first to the work of Johannes Lotz because he defends the radicality of St. Thomas as a philosopher of Being, and therefore as the foremost exception to Heidegger's pronouncements about metaphysics, in precisely the way in which one would expect: that is, in terms of St. Thomas' notion of God as subsistent Being itself (*ipsum esse subsistens*). Lotz is no casual commentator on these matters. During the '30s he and Karl Rahner attended the lectures of Heidegger—as did Siewerth and Müller—and this was the beginning of a lifelong confrontation which he was to carry out in his writings between the metaphysics of St. Thomas and Heidegger's thought of Being. In 1975 he published *Martin Heidegger and Thomas Aquinas: Man, Time, Being*, a volume which consummates a lifetime of reflection on this issue.[2]

Lotz views Heidegger and Aquinas as the philosophers of Being *par excellence* in the Western tradition, in comparison with whom the entire history of metaphysics stands in the oblivion of Being. Even so, the two thinkers are not on a par in Lotz's view, for Heidegger's thought on Being (*Seinsdenken*) attains only finite, historical Being. Heidegger does not make the breakthrough to the innermost core of Being, to infinite, eternal, and subsistent Being. To that extent, even Heidegger himself, the most probing thinker of our time, remains a victim of the oblivion of Being:

> To be sure, he [Heidegger] overcomes that oblivion of Being which lies prior to the turn [from the representation of beings to the thought of Being] and in which Being disappears in beings. Yet at the same time this turn, as he carries it out, contains that *higher-level oblivion of Being* which does not discover in temporal beings its supratemporal or eternal core. Heidegger's service is to have worked out temporal Being. But his limitation is that he remains there and takes the supra-temporal mystery which is announced there to be inaccessible. . . . Despite his turn to Being itself Heidegger does not truly arrive at Being itself because Being remains subordinated to a mode of beings—namely, to temporality—and he does not attain the mode which is innermost and proper to it: namely, eternity [pp. 124–25].

Heidegger thus is not to be given any final authority. It is St. Thomas who holds the upper and guiding hand in this confrontation of the two thinkers. Lotz is a Thomist (a Transcendental Thomist) who, like Rahner, Coreth, Müller, and Siewerth (p. 41), belongs to what might be called a "Heideggerian school." He takes Heidegger somewhat the way St. Thomas might have regarded any of his own sources, as a thinker to be used in articulating the true synthesis, while remaining mindful of the thinker's limitations. Heidegger is the great thinker of the present age precisely because he has reawakened the most important of all philosophical questions, the question of Being, and on this point he has served to remind us of depths in the philosophy of Being of St. Thomas himself which we might otherwise have missed. He has formulated the question of Being, and opened up the distinction between Being and beings, with a sharpness which is not to be found in Thomas himself. But when this distinction is made and this question is asked, it is to Thomas himself that we must turn to work out in a truly radical and comprehensive way the issues which Heidegger has raised.

The fundamental difference between Lotz and Heidegger is brought out in a telling way in the third essay of Lotz's volume, a discussion of the problem of "ground." This issue is a focal one in the confrontation of Heidegger and Aquinas, for it is in terms of "grounds" that one can formulate the *Seinsvergessenheit* which each thinker would object to in the other. From St. Thomas' point of view Heidegger has meditated the Being of creatures, that is, of finite and limited beings, and has attained an insight into their common Being (*esse commune*). But he fails to penetrate beyond common Being to its ground in absolute, subsistent Being. From the point of view of Heidegger, on the other hand, St. Thomas is a classic example of onto-theo-logic, of a metaphysics wholly given over to a causal account of the origin of finite beings in the highest and most perfect being, thereby leaving Being itself, the ground which itself is without ground (*Ab-grund*), entirely unthought. Each thinker takes the other to have fallen into ground-lessness, which is, if I may say so, Being-lessness (*Grund- oder Sein-losigkeit*).

In Lotz's view the critical flaw in Heidegger's account of Being as ground is his notion of Being as a groundless ground, as a veritable abyss (*Ab-grund*) (pp. 79–82). Being is indeed an abyss, Lotz holds, only if one means thereby that Being is a ground which rejects any ground other than itself, that is, if Being is self-grounding (*ens a se*), a *principium sine principio*, as Meister Eckhart says.[3] For Being in contradistinction to beings is the absolute fullness of all possible ways to be, and so there can be nothing other than itself upon which it is founded. If there were, Being would not be Being. But this is clearly not Heidegger's view. For Heidegger takes Being as a ground which is altogether lacking in any ground, internal or external to itself. That is why he calls Being a play (*Spiel*). But to call Being a play is, for Lotz, to make of it a naked fact which, in the case of Being itself, the ground of all beings, is no more than an *Un-sinn*, a self-refuting piece of literal non-sense. For in that case, Being is reduced to nothing in the negative sense. If Being as opposed to beings has any meaning at all, then Being is the absolute fullness of possible ways to be; it cannot be ground-less in Heidegger's sense but only in the Scholastic sense of what is self-grounding.

All this is another way of saying that Being is not simply the Being of beings, that Being is not always and only confined to the sphere of concrete things. For then multiplicity and limitation would be built into the very structure or meaning of Being, and the fullness of Being would be denied. Indeed, Being itself would be denied and thus disappear (pp. 84–85). One must break through the Being of beings, Heidegger's immanent transcendence (*esse commune*), to the absolutely transcendent, to the Being which is loosened from (*ab-solvere*) all attachment to beings and subsists in itself and through itself. Heidegger's mixed transcendence must give way to pure transcendence. The alternative is a causally unintelligible Being.

But does not Heidegger precisely want to avoid such a causal account to begin with, Lotz asks (pp. 85–86)? Indeed. But that is so only because Heidegger takes causality to be an intrinsically ontic relationship which leads from one being (effect) to another (cause) and never attains Being itself. Yet what if one conceives of a veritable ontological cause, that is, of a cause which is not a being but is causal precisely in virtue of its status as Being itself? Ontic causes produce only modifications in the Being of their effects; but an ontological cause is responsible for the whole Being of its effect. Ontological causality signifies the giving of Being (*esse participatum*) to beings by Being itself (*esse subsistens*). Such an account, being causal, would indeed be metaphysics, although not a metaphysics such as Heidegger conceives, but a truly ontological metaphysics, a metaphysics which reaches subsistent Being itself. Indeed, in comparison to this metaphysics, Heidegger's own thought of Being, remaining on the level of mixed or immanent transcendence, the Being of finite beings, is itself still a captive to the oblivion of Being (pp. 87–88).

Lotz's argument in this essay is very important, and it represents, in my mind, the precise kind of response which a thinker in the Thomistic tradition would want to make to Heidegger. Yet I do not find it persuasive from a Heideggerian standpoint. It is true that Heidegger objects to causal accounts because they merely lead us about from one being to another. And as long as one formulates Heidegger's position in this way Lotz's response has some merit. But we saw in Chapter 5 that thinking in terms of "Being" and "beings" is no longer the ultimate framework in Heidegger's later writings. His interest ultimately lies in the event of opening up that difference, the light process which discloses these terms to the thinker of a given age. His interests, in other words, are ultimately alethiological, and all causality, be it ontic or ontological, is objectivistic. All "causal" accounts differ radically from an "alethiological experience" of Being. A causal metaphysics is a function of Being as ἀλήθεια, a particular withdrawal of the primordial experience of the "presencing" of Being in beings in favor of a Romanized account of beings in terms of efficiency and productivity, as we saw in the preceding chapter.

In the last and most important essay in his volume, Lotz introduces the thematic of "man–time–Being" which is mentioned in the subtitle of his book. On the one hand, Lotz holds, man makes his way to Being through time. For Heidegger this means that man gains access to the meaning of Being through the horizon of time, and for St. Thomas it means that man rises to subsistent Being through the mediation of Being in time. But, on the other hand, man's ascent to Being through time is made possible only because Being itself gives itself to man in the form of time. For Heidegger this means that Being as *Ereignis* bestows itself upon man in the successive epochs of the history of Being; for Aquinas, that subsistent Being reveals itself in time in the form of created or participated Being. It is through this overarching structure—from man through time to Being, and from Being through the time of man—that Lotz works out his main confrontation of Heidegger and St. Thomas.

The first movement, which belongs to the *Being and Time* period in Heidegger's writings, consists in showing the temporal dimension of man's ascent to subsistent Being in St. Thomas. Lotz begins by arguing that the senses, both internal and external, operate within the horizon of time. While the outer sense and the common sense deal with what is sensibly present, the imagination and memory deal with past objects, and the cognitive power (*vis aestimativa*) with the future. Now, human reason, as the lowest among intellectual substances, is touched by time. Its own operations (conceiving, judging, reasoning) are in time, and its objects are drawn from the flowing world which the time-bound senses present to it. Man is spirit in the world, even as for Heidegger Dasein is Being-in-the-world, an intelligence whose roots are planted in the world of time, but whose uppermost reaches extend to eternity (pp. 147–48). For human *ratio* is a participation in pure *intellectus*, an order of knowing which transcends the abstractness and the successiveness of ratiocination. Reason is proportioned to the Being of the flowing world of temporal beings, to the Being of beings. But *intellectus* is ordered to Being itself, to the eternal, unchanging, and pure act of Being which subsists through itself (*ipsum esse subsistens*). From Lotz's point of view, by confining man to temporal Being, Heidegger contracts both *intellectus* to *ratio* and *ratio* to the order of sensibility and hence makes the ascent—from time to Being—impossible (p. 153). Thus one cannot compare *ratio* to Heidegger's representational thinking (*vorstellendes Denken*) and *intellectus* to essential thinking (*wesentliches Denken*) because both modes of *Denken* for Heidegger are time-bound, and *intellectus* is an intuition of eternal Being itself. Heidegger cannot make the ascent to Being, and so remains locked in his own form of *Seinsvergessenheit* (pp. 162–66).

The first moment in Lotz's architectonic corresponds to the early Heidegger. It represents an attempt on Lotz's part to integrate a transcendental structure—in particular, a transcendental–temporal structure—into the way in which the human spirit rises to a knowledge of Being in St. Thomas. The second half of the essay, however, is slightly more pertinent to the present study, for I have maintained all along that the essential issue in the confrontation of Heidegger and Aquinas is centered in the later Heidegger. Moreover, even a fellow-Thomist who is sympathetic to Heidegger, like Gustav Siewerth, argues that all versions of "Transcendental" Thomism, issuing from Maréchal as they do, fall victim to Heidegger's critique of "subjectism" and of transcendental–horizonal thinking.[4] In the movement from Being to man, in the way in which Being gives itself to man through time, Lotz establishes a correlation of *Ereignis* and *creatio*. We have already seen that for Lotz the event of Being, the emergence of beings into Being, is a causal–ontological bringing forth of beings into Being (*esse participatum*) by Being itself (*esse subsistens*). Hence, the *Ereignis* is transmuted by Lotz into the metaphysical act of creation, which is for him its genuine and true sense. In either case, though the first moment was one of ascent (from man to Being), the second is one of descent (Being's self-giving to man).

Now, Heidegger says in the most unequivocal terms in "Time and Being" that the *Ereignis* is not to be conceived in terms of causality and making (*Machen*): "There is no making here. There is only giving in the sense of the extending which opens up time–space" (SD 17/16). But Lotz thinks it possible to avoid Heidegger's objection to interpreting the *Ereignis* in terms of making by introducing the distinction between *mutatio* and *creatio*. *Mutatio* is making in the proper sense, for it is the production of a change in a pre-existing thing; *creatio* is a production of the whole being of its effect without the presumption of anything pre-existent. Creation is not making, for there is nothing to create "out of." Whatever is made is made out of something. Hence creating is not making. Creation belongs to an entirely different sphere. It is the very bringing into presence of the whole Being (*totius esse*) of its effect. Hence, it is an event (*Ereignis*), not a making (*Machen*). Lotz thus reverts to the distinction which he has already drawn between ontic and ontological causality. But, as we have seen, Heidegger is critical of all causal thinking, be it ontic or ontological.

Lotz adds that once *Ereignis* is taken to mean creation it is clear that it is not only an event of power—in the sense that φύσις is the power of emergence—but also an event of truth and love, for it is an event springing from the knowledge and will of God. *Scientia dei causa rerum*: God's knowledge is the cause of things. Far from being a purely speculative knowledge, God's knowledge is actually productive of creatures, and so is to be likened to the knowledge of an artist. Created things, on the other hand, spring from God's creative knowledge as from an exemplar and ideal which they strive to imitate. They imitate the purity of the light with which they shine in the divine mind. (This is as close as Lotz comes to addressing the ἀλήθεια issue in Heidegger's thought.) At the same time it is an event of love, for creation springs from the bountiful goodness of God, His loving will to share Being. To this there is no counterpart in Heidegger's thought, for he steadfastly resists thinking the *Ereignis* in personalist terms. The *Ereignis* is an "it" (*das "Es"*), not a he (*ein "Er"*).

Lotz also finds a dialectic of revelation and concealment in this event of creation. For the revelation of the divine *esse* which is effected by creation is at the same time a concealment of it. I have already articulated such a structure in Chapter 5 in my discussion of "arrival" and "coming over." The concealment of Being (*Seinsverborgenheit*) in Heidegger is for Lotz the concealment of the divine being by the world. This explains the possibility of atheism and of "worldliness" in general, that is, the whole attitude by which men turn away from their creator and toward the world which He has created. It is as in Heidegger, when he says that man is inclined to accept that which is given and neglect the It which gives. But by the same token the world which conceals God is also the world which, by participating in the divine Being, likewise reveals it. Thus this dialectic not only explains worldliness; it also explains a Saint Francis who finds God in all things, in all nature, in the living creatures which God has made and even in sister death.

It is here that Lotz parts company with Heidegger. For Heidegger, he thinks, is content with the Being given in the event of creation (*Ereignis/creatio*) without pressing on further to the more primordial level of the source of the *Ereignis* (pp. 194–95). For Aquinas, subsistent Being itself is the origin of the *Ereignis*, and hence, Lotz says, *das Ereignende*, that which events, that which gives the Event (p. 196). Heidegger, on the other hand, remains on the level of the Being which is given by the Event without pressing further. As such, Being for Heidegger is always subordinate to the *Ereignis*. But Aquinas has penetrated to the origin of the *Ereignis*, to the subsistent Being which is prior to the *Ereignis* and to which the *Ereignis* itself is subordinate.

The same kind of treatment is afforded the question of creation and time. Heidegger's Being is essentially temporal because it is the Being which is given in the event of creation. Heidegger thinks the Being which is given to man and as it is given to man without thinking Being itself. For Being itself, subsistent Being, is not temporal but eternal (pp. 222–23), even as *human ratio* is but a temporalized version of *intellectus*. The finitized, epochal nature of Being is a condition, not of Being itself, but of created Being. These finite dispensations of Being are themselves proportioned to the finitude of human reason which, being subject to time itself, can accept only partial revelations of Being. Temporalized Being is proportioned to a temporalized understanding. But it is in principle possible to terminate the partial and historical revelation of Being and to overcome the limitations of a time-bound understanding. It is possible to eradicate all *Seinsverborgenheit*, all concealment, all darkness, in a moment of total revelation in which subsistent being and *intellectus* are joined face to face, in which history draws to a close and human time is transcended. That indeed is the ideal toward which all metaphysical knowledge points. It is the essential failure of Heidegger, Lotz thinks, not to have penetrated thus far but to have remained on the level of participated Being while leaving the sphere of subsistent Being unexplored. Heidegger thinks on the level of the "Being which sends itself to man," not on the level of Being itself, which is subsistent Being (p. 259).

Although one must admire the attempt which Lotz has made on behalf of the standpoint of St. Thomas to come to grips with Heidegger's thought, it seems to me to fall short of its goal. For Lotz has underestimated the radicality of Heidegger's critique of causality and made too facile a shift into the causal mode of thought. Lotz asks about the causal ground of the *Ereignis*, whereas Heidegger has made it abundantly clear that causality itself is one of the *essential* transformations in the history of Being which have been bestowed upon us by the *Ereignis*. Causal thinking, the chief tool with which Lotz would make his way beyond Heidegger's *Ereignis*, is itself a function of the *Ereignis*. In the earliest dispensation of Being, prior to the age of the philosophers, Being is not thought at all in terms of cause and effect. According to "The Question Concerning Technology" (VA 18–19/292–93), it is even a mistake to understand Aristotle's αἰτία in terms of *causa*. "Causal thinking" occurs only in the Roman—medieval period; it is introduced in the Latin language, the language of the Empire and the Curia. It is a dispensation of the history of Being, a move on the part of Being as ἀλήθεια, a shift in the way in which language speaks to us. So Lotz's distinction between ontic and ontological causality is to no avail. For although it meets the objection that causal relations are between one being and another, it nonetheless continues to treat Being itself in terms of production, bringing about, and "making," even if it is indeed a making out of nothing (*aliquid ex nihilo facere*) (ST, I, 45, 2). All causal thought is objectivistic and misses the simplicity of a sheer emergence into presence. This is a point which deserves to be stressed, for there can be no meeting between Heidegger and Aquinas so long as causal thinking holds sway.

Lotz contends that Heidegger's thought has to do with a merely phenomenal, experienced, man-related Being, whereas St. Thomas has moved beyond phenomena to Being in itself. But for Heidegger the whole realistic, objectivistic, causal, and metaphysical orientation of St. Thomas, and of Lotz's more contemporary version of St. Thomas, belongs to a dispensation of Being, a way Being was dis-

closed in the medieval epoch. From Heidegger's standpoint one cannot argue that Being as ἀλήθεια is merely man-related, while *esse subsistens* is Being itself. On the contrary, *esse subsistens* is an historically
bestowed way of thinking the Being of God, and causality and metaphysical creation are but historically bestowed ways of thinking the
relationship of the world to God. *Creatio* does not therefore lead us
back to a creator who lies deeper than the *Ereignis*. It leads back to
the *Ereignis* which has bestowed upon us the metaphysical terms of
cause and effect, creator and created, eternal and temporal.

And the same kind of argument can be made in response to Lotz's
claim that eternity is the inner core of time and that Heidegger, con-
tenting himself with temporal being, falls short of real Being, which
is eternal. For Heidegger eternity is a mode of time, a structure which
can be thought only within the horizon of time, as the *nunc stans*,
the negation of the flowing now which we all experience. Eternity is
thought when the flowing process of presencing, the emerging into
the presence which begins and ends in absence, is congealed into a
static endurance, a perduring presence in which presence clings to
presence and all absence is expurgated. Eternity is a mode of time,
and the metaphysics of eternity is a dispensation of the *Ereignis*.
Eternity for Heidegger is not the inner core of time; it is a modification and a derivate of time. The philosophy of *ipsum esse subsistens*
does not go deeper than the thought which turns into the *Ereignis*
(*die Einkehr in das Ereignis*) (SD 44/41), for the metaphysics of
changeless Being is a dispensation of Being which the *Ereignis* itself
grants, an "epochal" (ἐποχή = withdrawal) falling out of the original
experience of Being as φύσις, as the lingering presence which joins
absence to absence. One can hardly speak of breaking through time
to eternity if one takes into account the radicality of Heidegger's
critique of all philosophies of eternity.

I do not think that Lotz responds to the full depth and radicality
of Heidegger's critique of metaphysics and I do not think his confrontation with St. Thomas is therefore successful. It is instead an
original and interesting attempt to articulate the metaphysics of St.
Thomas in noticeably Heideggerian accents. But I do not think that
it is a convincing response to Heidegger. It does not persuade me that
St. Thomas does not belong to the history of the oblivion of Being—
which is really the oblivion of the dif-ference—in the sense that Heidegger means this. It does not show us that there is indeed a radically

alethiological dimension to St. Thomas. St. Thomas remains a causal thinker, the author of an objectivistic metaphysics, and the only *rapprochement* which has been made is that all this is cast in the language of *Ereignis*.

BEING AND THE TRANSCENDENTAL *Verum*

If the objection which I have made to Lotz's interpretation of Heidegger's relationship to Aquinas is that he has failed to bridge the gap between the objectivistic and the alethiological modalities of these thinkers, then it would seem that the place to turn for a deeper-level *rapprochement* would be the Thomistic idea of truth and of Being as truth. The Heideggerian correlate in St. Thomas would then be found not only in what he says about Being but particularly in what he says about the Being of truth and the truth of Being. It is not only to *esse* but also to *verum* that one must turn to find the depth dimension in St. Thomas which excepts him from the Heideggerian critique. That is precisely the route which Rioux follows in his *Being and Truth in Heidegger and Thomas Aquinas*.[5] For one must avoid a head-on confrontation of Heidegger's *Sein* with the Thomistic *esse* because of the radically phenomenological and post-phenomenological character of Being in Heidegger. One must not be misled by the grammatical and lexical isomorphism of these two words into thinking that both words are thought in the same terms. Now, I myself pursued this strategy in the preceding chapter and found it wanting. Let us see now what Rioux makes of it.

Rioux's argument about the *verum* in St. Thomas is preceded by an argument about *esse* itself. Hence Rioux makes two central and closely related claims about St. Thomas. First, he argues, in the spirit of Lotz and of Cornelio Fabro, that, contrary to Heidegger's claims, there is a penetrating insight in St. Thomas into Being *as Being* which can in no way be associated with any so-called "oblivion of Being." Secondly, and this follows from the first point, St. Thomas does not have a merely ontic, correspondence theory of truth; he has thought truth—the transcendental *verum*—strictly in terms of Being, and he has the strongest appreciation of the belonging together of Being and thought of which Heidegger speaks. Nor is Rioux content to measure the value of St. Thomas' thought against the rod of Heidegger's work.

For in Rioux's view Heidegger's "alethiology" remains captive to idealism, inasmuch as Being is tied to Dasein, so that "Being" is neither the concrete absolute of the Thomistic *esse subsistens* nor any particular being, but nothing more than the abstraction which the Scholastics call *esse commune*. Rioux develops these ideas on the basis of a thorough and probing analysis of the texts of Heidegger which cuts off the easy escape which Heideggerians frequently invoke: that all criticisms of Heidegger are based on a misunderstanding. Let me therefore examine first what Rioux has to say about *esse* and then about the *verum*.

Borrowing I think rather heavily from an article by Cornelio Fabro which I shall discuss below, Rioux emphasizes that in the Thomistic notion of Being as the *actus essendi* there is to be found a vivid intuition of Being in its active upsurge which meets all of Heidegger's objections against the metaphysical oblivion of Being. For Thomas, Being does not mean οὐσία, as in Aristotle, but the very act of Being. Thomas found in *esse* a *principium quo* (a principle by means of which) which was unknown to Aristotle, for whom form was the highest principle of substance. As St. Thomas writes: "Form is able to be called a *quo est*, according as it is a principle of being [a substance]. But the whole substance is itself a *quod est* [something which is]. And *esse* itself is that by which [*quo*] substance is called a being" (SCG, II, 54). In his discovery of *esse* as an act of being (*actus essendi*), as that principle by which the essence is brought forth into being, Thomas has broken with the oblivion of Being which precedes and follows him. Rioux says: "In this fundamental relationship of essence to the act of being which perfects it intrinsically, there resides the ontological difference underlined with so much depth by Heidegger. Being is that which is [*ens*] on the foundation of the act of being (*esse*) . . ." (p. 218). Elsewhere Rioux refers to *esse* as "that energy which animates every being and makes it appear in a concealed Presence" (p. 251). *Esse* as act means Being as upsurge, the active emergence into Being which is what Heidegger means by φύσις. As such *esse* means the emergence into presence and manifestness signified by ἀλήθεια.

Now, there is some truth to the claim, as we saw in the preceding chapter, that there is a trace of Being as φύσις, as active upsurge, in Thomistic *esse*. And to this extent one can agree with Rioux. But Rioux seems wholly to ignore Heidegger's critique of *actualitas* and of the causal character of any conception of Being within the horizon of making and acting (*agere*). The translation of ἐνέργεια into *actualitas* is precisely a fateful concealment of the meaning of original φύσις for Heidegger. Rioux nowhere addresses this point, which is explained no doubt by the absence of the *Nietzsche* volumes from his bibliography, although they had been published two years before his book appeared.

Rioux's argument is inspired by Fabro's essay entitled "The Currency and Originality of the Thomistic *Esse*."[6] Fabro wrongly takes it that the oblivion of Being spoken of by Heidegger is essentialism and that the antidote to essentialism is the Thomistic notion of *esse* as the *actus essendi*. This claim is at the heart of all the diverse responses on the part of the Thomists to Heidegger's charge of *Seinsvergessenheit*, yet from Heidegger's point of view it misses the mark in a very basic way. Fabro writes:

> Our research begins with the firm conviction (which we intend to establish) that it is only in the perspective of creation that the radical foundation of *a theory of Being as the act of the being is possible*, an expression which (if it is properly understood) enables us to see the originality of Thomistic metaphysics with respect to the Aristotelian metaphysics of "the being as a being," which is the target of Heidegger's critique.[7]

Heidegger would indeed agree that Thomas' thought is a metaphysics of act and actuality and that it is entirely circumscribed by the doctrine of creation. But far from taking this to prove that Thomas is thereby extricated from *Seinsvergessenheit*, he would take it as a decisive testimony that he is not. Fabro's mistake is to think that for Heidegger Being means act—and I think that this mistake is rather commonly made by the Thomists:

> The Being of Heidegger, like that of St. Thomas, is neither phenomenon nor noumenon, neither substance nor accident; it is simply act. But while Heideggerian Being is given in the flux of time by the consciousness of man, Thomistic Being expresses the act which is possessed essentially (God) or which rests (*quiescit*) in the heart of all being, as the primordial participated energy which sustains it outside of nothing (in the creature).[8]

And since Heidegger has attained only a finite act, not the infinitely creative act, he himself remains in the very oblivion of Being of which he speaks.[9] But Being for Heidegger is precisely *not* act, neither *actus purus* (EM 14/14) nor *actus creatus*, but the quiet splendor and simple radiance of what shows itself, which is wholly removed from all the categories of causality and actuality. The entire response which Fabro makes to Heidegger's critique of the metaphysics of *esse* as the *actus essendi* is vitiated, in my judgment, by his failure to come to grips with this central point and to have presented a Thomistic response to it. As Beaufret points out so lucidly, the very discourse of St. Thomas about Being in terms of *actus* and *actualitas*, far from extricating him from the oblivion of Being, thrusts him into it all the more deeply.

On the basis of his authentic understanding of Being, Rioux argues, St. Thomas develops an equally authentic conception of truth. He defends the Thomistic theory of judgment as having an ontological and not merely an ontic validity, as attaining the level of Being (the "is"). And he holds that this judgmental truth is rooted in the strictly ontological conception of truth found in the transcendental *verum*. The truth of judgment is founded on the truth of Being.

The judgment in St. Thomas is indeed the formal locus of truth properly so called. Truth is to be found formally only in the mind, not in things. But this does not open St. Thomas to all of Heidegger's criticisms of this theory. For the mind or intellect which judges is a faculty of Being (p. 181). It must not be understood as a faculty which erects pictorial representations within itself of the outer world, as in the Cartesian paradigm which Heidegger has in mind, but as a faculty which reaches the "is," the *est* in the *quod est*. The intellect for St. Thomas, in virtue of its intentional structure, is thrust into the world and so it never suffers from the usual objections made against all Cartesian and post-Cartesian "correspondence" theories. Unlike the theory of judgment entertained by the young Heidegger, which I examined in Chapter 1, St. Thomas' theory is "existential," intentionally directed at Being itself, the Being of what is. Judgment is not confined to the level of "meaning" and "validity" but attains to Being itself. Hence, though St. Thomas may have an *adequatio* theory of truth, he does not have a correspondence theory in the modern sense.

Heidegger thinks that the judgment, insofar as it is derived from the pre-predicative level, is essentially "fallen," while St. Thomas, who also takes the judgment to arise from the pre-predicative, perceptual level (*omnis scientia oritur in sensu*), considers the judgment to be "perfective" of the perceptual, raising it for the first time to a genuinely ontological level (pp. 188–89). By means of the existential "is," the mind first explicitly affirms and encounters Being. It is in this judgmental "is" that the pre-ontological becomes ontological, that the Being which is implicitly known becomes explicitly affirmed. Rioux therefore goes on to say that Heidegger's opposition to discursive and judgmental reason results in a Manichaean dualism in which "thought" and reason are essentially at odds. This can be corrected by a more sober and ontological theory of judgment which does not relegate it to the ontic and put it hopelessly at odds with the ontological (pp. 130, 220–21).[10]

However, the truly ontological character of St. Thomas' conception of truth is found not in his theory of judgment, which is for St. Thomas a defective operation peculiar to the lowest (human) level of intellects, but in his theory of the transcendental *verum*. For Rioux the *verum* signifies "the rapport of the intellect and being" (p. 133). Heidegger's enlivening insight is into the essential belonging together of Being and mind in the notion of truth, the necessity of mind for Being to be revealed. Without mind there can be no *esse manifestivum*, which is one of the definitions of the truth which Thomas invokes (*De ver.* I, 1). Now, Heidegger himself acknowledges that in the Thomist conception of the mind as that whose nature it is to come together with all beings, to become all things in knowledge (*convenire cum omni ente*), there are contained the essentials of his own idea of Dasein (SZ § 4, 14/34). St. Thomas has already worked out a definition of man in terms of his relationship to and understanding of Being. The highest and defining characteristic of man is his participation in intellectuality, and the intellect is a faculty of *esse* (pp. 152–54; ST, I, 5, 2, c).

But Heidegger's essential failure is to have confined the relationship between Being and mind to a relationship between Being and Dasein, and not to have seen that what he is talking about, the essential need of Being to be manifested, the essential identity between Being and thought, is to be found only in the relationship between the divine Being and the divine mind (pp. 240–42). There alone, in the identity of *intelligere* and *esse* in God, does one find the essential belonging together of Being and thought. There alone is Being necessarily manifested. The openness of Being is not its relative and contingent openness in Dasein, but its absolute openness in God. Heidegger thus, in Rioux's view, remains under the vestigial influences of idealism (pp. 250ff.), and because of this his thought is caught up in a serious contradiction. For although Heidegger affirms the transcendence of Being, he must at the same time affirm its dependence on Dasein. Being "needs" Dasein for its epiphany, yet Being is called the "simply transcendent." Indeed, Rioux adds, there is some question as to just what Heidegger's "Being" can possibly signify. It is not the separate absolute of St. Thomas' *esse subsistens*, yet it is more than just the *esse* of this or that individual. What else can it possibly signify but an abstraction which the Scholastics call *esse commune*, that which all beings have in common without regard to their mode of concretion, without regard even to whether they are infinite or finite? And what a high irony it would be if the upshot of Heidegger's attempt to rethink the question of Being in a more radical and concretely phenomenological way would have been to have succumbed to an abstraction, to the illusory reality of a creature of our own making!

I am impressed by the knowledgeability of Rioux's renderings of Heidegger and Aquinas and by the incisiveness of his criticism of Heidegger from a Thomistic standpoint. But I remain unconvinced by his argument. I think that the main merit of this work is to have exposed the nerve of the disagreement between Heidegger and Aquinas. It is true that in the judgment the ontological level becomes explicit, but for Heidegger this is at the cost of the original integrity of the encounter with Being. For it has become explicit in the form of an objectivistic discourse *about* Being. Heidegger's objection against the judgment is that in it the original experience of Being, the face-to-face encounter with Being in all its pristine originality, is transformed into a statement which is uttered from the standpoint of one who has disengaged himself from the experience, and who then seeks to "represent" it. This "representation" need be taken not in the strong Cartesian sense, but in the minimal sense of speaking *about* (*über*) the experience instead of *from out of* (*aus*) it—whence the title of Heidegger's little poetic piece "out of the experience of thinking," "*Aus der Erfahrung des Denkens.*" That title expresses in a single phrase Heidegger's "method," that is, his way of making his way. Heidegger

objects to the proposition, not because it makes the "is," the ontological, explicit, but because it makes it explicit in the manner of objective discourse. He prefers the thinker's or the poet's way of "naming"
Being, that is, of making it explicit. The "is" must be named, not in
the manner of "existential judgments," but by poets and thinkers who
have been touched by it.

And that is why the rest of Rioux's argument against Heidegger is
in vain. Heidegger would meet the claim that his thought suffers from
an inevitable anthropomorphism, that what he calls the belonging together of thought and Being is to be found not in Dasein but in God,
by questioning the standpoint from which such a claim is made. Such
theories for Heidegger are theories only, speculations, theoretical
contrivances, which from the "phenomenological" standpoint are
free-floating (*freischwebend*), without phenomenal base, lacking in
a birth certificate in the things themselves. Heidegger would disallow
the distinction which Rioux wants to draw between *esse reale* and *esse
manifestivum* as an invention of the disengaged and ultimately worldless subject. Lotz, Rioux, and Fabro complain that Heidegger fails
to make the move from the experienced world of phenomenal Being
to the realm of "real" Being which is the cause of the world of Being
in time. Yet to make such a move, to "ascend" to an explanatory and
causal ground of Being, is essentially at odds with Heidegger's path
of thought and can have nothing to do with it. Being, the Event, can
mean only what we hear and see it to mean, and we can speak of it
only insofar as we have been touched by it.

From Heidegger's standpoint it is Rioux's objectivism which represents the true abstraction, not Heidegger's Being. For this objectivism
is possible only if one disengages oneself from the actual situatedness
of human Dasein and attempts to speak of Being as it is, apart from
Dasein. Objectivism is a possibility only for a thus abstracted Dasein.
The Being of which Heidegger speaks is the Being which gives itself
up into presence. He has forsworn to speak of any other possible kind
of "Being."

And so I am, as I said, unconvinced by Rioux's fine book, although
I am grateful to the author for having so ably exposed the nerve of the
disagreement. The abyss which separates Heidegger from Aquinas is,
in the parlance of philosophy, a "methodological" one. It is the difference between alethiological experience and an objectivistic explanation, between encounter and disengagement, between being

touched by the grace of Being and explicating it in causal categories. One must show that one of these two "methods" must give way, must break down. For if they are taken in their separate integrity, there is no bridge between objectivism and alethiology.

BEING AND *Esse Intentionale*

Rioux's work raises an important issue which must be discussed further. Rioux claims at the end of his book that Heidegger "does not make the distinction between a manifestation of Being according to the *esse* which is proper to beings and according to their intentional *esse* . . ." (p. 258). John Deely has taken up this point and made it the theme of his interpretation of Heidegger and Aquinas.[11] This is an interesting strategy, for it recognizes the mistake of thinking that the realist *esse* of St. Thomas and the phenomenological *Sein* of Heidegger are spoken in the same mode, and it looks instead for the properly Heideggerian correlate in St. Thomas in his conception of Being as known, not Being "in itself." What Heidegger has discovered or, more properly, recovered, on this interpretation, is not Being itself, as Heidegger would have us believe, but the traditional idea of *esse intentionale*, Being as it enters into the intentional life of man (= Dasein). Though the Scholastics first articulated the notion of intentional being, it was not until Heidegger that this "wholly unique sphere" (as Maritain, whom Deely greatly favors, put it) was fully thematized and elaborated. The structures of culture and history, long absent from Scholastic analyses, can be properly treated only within the framework of intentional life. Deely therefore offers us a translation of certain basic terms in Heidegger's vocabulary into the language of St. Thomas in order to make Heidegger's insights accessible to the Thomists and then to show how Heidegger has deepened and elaborated these ideas.

This is not to say that Heidegger's work leaves nothing to be desired in Deely's mind. Rather he wants to argue that Heidegger's success is limited because his method, phenomenology, is in principle so unable to accommodate "the aboriginal questioning of Being" (p. 176), that Heidegger himself must in the end be the victim of, and not the liberator from, *Seinsvergessenheit*. Heidegger's Being is Being as meant, Being as intended (= *esse intentionale, esse quod est intra animam*), and so Heidegger is unable to address himself to Being in itself, Being as it actually exists outside the mind (*esse reale, esse naturale, esse quod est extra animam*). There is even a theory of the reversal in this interpretation. For Deely, like his teacher Ralph Powell,[12] contends that although *Being and Time* at least wrestled with the tension between real and intentional Being, the problem is wholly obliterated in the later works. There Being simply evaporates into intentional being. Being volatilizes into appearance, into meanings, which have no greater claim on reality than myths and fictions (p. 158). A genuine and fully grounded thought of Being must be able to account for the complementarity between Being in itself and Being as known; but this is a charge which phenomenology is in principle unable to carry out.

Thus Deely, like Rioux, Lotz, and Fabro, comes back to the same point: that Heidegger's thought of Being is limited to a finite sphere of beings (temporal beings, *esse in commune*, intentional Being), but does not break through to real and finally to subsistent Being.

The importance of Deely's book is its sensitivity to the phenomenological or alethiological character of Heidegger's thought. He is aware of the mistake of forging blindly ahead, looking for equations between *Sein* and *esse*, without ever taking into account that in *Being and Time*, and later, Being is always something which is understood by Dasein. "Being 'is' only in the understanding of those entities to whose Being something like an understanding of Being belongs" (SZ, § 39, 183/228), a text which Deely frequently presses into service (pp. 70, 76, 150, 159–60). This sensitivity enables him to cast Heidegger's work in an illuminating light for the Scholastic thinker. Thus in the entitative order things are self-identical and distinct from one another, but in the intentional order the knower becomes the known. In the entitative order, meadows do not smile; in the intentional order they do, or perhaps they brood. The entitative order is explicated in terms of the categories of substance and accident; but such categories do not befit the intentional order. Both Deely and Powell point to the later Heidegger's analysis of the "thing" and the intersection in it of the fourfold (p. 164).[13] Entitatively earth and sky are distinct substances, but intentionally they intersect in the jug. The world which appears in intentional life is not governed by identity and contradiction, substance and accident. It is of course true enough that the intentional species is an accidental form inhering in the intellect. But, as Maritain points out, we must carefully distinguish the entitative being of the species in the soul from its intentional role in knowledge. Failure to do so will lead us down the road of Descartes and modern philosophy, for whom the species is a *Vorstellung* which somehow depicts or represents the outer world. This is a point upon which Heidegger, Maritain, and Husserl alike insist. The species *qua* species is a *medium quo*, not a thing but a means of knowing things. It possesses not *esse in* but *esse ad*.

Deely wants to show that, far from finding the ground of traditional metaphysics, as William Richardson suggests,[14] Heidegger's thought of Being must instead be grounded by the traditional philosophy of Being. Phenomenological metaphysics is in principle unable to account for itself and must have recourse to traditional ontological categories in order to explicate itself. Deely's argument is drawn from the following passage from *Being and Time*: "Entities *are*, quite independently of the experience by which they are disclosed, the acquaintance in which they are discovered, and the grasping in which their nature is ascertained. But Being 'is' only in the understanding of those entities to whose Being something like an understanding of Being belongs" (SZ, § 39, 183/228). For Deely, the sphere of the ontic, of beings, is the sphere of the real, of what is independent of Dasein, of Being in itself, of the present-at-hand (all of which are equivalent for him). The ontological, on the other hand, is the sphere of Being as meant, intentional Being. Thus the ontological difference for Deely, the difference between the ontological and the ontic, is the difference between intentional and entitative or real Being (pp. 2, 58–59, 75 et passim). But the ontological must have an ontical base. It must take its point of departure from the concrete being in whom the understanding of Being has become a fact. Yet this is methodologically impossible. For only a predicamental (categorial) analysis befits the ontic (real) sphere. Phenomenology, which cannot distinguish *esse intentionale* from *esse reale*, cannot account for beings and remain consistent. Thus *Being and Time* is brought to a critical turning point (p. 153). *Either* give up the phenomenological method and openly introduce the hitherto forbidden metaphysical analysis, thereby saving the category of the ontico-ontological which Heidegger uses in his early works; *or* give up the ontico-ontological analysis (for it cannot be explicated without traditional metaphysics) and then embrace a total lack of structure (Powell) and an exclusively ontological–intentional philosophy which loses its grips on *ens reale* (Deely). The actual course of Heidegger's thought proves that he took the latter alternative. According to Powell, Heidegger's later thought is unstructured and amorphous; things which are distinct merge into one another; confusion reigns. For Deely, any attempt to relate the various intentional faces which beings show us in the history of Being to an underlying Being which is not relative to any particular mittence of Being is impossible. All there is is intentional Being, the various successive historical epochs, but without a permanent substrate of reality.

Although I admire the frequently illuminating attempts of Deely to "situate" Heidegger within the Scholastic tradition (p. 100) and to make his work accessible in Scholastic terms, I believe that his interpretation and realist critique of Heidegger do not succeed. I should like to discuss this somewhat further, because, even though Deely's book is almost wholly devoted to an analysis of *Being and Time*, and I have concentrated on the later work, it has implications for understanding the whole of Heidegger's work and therefore for the thesis of the present study.

I think the trouble lies in Deely's interpretation of the distinction between the ontological and the ontic. The "ontological" in *Being and Time* must, in my view, be understood in terms of "projection": "Ontological interpretation projects the being presented to it upon the Being which is proper to that being, so as to conceptualize it with regard to its structure" (SZ, § 63, 312/359). To understand a being is to project it upon (*auf*) the kind of Being which renders it manifest as the sort of being which it is. The Being of beings is the horizon upon which they are projected. There are as many horizons of Being as there are regions, that is, kinds or understandings of Being (*Seinsarten*). This is clarified by § 14, where Heidegger wants to find the meaning of the "world." If we merely enumerate things in the world (houses, mountains, stars, etc.), Heidegger says, our account is both "pre-phenomenological" and "ontical" (SZ, § 14, 63/91). The account becomes ontological only when we analyze these beings in their Being. Now, the Being of the things of nature is "thinghood" and "substantiality." Such a determination is "undoubtedly ontological" (SZ, § 14, 63/92), Heidegger says, for it has projected natural beings upon their Being, where Being is conceived in terms of Nature.

But it has not succeeded in speaking ontologically about the "phenomenon" of the world. The account is ontological but pre-phenomenological. The whole analysis must be shifted from an objectivistic to a phenomenological framework. An adequate idea of the world must be at once ontological and existential; it must project innerworldly beings upon their Being where Being is thought in terms of existence. However, such an analysis must take its point of departure from innerworldly beings; that is, it must have an ontical base, not an ontical-categorial, but rather an ontical-existentiell, base. The ontological-existential concept of the worldhood of the world takes its point of departure from the ontical-existentiell world, the *Umwelt* "in which factical Dasein can be said to live" (SZ, § 14, 65/93). There are then four possible ways to conceive the world:

1. Ontical-categorial;
2. Ontological-categorial;
3. Ontical-existentiell;
4. Ontological-existential.

The first two are pre-phenomenological, for they move within an understanding of Being as objective presence (*Vorhandensein*); the second two senses are phenomenological, for they deal with the lived world and interpret the life of Dasein appropriately, that is, in terms of existence.

In *Being and Time* there are two predominant and competing understandings of Being, and hence two competing ontologies, the ontology of Being as presence-at-hand and the ontology of Being as existence. The latter is shown to be primordial and the former to be founded (*Fundierungszusammenhang*) (SZ, § 43, 201/245), in Husserl's sense, upon the former. The existential horizon is then shown to be projected upon the horizon of time and the horizon of mere presence-of-hand to be a temporal distillate of the horizon of existence.

Deely's equation of the ontological with the intentional or phenomenological, and of the ontic with the present-at-hand (*realia*), cannot be sustained. For the ontological may be either existential or categorial (the competing ontologies in *Being and Time*); and the ontical may be projected upon either the horizon of existence or the present-at-hand. There are thus the four possibilities which I enumerated above, which Deely has tried to reduce to two:

1. Ontological-existential;
2. Ontico-categorial.

Deely thinks it a violation of the phenomenological method, for example, to speak of "ever-mineness," which, being ontic, is "entitative." But the entitative (categorial) analysis of the individual yields the idea of an interchangeable instance of a species, whereas the existentiell phenomenon is of a unique, non-interchangeable "I myself." Clearly, contrary to Deely's interpretation, the ontic–ontological distinction cuts across the distinction between the existential and the present-at-hand.

Heidegger does not take Dasein, or another entity, to be a complex of phenomenon-*cum*-reality, of existence-*cum*-presence-at-hand. Existence and presence-at-hand do not differ as the ontological and the ontic do. Each is a different ontological framework, and the ontological–ontic distinction occurs within both. Now, it is true that Dasein can be taken as something present-at-hand. The physicist may interest himself in Dasein only insofar as Dasein is able to displace water. What happens then is not that a second "irreducible" aspect of Dasein emerges, as Deely contends (p. 60). Rather, Heidegger thinks, there has been a "change-over" (SZ, § 69b, 361/412) in ontological frameworks, a shift in the understanding of Being, so that Dasein is now projected not upon existence but upon presence-at-hand. So far from lying outside the purview of phenomenology, the attempt to treat Dasein as something present-at-hand is alone explicable by phenomenology. Deely thinks that all talk of "real" beings, of "presence-at-hand," lies outside the scope of phenomenology, and any attempt on Heidegger's part to relate phenomena to *realia* is in principle a violation of the phenomenological method. Deely thinks that Heidegger needs to talk about real beings, and that his method prevents him from doing so (pp. 159–60). But that is precisely not the case, for one of the principal goals of Heidegger's phenomenology is to explain the derivation of the understanding of Being in terms of "reality," even as it was Husserl's goal to explain how beings are "constituted" as real or "transcendent." "Reality" for Husserl is the correlate of certain kinds of noetic acts which he calls "doxic." And just as Husserl wants to explain how the transcendent is built up in consciousness, Heidegger shows in § 43 how "real" beings are "projected" in terms of Dasein's understanding of Being as reality or presence-at-hand.

A being can be thought to be "independent" or "real" only within a certain horizon or understanding of Being. Without Dasein there is neither "independence" (realism) nor dependence (idealism), both of which are for Heidegger meta-phenomenological interpretations or constructions with no phenomenal base. This point is clearly made in § 43c, where Heidegger writes: "When Dasein does not exist, 'independence' 'is' not either, nor 'is' the 'in itself.' In such a case, this sort of thing can be neither understood nor not understood" (SZ, § 43c, 212/255). Without Dasein's understanding of Being as presence-at-hand, it would not be possible to project beings as independent or as being in itself. He continues: "Then (i.e., if there is no Dasein) it can be said neither that the entity is nor that it is not." This contradicts Deely's claim that the order of entities present-at-hand is independent of Dasein and is real with or without Dasein. Heidegger adds: "But *now* (i.e., while there is Dasein) as long as there is an understanding of Being as presence-at-hand, it can indeed be said that in *this case* (i.e., if there were no Dasein) entities will still continue to be." Thus Dasein not only can project beings which are other than itself; it can even project them at some hypothetical time when it, Dasein, does not exist. Thus presence-at-hand, objective, independent being, is accounted for perfectly by the phenomenological method, viz., as a projection which issues from Dasein's understanding of Being. How beings are apart from Dasein is a way Dasein has of thinking about beings when it thinks in terms of presence-at-hand. None of this trespasses beyond the limits of phenomenology or constitutes an "eminently metaphysical acknowledgement" as Deely contends (pp. 159–60).

Thus for Heidegger *both* existentialia and predicamenta belong to the realm of intentional being. Existentialia are the most primordial structures in our experience, for they name the world and Dasein in our primitive engagement with the world, before reflective thought has set about analyzing and unpacking it. Predicamenta, on the other hand, are derivative names for things which result from stepping back out of our original engagement with things, adopting a disinterested posture, and speaking, in general, "as if" we had somehow acquired a leave of absence from our being-in-the-world. Existentialia and predicamenta differ as do the primordial and the derived, the original and the founded, the concrete and the abstract—but not as the subjective and the objective, or the merely cognitive and the actually real, as Deely makes out. Realism is the forgetfulness of the change-over which results in the appearance of the "objective" world. It forgets that the "real" world which would be there "then" (without Dasein) is itself founded on the projection which Dasein makes "now." Having forgotten the origins of this world in Dasein's projective understanding, the realist takes the world to be ready-made, there all along, in itself. But in truth existentialia and predicamenta are for Heidegger two different ways to understand the Being of beings. Neither lies outside the sphere of intentional being, that is, of Being as it is understood by Dasein. It is just that one names the world which is aboriginally given while the other is theoretically constructed. They differ as the primordial and the derived, not as appearance and reality.

Deely's approach to Heidegger is undisguisedly a "realist retrieve" of Heidegger which at best gives Heidegger credit for filling in a gap in Scholastic analyses. But in the end Deely thinks that, although Heidegger is the master of appearances, Thomas is the doctor of real things. And he tries to cast Heidegger's thought in terms of a dichotomy which it was the direct aim of *Being and Time* to overcome. He thinks that intentional being, for example, "supervenes over" (p. 140) the real existence of things in themselves, whereas Heidegger states unequivocally that we must be on guard against thinking that there is some world stuff over which we have laid a subjective coloring (SZ, § 15, 71/101). He has attempted a critique of Heidegger, but the responses to his criticisms are already stated in *Being and Time*.

I think that the issue Deely raised is not restricted to *Being and Time* but is of general significance for understanding Heidegger's work and therefore for understanding his relationship to St. Thomas. For what I have said here on behalf of phenomenology holds also, *mutatis mutandis*, of alethiology. What I have said here vis-à-vis Deely applies as well to the efforts of Lotz, Rioux, and Fabro. The argument that Heidegger deals with the given world, the temporal world, the world which appears, and that Thomas touches the metaphysical bottom of "real" being cannot be made to stick against Heidegger. For although the later Heidegger would not say that "real Being" is a way in which Dasein projects Being, he would later say, in accord with the dynamics of the reversal, that the conception of Being as reality is an epoch in the history of the concealing revelation of Being, an epochal way in which Being disclosed itself in the Latin Middle Ages (*actualitas*) and modernity (*Wirklichkeit*). *Esse subsistens, esse reale vel naturale,* are so many historical sendings, epochal dispensations, of a Being whose only proper name is ἀ-λήθεια, dis-closure. "Real Being" is an historical name of Being, a way Being reveals itself, and as such it is subordinate to the "Event." Whether we speak of presence-at-hand as the way Dasein projects beings in their Being, or of *esse reale* as an historical mittence of Being as ἀλήθεια, it comes down to the same thing. There is no sphere of "real" Being over, under, or behind Heidegger's *Sein.* And one cannot pin on Heidegger some kind of neglect or omission of this sphere as if he suffered from a kind of ontological shortsightedness or an obstinate this-worldliness. He has seen very clearly the claims of realism and subsumed them within his own phenomenology become alethiology. He has not missed this point; he has deconstructed it.

As illuminating as their studies are, I do not think that Rioux and Deely have found the bridge between Heidegger and Aquinas, although they do elucidate the points of difference between them. Nor do they extricate Thomas from Heidegger's notion of *Seinsvergessenheit,* for they argue positions which Heidegger is aware of and rejects. If there is a depth dimension in St. Thomas which even Heidegger himself must concede, it has not yet been shown to us.

Ἀλήθεια AND THE PARTICIPATION OF BEING

I turn my attention now to the work of Gustav Siewerth and Max Müller, the two authors who have both gone the farthest in attempting to appropriate the insights of both Heidegger and Thomas Aquinas into a single vision. Müller in particular fully appreciates the radical nature of Heidegger's critique of metaphysics and, especially, of the metaphysics of *actualitas* as the Romanization of the Greek experience of ἀλήθεια. Müller concedes that St. Thomas belongs to the history of *Seinsvergessenheit*—an admission which is unthinkable for Lotz, Fabro, Deely, and Rioux—and he thinks it necessary to undertake a rethinking of St. Thomas' teachings in order to evade Heidegger's critique. This, as we shall see, is an important contribution to the argument which I shall make in the last chapter of this study, in which I propose to undertake a "deconstruction" of St. Thomas' metaphysics. For it seems increasingly clear that one cannot at once adhere to St. Thomas' thought in its own historical actuality and integrity and also defend him against Heidegger's critique of metaphysics. St. Thomas does indeed belong to the tradition which Heidegger describes. The question is whether that is the last word in this dispute, or whether there is not a depth dimension to St. Thomas which needs to be wrested from his writings, rather in the mode of a Heideggerian retrieve or deconstruction. That is why I treat Siewerth and Müller last, because they serve as a transition to the argument which I shall make in Chapter 8.

Siewerth's interpretation of the relationship between Heidegger and St. Thomas is, as Father Richardson described it, "the most ambitious attempt thus far [1963] to let Heidegger's experience shed light on another type of thought, and . . . [it] offers the most edifying spectacle of one of Europe's most powerful minds exuberantly engaged in his task."[15] But Siewerth, in my judgment, falls prey to a tendency which one frequently encounters in studies of Heidegger and Aquinas, viz., to slip into an easy assimilation of *esse* and *Anwesen*, of Being as reality and actuality in St. Thomas and the emergent presencing of Being in Heidegger, something which I warned against doing in the previous chapter. In *The Destiny of Metaphysics from Thomas to Heidegger*, Siewerth enthusiastically endorses Heidegger's conception of the history of metaphysics as a history of the oblivion of Being.[16] But like Gilson, Rioux, and others, he takes St. Thomas to be a salient exception to this oblivion, a high point in the history of metaphysics which was not attained before or after his work. In support of this contention, Siewerth offers a history of the development of metaphysics from Meister Eckhart to the present time, including an account of the Maréchalian school of "Transcendental" Thomism. Like Gilson he argues that the history of metaphysics after St. Thomas is a history of the conceptualization of Being in which Being comes to mean *ens ut sic*, the abstract conception of the emptiest and most universal class (p. 406). He is especially critical of Suárez in this account, whom he sees as a pivotal figure mediating metaphysical conceptualism to the modern world (pp. 119ff.). The Maréchal or Transcendental school of Thomism is accused of "subjectivism" in the Heideggerian sense (pp. 207–43), and Siewerth's critique of the theory of intellectual dynamism is actually a mirror of Heidegger's own self-criticism when Heidegger speaks of the necessity of overcoming all transcendental–horizonal thinking (G 50–51/72–73).

But if Being is not something conceptual, it is because Being means emergence, letting-originate, the upsurge into Being which is captured in Heidegger's interpretation of φύσις. The actuation of a being by *esse* is a process of letting-arise or -go-forth. Siewerth actually identifies *Aktuieren* with *Hervorgehenlassen* (p. 406). But this equation, which Siewerth makes use of throughout his book, and which we have already met in Rioux's book, is in my judgment quite gratuitous, as I have already shown. Siewerth simply imposes a Heideggerian sense on St. Thomas' words without adverting to the fact that this is not what Thomas means. He holds that the experience of the fourfold (*das Geviert*) is harbored within his Heideggerianized *esse* (pp. 408–15). That is possible only if *esse* has been thoroughly dismantled and replaced by φύσις and ἀλήθεια. Siewerth seems to me to ignore the difference in the *Seinsgeschick* of Heidegger and Aquinas, and he does this at the peril of the credibility of his account.

Nonetheless Siewerth departs from Heidegger on one central issue. He argues in the manner of Gilson that the reason St. Thomas' metaphysics constitutes an exception to the history of the oblivion of Being is that his thought was conducted under the full light of divine revelation. Thomas' metaphysical insight was augmented by the knowledge of truths which, though accessible to reason, were factually unknown prior to Christian revelation. One cannot separate the history of Being from revelation. One must instead find out what the understanding of Being is which is harbored in revelation (pp. 68ff.). Revelation thus represents a pre-eminent case of the unveiling of Being. And when the claims of revelation are taken seriously, we find disclosed there a conception of subsistent Being, Being which is not the Being of beings, not an abstract representation of Being, but a Being removed from all finitude and limitation, subsisting purely in itself. Siewerth thinks, not that Heidegger denies such a Being, but that he simply fails to attain it. He sees the later Heidegger's discussion of the holy and the truly divine God as preparatory for the naming of God in a truly appropriate, non–onto-theo-logical way, a way which he thinks has already been announced in St. Thomas. Thus the five ways are interpretated as eluding Heidegger's criticism of onto-theo-logic. This strains my credulity and is an example of the precipitous equation of St. Thomas' objectivistic and Heidegger's aletheiological modes of thought to be found throughout this book.

Once again, I think that Siewerth underestimates the differences separating St. Thomas from Heidegger. I wonder if Heidegger has not so radically finitized God and the gods that they become offspring of the *Ereignis*, which is something to which no Christian, not to say any Thomist, Transcendental, Heideggerian, or whatever, can consent. For Heidegger God is not subsistent Being itself over and beyond the Being of beings, to which his phenomenological or aletheiological method has no access and about which he simply remains silent. Rather, the notion of God as subsistent Being is a particular metaphysical conception, a particular way of breaking open the difference between Being and beings to be found in the High Middle Ages, and thus a particular way in which the *Ereignis* has come to pass. It is subordinate, not superordinate, to *Ereignis*. I do not see that Siewerth addresses this point, which was also true of Lotz.

Müller is rightly suspicious of the ease with which Siewerth assimilates Thomas to Heidegger and of his confidence that Thomas is indeed to be excepted from the history of the oblivion of Being (p. 241).[17] It is true that, in virtue of the doctrine of creation, Thomas has broken through to the level of Being. But the Being which is thought in the doctrine of creation is Being as "actuality" (*Wirklichkeit*), that which brings forth or is itself brought forth by an efficient cause: "This [causal ground, *Wirkgrund*] is not considered further by Thomas, but rather only the 'how' of such producing, which is analyzed in its moments and conditions" (pp. 241–42). It did not belong to the historical possibilities of Thomas' moment in history to put the meaning of Being into question. He does not belong to the first beginning of Western thought, to the initial wonder from which all subsequent thought set out. Nor does he belong to the present age, in which the gradually transforming sense of Being has fully spun itself out, so that the question of the meaning of Being has once again become questionable. Accordingly, he came either too early or too late. He thinks instead in terms of principles of Being which he regards as *per se nota*, self-evident (*selbstverständlich*). He assumes that Being means what in *Being and Time* is called *Vorhandensein*, the objective presence of what is simply "there." His thought is bent on unraveling the dynamics of the "is," the way in which Being is brought forth and sustained in creatures, the way in which it subsists of itself in God. But what *est* (is) means never became a question for him (pp. 242–43).

Müller thus goes farther down the road with Heidegger than any of the other major commentators on Heidegger and Aquinas. For Müller agrees that as long as Thomas' thought is read in causal terms —in cosmological or, as he says, "aetiological" terms—he remains a captive to what Heidegger regards as the oblivion of Being. But there is more to Thomas than this causal–Aristotelian dimension, Müller claims, for there is also to be found in St. Thomas a Platonic and Augustinian doctrine of participation. In Book X of the *Confessions*, Müller argues, beings are led back to God, not as to a cause, but as to the source in which they participate. God shines in all things; things are the words which God speaks. God is the hidden source of which all things speak in disguised and muted terms. God is the presence which is concealedly present in everything present in the world. Now, if Müller can find such discourse in St. Thomas' treatment of *esse*, then he has discovered what I would take to be the one really genuine instance in which Thomas has met Heidegger's objection head on and has broken through the barriers of all onto-theo-logic in order to recover the experience of the presencing of Being in beings in a way which Heidegger could not fault.

Müller thinks that such a doctrine is to be found in the Thomistic theory of the participation of Being, and he cites St. Thomas' "fourth way" as a case in point (ST, 1, 2, 3, c), at least the first half of this argument. For here Being is thought as the Presence which permeates and is present in a concealed way in every being before Being is divided into cause and effect. Müller writes:

> As soon as metaphysics does not merely *use* participation as an expedient and an explanation, but rather actually *meditates* it, then it transcends all considerations of the being as a being and all consideration of its beingness, and it moves forward to a real thought of Being as such in the wonder of that presence which gives every being its essence ... [p. 245].

It was by means of such thinking that Heidegger thought the "thing" of the fourfold as opposed to the thing produced by the four causes.

It is precisely such an alethiological meditation on Being, stripped of all "aetiological" (p. 243) considerations, which Müller calls for and which he designates, counter to Heidegger's usage, the "new metaphysics." Such a metaphysics will try, not to interpret and explain, but meditatively to think the doctrine of participation. Such a thought will go to the heart of the being in its Being, and will not skirt its perimeter with causal considerations. For in the classical metaphysical doctrine of the different causes, form refers to a determination *in* the being, and matter something "under" it; and the efficient cause reaches something "before" it, while the final cause has to do with something "after" it; the exemplary cause, on the other hand, touches something "above" it (pp. 251–52). But prior to "in," "under," "before," "after," and "above," there lies the being itself, the being which lies before us (*vor-liegt*) and whose Being we must learn to think, to let-lie (*vor-liegen-lassen*). We must learn to think the being in its Being prior to all causal determination, before we have allowed it to be subjugated by calculative reason. Such a noncausal account of Being is in the end better suited to the needs of Christian belief and to the mystery of faith. For we cannot conceive Being; we must take up instead a non-conceptual thought. Concepts befit beings, not Being itself.

One can find nothing to fault, from a Heideggerian standpoint, in Müller's proposals. The one question which arises is: What kind of violence, hermeneutic or otherwise, does this do to St. Thomas? For it can hardly be clearer that in St. Thomas causality and participation are not opposed. On the contrary, participation represents a central and important kind of causality. In the "fourth way" to which Müller refers, in a pivotal sentence in the middle of the argument, after setting forth a purely "participational" argument, Thomas shifts into decidedly causal terms: "Now the maximum in any genus is the cause of all that is in that genus; as fire, which is the maximum of heat, is the cause of all hot things" (ST, I, 1, 2, c). The distinction between pure Being and the limited participations in it is not treated by St. Thomas as the distinction between presence (*Anwesen*) and the things which are present, but it is understood in terms of a *causal* relationship. That which is maximally perfect in any order is the cause of the other things in that same order. Hence, the being which is Being itself, which is possessed of the whole power of being (*tota virtus essendi*), is the cause of all limited participating beings (SCG, I, 28).

The only question which is raised by Müller's suggested reading of St. Thomas is: What does it have to do with St. Thomas? Is it a Heideggerian retrieve of so violent a sort that it asks us to take up a possibility which is not only unknown but even foreign to St. Thomas? Is it a retrieve which is without rules and which allows us to read in St. Thomas what we have first read in Heidegger? Is it simply the case that having read in Heidegger that Aristotle is not a causal thinker, we now read in Müller that Thomas Aquinas is not either? Or does this suggestion have something to do with Thomas' authentic teaching? Does it point us in the direction of a depth dimension which is genuinely present in St. Thomas, even if it needs to be wrested from him and is not entirely clear even to Thomas himself? Is there something in the texts of St. Thomas himself which opens up the possibility of a non-causal and strictly alethiological meaning of Being?

I shall try to establish in the concluding chapter that this is precisely the case, that there is in Thomas a dimension which is largely concealed by his texts, but which is nonetheless concealedly present there, which is why it is missed with such regularity by his commentators. There is, I shall try to show, a mystical element in St. Thomas' thought which belongs to his profoundest and most genuine teaching. And I shall show too that it is here that an authentic alliance between St. Thomas and Heidegger is able to be seen. And that much established, the argument of the present study will be concluded.

NOTES

1. I have not found, e.g., that Hans Meyer's book *Martin Heidegger und Thomas von Aquin* (Munich: Schöningh, 1964) illuminates the question of Heidegger and Aquinas. Its usefulness is severely curtailed, if not entirely destroyed, by its disputatious and polemical tone, by its defensiveness about St. Thomas, and by its questionable judgments. What can one say of an author who writes: "Existential philosophy in its radical form is the final word of modern autonomism, the unrestricted autocracy of existential man. The denial or estrangement from God and anxiety before the world spring from the same root and are brought into one system. . . . Perhaps one will object that Heidegger is no existentialist, but rather a fundamental ontologist. Leave the terminology to itself. The determinations of human existence take in so broad and fundamental an area that existentialism can claim him for itself" (pp. 4–5). This is no thoughtful confrontation of Heidegger and St. Thomas, no attempt at dialogue, merely a good example of what Heidegger calls "parading polemical opinions" (AED 11/6), and I have therefore omitted any further reference to it. Apart from the works which are discussed in this chap-

ter, I refer the reader to the Bibliography in which I have supplied a more complete list of studies in the area of Thomas and Heidegger. In particular I find Sheehan's "Notes on a 'Lovers' Quarrel': Heidegger and Aquinas," to be very rich in insight although unfortunately short. My aim in the present chapter has been to discuss not everything, but only the most important studies and the ones which give us the best sampling of the diverse issues involved.

2. Johannes Baptist Lotz, *Martin Heidegger und Thomas von Aquin: Mensch, Zeit, Sein* (Freiburg: Herder, 1975). All page numbers in parentheses in the body of the text in this section will be to this volume unless otherwise noted. Because of its comprehensiveness I have based my exposition of Lotz's views upon this work. His essay "Das Sein selbst und das subsistierende Sein nach Thomas von Aquin," in *Martin Heidegger zum siebzigsten Geburtstag*, ed. Günther Neske (Pfullingen: Neske, 1959), pp. 180–94, is an adumbration of the present volume. A fuller sketch may be found in *"Being* and *Existence* in Scholasticism and in Existence-Philosophy," trans. Robert E. Wood, *Philosophy Today*, 9, No. 1 (Spring 1964), 3–45. The essays included in *Sein und Existenz* (Freiburg: Herder, 1965), pp. 97–242, except for the previous essay (pp. 340–408), tend to be in the nature more of book reviews than of a critical confrontation with St. Thomas. See also "Heidegger und das Christentum," *Doctor Communis*, 4 (1951), 63–73.

3. *Mystical Element in Heidegger's Thought*, pp. 108–109, 247–48.

4. See the last section of this chapter, "Ἀλήθεια and the Participation of Being"; see also G 38/63.

5. Bertrand Rioux, *L'Etre et la verité chez Heidegger et saint Thomas d'Aquin* (Paris: Presses Universitaires de France, 1963). All page numbers in parentheses in the body of the text in this section will be to this volume unless otherwise noted.

6. Cornelio Fabro, *Participation et causalité selon saint Thomas d'Aquin* (Louvain: Publications Universitaires de Louvain; Paris: Editions Beatrice-Nauwelaerts, 1961), pp. 13–83. This chapter originally appeared as an article in the *Bulletin Thomiste* in 1956. See also his "Il nuovo problema dell'essere e la fondazione della metafisica," in *St. Thomas Aquinas, 1274–1974*, ed. Maurer, II 423–57.

7. Fabro, *Participation*, p. 51.

8. Ibid., p. 52.

9. Ibid., p. 176.

10. See also my critique of the distinction between "thought" and "reason" in the later Heidegger in *Mystical Element in Heidegger's Thought*, pp. 264–70.

11. *The Tradition via Heidegger: An Essay on the Meaning of Being in the Philosophy of Martin Heidegger* (The Hague: Nijhoff, 1971). This book evolved from an article entitled "The Situation of Heidegger in the Tradition of Christian Philosophy," *The Thomist*, 31, No. 2 (April 1967), 159–244. All page numbers in the body of the text in this section will be to *The Tradition via Heidegger*, unless otherwise noted.

12. See Powell's "The Late Heidegger's Omission of the Ontico-Ontological Structure of Dasein," in *Heidegger and the Path of Thinking*, ed. John Sallis (Pittsburgh: Duquesne University Press, 1970), pp. 116–37.

13. Powell, "The Late Heidegger's Omission," pp. 119–20.

14. *Heidegger*, p. 154.

15. Ibid., p. 687.

16. Gustav Siewerth, *Das Schicksal der Metaphysik von Thomas zu Heidegger* (Einsiedeln: Johannes Verlag, 1959). All page numbers in the body of the text in the next three paragraphs of this section will be to this volume unless otherwise noted. See also the interesting portrait of Siewerth's relationship to Heidegger in Fischer-Barnicol's recollections of Heidegger in "Spiegelungen —Vermittlungen," pp. 98–100.

17. Max Müller, *Existenzphilosophie im geistigen Leben der Gegenwart*, 3rd ed. (Heidelberg: Kerle Verlag, 1964). All page numbers in the body of the text in the remainder of this section will be to this volume unless otherwise noted. For a commentary on the earlier editions of this book, see Jean Langlois, "Heidegger, Max Müller et le Thomisme," *Sciences Ecclésiastiques*, 9 (1957), 27–48.

8

The Mystical Element
in St. Thomas' Thought:
A Retrieval
of Thomistic Metaphysics

WHAT IS UNSAID IN ST. THOMAS' THOUGHT

Up to now I have treated St. Thomas' thought as metaphysical theology, taking it in the terms in which it was written and in the way in which it was intended by St. Thomas himself. By my so doing, we have seen that this metaphysics does not escape the criticisms which Heidegger makes of metaphysics. Every attempt to relate the metaphysics of *esse* with the turn into the *Ereignis*, to compare St. Thomas' "existential" metaphysics with Heideggerian "alethiology," is bound to fail. So long as we remain on the level of the Thomistic text in its historical *actuality,* on the level of what St. Thomas himself actually said and intended to say, of the actual metaphysical doctrine which he developed in the Scholastic mode, then we shall never be able to bring Heidegger and Aquinas into living relationship with one another. We become capable of that only insofar as we see in St. Thomas' thought a constellation of *possibilities* which remain to be thought. Then we see in what St. Thomas actually said the possibilities which he opens up, possibilities which as a matter of necessity he himself left unsaid. Our relationship to St. Thomas then becomes less historical and more philosophical, and we enter into a philosophical dialogue with him. As Heidegger says, speaking of the interpretation of the Heraclitean fragments: "Wishing to pursue the 'objectively correct' teaching of Heraclitus means refusing to run the salutary risk of being confounded by the truth of a thinking" (VA 261/106).

In the pages which follow I want to run the risk of thought, the risk of a thoughtful dialogue with St. Thomas. I want to show that there is more to St. Thomas' thought than the metaphysical theology which we have thus far encountered. I want to distinguish an enlivening insight, a motivating tendency, from the metaphysical casing in which it is enclosed. I want to distinguish the kernel from the shell. My argument will be that there is a more profound and non-metaphysical tendency inscribed within the essence of St. Thomas' metaphysics which needs to be made explicit. In its own historical actuality, St. Thomas' thought, as a metaphysical theology, is "guilty"—there is, of course, no question of personal failure here—of the charges which Heidegger makes against metaphysics. But there is an orientation within his metaphysics toward a non-metaphysical experience of Being, a tendency within Thomistic metaphysics to transform itself, not, to be sure, into what Heidegger calls "thought," but into mysticism. Now, mysticism is not thought, as I have tried to show on another occasion, but like thought, it lies beyond the sphere of influence of the principle of sufficient reason.[1] It abjures concepts and ratiocinations; it is a simple immediacy and pristine contact of the soul with God. It has nothing to do with "calculative thought," as Heidegger uses the expression. Genuine and great mysticism, Heidegger insists —not the irrationalist extravaganzas which sometimes parade themselves as "mysticism"—enjoys the sharpness and depth of thought itself (SG 71), and it has been, in the form of Meister Eckhart, of decisive influence on Heidegger himself.

I should like, therefore, in the present chapter to retrieve or, if you will, to "deconstruct," Thomistic metaphysics, to break open its metaphysical encasement and to expose the contents of its essentially mystical significance. To retrieve or deconstruct is, not to destroy, but to shake loose from a text its essential tendencies, tendencies which the text itself conceals. I much prefer the word "deconstruct," which is used by Jacques Derrida, to "*Destruktion*," which Heidegger used in *Being and Time*.[2] Deconstruction, or in German *Ab-bauen*, a word which Heidegger himself uses, has primarily for us, not the negative sense of leveling or wrecking a text, but rather the positive sense of taking a text apart in order to find its most essential and enlivening insights and then reconstructing the whole around them. I believe that the uninterruptedly metaphysical mode of St. Thomas' discourse effectively covers over the truest tendencies of his thought.

I want to break this metaphysical mode open in order to retrieve and set forth in a place of prominence the mystical content of his work. In so doing I believe that we shall discover, not that I have constructed a purely hypothetical and capriciously contrived Aquinas, but rather that I have laid hold of something more essential about Aquinas than is conveyed to us by any strictly metaphysical presentation of his thought.

We shall not—and upon this I insist—we shall not find that this more essential Aquinas is in fact Heidegger—any more than those old doctoral dissertations from the first half of this century succeeded in convincing us that if we understand Leibniz or Hegel more essentially we shall find St. Thomas. The mystical element in St. Thomas is, not Heideggerian "thought," but an essentially religious mysticism which focuses entirely on the ultimate unity of the self with God. But this mysticism is non-metaphysical, non–onto-theological. It is a matter, not of *ratio* at all, but of an experience of Being—one, indeed, which rivals Heidegger's in its claim to authenticity. It is, in its own way and on its own terms, an alethiology of Being, an encounter with the power ($\phi\acute{v}\sigma\iota\varsigma$) and light (*Lichtung*) of Being. This Thomistic mysticism shows in a decisive and in the only really adequate way how inappropriate and inaccurate it is to write off St. Thomas' metaphysics as one more metaphysics, one more onto-theo-logic. And it provides us with the genuine point of contact between these two thinkers. I shall argue, not that St. Thomas' *metaphysics* is innocent of the oblivion of Being which Heidegger describes, but that there is more to St. Thomas than metaphysics, and that this metaphysics tends by a dynamism of its own in the direction of a non-metaphysical experience of Being. And in this sense there is an overcoming of metaphysics in St. Thomas as well.

All this amounts to finding something unsaid in what St. Thomas has said. Now, something of this sort is discussed by the distinguished German Thomist Josef Pieper when he speaks of "the silence of St. Thomas," that is, what St. Thomas left unexpressed. Pieper writes that "certain notions remained unexpressed because they were self-evident to the author, whereas they are in no way self-evident to the man who is interpreting the text." Then he adds that our aim must be:

> to grasp those basic assumptions which, remaining unexpressed, nevertheless permeate all that is actually stated; to discover, so to

speak, the hidden keynote that dominates whatever has been explicitly said.

It could be positively maintained that the doctrine of a thinker is precisely "*das im Sagen Ungesagte,* the unexpressed in what is expressed." This is how Heidegger begins his own interpretation of a Platonic text. The phrase is no doubt deliberately strained, but it is clear than an interpretation which does not reach the unspoken assumptions underlying the actual text must remain, in essence, a misinterpretation, even if in other respects the letter of the text be commented upon with considerable learning; this latter fact may, indeed, make things worse.[3]

Though I agree heartily with Pieper's hermeneutical recommendation, I believe that he himself does not go far enough in locating the silence of St. Thomas. For he finds the unspoken theme of St. Thomas' metaphysics to be the doctrine of creation. Creation is the everpresent, but implicit, horizon of Thomistic metaphysics, a claim which, as far as it goes, Heidegger would indeed accept (GP 115/ 82). But the doctrine of creation itself remains on the level of metaphysical theology; it is an unspoken horizon of St. Thomas' metaphysics which nevertheless belongs *to* that metaphysics. I would look for the unspoken horizon of St. Thomas' thought outside metaphysics, in a certain kind of non-metaphysical experience, of which the metaphysics is an objectivistic conceptualization and toward which it tends. I would look for the unspoken horizon of St. Thomas' thought in the mystical–religious experience of life which animates his works, an experience which does not come to words because it cannot. Indeed, the more St. Thomas talks, the more likely it is that this mystical element will be concealed. For Thomistic doctrine is very strongly cast in the form of what Heidegger calls an "onto-theo-*logic*"; it is very much a captive of *ratio,* very much what Heidegger calls a thing of *ratio* (*eine Sache der ratio*) (WdP 22–23). Now, what is unspoken in the imposing machinery of this erudite and skillful *magister*'s texts, what one almost never hears amid the clatter of syllogisms and *respondeo*s, is the silent call which speaks in St. Thomas' works to suspend *ratio* and enter into the intuitive unity of *intellectus.* Yet the whole point which this elaborate exhibition of Scholastic *ratio* leads up to is precisely that *ratio* is a weak and defective instrument which must be laid aside for a higher way. What is unspoken in all that St. Thomas says is that the metaphysical–theological way to think is a ladder which is to be thrown away, that metaphysics is something to be overcome.

It cannot be overlooked that St. Thomas' metaphysics is pre-Cartesian and hence that it is not an onto-theo-logic in the strong sense of the post-Cartesian systems. St. Thomas' conception of reason differs markedly from that of the post-Cartesian thinkers and should never be confused with rationalist reason. The ὕβρις of "subjectism" (*Subjektität*) (N II 452) which Heidegger criticizes in metaphysics, the arrogant claim of subjectivity to hold court over Being itself, never characterizes the reason of St. Thomas. There is no Cartesian subjectivism in St. Thomas which groups the whole of Being around the thinking self, no *principium reddendae rationis* which refuses to grant permission to be unless the being can present its credentials before the jurisdiction of reason (Leibniz), no Hegelian absolutizing of rational categories. In St. Thomas, reason is subordinate to faith, to mysticism, and, in the end, to the eschatological consummation of intelligence in the beatific vision. Everything St. Thomas wrote he wrote as a Christian believer, as a friar, and, we have reason to think, as a practitioner of mystical prayer. That is why one need only find the quiet spot in his metaphysical treatises, that point in his metaphysical theology at which he himself unmasks the pretension of *ratio* to absolute validity, in order to see that this metaphysics, unlike all post-Cartesian systems, *invites* deconstruction. The elaborate scaffolding of Thomistic metaphysics conceals what it attempts to reveal—and hence reveals what it conceals: that the end of the self is a non-metaphysical union with God.

It is a matter of no little irony to me that Heidegger was able to find a more gentle nature in Aristotle but not in St. Thomas. He finds in Aristotle's *Physics* an echo of the original Greek experience of φύσις. He sees in the doctrine of the four causes not a metaphysics of making—although he changed his mind on that point, as we saw—but an alethiological doctrine of the bringing forth of truth into the work. But in the High Middle Ages he finds only the metaphysics of making, a tough-minded logicism and ontology which is only one step removed from technology and the will-to-power. Now, I find this as surprising an interpretation of Aristotle as it is of medieval philosophy. And it is astonishing to me how the Heideggerians have fallen on Heidegger's breast in this matter and repeated his *dixit*s so unquestioningly. I take Aristotle to be one of the more tough-minded, rationalistic thinkers the West produced prior to the emergence of the modern post-Cartesian systems. He spawned in Averroës the most anti-religious and rationalistic thinker of the Middle Ages. He is the virtual inventor of the principle of causality, the causal thinker *par excellence* in the ancient world. Were he alive today, I dare say, his interests would be in theoretical physics, astrophysics, DNA-molecule research, and the other natural and social sciences which collectively go together to make up what Heidegger calls "cybernetics" (SD 64/ 58). Men like Bonaventure, Albert the Great, Thomas Aquinas, and the entire German Dominican school, on the other hand, were of an entirely different stripe. St. Thomas' thought in particular is dominated by a strong sense of the limits of reason, of the primacy of Being (*esse*), of filial *pietas* toward Augustine and the other sacred Doctors. He belongs to an age of the holy—if ever there was one. His world is filled with gods (angels), who are constantly before his mind, with saints, miracles, and the multiform signs of God's *presence* among men. There is every bit as much, indeed considerably more, motivation to suspect a deeper dimension, an unspoken horizon of meaning in St. Thomas' metaphysics, and therefore to undertake a hermeneutic retrieve of his writings, than there is with Aristotle. The basis of Heidegger's deconstruction of Aristotle is that Aristotle lived in the afterglow of the early Greeks, that he still spoke the language which once burned white hot, in Heidegger's view, in Anaximander, Heraclitus, and Parmenides. But Aristotle had as much to do with the onset of "onto-theo-logic" as any thinker before Descartes. Sometime around 1920 Heidegger's attitude toward medieval thinkers began to change: he chose, not to seek out the depth dimension in the medieval experience of Being, but to take the thinkers of the Middle Ages at their face value, to take them at their word, whereas, by his own account, one ought to listen to what they do *not* say. At this point, Heidegger ceased to heed his own good advice in the *Habilitationsschrift*: that one ought not to take medieval Scholasticism and medieval mysticism to be opposites and that one ought not to try to understand Scholasticism apart from its mystical and moral underpinnings, its rootedness in the mystical life of the soul with God (FS² 205–206, 410). In 1916 Heidegger possessed the key with which to unlock the depth dimension in Scholasticism; sometime after 1919 he threw the key away.[4]

For if one listens only to what St. Thomas says, and if in particular one focuses on how he says it, one will come away convinced that here indeed is onto-theo-logic, indeed perhaps even a paradigm of it. There is no denying that St. Thomas' experience of Being is heavily encased in a species of onto-theo-logic.[5] But the task of thought is to probe this onto-theo-logical structure to find the point at which the dismantling which exposes its more essential meaning can begin. And the surprising result which emerges from such an undertaking in deconstruction is that, in St. Thomas, metaphysics is meant to wither away. The whole elaborate texture of *disputatio* which he weaves is an exercise in showing the deficiency and infirmity of *ratio*, in showing that metaphysics is something to be overcome.

"*Raynalde, non possum*": St. Thomas' Mystical Life

The principle and point of departure of the deconstruction of St. Thomas' metaphysics are supplied to us by no less an authority than Thomas himself. For we are told by the ancient biographers that at the end of his life St. Thomas experienced a personal breakthrough, an overcoming of his metaphysical theology, which led him to break off his writing and to take up an almost uninterrupted silence until his death three months later. The story is handed down to us by Bartholomew of Capua, who gave the information to William of Tocco, but its source is said to have been Reginald of Piperno, Thomas' personal secretary (*socius*), who would have been an eyewitness to the events. Let us listen to Weisheipl's account of the story:

> On Wednesday morning, December 6, the feast of St. Nicholas, Thomas arose as usual to celebrate the Mass of the feast in the chapel of St. Nicholas. During Mass, Thomas was suddenly struck (*commotus*) by something that profoundly affected and changed him (*mira mutatione*). "After this Mass he never wrote or dictated anything." In fact, he "hung up his instruments of writing (an allusion to the Jews who hung up their instruments during the exile) in the third part of the *Summa*, in the treatise on Penance." When Reginald realized that Thomas had altered entirely his routine of more than fifteen years, he asked him, "Father, why have you put aside such a

great work which you began for the praise of God and the enlightenment of the world?" To which Thomas answered simply, "Reginald,
I cannot." [*Raynalde, non possum.*] But Reginald, afraid that
Thomas was mentally unbalanced from so much study, insisted that
he continue his writing and return to his former routine, at least at
a slower pace. But the more Reginald insisted, the more impatient
Thomas became until he replied, "Reginald, I cannot, because all
that I have written seems like straw to me." Reginald was mystified
at this reply. But Thomas was serious; he could not go on. He was
physically and mentally unable to do so. The only recourse he had
was to pray for himself, and acceptance of his inability to work.[6]

When pressed again by Reginald, Thomas added this explanation:
" 'Everything which I have written seems like straw to me compared
to what I have seen and what has been revealed to me' " (*Omnia,
quae scripsi, videntur mihi paleae respectu eorum, quae vidi et revelata sunt mihi*). According to the story which has been handed
down to us, the one time that Thomas did break his silence after that
was to write a commentary on the *Canticle of Canticles* (but if he
composed such a commentary, it has been lost). And the *Canticle*,
of course, is a mystical poem from the Old Testament about the love
of the soul for God. The last days of Thomas' life, then, are given
over to mystical silence and a commentary on a mystical poem. Now,
we certainly do not hear of these events in Heidegger's version of
Scholasticism and St. Thomas; nor, for that matter, do we hear much
about it in most renderings of St. Thomas by his own disciples.

The story of Thomas' final days illustrates precisely the point
which I am trying to make in this chapter. At the end of his life,
Thomas underwent an experience of Being itself (of *ipsum esse subsistens*) in comparison with which his metaphysical–theological writings appeared to him as straw. And what is this straw except the straw
of onto-theo-logic? We cannot but be struck by the language to
which Thomas has recourse in attempting to disclose the new sphere
which has been opened up for him. The straw of metaphysics is compared to "those things which I have seen and which have been revealed to me" (*quae vidi et revelata sunt mihi*). That with which onto-
theo-logic is so unfavorably compared is formulated in the language
of sight, seeing, and revelation. This is to say that Thomas has passed
from the sphere of representational thinking, from the sphere of the

concepts, judgments, and ratiocinations of the *Summa*, into the realm of the unconcealed, the clearing (*Lichtung*), the sphere of light and manifestness. He passes from the chatter of discursive reason to the silence of thought, from calculation to thought. And when he chooses to speak, it is about a song, a singing, a poem which poetizes the relationship of the soul to God. He invokes the language of the mystical poet rather than the language of the Philosopher. The language of the poet is the language of the clearing, of the open place in which the Being of God lights itself up and shows itself as a primordial φαινόμενον. In the clearing one sings, although only after a long silence and as a result of a great silence. Outside the clearing there is the straw of scientific discourse.

The story of Thomas' last days is the story of a "step back" out of metaphysics which enables him to see the "essence" of metaphysics, to see metaphysics for what it is, the straw of *scientia*. Metaphysics attempts to encase the Being (*esse*) of God, the world, and the soul within concepts of its own making. Thomas has been admitted into the very *Sache* of metaphysics, which metaphysics itself is unable to name without distortion. The clearing is the sphere which can be entered by the saint, whereas the sphere of the *Summa*, of *ratio*, may be entered by any *magister* (by the *Privatdozenten!*). If the *magister* speaks in the language of the onto-theo-logician, the saint has entered an altogether different sphere.

Were we able to take the ancient biographers at their word, the argument of the present chapter would be complete and this book would be finished. For we would have it on no less an authority than Thomas himself that metaphysics is something to be overcome, that all *scientia* is straw compared to mystical experience. Our modern temperament, however, compels us to be somewhat critical of such legends. After all, the whole purpose which William of Tocco had in writing his *vita* was to support the canonization process of his Dominican brother. And we know how competitive the orders were in the Middle Ages when it came to such matters. Moreover, some rather extraordinary things indeed are said to have happened to this candidate for sainthood, including discoursing with a recently deceased *magister*, Romanus, whom Thomas quizzed about the answers to one of the *questiones* they had discussed when Romanus was still alive. Edmund Colledge makes a telling point in connection with the story of Thomas' mystical life:

Of the whole legend, no other incident suggests more clearly a purely natural explanation. Several medical authorities with whom the present writer has discussed it have independently said that it presents the standard symptom of severe brain damage through haemorrhage: impaired speech, manual dexterity and gait, expectation of further such attacks, and violent mental disturbance.[7]

Mystical experience or cerebral hemorrhage? Mystical breakthrough or mental breakdown? Or both, as Weisheipl seems to suggest?[8] St. Thomas followed a punishing routine which could easily have brought on a stroke or driven him to exhaustion. And his death just three months later suggests more than anything else the physical rather than the mystical explanation.

For us modern thinkers, the legend of St. Thomas' final days may be no more than μῦθος(it would be "temerarious," as Colledge says, to try to rule on it). But every μῦθος has a λόγος. The wholly undecidable question of whether such miraculous and mystical things did indeed occur to St. Thomas is not the important thing; that these things were part of the total figure which Thomas cut in his own day and shortly after his death is. His Dominican brothers, his students, the ecclesiastical leaders of the day, the Cistercians at Fossanova who wanted to keep his remains, found it eminently meaningful that this man so renowned as a *magister* should have been a sainted mystic, a seer of eternal things, a blessed and holy monk. They were not scandalized that this famous *magister* thought his *Summa* to be like straw; on the contrary, they considered it an edifying story. St. Thomas was held by his contemporaries to be a man endowed with contemplative gifts, with religious and mystical grace, and not merely with theological intelligence. His own life and habits supplied a *fundamentum in re* for the legend. Those who knew St. Thomas were fully prepared to believe that he would have considered the *Summa* to be as straw. They did not think that this refuted everything he stood for; on the contrary, they took it to mean that he had attained the crown for which he strove.

The legend of St. Thomas does not *demonstrate* anything, but it does *illustrate* that the meaning, the *sens*, of St. Thomas' metaphysics, is to be located in an essentially religious mysticism. For an effective demonstration of this thesis one must undertake a deconstructive reading of his texts. For even the legend recounts that when the Lord appeared to St. Thomas, He told the saint that he had written well of Him: *Bene scripsisti*. Hence, it is in the texts of St. Thomas that one must find the ultimately mystical meaning of his metaphysics. Thomas has written well; now it is our task to hear well. The writings are not, after all, straw; they are simply likened to straw in comparison to the vision. The vision is the meaning of the writings, their *sens*, in the French sense of direction and tendency, their innermost τέλος. They express in the mode of *ratio* that which altogether transcends *ratio*. The silence and the mystical song of which the legend speaks are to be taken, not as the contradiction of the writings, but as their innermost meaning and final fruit. The silence is, not the opposite of the words, but their true sense. We are to read the *Summa*'s with silence in mind, for the silence teaches us how to read the book. The greatest danger would be to listen to the *questiones* of the *Summa* and not to hear the silence. Then one would hear only the outer rattle of Scholastic machinery. Then one would have straw indeed.

The Unsayability of *Esse*

The task of the deconstruction of Thomistic metaphysics must be carried out on two fronts: that of the interpretation of *esse* and that of the interpretation of *intellectus*. I hope to show that in St. Thomas' metaphysics the unmediated unity of *intellectus* and *esse*—of what Heidegger would call the belonging together of thought and Being— is an enlivening if unstated goal toward which the whole is striving.

In this section, I wish to show how St. Thomas' notion of *esse* tends to surpass metaphysics, how it cannot be contained within the boundaries of metaphysical discourse. This will come as a surprise to those who know of St. Thomas only through accounts which depict him in terms which befit the Scholasticism of the seventeenth and eighteenth centuries. It is this paradox—namely, that at the heart of this "Scholastic metaphysics," this creature of metaphysical reason, there should be found the wholly non-conceptualizable notion of *esse* —which Gilson exploited with so much skill and acumen in *Being and Some Philosophers*. For it is precisely the need of the intellect to formulate conceptual definitions which the Thomistic doctrine of *esse* frustrates. Reason is at home with form, structure, essence, definition; but *esse* is none of these. The crowning point of Thomistic metaphysics in Gilson's view is the steadfastness with which Thomas resists the metaphysical temptation to reduce *esse* to an essentialist structure. The strictness of thought, Heidegger says (*Weg.*[2] 315/ 195), is to abide strictly within the element of Being. The strictness of St. Thomas' thought is to abide rigorously within the element of *esse* and not to think *esse* as if it were form or structure. Indeed, it is this comparable passion in both thinkers to abide strictly within the element of Being and to avoid every temptation to make it something less than it is which lies at the heart of the confrontation of these two thinkers.

Insofar as *esse* is something other (*aliud*) than essence, it cannot be treated in the manner of an essence (ST, I, 29, 2, ad 3). Essence is what is signified by the definition of a thing, which means that *esse* falls outside the realm of definition. It is impossible to ask or to say "what" *esse* is. For it is essence which answers the question "What is it?" (*Quid sit?*). Essence is constituted by form, whether this means, in the case of the separate substances, that essence is form alone, or, in the case of material things, that form is conjoined to matter. But *esse* is in nowise a form, although Thomas says that it is "formal" in relation to essence, meaning that it is the act of the essence. But even though *esse* is the perfection and actuality of all forms, it itself is not a form (ST, I, 4, 1, ad 3). It cannot therefore be conceived in the strict sense of the word; it does not yield itself to the first act of the mind which wants to seize and apprehend.

Thus, we find embedded in the heart of Thomistic metaphysics an enigmatic and non-conceptual element. What is *esse* if it is not definable and if it does not even permit the question "What?" to be raised in its regard? Clearly there must be some other way of access to the meaning of *esse*. As Heidegger says in § 1 of *Being and Time*, even if Being does not have a definition, this is not to say that it is without meaning. *Esse* has a meaning (*intelligibilitas*) which is not conceptual (*conceptus*).[9] Its meaning is to be the act in virtue of which every being stands outside of nothingness. And if this act is not circumscribed by a definition, it is reached by the intellect in the act of judging. The intellect attains—without conceiving—the act of existence in a judgmental act which, for its part, is a response to the act exercised by the thing itself. There is here a νόησις and νόημα of act, an intentional correlativity such that act is known only by act, existence by affirmation, Being by the acclaiming "is" of the intellect, even as there is an intentionality of structure and form between essence and the conceiving apprehension. To the structural quality of the real (*essentia*), the intellect responds by conceptual circumscription, with which it is entirely at ease. But to the active upsurge of the real, the intellect responds with affirmation, acclamation, and it understands that it has thereby entered a different sphere, that it is set on a different course, one in which it must dispense with the comfort of definitions and expose itself to the hazard of thinking the "is" in that which is.

The non-definability of *esse* is brought home to us with particular force when we turn to St. Thomas' doctrine of God as *ipsum esse per se subsistens*. For if *esse* eludes the defining power of the intellect, then God, who is maximally *esse*, is maximally indefinable. If *esse* is beyond form and structure, then God is maximally foreign to the conceptualizing powers of the mind. The outstanding American Thomistic metaphysician W. Norris Clarke has expressed this dimension of Thomas' metaphysical theology in an especially sharp way. In a remarkable article on the indefinable character of the ultimate principles of Thomistic metaphysics, Father Clarke argues that St. Thomas' view of *esse* "points beyond to something that cannot properly be said, but can only be recognized, not conceptualized, in a flash of synthetic insight."[10] In fact, Clarke maintains, what St. Thomas wants to say about *esse* strains the limits of language. If God means *ipsum esse subsistens*, it is barely possible to say that God "is." And this is because it strains against the noun–verb structure of grammar, and not just against the empirical limits of English grammar, but against what Husserl called in the *Fourth Investigation* noun–verb "categories of meaning." For in the case of God, *what* is and the *is* itself are the same. This is to say that in the Thomistic version of the simple sentence "God is," the subject functions as its own verb and the verb is the subject of its own activity. For if we say "the subsisting act of existence is" (*ipsum esse subsistens est*), we are in fact invoking a grammatical distinction in order to signify something which repudiates that distinction. In this case, the *esse subsistens* and the *est*, the subject and the verb, are the same. What is named by the subject and what is named by the verb are the same. Hence, "the core of St. Thomas' teaching on the nature of God is something that cannot be directly said at all."[11]

Father Clarke shows the reverberations on the level of language of the non-conceptualizability of Thomistic *esse*, and, therefore, of the eminent non-conceptualizability of God's *esse*. That is why it is not surprising that there is an all-too-easily overlooked "negative theology," a *docta ignorantia*, in this theologian who is frequently identified with theological rationalism. Gilson puts it best:

> the negative theology of Thomas Aquinas is an energetic and eminently positive effort of the mind against the self-deception that it knows the essence of the highest object. . . . Everything in man's intellect rebels against such an attitude. It is not natural to man to busy himself about its objects in order to make sure that he does *not* know them. . . . In deep agreement with the most radically imageless mysticism there ever existed, that of Saint Bernard of Clairvaux, Thomas Aquinas invites us to transcend all representation and figurative description of God.[12]

Gilson is referring to the repeated assertions of St. Thomas that we know of God only that He is, that we know, not what He is, but what He is not (ST, I, 3, Introd.; SCG, I, 14; *Exp. Boeth. De Trin.*, I, 2).[13] If *esse* is what is non-conceptualizable in the creature, which we know, then God, who is pure and subsistent *esse*, is the most removed of all from the powers of our mind in their present state. The best one can do within the limits of metaphysical theology is to say what God's *esse* is not, that it is not temporal, composite, bodily, etc. That is why St. Thomas writes: "This is the ultimate in human knowledge of God: to know that we do not know Him" (*De pot.* 7, 5, ad 14).

It is clear that there is, if not an exigency, at least a yearning in the metaphysics of St. Thomas for something beyond metaphysics, a tendency for an encounter with the divine *esse*, for an immediate vision which, to the extent that it is possible in this life, is permitted only to the mystic and is, in the end, fully possible only in the beatific vision. In metaphysics, we know only representationally and deductively *that* a first cause whom men call God does indeed exist; we know abstractly *about* the divine *esse*. There is required a mystical intimacy which St. Thomas calls "rapture" (*raptus*) (ST, II–II, 175, 5) which is possible only to those who have laid aside all phantasms and concepts and all the tools of deductive metaphysics and have abandoned their wills to God.[14] There seems to be little doubt that St. Thomas knew of such an experience in a firsthand way. Nor is it surprising that the author of the *Summa theologica* is at the same time

the author of the hymn *Adoro te devote, latens deitas*. As Gerald Mc-
Cool has written of Scholasticism in the early part of this century:

> the intelligible connection which links Thomas' metaphysics of God
> to his personal religious experience was not observed, much less
> exploited. In this misleading presentation, Thomism could not fail
> to give the impression of being a highly rationalistic system. It was
> [taken to be] in fact an impersonal Aristotelian science. . . . Little
> appreciation was shown for the vital role of personal experience and
> non-conceptual intuition in religious knowledge of God.[15]

It is this "personal religious experience" of which Father McCool
speaks which constitutes the true silence of St. Thomas and which
forms the indispensable horizon for any interpretation of his thought.

Intellectus AND *Ratio*:
ST. THOMAS' CRITIQUE OF METAPHYSICAL REASON

We must turn our attention now to the life of *intellectus* as St. Thomas
conceives it. For as I said above, just as *esse* cannot be contained
within the limits of metaphysics, so human *ratio* must give way to
the simplicity of *intellectus*. Just as *esse* cannot be contained within
the limits of rational conceptualization, so the mind itself is not
content with conceptual, judgmental, and discursive knowledge of
reality. The mind itself is driven on by a dynamism of its own to seek
a life beyond *ratio* in the sphere of pure *intellectus*. There alone all
ratio, and hence all philosophy as a thing of *ratio* (*eine Sache der
ratio*) (WdP 22–23), are left behind. As *esse* tends to resist rationalization, so reason itself tends to be driven beyond itself. Hence, the
task at hand is to show that in St. Thomas there is a critique of *ratio*,
and that means of *scientia* and of metaphysics, in favor of a more simple and unmediated unity of *intellectus* and *esse* in which metaphysics
is overcome. If St. Thomas does not say this with explicit clarity, this
is because it belongs more to the realm of what is unsaid in St.
Thomas than to what he explicitly proclaims.

I begin with the distinction which he draws between *ratio* and *intellectus*. To do this, let us turn, as we did in Chapter 4, to St. Thomas'
treatise on the angels. For just as Thomas' insight into the separa-
bility of *actus* from *forma*—that there is an act beyond form—is oc-

casioned by his reflections on the created character of the angelic being, so his insight into the analogical amplitude of *intellectus* is deepened by his consideration of angelic intellectuality. Thomas wants to know, first, whether angels know by way of discursive reason, as men do, and, secondly, whether they make use of propositional or judgmental knowledge, again as we do. In each case, he answers in the negative and in so doing differentiates angelic *intellectus* from human *ratio*.

Angelic knowledge is not discursive because of the perfection with which the angelic being subsists in its essence. Inasmuch as its essence is not received into matter, and hence individuated, its essence —not its being—is unlimited. The angelic nature is not spread out in time and limited by the conditions of sensibility and spatiality. The angel's consciousness, to speak phenomenologically, is not a flow (*Strom*). He has no perceptual consciousness and hence makes no use of perspective, protention, or retention. Nor are his intellectual acts "founded" on perception; they are, rather, originary and intuitive. Hence, there can be no movement, no dis-course (*dis-currere*, running through) from one assertion to the next, no genesis of the object of knowledge. Whatever the angelic mind is capable of knowing, it knows at once (*statim*) and by simple insight (*intuens*), and that is the perfection of its *intellectus*. But with human *ratio* everything is different because of the weakness of the intellectual light in men (*ex debilitate intellectualis luminis*). Our grasp of principles is so weak that we do not see all that is contained in them, but must reason from one assertion to the next until we have made all their implications explicit. Insofar as we have insight at all, we have a share in *intellectus*; but insofar as this insight is infirm and must be completed by discursive argument, our participation in *intellectus*, which is the lowest among intellectual beings, is called *ratio*. St. Thomas says all of this as follows:

> the lower, namely, the human, intellects obtain their perfection in the knowledge of a truth by a kind of movement and discursive intellectual operation. That is to say, they obtain their perfection by advancing from one thing known to another. But if from the knowledge of a known principle they were straightaway to perceive as known all its consequent conclusions, then there would be no place for discursiveness in the human intellect. . . . But human souls which acquire the knowledge of truth discursively are called *rational*; and

this comes from the feebleness of their intellectual light. For if they possessed the fullness of intellectual light, like the angels, then in the first grasping of principles they would at once comprehend all their virtualities, by intuiting whatever could be gotten out of them by a syllogism [ST, I, 58, 3, c].

A similar line of reasoning leads St. Thomas to deny that angelic cognition proceeds by way of "composing and dividing" (judgment or assertion). For just as the strength of their intellectual light rules out the multiplicity of premiss and conclusion, so it rules out the multiplicity of subject and predicate:

if the intellect in apprehending the quiddity of the subject were at once to have knowledge of all that can be attributed to, or removed from, the subject, it would never understand by composing and dividing but only by understanding the essence. Hence, since the intellectual light is perfect in the angel, for he is a pure and clear mirror, as Dionysius says, it follows that as the angel does not understand by reasoning, so neither does he by composing and dividing [ST, I, 58, 4, c].

Angelic cognition is thus an ideal which human cognition can only vainly approximate. Angelic intellectuality is compared to human reason as the perfect to the imperfect, the strong to the weak, the simple to the complex, and as what is at rest to what must continue to strive. This differentiation of angelic and human intelligence is St. Thomas' version of a critique of reason, a setting forth of its limits, and hence, implicitly, a setting forth of the imperfection of any metaphysical science. In so doing, Thomas refers to the weaknesses of the intellect and the lowliness of human reason: surprising words from a thinker who is so widely taken to be a rationalist!

It is worth noting, in connection with our discussion of Father Clarke's thesis on the unsayability of *esse*, that the limitations which he points out are strictly "rational," that is, they apply only to human *ratio*. Clearly, an intellect which is not bound by the tripartite structure of concept, judgment, and ratiocination does not suffer from the inability to join subject and predicate of which Father Clarke speaks. For such an intelligence enjoys a simple *intuitus* or *intellectus* in which *esse* is apprehended in its simple reality. Here there is in principle no need to compose that which is with the act of being, no need to utter the proposition "God is"; there is only a simple vision of His reality.

But are we to understand that metaphysics belongs to the realm of *ratio* or of *intellectus*? Clearly, I think, to *ratio*, for metaphysics is a discursive science. Yet St. Thomas does not think that this is the last, or the most important, word about metaphysics. In discussing the division of the sciences, St. Thomas argues that natural science proceeds rationally (*rationabiliter*), mathematical science systematically (*disciplinabiliter*), but metaphysics intellectually (*intellectualiter*) (*Exp. Boeth. De Trin.* VI, 1). Though all the sciences use logic or discursive reason, the "rational" procedure is attributed to natural science with a special appropriateness. For "reason" is the specific difference of man and the uniquely proper mode of knowing. Now, in St. Thomas' Neo-Aristotelianism the distinctly "human" character of knowledge is found in its dependence upon perception. And it is in natural science above all that man moves from one object to the next, from effects to cause, discursively from one thing to another, laboriously building up a knowledge of the physical world. Similarly, all sciences proceed with scientific "discipline," that is, with a sense of rigorous proof and demonstrative certainty, but none exemplifies this as pre-eminently as mathematics.

Now, just as *ratio* is what is most in evidence in natural science, so the mode of *intellectus* is most in evidence in metaphysics. It is proper to *ratio*, St. Thomas says, to concern itself with the multiple things and "from them to gather [*collegere*] one simple knowledge"; reason tries to gather unity from the multiple. (No Heideggerian will fail to notice St. Thomas' association here of *ratio* with *collegere*, to collect.) St. Thomas writes: "But intellect conversely first considers one simple truth and in this grasps a knowledge of a whole multitude, as God, by understanding His essence, knows all things." Thus, as reason moves backward, by way of "resolution," from the many to the one, intellect moves forward, by way of "composition," from the one to the many. But it is the task of metaphysics to treat of that highest unity toward which all the sciences tend, and into which they are resolved, for metaphysics treats of the highest principles and supreme causes of all things. Though metaphysics, like every science, must make use of reason, and though it is permeated by rational and demonstrative argumentation, what is most distinctive about metaphysical knowledge is its character as the beginning (*principium*) and end (*terminus*) of reason. If natural science is in continual discourse from effect to cause, from accident to substance, metaphysics signifies, in its idea at least, a simple insight into the highest principles and ultimate causes under which all other things are comprehended.

St. Thomas appears to say that although metaphysics is embedded in reason and must carry out its life within the framework of discursive argumentation, it nonetheless strives to extricate itself from *ratio* and to transform itself into *intellectus*. For it can never be forgotten that it is impossible for metaphysics, as long as it is metaphysics, to lay aside the procedures of *ratio*. The insight of human metaphysical reason into its own first principles is so weak, its share in the intellectual light so small, that it cannot comprehend what is contained in its principles. It cannot comprehend what *esse* means apart from the multiplicity of composition and division. Its grasp of things is so frail that it must continually be filled out by rational discourse. Hence, the necessity for the demonstrations of God's existence, of His attributes, of the distinction between *esse* and essence, etc. The pages of St. Thomas' treatises are filled with a body of arguments which collectively go to make up what is called "Thomistic metaphysics." Even the painting of St. Thomas by Justus of Ghent which hangs in the Louvre portrays a composed and contemplative figure who appears to be enumerating arguments on his fingers! Hence, nothing has been easier for the students of St. Thomas—and sometimes even for St. Thomas himself—than to overlook the ultimately intellectual character of metaphysics in favor of its rational mode, or what Heidegger would call its onto-theo-logical nature. Nothing has been easier than to allow the element of simple, intuitive insight in metaphysics to be overshadowed by the noisy machinery of its elaborate and clever ratiocination.

St. Thomas is saying, not that metaphysics is *intellectus*, but that metaphysics wants to become *intellectus*. He seems to tell us that however much metaphysics is embedded in *ratio* it wants to extricate itself from *ratio*. There is a tendency within metaphysics to pass beyond itself, to overcome itself, and to become a simple vision. Metaphysics tends by its own nature to pass from the calculative to the meditative mode. But this remains forever impossible for metaphysics so long as metaphysics is a *scientia* practiced by men whose characteristic mode of thinking is "rational." What is needed to carry out this inner tendency of metaphysics, of which metaphysics itself remains incapable, is for man to take up an altogether new way of thinking, that of *intellectus* itself. This is possible for Thomas in a thoroughgoing and complete way only after death. But it is possible in the present life, as a foretaste and foreshadowing, in mystical experience. Metaphysics thus points toward mysticism. Mysticism is the terrestrial fulfillment of metaphysics, even as union with God is its celestial fulfillment.

INTELLECTUALISM AND MYSTICISM IN ST. THOMAS

Insofar as we take St. Thomas' metaphysics to be a species of rationalism, to be wedded to and infatuated with human *ratio*, we miss the radical critique of reason which is to be found in his works. St. Thomas' metaphysics is not a "-logic" in the strong sense in which Heidegger means this, where logic means *ratio*, precisely because Thomas takes *ratio* to be the lowest and most debilitated form of intellectuality. If one understands the deepest intentions of St. Thomas' metaphysics, one sees that it has more to do with mysticism than with logic and reason. Reason (*ratio*) is a form which metaphysics would shed *en route* to becoming *intellectus*. Now, no one has diagnosed St. Thomas' reflections on *ratio* with respect to *intellectus* more penetratingly than Pierre Rousselot has in his memorable, even if often forgotten, treatise of 1908, *The Intellectualism of St. Thomas*. No one has seen more clearly how the differentiation of *ratio* and *intellectus* is in fact a critique of reason. And no one has shown more forcefully the internal dynamism of St. Thomas' teaching on *intellectus* toward mystical experience. "Intellectualism"—a word which can hardly *not* be misunderstood today—means for Rousselot that the highest end of man is to be found not in *ratio* but in *intellectus*, where *intellectus* means not just simple "seeing" but unity, or what Heidegger might want to call the "identity" or "belonging together" of Being and thought. As Rousselot writes at the end of his extraordinary treatise:[16]

> Christian life seems to have developed in the soul of St. Thomas an enthusiasm for intelligence side by side with a disdain for mere human reasoning. In the last days of his life, therefore, he cannot be said to have abandoned his own theories, but rather to have made a practical application of them, when he prolonged his hours of con-

templation and ceased to study, *suspendit organa scriptionis*, as the rather untranslatable Latin of the Chronicler puts it. The *Summa* had not been completed and his companion pressed him to take up his pen again. "Impossible," St. Thomas told him, "all I have written now appears to me as so much straw." *Raynalde, non possum: quia omnia quae scripsi, videntur mihi paleae*. In these words, one may say without fear of paradox, we possess an exact formula in which to express the intellectualism of St. Thomas [p. 223].

In my judgment, Rousselot here touches bottom in terms of understanding the ultimate import of St. Thomas' thought. We are now for the first time in a position to begin to understand in what sense there is a community of insight and a genuine rapport between the two great thinkers whom I have taken as the theme of this study. The genuine point of contact is opened up by consideration not of *esse* but of *intellectus*, by means not of the Gilsonian thesis but of Rousselot's.

For Rousselot, St. Thomas' philosophy is essentially religious, and its religious character is not at odds with its "intellectualism," but identical with it. The intellect is not a faculty of generating concepts and weaving arguments, but a faculty of the divine, a *capax dei*. For it is in the intellect that the unity of the soul with God takes place. And since the essence of religion lies in unity with God, the essence of intellectualism and of religion coincide (pp. 217 ff.). Rousselot has in mind here St. Thomas' view of the beatific vision, in which God Himself serves as the intelligible species or *verbum mentale* in which the soul beholds the divine being (pp. 43–50; SCG, III, 51). Thus, the soul and God are united in the *visio dei*, fulfilling in a pre-eminent way the Scholastic dictum that to know is to become the other as other. The will tends toward God with love, and rejoices in the possession of God, but the formal character of union is nonetheless intellectual. The intellect is not primarily a rational faculty for Thomas but an intuitive one, and not merely intuitive but unitative. Thus, the theory of *intellectus* is a metaphysical elaboration of the essentially mystical and religious core of St. Thomas' thought. This illustrates quite exquisitely the unity of mysticism and metaphysics in medieval thought of which the young Heidegger spoke. That is why Rousselot will often contrast St. Thomas' "poetic vision" with his actual practice as a *magister*, in which he tended to succumb to "an unconscious fascination for the conceptual mode of thinking" (p. 12). This contrast is the very heart of my deconstructive reading of St. Thomas. Beneath the elaborate argumentation, the tantalizing distinctions and subtle technical discourse, there lies the mystical relationship of the soul to God. But this mystical vision is encased within *ratio* and hence easily forgotten by St. Thomas' readers and sometimes even by St. Thomas himself. Rousselot's book is therefore a retrieval, a *Wiederholung*, of what has fallen into oblivion in St. Thomas' metaphysics.

Because the ultimate meaning of *intellectus* is unitative, Rousselot also holds that the conception of truth as *adequatio* represents only a preliminary and transient notion of truth which does not touch its genuine sense:

> its [truth's] deep and ultimate meaning is less an *adequatio rei et intellectus* than an assimilation and union of mind with things. It is due to the infirmity of our minds that truth cannot be attained without recourse to the manipulation of many terms and to the process of *componendi et dividendi* [pp. 32–33].

Insofar as our intellects, in the present state of life, must draw intelligible sustenance from perception, and so are prohibited from functioning with the characteristic intuitiveness of *intellectus*, our intellectuality fails to be unitative and tends rather to be abstractive and representative. Yet even this *adequatio* is not a Cartesian subjectivism in which an interior self represents to itself the likeness of exterior things. Even on this level the mind is intentionally borne into knowledge of the world. Hence, even this *adequatio* aims at the *unio* and *assimilatio* which is achieved perfectly in the angelic and divine intellectuality. It would make no sense to speak of the intellectual union of the soul with God in the beatific union as an *adequatio*. For there one finds only direct union, possession, identity (*fieri quodammodo aliud*). The truth of *intellectus* is unitative not representational, experiential not objective. God is not an object grasped at a distance but a presence which envelops the soul. And the essence of truth is *assimilatio, Identität*.

Now, one might well argue that all this only proves Heidegger's point. For St. Thomas is saying that truth is *adequatio* in this life, which is after all the only one which Heidegger has in mind. But Rousselot wants to say that the overcoming of truth as *adequatio* is an intrinsic dynamism of the intellect even in its present state, and furthermore that it is a dynamism which is not without a certain realization here on earth, viz., in the mystical life of the soul. For what else is mystical experience but an overcoming of representationalism in favor of an immersion of the soul in the encompassing presence of the divine, in the only possible analogue in St. Thomas to ἀλήθεια?

In Rousselot's view, the actual conditions under which intellectuality is exercised in this life are seriously deficient and force the intellect to generate certain substitutes and imitations in order to make good for them (pp. 69–70). He studies four such substitutes: concept, science, system, and symbol. Thomas has disdain for such modes and takes them to arise from a defectiveness of the intellect. To this extent, then, Thomas has a strong sense of the onto-theo-*logical* character of metaphysics and of the need to overcome metaphysics. The *concept*, in Rousselot's reading of St. Thomas, is a most imperfect instrument. It lacks intuitiveness and determinateness—and this because it is drawn by abstraction from perception. This is to be contrasted with the creative intellectuality of God and the infused knowledge of angels in which there is a true intuition of the individual. Every "definition" of an "essence" in St. Thomas is an imperfect substitute on the part of the human intellect for its failure to grasp the individual in the fullness of its concrete being. Yet even Thomas himself exhibits a certain tendency to cling to his definitions and to become enamored of constructions which, on the basis of his own more "profound" and "poetic principles" (pp. 106, 108), must be understood as radically defective. Hence, any attempt to formulate a "definition" of the "essence" of Being can result only in an abstract and general concept which is quite unable to express what Being means. *Esse* can be grasped only by that face-to-face intellectuality in which the distinction between concept and judgment has been superseded, in which there is a simple intuition of Being. Hence, even the argument of Gilson and others that *esse* is grasped not in concept but in judgment does not go far enough, for this very distinction belongs to *ratio*.

Concepts are formed into judgments, and judgments are elaborated into a *science*. Science is but "a logical skeleton of the scheme of things" (p. 134). Hence, any attempt to articulate the meaning of *esse* within the limits of a science must fail, for it lacks intuitiveness and a firsthand quality. Finally, St. Thomas attempts to make good for the shortcomings of *ratio* by rounding off the edges of his *scientia* into a *system*, a complete elaboration of all assertions into a harmonious picture of the universe.[17] To illustrate this, Rousselot cites

Thomas' "argument" that, as Adam was born from neither man nor woman, and Eve from man without woman, so it is "appropriate" that Jesus be born from woman but not man. St. Thomas' works are filled with such arguments from convenience. These go together with the more serious demonstrations contained in his treatises to make up an aesthetic picture of the world. The method is "artistic," because "it would seem to have satisfied needs in the mind of that epoch for which art caters at the present day" (p. 148). St. Thomas wanted to bring the world into a harmony which satisfied the yearnings of the mind for that unity of vision which could only be supplied by *intellectus* and of which *ratio* remained forever incapable. These arguments are to be taken critically, as attempts of *ratio* to simulate the life of *intellectus*.

St. Thomas' thought is centered on a native dynamism of the mind toward the beatific vision, a dynamism which to be sure requires a supernatural aid in order to be satisfied (pp. 176–83; *Comp. theol.* 104). On earth this dynamism is felt in the natural need of the soul for mystical union. The life of St. Thomas, Rousselot thinks, bears testimony to his increasing distrust of merely earthly knowledge and an increasing recourse to contemplation and mystical prayer. Rousselot writes:

> We cannot but notice how naturally "mysticism" appears as the crowning part of "intellectualism" of which it is in reality the fruit. No matter how legitimate the opposition of mysticism and intellectualism may be in other respects and for other thinkers, no opposition is more superficial or more false when it is a question of orthodox mysticism and of the classical philosophy of Catholicism [p. 190].[18]

Unfortunately, Thomas does not elaborate upon the conditions and nature of mystical union. The closest he comes to it is the question on prophecy in which he discusses the nature of knowledge without images (ST, II–II, 171).

At this point, I should like to supplement Rousselot's argument about the lack of a theory of mysticism in St. Thomas. The word *mysticus* in St. Thomas' Latin means mysterious or hidden as well as parabolical or figurative. The doctrine of the immediate relationship of the soul to God is found in St. Thomas' treatment of *raptus*, rapture, to which he devotes two important questions (*De ver.* 9; ST,

II–II, 175). St. Thomas had it on the authority of Scripture itself that there were at least two cases of mystical experience, that is, of an immediate vision of the essence of God (we would prefer to say: experiences of the *esse* of God), while remaining bound to the body and the conditions of mortality. The first was that of St. Paul who was "caught up . . . into the third heaven" (*raptum usque ad tertium caelum*) (2 Co 12:2–4). Inspired by Augustine's gloss on this text, Thomas took up the question of "rapture." The other Scriptural case was Moses' encounter with God on the mountain. Thomas wants to know how the vision of God, which is the essential state of the blessed in heaven, can be realized on earth.

To begin with, he defines rapture as a kind of violence, that is, an exertion applied to a nature by an external agent which impels that nature beyond the limits of what it is capable of by its own natural powers (ST, II–II, 175, 1). He uses the example, possible only in medieval physics, of the natural place of a stone which tends by nature to fall downward. The stone may be violently propelled by an external agent either upward—which is against its nature—or downward—which carries out its own natural tendency in a way which far exceeds its own limits.[19] Mystical rapture is of the latter type, when the soul is impelled or elevated to a level of intellectuality which exceeds that of which it is of itself capable, although it tends naturally in that direction. Man tends naturally toward the divine, but always by means of the gathering of intelligible knowledge from the senses. But in rapture this mediation of the senses is suspended (*alienatus a sensibus*), and the soul is granted a face-to-face vision.

But then why was the vision of Paul not a fatal blow to his mortality which would have at once terminated his earthly existence by initiating him into eternal life? No man can see God and live. St. Thomas' answer is the key to his theory of mystical experience. The vision is possible only if the light of glory (*lumen gloriae*) is granted to the soul, that is, only if that light which is the divine essence itself shines upon the soul. This can come about in two ways: "In one way through the mode of an immanent form and that is how it makes the blessed holy in heaven. But in another way in the mode of a transient passion, as was said about the light of prophecy" (ST, II–II, 175, 3, ad 2). Paul was entered among the blessed, not *simpliciter*, but only *secundum quid*. He was given a passing participation, a fleeting initiation, into what the blessed possess habitually. Paul shared, not in the habit of the beatific vision, but in a transient act, while retaining here the habit of faith which does not see except darkly, through a glass: "It must be said that because Paul in his rapture was not made blessed habitually, but only had the act of the blessed, it follows that there was not simultaneously in him an act of faith. But there was simultaneously in him nevertheless a habit of faith" (ST, II–II, 175, 3, ad 3). This experience is the most perfect fulfillment of *intellectus*, its most complete and total actualization. On earth one can have, if not the habit, at least the act, the transient share, of the beatific vision.

Now, I do not think that one must read these questions as if it were Thomas' opinion that one must be a Paul or a Moses to enter into mystical experience. St. Thomas is seeking to explain here the fact of evident mystical experiences recorded by the Scriptures. But the conditions under which these experiences were possible apply to all men and can be realized by everyone to a greater or lesser extent—if not to the "third" heaven, then to a lesser heaven. Mysticism is nothing exotic, merely the natural terminus of nature and grace.[20] St. Thomas gives us here an account of how the soul is borne totally into God (*totaliter fertur in deum*) (ST, II–II, 175, 4, c), and what he says applies in varying degrees to every intellectual being, for the tendency toward an immediate experience of God is the natural and supernatural end of *intellectus* itself.[21]

Hence even if, on the most cold-blooded reading, St. Thomas' mystical experience was no more than a cerebral hemorrhage, Rousselot has demonstrated in the texts themselves the existence of a mystical element in St. Thomas' thought. For just as Heidegger wants to make the step back out of metaphysics, so there is in St. Thomas a tendency, a *desiderium naturale*, to divest oneself of the concepts, judgments, and ratiocinations of metaphysics in order to enter into the simplicity of *intellectus*. To Heidegger's *Seinserfahrung* I offer the mystical *pati divina* in St. Thomas. Here it seems to me is the heart of the relationship between these two thinkers.

FROM THOMAS TO ECKHART

I have shown that in Thomas' metaphysics there is a natural movement by which the imperfect instrument of *ratio* tends to fall under its own weight and to give way to a more perfect experience of Being. Thus far the mysticism which we have had in view is the crown and perfection of metaphysics, and hence the metaphysics we have had in view has remained intact, at least inasmuch as it has been granted a *provisional* justification as a ladder to be climbed and then discarded. Now, that is a crowning of metaphysics, but not a deconstruction of it. The mysticism in question is a mysticism of seeing and vision, of light and presence. But even if such a mysticism has laid aside the instrumentality of representational discourse, it nonetheless remains under the influence of the metaphysics which Heidegger criticizes. For metaphysics for Heidegger is not merely a methodological notion (it is "calculative" rather than "meditative" thinking), but also a "substantive" one (the matter [the *Sache*] of traditional metaphysics is pure Being and pure presence). Hence, the mysticism of pure presence does not overcome the metaphysics of pure presence, in Heidegger's view, but only extends it, completes it, crowns it. There is nothing "alethiological" about mystical experience so conceived, for there is no trace of λήθη, of the concealment of Being, of the Mystery.

Thus Heidegger does not hesitate to criticize the notion of *beatitudo* in St. Thomas (ST, III, 3, 5, c) on just these grounds.[22] The notion that knowledge is primarily and paradigmatically intuition is not new with Husserl, Heidegger says, but belongs to the mainstream of modern metaphysics. It is found in Kant and in the Rationalists. In particular he points out that the Cartesian distinction between *intuitus* and *deductio* is drawn from the Scholastics, where it is found not only among mystical thinkers, as one would expect (!), but even in the Aristotelian tradition, in St. Thomas. For in Aquinas intuition is not only the highest mode of knowledge but also the highest mode of Being of which man is capable. By means of it man is united with God Himself. The end of man is the *visio dei*, which is "a pure seeing and pure having present of God." The will, which *tends* toward God by love, does not *have* God *present* (*gegenwärtighaben*) as the intellect does. (Intuition, as Husserl points out, is fulfillment [*Erfüllung*].) The beatitude of man consists in the most perfect act of the most perfect faculty of man directed at its most perfect object—and this is the intellectual intuition of the divine being. Intellection for Thomas is nothing other than a certain way of having present (*intelligere nihil aliud est quam presentia quocumque modo*) and, as Heidegger explains, this means the presence of the knowable relative to knowledge.

Now, for Heidegger—who is objecting here not to eternal happiness but to Thomas' articulation of it—this conception of eternal happiness is not Christian but Greek. It moves within the framework of the Greek conception of θεωρεῖν and hence of the metaphysical conception of Being as presence and of thought as pure seeing, "looking at." In metaphysics Being means what is permanently and enduringly present (*stetige Anwesenheit*), and thinking means making it present. It assumes a temporal conception of Being where time is conceived primarily in terms of the present: time is a series of present moments, the past and future are a lack of presence, and eternity is a present which does not flow. But in a genuinely alethiological conception, absence and concealment belong to the very structure of appearance. Hence, in *Being and Time* the primary relationship of Dasein to the world is not theoretical: the "things" which are closest to Dasein are tools whose Being consists in withdrawing into inconspicuousness. Once they become conspicuously present they have lost their use. And so what *Being and Time* and the later works ever more clearly say is that Being is an emergent process in which the concealment from which they emerge is intrinsic to their appearance. Absence is inscribed in the essence of Being; concealment, in the essence of un-concealment. Being is a presence which lingers for a while between absence, and thinking is a continual openness toward absence, a resistance to the illusion that thought makes present, renders transparent. Thinking releases itself to the emergence of things and stays open to their ever-concealed depths, the mystery from which they spring.

Scholastic metaphysics, metaphysical theology, and mystical theology, Heidegger contends, are dominated by the paradigms of Being as presence and of thinking as the beholding (*intuitus*) of pure presence. So far from overcoming metaphysics, a mysticism so conceived in fact represents the jewel in its crown. And I do not think that there is anything in the argument which I have presented thus far which meets that critique. I have shown that there is an implicitly mystical tendency animating Thomistic metaphysics which overcomes the *modality* of metaphysics: it is no longer representational thinking; it lays aside discursive argumentation in order to enter into a deeper union. But the movement from metaphysics to union as it is portrayed by Thomas and his commentators is always a movement of progressive enlightenment, an ascent to an ever-more-perfect light and presence. It is a movement from light to light, from the light of reason (*lumen naturale*) to the light of faith (*lumen fidei*) to the light of glory (*lumen gloriae*). But once the Heideggerian notion of ἀλήθεια is given serious consideration, as I think it must, then we are forced to rethink these notions and to ask whether they are not simply a residue of Greek metaphysics rather than indigenous products of Christian life and religious experience. That is why I am now compelled to take another and more decisive step in the deconstructive reading of St. Thomas. For even if I have shown that *ratio* leads to *intellectus*, and that *intellectus* is the seat and site of mystical (and indeed of beatific) union, still the intellectual union of the soul with God belongs to the metaphysics of seeing and presence. This is true even if it is no longer a question of *conceptual* seeing and even if what is present is not an *object*. So long as we remain under the spell of Rousselot's religious intellectualism, or of St. Thomas' doctrine of *raptus*, Heidegger's critique of Thomas' understanding of Being is still not met. Hence, what I want to say now belongs, not to the *actuality* of Thomas' own teachings, but to the sphere of *possibilities* which inhere in his thought, possibilities which can be brought forth only by the hermeneutics of retrieval (*Wiederholung*). This is not to say that I am left entirely without direction in this undertaking. For I am able to turn to Thomas' successor in the Dominican chair at Paris a quarter of a century after his death, Meister Eckhart of Hochheim. From Meister Eckhart we shall learn that the Being of God is as much absence as it is presence, that it is presence in absence and absence in presence, that *intellectus* properly understood is not a matter of seeing but of letting-be and of openness to the Mystery. And lest the reader fear that I am putting words in Meister Eckhart's mouth, let him only recall that the talk of the divine abyss (*Abgrund*), of the nothing (*das Nichts*) and letting-be (*Gelassenheit*) belongs to the original vocabulary of Meister Eckhart, to whom Heidegger has often expressed his debt. And if Heidegger does not have a merely casual relationship to Meister Eckhart, neither does Meister Eckhart have a merely passing relationship to St. Thomas. Eckhart's work consists in no small part in driving the Thomistic theses (which he was committed to defend by reason of the professorial post which he held) to their mystical extreme, radicalizing them, pressing them so tightly as to make them yield their mystical sense. What is said in Thomas' writings remains too much under the spell of metaphysics, and that is why I must at this point look to what is unsaid in these writings. And for that I turn to Meister Eckhart. Meister Eckhart is the middle term in this study, the point of interaction between Thomas and Heidegger, and it is only with the move from Thomas to Eckhart that the argument of the present study is completed. Eckhart was no commentator on the mystical element in Thomas' writings, like Rousselot or Maréchal or Maritain, but an independent preacher and practitioner of the mystical life who drew his inspiration from St. Thomas. Eckhart preached and wrote out of the experience of mystical life, as Heidegger taught and wrote out of the experience of thought (*aus der Erfahrung des Denkens*). As Bernard Welte claims, in the actuality of Meister Eckhart there unfolds a possibility in Thomas Aquinas.[23] Hence, if my deconstructive reading of St. Thomas was initiated by listening to Rousselot, it can be completed only by listening to Meister Eckhart.

Under the influence of Eckhart's mystical hand, both *esse* and *intellectus* undergo a transforming change in which their mystical sense is finally made explicit. I shall take up each of these notions in turn.

Eckhart says that Being is God (*esse est deus*); this is the more radicalized version of the Thomistic thesis that God is His own act of being (*deus est suum esse*).[24] And it is meant to stress the way in which the creature is dependent through and through upon the pure Being of God. But Eckhart is also able to deny Being of God, for the Being of God is so pre-eminently pure and perfect that if beings (creatures) are, then God is not. Hence, if God is the ground of beings, then He is also an abyss which withdraws from view. If God is Being—the Being from which beings emerge—He is also Nothing, the Mystery which is concealed by beings. Hence, there is considerable talk in Meister Eckhart's sermons of the divine abyss, the divine nothingness, and quite frequently of the divine "wasteland" (*Wüste*), that absolute desert in which no conceptual being can grow, in which every construct of the understanding withers and is desiccated by the intensity of the divine heat. Eckhart has a strong and lively sense of the debility of human thought, the inability of the constructs of human subjectivity to gain access to the genuine depths of the divine Being. He writes of our need to lay aside the purely thought-up God (*der gedachte Gott*) for the sake of the truly divine God (*der göttliche Gott*). The God whom human thoughts and words think they lay hold of is precisely *not* God. The depth of the divine God is such that it continually withdraws behind every name which is addressed to it, eludes every conceptual net which is thrown over it.

The strongest formula which Eckhart uses to express the transcendent mystery of the divine abyss is found in his famous sermon on the "poverty of spirit." Not only must the soul become poor in spirit in order to receive God, stripped naked of all attachment to creatures, to its own thoughts about God and personal desires, but God Himself must also become poor, that is, stripped down of all His attributes and "properties," of everything which we call "God." Hence, Eckhart writes "I ask God that He rid me of God." Here, in what I have elsewhere called Eckhart's "mystical atheism," is Eckhart's strongest formulation of the abyss and nothingness of God's Being and of the utter impotence of any metaphysical theology to seize Him with its concepts.[25] This God beyond God, this absolutely transcendent and hidden depth in God, is called by Eckhart the Godhead within God (the *deitas* in *deus*, the *Gottheit* in *Gott*), and it functions quite explicitly for him as the λήθη in ἀλήθεια, the concealed and withdrawn depths in the manifest God. Hence, Eckhart prays that he be rid of the manifest God in order to remain open to the hidden God. "God" is everything we say of Him, whereas the Godhead remains behind, its essential Being untouched by this discourse. For if "God" is Father, Son, and Spirit, *causa prima*, creator, omniscient and omnipotent, then the Godhead is none of these things; it is *prior* to these things, deeper, not *yet* manifest, the concealed *Wesen*, the *Ab-wesen*, in the manifest God (*An-wesen*). All the names of "God," whether they are drawn from philosophy or faith, metaphysics or theology, fall short of the divine abyss.

Eckhart's formulations of the divine abyss were profoundly shocking to the churchmen of his day, perhaps because they sensed that there was underway here a deconstructive attack upon metaphysics which would undo the objectivism to which the ecclesiastical bureaucracy, which knows nothing of *Gelassenheit*, is so closely wedded. And so on this point too Eckhart followed in the steps of Brother Thomas, and his thought was officially censured! In that papal Bull is expressed the condemnation of thought by onto-theo-logic.

But if Eckhart speaks on the one side of the naked poverty and the wasteland of the divine *esse*, he also understands the poverty and nothingness of *intellectus*. If *intellectus* means *intuitus* for Thomas

Aquinas, it comes to mean "detachment" in Meister Eckhart. In a brilliant set of questions argued at Paris in 1301 Eckhart defends the "nothingness of the intellect" as opposed to the plenitude (presence) of Being. Following up the Aristotelian formula that the soul is a *tabula rasa*, Eckhart argues that it is not Being, but what knows Being, an openness to Being which is divested of Being in order to be taken over by Being.[26] Here Eckhart argues for a Scholastic thesis which articulates on the metaphysical level the very mystical deconstruction of metaphysics which is at work in his sermons. For he argues philosophically that *intellectus* means emptiness, openness, just as he thinks that mystically it means detachment, self-divesting. The intellectual soul is most truly itself when it has divested itself of all its images, all its desires and affects, and become a purely open space into which God alone can enter.

Hence, in these perfectly extraordinary *questiones* Eckhart makes the astonishing transformation of an Hellenically inspired *intellectus* into religious detachment, and detachment is *Gelassenheit*. The fully radicalized meaning of *intellectus* in Meister Eckhart then is *Gelassenheit*. And with this move, with this transformation, the argument of the present study reaches its climax. For here the implicitly mystical sense of the Thomistic metaphysics of *intellectus* and *esse* is made explicit, and the bridge is built from Heidegger to Aquinas, a bridge which simply cannot be found so long as one remains on the level of the historical actuality of Thomas' own teachings.

In *Gelassenheit* the soul surrenders itself to the divine Being and does not merely "look on" from a safe distance. In the authentic mysticism of Meister Eckhart, the whole "judicial" posture of metaphysical thought is broken; the soul gives itself over to God, lets God be God. It does not keep its distance from God but yields itself up to Him. The paradigm of the Greek spectator, of the onlooker, which reaches all the way from Parmenides to Husserl, is entirely overcome. We are at least as likely to hear erotic discourse in Meister Eckhart— the naked unity of the soul and God—as Hellenic visual metaphors. There is a question, not of looking at God, but of yielding to His embrace.

Now, the lethic dimension, the element of concealment and hiddenness, is preserved only in a doctrine of *Gelassenheit*. For in *Gelassenheit* we put ourselves at the disposal of the matter and no longer attempt to reign over it with our concepts. In our surrendering to it, *it alone* holds sway; the matter is not seized about, but let-be and hence preserved in its inexhaustibility. That is why Heidegger exploits the twofold sense of the German *ver-borgen* as both concealing and protecting, as in the English "sheltering" or "harboring." If the matter were wholly subject to thought, it would vaporize into a thought-construction, lose itself in our thought. Λήθη is lost therefore the moment that thinking detaches itself from the thing and assumes the posture of onlooker, of the judge and jury of the "object." The "thing" (in Heidegger's terms) becomes an "object," λήθη is lost, and we are left with a metaphysical construction of a transparently present object.

Gelassenheit is openness to the Mystery, as Heidegger says (G 26/55). And mystical *Gelassenheit* is openness to the divine transcendence, to the Mystery of the divine abyss. Mystical *Gelassenheit* is the sheltering of the mystery of God from the assault of metaphysics. It is a letting-be which lets the divine λήθη hold sway, which releases the divine God and detaches itself from the God which subjectivity has constructed. Mystical *Gelassenheit* is an openness to the Word which preserves that Word in its unnamability.

Hence, if in Thomas and his commentators we are more likely to find an ascent to enlightenment, a movement from light to light, we find in Meister Eckhart rather a *descent* into the divine depths, into the unknown. Mysticism is for Eckhart a shattering of every human idol, of the whole positivity of metaphysics. It is detachment—from our concepts, our desires, our selves. It breaks the illusion of clarity and transparency. Mysticism is μύειν, closing one's eyes and lips to the idols of subjectivity in order to let the truly divine God be heard. This mystical atheism is closer to the truly divine God, as Heidegger says, than is the God which is spoken of in onto-theo-logic (ID 141/72).

It is therefore in Meister Eckhart that the overcoming of metaphysics which is implicit in Thomistic metaphysics is made explicit, that a possibility which is *in* St. Thomas (if not altogether a possibility *for* St. Thomas) gets worked out. And although this is not the place to work out the full debt of Eckhart to Thomas,[27] the full measure of the impetus which he received from Thomas, let me only emphasize that Eckhart considered himself not to be controverting Aquinas but to be radicalizing and extending him. Eckhart saw beneath the cool prose of St. Thomas' Scholasticism a vibrant mysticism. Perhaps he was prompted in this direction in the first place, as Matthew Fox suggests,[28] because he had heard from his earliest years in the Dominican Order of the celebrated mystical experience of St. Thomas, a point the Dominicans vigorously promoted in Thomas' canonization process. But be that as it may, there are lines of force reaching out from Thomas directly into Eckhart's sermons. It is not hard to hear beneath Eckhart's mystical formula, *esse est deus*, Being is God, Thomas' more restrained *deus est suum esse*, God is His own act of Being. It is not hard to hear in Eckhart's doctrine of the ground of the soul (*Seelengrund*) echoes of the Thomistic theory of the substance of the soul as the root from which its faculties flow. Eckhart would have read of the *scintilla rationis* in St. Thomas (*In II Sent.*, d. 39, II, 1), an obvious ancestor of his teaching about the "little spark in the soul" (*Seelenfünklein, scintilla animae*). And Eckhart's teachings about the birth of the Son draw in no small measure upon Thomas' teachings on grace. Eckhart also cites Thomas' question on rapture.[29] It is no wonder that Eckhart answered his accusers in the Inquisition by saying that he said no more than is taught in the *Summa* of Brother Thomas. And indeed this *is* what is said *in* Thomas if not *by* Thomas, now stripped of its onto-theo-logical encasement, pushed to mystical conclusion and now recast, not in the terms of Scholastic objectivism, but in terms of a living alethiology.

HEIDEGGER VS. ST. THOMAS

What, then, is the difference between Heidegger and this metaphysically deconstructed and mystically reconstructed Thomas Aquinas? Let me emphasize again that I think there is nothing to gain from easy syncretisms and historical conflations. I do not say that Eckhart and Aquinas are to be identified; I do say that Eckhart works out a possibility which is latent in the historical actuality of Thomas Aquinas. But I have labored earnestly in the preceding chapters to keep the historical actuality of Thomas in focus. Now I must add, and this is more important still, that I do not want to identify this mystical tendency which is latent in Aquinas and overt in Eckhart with Martin Heidegger. I have set this forth in my study of Eckhart and Heidegger,[30] but it is well to reaffirm it here, and in the terms which are proper to this study.

This can be done by returning to the all-important issue of the λήθη in ἀλήθεια. In Heidegger the hiddenness of Being, the withdrawn depths from which beings emerge into presence, is something final. There is no further dimension which can be anticipated in which it would be possible to shed light on this darkness. *Gelassenheit*, the openness of thought to these mysterious depths, is the ultimate attitude which one can adopt. But in a religious mysticism such as is implicit in Thomas and explicit in Eckhart, this is not the case. For in these thinkers the hidden depths are the depths of the divine Godhead itself, and if they are hidden *from us*—permanently and in principle—they are not hidden from the Godhead itself. There, in the depths of the Godhead, God is known *to Himself*. There, in the Godhead itself, a concealed unity of Being and thought holds sway, which eye has not seen nor ear heard. There can be talk of mystery and abyss *in* God but not *for* God. God is the Mystery, but the mystery is not mysterious to itself. The concealed depths of the Godhead are not concealed from God; they *are* God. There the eternal Word is spoken which no human word can name; there is God's unnamable self-knowledge. How God is in Himself, in His withdrawn depths, cannot be named by us, but His own presence to Himself and knowledge of Himself in these depths is what all men call God, and it is definitive (negatively!) of His Being. The believer cannot suppose that the Being in whom he puts his faith is subject to the same limitations as the believer himself. That is to make foolery out of faith and religious experience. Religious *Gelassenheit* is openness to the mystery, but the mystery is not concealed from itself. It is, and this is the believer's faith, a sphere of self-openness, self-presence.

Hence, at the risk of shocking the Heideggerians who are accustomed to bend their knee at the mention of λήθη, I must say that λήθη and absence are nothing to be sought in themselves. They are the conditions of finite thinking and the only way we can preserve the integrity and independence of the matter for thought. But for a thinking which has been released from the conditions of finitude—a standpoint which we can never adopt and which belongs exclusively to God—there is only presence and only manifestness. There is after all nothing intrinsically to be preferred about concealment, a point at which some Heideggerians are apt to rend their garments. And it belongs to the believer's faith and his trust in the light—or in the darkness—that whatever God may be like in His hidden Godhead, there is nothing to fear in God but only to love, as Meister Eckhart said. The important thing to bear in mind, and this is a point which religious thinkers are wont to forget, is that this is a standpoint which we are incapable of assuming. We can never pretend to have seen the light, to have penetrated the darkness, to have been liberated from the conditions of finitude. That indeed is what Kierkegaard was always protesting to Hegel: I assume, he said mockingly, that I have the honor to address a fellow human being, one who is subject, that is, to the conditions of finite thinking.[31]

Hence, while for the believer God is an ever-deepening mystery, a darkness, this is a darkness in which the believer has a certain trust, in which he believes himself to sense a loving if inscrutable hand. But nothing like that can be so for Heidegger, because the mystery of ἀλήθεια is not for him the mystery of a person whose depths we cannot fathom, but the mysterious play of presence and absence, of Being's emergence into presence for us. Heidegger's ἀλήθεια is emphatically not God even if the believer's God has an alethiological dimension. Ἀλήθεια is the play of Being for Heidegger, the successive movements of Western history. In a religious mystic, *Gelassenheit* is a loving trust in an impenetrable mystery; in Heidegger it is the openness of thought to an inscrutable play.

For the religious thinker, to put it in onto-theo-logical terms, God is a mystery *quoad nos* (for us) but not *quoad se* (for Himself). But we can*not* say of Heidegger's Being that it is a mystery not only *quoad nos* but also *quoad se*. For it makes no sense to speak of Being *quoad se* for Heidegger. Heidegger's Being is not a person which is capable of self-knowledge, but a process which achieves self-manifestation only in and through human thought. Hence, Being is always and in principle taken as Being *quoad nos* in Heidegger, that is, in its belonging together with human thought. Heidegger's thinking is irrevocably committed to its experiential and finite standpoint, and so there is no possibility in Heidegger of speaking, even with the uncertainty of faith, of Being *quoad se*. Being is always Being in its belonging together with thought. Both Being and thought then are taken in their irrevocably finite sense.

That is why Heidegger says that Being *needs* thought, that it requires thinking for its self-manifestation. For, all along, Being for Heidegger is the Being which reveals itself in and through human thought. If there is no humanism in Heidegger in the sense which he rejects (viz., a subjectivism which simply subjects Being to human requirements), there is a humanism in the higher sense, that he always thinks a Being which needs and uses man (*Weg.*[2] 342–43/222). But the God of the religious thinker is under no such necessity. His self-revelation to man is an act of unmotivated love, an overflowing of His riches into the soul, a loving outpouring which admits man into a privileged nearness with the divine Being. The Being of Heidegger is always finite, needful of man; the Being of the religious mystic is the divine plenitude and sufficiency.

Heidegger does not think an eternal and loving Father, an all-perfect and personal Being; he thinks a world power which governs over the succession of world epochs, the original source from which the successive grantings of Being from age to age issue. Heidegger is intent on thinking the meaning of Western history, a history which he conceives not in the ordinary sense as a sequence of happenings, but as a history of truth and un-truth, as a play of light and darkness, of successive clearings in which the various "worlds" of Western historical man are rendered open and manifest. For Heidegger "God" makes an appearance within this clearing—or remains absent from it. But God is not the clearing itself; nor is the clearing the gift of God. Heidegger's thinking has something of a "secular" character in the sense that he is concerned with the *saeculum*, with past and coming ages, and not with eternity.

But the simple unity of *esse* and *intellectus* which stands at the summit of St. Thomas' doctrine is essentially found beyond time and history. This *unio* takes place most perfectly in eternity, in *patria*, in the homeland of the soul outside of time. To the extent that it is anticipated on earth, there is an anticipation of eternity, a shrouded and momentary experience of eternal things. There can be no confusing the mystical unity with God in Thomas or Eckhart with the belonging together of Being and thought in Heidegger. Even though both experiences are of a profoundly non-metaphysical character, even though both lie beyond the borders of onto-theo-logic, they inhabit nonetheless very different regions within this sphere. God for St. Thomas is not taken to be a function of the historical clearing; rather He rules over time and is the Lord of history. The created world is an imitation of the divine Being and the goal of the creature is to re-enter that original union which it possessed with God, as Meister Eckhart says, before it was created, when it was no more than an idea in the mind of God. *Exitus* is to be followed by *reditus*; that is the architectonic principle of the *Summa theologica* and of Eckhart's sermons. Heidegger's *Ereignis*, if it can be anything at all for St. Thomas, must be subordinate to God. Aquinas' God, if He can be anything at all for Heidegger, must be granted by the *Ereignis*.

CONCLUSION:
TOWARD A RELIGIOUS ALETHIOLOGY

Behind the discursive arguments, the conceptual distinctions, the whole impressive display of *ratio* which is found in St. Thomas, there lies hidden an experience of Being. Behind the sober and cool-headed account of God and the soul and the world, there lies a profound, if implicit, mysticism. In the end, St. Thomas is properly understood only by converting the coin of his metaphysical theology into its religious and alethiological equivalent. Scholastic objectivism must give way to a religious alethiology. We must learn to hear St. Thomas' words anew, divested of their onto-theo-logical significance and re-invested with their experiential value. We must hear in *esse*, not the Roman *actualitas* described by Heidegger, but the intensely Christian experience of Being, a religious experience of God's presence in the world and in the soul. We must hear in *esse* upsurge, coming-to-presence, *An-wesen*, not the *sistere extra causas* of Scholastic metaphysics. We must find in God's relationship to the world not causality but presencing. For if God is in all things inasmuch as all things have *esse*, then God, from whom their *esse* is shared, is present to them. We must learn to think of God not as the cause of the world but as that fullness of presence which is intimately present to the Being of things: "as long as a thing has *esse* God must be present to [*adest*] it, according to its mode of Being. But *esse* is what is innermost in all things. . . . Hence, it must be that God is in all things and intimately so" (ST, I, 8, 1, c). The *esse* of creatures is their coming-to-presence in the world; the *esse* of God is the mystery of presence which is intimately present in everything which is present. The doctrine of participation must cease to be a causal theory which articulates the dynamics of the creative action and become a doctrine of presencing, as Max Müller has argued.[32] This means that the task of thought must be, not to account for things by means of a causal reckoning, but to savor the Being of things, to meditate their presence, to learn to see in the reflected light of creatures the light of Being itself, a light which is also a primordial darkness. We must reinvest God and the world with their religious mysteriousness. We must acquire a sense of the weakness of *ratio* in order to esteem the splendor of *intellectus*, and abjure the cleverness of *ratio* to protect the simplicity of *intellectus*. For *intellectus* is the splendor of the simple (AED 13/7). And we must learn that in the end the simplicity of *intellectus* has nothing to do with the Greek "intuition," that it is religious *Gelassenheit*, letting-be, that openness which puts concepts aside and lets God be God and thus lets the Mystery hold sway.

It is a great mistake to conflate the metaphysics of St. Thomas with the rationalist systems of modern metaphysics, to forget its essentially religious and mystical inspiration. It is a mistake to remain only on the level of what Thomas has explicitly said and to pay no heed to what is unsaid. And if the Thomists are wrong to insist that the doctrine of *esse* as the *actualitas omnium actuum* is as it stands a response to Heidegger—instead of a confirmation of his worst suspicions—the Heideggerians are wrong to think that the doctrine of *actualitas* is all there *is* to this thinker. Oddly enough, the Heideggerians have not listened attentively enough to what is unsaid in these sayings, *das im Sagen Ungesagte*, not even when they are put on warning by Thomas himself. For in Thomas' exclamation to Reginald, "*Raynalde, Raynalde, non possum*," there lies the highest possibility in St. Thomas' thought. And possibility is always higher than actuality, *sicut Martinus dixit*.

NOTES

1. This is the principal argument of my *Mystical Element in Heidegger's Thought*, especially in the last chapter.

2. See the "Translator's Preface" in Jacques Derrida, *Of Grammatology*, trans. Gayatri Chakravorty Spivak (Baltimore & London: The Johns Hopkins University Press, 1974), pp. xlviii–xlix. See also Heidegger, *Vier Seminare*, trans. Ochwadt, p. 75.

3. *The Silence of St. Thomas*, trans. John Murray, s.J., and Daniel O'Connor (New York: Pantheon, 1957), pp. 45–46.

4. Consider the following passage from the *Habilitationsschrift*: "If one reflects on the deeper essence of philosophy, its essence as a world view, then

the conception of the Christian philosophy of the Middle Ages as a Scholasticism which stands in opposition to a contemporaneous *mysticism* must be exposed as fundamentally mistaken. In the medieval world view, Scholasticism and mysticism essentially belong together. The two pairs of 'opposites,' rationalism–irrationalism and Scholasticism–mysticism, *do not coincide*. And where their equivalence is sought, it rests on an extreme rationalization of philosophy. Philosophy as a rationalist structure, detached from life, is *impotent*. Mysticism as an irrationalist experience is purposeless" (FS² 410). Heidegger's views at that time seem to coincide nicely with those of Pierre Rousselot, who wrote a few years earlier: "only a pronounced mental rigidity and the lack of psychological imagination would prevent one from seeing the possibility of a subjective co-existence, and even compenetration, of rational Aristotelianism and a mysticism such as that of the Victors or of a St. Bernard. Speculative thought was not, and could not have been, isolated from the religious life which was so intense in the Middle Ages; the *Itinerarium mentis ad Deum* and the *Incendium amoris* [of St. Bonaventure] are not fully appreciated independently of the *Breviloquium*" (*The Intellectualism of St. Thomas*, trans. James E. O'Mahony, O.M.Cap. [London: Sheed & Ward, 1935], p. 7n3).

5. I do not think that Thomistic metaphysics is onto-theo-logic in the strong sense. It is not an onto-logic insofar as its focus is on *esse*, not *ens*; not a theo-logic, insofar as God is not a highest being so much as pure Being; not an outright -logic, inasmuch as it admits of the deconstruction of which I am speaking here. But it is an onto-theo-logic in the weak sense inasmuch as it belongs to the objectivistic mode of discourse which thinks short of the *Ereignis*.

6. James A. Weisheipl, o.p., *Friar Thomas d'Aquino: His Life, Thoughts, and Works* (Garden City, N.Y.: Doubleday, 1974). p. 321. The relevant Latin texts are found in the footnotes of the old biography by Roger Bede Vaughn, o.s.b., *The Life and Labours of St. Thomas of Aquin*, 2 vols. (London: Longmans, 1872), II 917–18, and in *Fontes vitae sancti Thomae Aquinatis*, ed. D. Prümmer (Toulouse, n.d.), pp. 376–78, originally published as supplements to *Revue Thomiste*, 1911–1934. See also Pieper's account of this story in *Silence*, pp. 38–40.

7. "The Legend of St. Thomas Aquinas," in *St. Thomas Aquinas, 1274–1974*, ed. Maurer, I 26.

8. Weisheipl, *Friar Thomas d'Aquino*, p. 323.

9. See the dispute between Gilson and Regis on the "conceivability" of *esse* in *Being and Some Philosophers*, pp. 216–27.

10. "What Cannot Be Said in St. Thomas' Essence–Existence Doctrine," *The New Scholasticism*, 48 (1974), 19.

11. Ibid., 25.

12. *Elements of Christian Philosophy* (New York: Mentor Omega, 1960), pp. 119–20.

13. I also recommend to the reader's attention Joseph Owens, "Aquinas— 'Darkness of Ignorance' in the Most Refined Notion of God," in *Bonaventure and Aquinas: Enduring Philosophers*, edd. Robert W. Shahan and Francis J.

Kovach (Norman: University of Oklahoma Press, 1976), pp. 69–86, which establishes a quite similar point. Owens discusses a remarkable text from the commentary on the Sentences (*In I Sent.*, 8, 1, 1, ad 4) in which St. Thomas speaks of the *confusio* and *tenebra ignorantiae* in which our knowledge of God is enveloped. The name of God is Being, St. Thomas says following Damascene, in the sense of an "infinite ocean of substance," or, to use more Heideggerian expression, an "abyss" (*Abgrund*), which is withdrawn from our concepts and representations. The notion of subsistent *esse* cannot be grasped in an act of conceptualization nor is it intuitively given to judgment, as in the case of a sensible existent. It is enshrouded in a supreme darkness which protects it from the distortions which the conditions of a purely human *ratio* would tend to impose upon it.

14. It should not be imagined, however, that in rapture or even in the beatific vision itself the incomprehensibility of God is overcome. On the contrary, there is an essential disproportion between the finitude of the human intellect and the infinity of the divine *esse*. Cf. Rahner's "Thomas Aquinas on the Incomprehensibility of God."

15. "Twentieth-Century Scholasticism," *The Journal of Religion*, 58 (Supplement 1978), S201–202.

16. All page numbers enclosed in parentheses in this section will be to Rousselot's work (see note 4), unless otherwise noted.

17. One notices the Kantian strains in Rousselot: the pure concept is empty; science (*Verstand*) wants to become system (*Vernunft*), which is a perfectly harmonious and ideal concatenation of scientific propositions. *Verstand* wants to become *Vernunft*, which is an infinite yearning, that is, the intellectual dynamism of which Rousselot and, with him, Maréchal speak. The Jesuit Rousselot belongs to the prehistory of Transcendental Thomism and is an antecedent of Maréchal. The philosophy of *intellectus* is a critique of reason (*ratio*).

18. Compare this text to the text of Heidegger cited above in note 4.

19. Hermeneutic violence is likewise a positive violence which propels a text beyond the level which it has attained by its own powers, yet nonetheless in the very direction in which the text itself tends—hence, in harmony with and not against its nature.

20. This is, in my understanding, traditional Catholic teaching. It was certainly the view of Maritain and Garrigou-Lagrange.

21. Cf. James E. O'Mahony, O.M.Cap., *The Desire of God in the Philosophy of St. Thomas Aquinas* (Cork: Longmans, Green, 1929). Father O'Mahony is the translator of Rousselot's book.

22. *Logik: Die Frage nach der Wahrheit*, Collected Works 21 (Frankfurt: Klostermann, 1976), pp. 121–23. See also John Sallis, "Into the Clearing" in *Heidegger: The Man and the Thinker*, ed. Thomas Sheehan (Chicago: Precedent, 1981), pp. 113–15.

23. "Thomas von Aquin und Heideggers Gedanke von der Seinsgeschichte," pp. 203–18.

24. For what follows on Meister Eckhart, see my "Fundamental Themes in

Meister Eckhart's Mysticism," *The Thomist*, 42, No. 2 (April 1978), 210–11, and chap. 3 of my *Mystical Element in Heidegger's Thought*.

25. See my "Fundamental Themes," 210–11.

26. See my "The Nothingness of the Intellect in Meister Eckhart's *Parisian Questions*," *The Thomist*, 39, No. 1 (January 1975), 85–115, for a discussion of the mystical meaning of *intellectus* in Meister Eckhart. See also Ruedi Imbach, *Deus est intelligere*. *Das Verhältnis von Sein und Denken in seiner Bedeutung für das Gottesverständnis bei Thomas von Aquin und in den Pariser Questionen Meister Eckharts* (Fribourg: Universitätsverlag, 1976).

27. I have made some comments in this direction in my "Fundamental Themes." See also Alois Dempf, *Meister Eckhart* (Freiburg: Herder, 1960), passim; and Bernhard Welte, "Meister Eckhart als Aristoteliker," *Auf der Spur des Ewigen: Philosophische Abhandlungen über verschiedene Gegenstände der Religion und der Theologie* (Freiburg: Herder, 1965), pp. 197–210.

28. *Breakthrough: Meister's Eckhart's Creation Spirituality*, ed. and trans. Matthew Fox (Garden City, N.Y.: Doubleday Image, 1980), pp. 26–30.

29. *Die deutschen Werke*. V. *Meister Eckharts Traktate*, ed. Josef Quint (Stuttgart: Kohlhammer, 1963), pp. 544, 452n68. See *De ver.* 13, 2, ad 9. See also my *Mystical Element in Heidegger's Thought*, pp. 14–15.

30. See the six points of difference between mysticism and thought enumerated in *Mystical Element in Heidegger's Thought*, pp. 223–40.

31. *Concluding Unscientific Postscript*, trans. David F. Swenson and Walter Lowrie (Princeton: Princeton University Press, 1941; repr. 1963), pp. 99, 272, 324, and passim.

32. *Existenzphilosophie*, p. 245.

BIBLIOGRAPHY

I · Primary Sources

A. MARTIN HEIDEGGER

The following Bibliography attempts, not to be exhaustive, but merely to provide the reader with references to the more important works of Heidegger and to existing English translations. Complete information through 1972 is available from Hans-Martin Sass, *Heidegger-Bibliographie* (Meisenheim: Hain, 1968) and *Materialien zu Heidegger-Bibliographie, 1917-1972* (Meisenheim: Hain, 1972). See also his more recent *Martin Heidegger: Bibliography and Glossary* (Bowling Green, Ohio: Philosophy Documentation Center, 1982).

Aus der Erfahrung des Denkens. Pfullingen: Neske, 1965.   (AED)
   "The Thinker as Poet." In *Poetry, Language, Thought.*
   Trans. Albert Hofstadter. New York: Harper & Row,
   1971. Pp. 1–14.
Einführung in die Metaphysik. Tübingen: Niemeyer, 1958   (EM)
   An Introduction to Metaphysics. Trans. Ralph Manheim.
   Garden City, N.Y.: Doubleday Anchor, 1961.
Erläuterungen zu Hölderlins Dichtung. Frankfurt: Klostermann, 1963.
   Pp. 7–30: "Remembrance of the Poet." Trans. Douglas
   Scott. In *Existence and Being.* Ed. Werner Brock. Chicago: Regnery, 1949. Pp. 233–69.

   Pp. 31–46: "Hölderlin and the Essence of Poetry."
   Trans. Douglas Scott. In *Existence and Being.* Pp. 270–91.
Der Feldweg. Frankfurt: Klostermann, 1962.   (FW)
   "The Pathway." Trans. Thomas F. O'Meara, O.P., rev.
   Thomas J. Sheehan. *Listening,* 8, No. 1 (Winter 1973),
   32–39.
Die Frage nach dem Ding. Tübingen: Niemeyer, 1962.
   What Is a Thing? Trans. W. B. Barton, Jr., and Vera
   Deutsch. Chicago: Regnery, 1967. (Excerpts from this
   translation also appear in *Martin Heidegger: Basic Writings,* ed. David Farrell Krell [New York: Harper & Row,
   1977], pp. 247–82.)

Gelassenheit. Pfullingen: Neske, 1960.   (G)
    Discourse on Thinking. Trans. John M. Anderson and E.
    Hans Freund. New York: Harper & Row, 1966.

Gesamtausgabe:

I. *Frühe Schriften*. Frankfurt: Klostermann, 1978.   (FS²)
    Pp. 1–15: "The Problem of Reality in Modern Philos-
    ophy." Trans. Philip J. Bossert. *Journal of the British
    Society for Phenomenology*, 4, No. 1 (January 1973),
    64–71.

II. *Sein und Zeit*. Frankfurt: Klostermann, 1977.

IV. *Erläuterungen zu Hölderlins Dichtung*. Frankfurt: Klos-
    termann, 1981.

V. *Holzwege*. Frankfurt: Klostermann, 1971.   (*Holz.*²)
    Pp. 1–74: "The Origin of the Work of Art." In *Poetry,
    Language, Thought*. Trans. Albert Hofstadter. New
    York: Harper & Row, 1971. Pp. 15–87. Repr. (in
    abridged form) in *Martin Heidegger: Basic Writings*. Ed.
    David Farrell Krell. New York: Harper & Row, 1977.
    Pp. 149–87.

    Pp. 75–114: "The Age of the World-View." Trans. M.
    Grene. *Boundary 2: A Journal of Postmodern Literature*,
    4 (1976), 341–55; and "The Age of the World Picture."
    In *The Question Concerning Technology and Other Es-
    says*. Trans. William Lovitt. New York: Harper & Row,
    1977. Pp. 115–54.

    Pp. 115–208: *Hegel's Concept of Experience*. New York:
    Harper & Row, 1970.

    Pp. 209–68: "The Word of Nietzsche: 'God is Dead.' "
    In *The Question Concerning Technology and Other Es-
    says*." Pp. 53–114.

    Pp. 269–320: "What Are Poets For?" In *Poetry, Lan-
    guage, Thought*. Pp. 91–142.

    Pp. 321–73: "The Anaximander Fragment." In *Early
    Greek Thinking*. Trans. David Farrell Krell and Frank A.
    Capuzzi. New York: Harper & Row, 1975. Pp. 13–58.

IX. *Wegmarken*. Frankfurt: Klostermann, 1976.   (*Weg.*²)
    Pp. 45–78: "Phenomenology and Theology." In *The
    Piety of Thinking*. Trans. James G. Hart and John C.
    Maraldo. Bloomington: Indiana University Press, 1976.
    Pp. 5–22.

Pp. 103–22: "What Is Metaphysics?" Trans. David Farrell Krell. In *Martin Heidegger: Basic Writings*. Ed. David Farrell Krell. New York: Harper & Row, 1977. Pp. 91–112.

Pp. 177–202: "On the Essence of Truth." Trans. John Sallis. In *Martin Heidegger: Basic Writings*. Pp. 117–42.

Pp. 203–38: "Plato's Doctrine of Truth." Trans. John Barlow. In *Philosophy in the Twentieth Century*. III. *Contemporary European Thought*. Edd. William Barrett and Henry D. Aiken. New York: Harper & Row, 1971. Pp. 251–70.

Pp. 239–302: "On the Being and Conception of Φύσις in Aristotle's Physics B, 1." Trans. Thomas J. Sheehan, *Man and World*, 9, No. 3 (August 1976), 219–70.

Pp. 303–12: "What Is Metaphysics? Postscript." Trans. R. F. C. Hull and Alan Crick. In *Existence and Being*. Ed. Werner Brock. Chicago: Regnery, 1949. Pp. 349–61.

Pp. 313–64: "A Letter on Humanism." Trans. Frank A. Capuzzi and J. Glenn Gray. In *Martin Heidegger: Basic Writings*. Pp. 193–242.

Pp. 365–84: "The Way Back into the Ground of Metaphysics." Trans. Walter Kaufmann. In *Existentialism from Dostoevsky to Sartre*. Ed. Walter Kaufmann. Cleveland: Meridian, 1956. Pp. 206–21.

Pp. 385–426: *The Question of Being*. Trans. William Kluback and Jean T. Wilde. Bilingual Edition. London: Vision, 1959.

Pp. 445–80: "Kant's Thesis About Being." Trans. T. E. Klein and W. E. Pohl. *Southwestern Journal of Philosophy*, 4 (1973), 7–33.

XX. *Prolegomena zur Geschichte des Zeitbegriffs*. Frankfurt: Klostermann, 1979.

XXI. *Logik: Die Frage nach der Wahrheit*. Frankfurt: Klostermann, 1976.

XXIV. *Die Grundprobleme der Phänomenologie*. Frankfurt: Klostermann, 1975. (GP)
The Basic Problems of Phenomenology. Trans. Albert

Hofstadter. Bloomington: Indiana University Press, 1982.

XXV. *Phänomenologische Interpretationen von Kants Kritik der reinen Vernunft.* Frankfurt: Klostermann, 1977.

XXVI. *Metaphysische Anfangsgründe der Logik im Ausgang von Leibniz.* Frankfurt: Klostermann, 1978.

XXXI. *Vom Wesen der menschlichen Freiheit.* Frankfurt: Klostermann, 1982.

XXXII. *Hegels Phänomenologie des Geistes.* Frankfurt: Klostermann, 1980.

XXXIII. *Aristoteles, Metaphysik Θ 1–3: Vom Wesen und Wirklichkeit der Kraft.* Frankfurt: Klostermann, 1981.

XXXIX. *Hölderlins Hymnen "Germanien" und "Der Rhein."* Frankfurt: Klostermann, 1980.

LI. *Grundbegriffe.* Frankfurt: Klostermann, 1981.

LV. *Der Anfang des abendländischen Denkens: Logik—Heraklits Lehre vom Logos.* Frankfurt: Klostermann, 1979.

Identität und Differenz.   (ID)
In *Identity and Difference.* Trans. Joan Stambaugh. New York: Harper & Row, 1969. The German text appears in the Appendix.

Kant und das Problem der Metaphysik. Frankfurt: Klostermann, 1965.
Kant and the Problem of Metaphysics. Trans. James S. Churchill. Bloomington: Indiana University Press, 1962.

Nietzsche. 2 vols. Pfullingen: Neske, 1961.   (N I, N II)
N I, pp. 11–254: *Nietzsche: The Will to Power as Art.* Trans. David Farrell Krell. New York: Harper & Row, 1979.

N II, pp. 399–490: *The End of Philosophy.* Trans. Joan Stambaugh. New York: Harper & Row, 1973.

" 'Nur noch ein Gott kann uns retten': *Spiegel*-Gespräch mit Martin Heidegger am 23. September 1966." *Der Spiegel*, 30, No. 23 (May 31, 1976), 193–219.

" 'Only a God Can Save Us': *Der Spiegel*'s Interview with Martin Heidegger." Trans. Maria P. Alter and John D. Caputo. *Philosophy Today*, 20, No. 4 (Winter 1976), 267–84.

Der Satz vom Grund. Pfullingen: Neske, 1965   (SG)
Pp. 191–211: "The Principle of Ground." Trans. Keith Hoeller. *Man and World*, 7, No. 3 (August 1974), 207–22.

Schellings Abhandlung über das Wesen der menschlichen Freiheit (1809).
Tübingen: Niemeyer, 1971.
Sein und Zeit. Tübingen: Niemeyer, 1971.   (SZ)
    Pp. 1–40: "Being and Time: Introduction." Trans. Joan
    Stambaugh. In *Martin Heidegger: Basic Writings*. Ed.
    David Farrell Krell. New York: Harper & Row, 1977.
    Pp. 41–89.

    Pp. 41ff.: *Being and Time*. Trans. John Macquarrie and
    Edward Robinson. New York: Harper & Row, 1962.
Die Technik und die Kehre. Pfullingen: Neske, 1962.   (K)
    Pp. 37–47: "The Turning." Trans. K. Maly. *Research
    in Phenomenology*, 1 (1971), 3–16.
Unterwegs zur Sprache. Pfullingen: Neske, 1965.   (US)
    Pp. 9–33: "Language." In *Poetry, Language, Thought*.
    Trans. Albert Hofstadter. New York: Harper & Row,
    1971. Pp. 189–210.

    Pp. 35ff.: *On the Way to Language*. Trans. Peter D.
    Hertz. Harper & Row, 1971.
Vier Seminare. Trans. (from French) Curd Ochwadt. Frankfurt: Klos-
    termann, 1977.
Vom Wesen des Grundes.   (WG)
    The Essence of Reasons. Bilingual edition. Trans. Ter-
    rence Malick. Evanston, Ill.: Northwestern University
    Press, 1972.
Vorträge und Aufsätze. Pfullingen: Neske, 1959.   (VA)
    Pp. 13–44: "The Question Concerning Technology." In
    The Question Concerning Technology and Other Essays.
    Trans. William Lovitt. New York: Harper & Row, 1977.
    Pp. 3–35.

    Pp. 45–70: "Science and Reflection." In *The Question
    Concerning Technology and Other Essays*. Pp. 155–82.

    Pp. 71–99: "Overcoming Metaphysics." In *The End of
    Philosophy*. Trans. Joan Stambaugh. New York: Harper
    & Row, 1973. Pp. 84–110.

    Pp. 101–26: "Who Is Nietzsche's Zarathustra?" Trans.
    Bernd Magnus. *Review of Metaphysics*, 20, No. 3
    (March 1967), 411–31.

    Pp. 145–62: "Building Dwelling Thinking." In *Poetry,
    Language, Thought*. Trans. Albert Hofstadter. Harper &
    Row, 1971. Pp. 143–61.

Pp. 163–85: "The Thing." In *Poetry, Language, Thought.* Pp. 163–82.

Pp. 187–204: "... Poetically Man Dwells ..." In *Poetry, Language, Thought.* Pp. 211–29.

Pp. 207ff.: "Logos." "Moira." "Aletheia." In *Early Greek Thinking.* Trans. David Farrell Krell and Frank A. Capuzzi. New York: Harper & Row, 1975. Pp. 59ff.

Was heisst Denken? Tübingen, Niemeyer, 1961.   (WD)
    What Is Called Thinking? Trans. J. Glenn Gray and Fred D. Wieck. New York: Harper & Row, 1968.

Was ist das—die Philosophie?   (WdP)
    What Is Philosophy? Bilingual edition. Trans. William Kluback and Jean T. Wilde. London: Vision, 1962.

Zur Sache des Denkens. Tübingen: Niemeyer, 1969.   (SD)
    On Time and Being. Trans. Joan Stambaugh. New York: Harper & Row, 1972.

B. THOMAS AQUINAS

For a detailed and annotated account of St. Thomas' writings, see "A Catalogue of St. Thomas's Works" by I. T. Eschmann, O.P., in Etienne Gilson's *The Christian Philosophy of St. Thomas Aquinas* (trans. L. K. Shook, C.S.B. [New York: Random House, 1956]), pp. 381–437. I list here only those works of St. Thomas which have been used in preparing the present study, and available English translations.

Expositio super librum Boethii De Trinitate. Ed. Bruno Decker. Leiden: Brill, 1959.
    QQ. V and VI: *The Division and Method of the Sciences.* 3rd ed. Trans. Armand A. Maurer, C.S.B. Toronto: Pontifical Institute of Mediaeval Studies, 1963.
In duodecim libros Metaphysicorum Aristotelis expositio. Edd. M.–R. Cathala, O.P., and Raymond M. Spiazzi, O.P. Rome & Turin: Marietti, 1950.
    On the Metaphysics. Trans. John P. Rowan. Chicago: Regnery, 1961.
In librum De causis expositio. Ed. C. Pera, O.P. Rome & Turin: Marietti, 1955.
In octo libros Physicorum Aristotelis expositio. Ed. P. Maggiolo, O.P. Rome & Turin: Marietti, 1954.

On the Physics. Trans. Richard J. Blackwell, Richard J. Spath, and W. Edmund Thirkel. New Haven: Yale University Press, 1963.

Liber De veritate Catholicae fidei contra errores infidelium seu "Summa Contra Gentiles." Edd. C. Pera, O.P., P. Marc. O.P., and P. Carmello, O.P. 3 vols. Rome & Turin: Marietti, 1961.

> *On the Truth of the Catholic Faith.* 4 vols. in 5. Trans. Anton C. Pegis, James F. Anderson, Vernon J. Bourke, and Charles J. O'Neil. Notre Dame, Ind.: University of Notre Dame Press, 1975.

Opuscula philosophica. Ed. Raymond M. Spiazzi, O.P. Rome & Turin: Marietti, 1954. (Contains: *De ente et essentia* et al.)

> "On Being and Essence." In *Selected Writings of St. Thomas Aquinas.* Trans. Robert P. Goodwin. Indianapolis: Bobbs-Merrill, 1965. Pp. 33–67.

Opuscula theologica. Edd. Raymond A. Verardo, O.P., and Raymond M. Spiazzi, O.P. 2 vols. Rome & Turin: Marietti, 1954. (Contains: *Compendium theologiae, In librum Boethii De hebdomadibus expositio,* et al.)

> *Compendium of Theology.* Trans. Cyril Vollert. Saint Louis, Mo.: Herder, 1957.

Quaestiones disputatae. Edd. Raymond M. Spiazzi, O.P., P. Bazzi, O.P., and M. Calcaterra, T. S. Centri, E. Odetto, and P. M. Pession. 2 vols. Rome & Turin: Marietti, 1949. (Contains: *De veritate, De potentia dei, De spiritualibus creaturis,* et al.)

> *On Truth.* Trans. R. W. Mulligan, James V. McGlynn, and Robert W. Schmidt. 3 vols. Chicago: Regnery, 1952–1954.
>
> *On the Power of God.* Trans. English Dominican Fathers. Westminster, Md.: Newman Press, 1952.
>
> *On Spiritual Creatures.* Trans. Mary C. Fitzpatrick and John J. Wellmuth. Milwaukee: Marquette University Press, 1949.

Quaestiones quodlibetales. Ed. Raymond M. Spiazzi, O.P. 8th rev. ed. Rome & Turin: Marietti, 1949.

Scriptum super sententiis. Books I–II. Ed. P. Mandonnet, O.P. Paris: Lethielleux, 1929; Books III–IV. Ed. M. F. Moos, O.P. Paris: Lethielleux, 1947, 1956.

Summa theologiae (theologica). 5 vols. Ottawa: Commissio Plana, 1953.

> Trans. L. Shapcote and the Fathers of the English Dominican Province. 3 vols. New York: Benziger, 1947.

Super epistolas s. Pauli lectura. Ed. Raffaele Cai. 2 vols. Rome & Turin: Marietti, 1953.

II · Secondary Sources

Barrett, William. *Irrational Man: A Study in Existential Philosophy*. Garden City, N.Y.: Doubleday Anchor, 1962.

Beaufret, Jean. *Dialogue avec Heidegger*. 3 vols. Paris: Editions de Minuit, 1973.

Bonaventure and Aquinas: Enduring Philosophers. Edd. Robert W. Shahan and Francis J. Kovach. Norman: University of Oklahoma Press, 1976.

Bonaventure, Saint. *The Mind's Road to God*. Trans. George Boas. Library of Liberal Arts. Indianapolis: Bobbs-Merrill, 1953.

Braig, Carl. *Vom Sein: Abriss der Ontologie*. Freiburg: Herder, 1896.

———. *Die Zukunftsreligion des Unbewussten und das Princip des Subjektivismus*. Freiburg: Herder, 1882.

———. "Die natürliche Gotteserkenntnis nach dem hl. Thomas von Aquin." *Theologische Quartalschrift*, 63 (1881), 511–96.

Breakthrough: Meister Eckhart's Creation Spirituality. Ed. and trans. Matthew Fox. Garden City, N.Y.: Doubleday Image, 1980.

Brentano, Franz. *On the Several Senses of Being*. Trans. Rolf George. Berkeley: University of California Press, 1975.

Caputo, John D. *The Mystical Element in Heidegger's Thought*. Athens: Ohio University Press, 1978.

———. "Fundamental Ontology and the Ontological Difference in Coreth's *Metaphysics*." *Proceedings of the American Catholic Philosophical Association*, 51 (1977), 28–35.

———. "Fundamental Themes in Meister Eckhart's Mysticism." *The Thomist*, 42, No. 2 (April 1978), 197–225.

———. "Heidegger's 'Dif-ference' and the Distinction Between *Esse* and *Ens* in St. Thomas." *International Philosophical Quarterly*, 20, No. 2 (June 1980), 161–81.

———. "The Nothingness of the Intellect in Meister Eckhart's *Parisian Questions*." *The Thomist*, 39, No. 1 (January 1975), 85–115.

———. "Phenomenology, Mysticism and the '*Grammatica Speculativa*': A Study of Heidegger's *Habilitationsschrift*." *Journal of the British Society for Phenomenology*, 5, No. 2 (May 1974), 101–17.

———. "The Problem of Being in Heidegger and the Scholastics." *The Thomist*, 41, No. 1 (January 1977), 62–91.

———. "The Question of Being and Transcendental Phenomenology: Heidegger's Relationship to Husserl." *Research in Phenomenology*, 7 (1977), 84–105.

———. "Time and Being in Heidegger." *The Modern Schoolman*, 50, No. 4 (May 1973), 325–49.

Carlo, William. *The Ultimate Reducibility of Essence to Existence in Existential Metaphysics*. The Hague: Nijhoff, 1966.

———. "The Role of Essence in Existential Metaphysics: A Reappraisal." *International Philosophical Quarterly*, 2, No. 4 (December 1962), 557–90.

Caspar, Bernhard. "Martin Heidegger und die Theologische Fakultät Freiburg, 1909–23." In *Kirche am Oberrhein: Beiträge zur Geschichte der Bistümer Konstanz und Freiburg*. Edd. Remigius Bäumer, Karl S. Frank, and Hugo Ott. Freiburg: Herder, 1980. Pp. 534–41.

Chenu, M.-D. *Toward Understanding St. Thomas*. Trans. A. M. Landry and D. Hughes. Chicago: Regnery, 1964.

Clark, Kenneth. *Civilisation*. New York: Harper & Row, 1969.

Clarke, W. Norris, S.J. *The Philosophical Approach to God: A Contemporary Neo-Thomist Perspective*. Winston-Salem, N.C.: Wake Forest University Press, 1979.

———. "The Limitation of Act by Potency: Aristotelianism or Neoplatonism?" *The New Scholasticism*, 26, No. 2 (April 1952), 167–94.

———. "The Meaning of Participation in St. Thomas." *Proceedings of the American Catholic Philosophical Association*, 26 (1952), 147–57.

———. "What Cannot Be Said in St. Thomas' Essence–Existence Doctrine." *The New Scholasticism*, 48 (1974), 19–39.

———. "What Is Really Real." In *Progress in Philosophy*. Ed. James A. McWilliams. Milwaukee: Bruce, 1955. Pp. 61–90.

Colledge, Edmund, O.S.A. "The Legend of St. Thomas Aquinas." In *St. Thomas Aquinas, 1274–1974: Commemorative Studies*. Ed. Armand A. Maurer, C.S.B. 2 vols. Toronto: Pontifical Institute of Mediaeval Studies, 1974. I 13–28.

Coreth, Emerich. *Metaphysics*. Ed. and trans. Joseph Donceel. New York: Herder & Herder, 1968. Repr. New York: Seabury, 1972.

Cox, Harvey. *The Secular City*. New York: Macmillan, 1965.

Deely, John. *The Tradition via Heidegger: An Essay on the Meaning of Being in the Philosophy of Martin Heidegger*. The Hague: Nijhoff, 1971.

———. "The Situation of Heidegger in the Tradition of Christian Philosophy." *The Thomist*, 31, No. 2 (April 1967), 159–244.

Del-Negro, Walter. "Von Brentano über Husserl zu Heidegger: Eine vergleichende Betrachtung." *Zeitschrift für philosophische Forschung*, 7, No. 4 (October–December 1953), 571–85.

Dempf, Alois. *Meister Eckhart*. Freiburg: Herder, 1960.

Derrida, Jacques. *Of Grammatology*. Trans. Gayatri Chakravorty Spivak. Baltimore & London: The Johns Hopkins University Press, 1974.

Diels, Hermann. *Die Fragmente der Vorsokratiker*. Rev. ed. Walther Kranz. 6th ed. 3 vols. Berlin: Weidmann, 1951–1952.

Doyle, John P. "Heidegger and Scholastic Metaphysics." *The Modern Schoolman*, 49, No. 3 (March 1972), 201–20.

Eckhart, Meister. *Die deutschen Werke*. V. *Meister Eckharts Traktate*. Ed. Josef Quint. Stuttgart: Kohlhammer, 1963.

——. *The Essential Sermons, Commentaries, Treatises, and Defense*. Trans. Edmund Colledge, O.S.A., and Bernard McGinn. The Classics of Western Spirituality. New York: Paulist Press, 1981.

Engelhardt, Paulus, O.P. "Eine Begegnung zwischen Martin Heidegger und thomistischer Philosophie?" *Freiburger Zeitschrift für Philosophie und Theologie*, 3 (1956), 187–96.

Erinnerung an Martin Heidegger. Ed. Günther Neske. Pfullingen: Neske, 1977.

Eschmann, I. T., O.P. "A Catalogue of St. Thomas's Works." In Etienne Gilson. *The Christian Philosophy of St. Thomas Aquinas*. Trans. L. K. Shook, C.S.B. New York: Random House, 1956. Pp. 381–437.

Fabro, Cornelio. *Participation et causalité selon saint Thomas d'Aquin*. Louvain: Publications Universitaires de Louvain; Paris: Editions Beatrice-Nauwelaerts, 1961.

——. "Il nuovo problema dell'essere e la fondazione della metafisica." In *St. Thomas Aquinas, 1274–1974: Commemorative Studies*. Ed. Armand A. Maurer, C.S.B. 2 vols. Toronto: Pontifical Institute of Mediaeval Studies, 1974. II 423–57.

——. "The Transcendentality of *Ens–Esse* and the Ground of Metaphysics." *International Philosophical Quarterly*, 6, No. 3 (September 1966), 389–427.

Fay, Thomas A. "Heidegger on the History of Western Metaphysics as Forgetfulness of Being: A Thomistic Rejoinder." In *Tommaso d'Aquino nella storia del pensiero. II. Del medioevo ad oggi*. Tommaso d'Aquino nel suo settimo centenario No. 2. Naples: Edizione Domenicane Italiane, 1975. Pp. 480–84.

Fellermeier, Jakob. "Wahrheit und Existenz bei Heidegger und Thomas von Aquin." *Salzburger Jahrbuch für Philosophie*, 15–16 (1971–1972), 39–70.

Finance, Joseph de. *Etre et agir dans la philosophie de saint Thomas*. 2nd ed. Paris: Beauchesne, 1945.

Fischer-Barnicol, Hans A. "Spiegelungen—Vermittlungen." In *Erinne-*

rung an Martin Heidegger. Ed. Günther Neske. Pfullingen: Neske, 1977. Pp. 99–103.

Fontes vitae sancti Thomae Aquinatis. Ed. D. Prümmer. Toulouse, n.d.

Franz, Helmut. "Das Denken Heideggers und die Theologie." In *Heidegger.* Ed. Otto Pöggeler. Cologne: Kiepenheuer & Witsch, 1969.

Franzen, Winifred. *Martin Heidegger.* Stuttgart: Metzler, 1976.

Gadamer, Hans-Georg. "Martin Heidegger and Marburg Theology." In *Philosophical Hermeneutics.* Ed. and trans. David Linge. Berkeley: University of California Press, 1976.

Geiselmann, Josef Rupert. *Geist des Christentums und des Katholizismus.* Mainz: Matthias Grünewald-Verlag, 1940.

———. *Die katholische Tübinger Schule.* Freiburg: Herder, 1964.

Geyser, Josef. *Neue und alte Wege der Philosophie: Eine Erörterung der Grundlagen der Erkenntnis im Hinblick auf Edmund Husserls Versuch ihrer Neubegründung.* Münster: Schöningh, 1916.

Gilson, Etienne. *Being and Some Philosophers.* 2nd ed. Toronto: Pontifical Institute of Mediaeval Studies, 1952.

———. *The Christian Philosophy of St. Thomas Aquinas.* Trans. L. K. Shook, C.S.B. New York: Random House, 1956.

———. *Elements of Christian Philosophy.* New York: Mentor Omega, 1960.

———. *L'Etre et l'essence.* 2nd ed. Paris: Vrin, 1962.

Glossner, M. "Die Tübinger katholische Schule, vom spekulativen Standpunkt kritisch beleuchtet." *Jahrbuch für Philosophie und spekulative Theologie,* 15–17 (1901–1903). Four articles.

Grabmann, Martin. *Der Gegenwartswert der geschichtlichen Erforschung der mittelalterlichen Philosophie.* Freiburg: Herder, 1913.

———. *Mittelalterliches Geistesleben: Abhandlungen zur Geschichte der Scholastik und Mystik.* 3 vols. Munich: Hueber, 1926, 1936, 1956.

———. "Der kritische Realismus Oswald Külpes und der Standpunkt der aristotelisch–scholastischen Philosophie." *Philosophisches Jahrbuch der Görresgesellschaft,* 29 (1916).

Heidegger. Ed. Otto Pöggeler. Cologne: Kiepenheuer & Witsch, 1969.

Heidegger and the Path of Thinking. Ed. John Sallis. Pittsburgh: Duquesne University Press, 1970.

Heidegger: The Man and the Thinker. Ed. Thomas Sheehan. Chicago: Precedent, 1981.

Herrmann, F. W. von. *Die Selbstinterpretation Martin Heideggers.* Meisenheim: Hain, 1964.

Husserl, Edmund. *The Crisis of European Sciences and Transcendental Phenomenology: An Introduction to Phenomenological Philosophy.*

Trans. David Carr. Northwestern University Studies in Phenomenology and Existential Philosophy. Evanston, Ill.: Northwestern University Press, 1970.

Ilting, K.-H. "Sein als Bewegtheit." *Philosophische Rundschau,* 10 (1962), 31–49.

Imbach, Ruedi. *Deus est intelligere: Das Verhältnis von Sein und Denken in seiner Bedeutung für das Gottesverständnis bei Thomas von Aquin und in den Pariser Questionen Meister Eckharts.* Fribourg: Universitätsverlag, 1976.

John, Helen James, S.N.D. *The Thomist Spectrum.* New York: Fordham University Press, 1966.

Kenny, Anthony. *The Five Ways: Saint Thomas Aquinas' Proofs of God's Existence.* New York: Schocken, 1969.

Kierkegaard, Søren. *Concluding Unscientific Postscript.* Trans. David F. Swenson and Walter Lowrie. Princeton: Princeton University Press, 1941. Repr. 1963.

Krell, David. "On the Manifold Meaning of *Aletheia*: Brentano, Aristotle, Heidegger." *Research in Phenomenology,* 5 (1975), 77–94.

Langan, Thomas. *The Meaning of Heidegger.* New York: Columbia University Press, 1961.

Langlois, Jean. "Heidegger, Max Müller et le Thomisme." *Sciences Ecclésiastiques,* 9 (1957), 27–48.

Lehmann, Karl. "Metaphysik, Transzendentalphilosophie und Phänomenologie in den ersten Schriften Martin Heideggers (1912–1916)." *Philosophisches Jahrbuch,* 71, No. 2 (April 1964), 331–57.

Lotz, Johannes Baptist. *Martin Heidegger und Thomas von Aquin: Mensch, Zeit, Sein.* Freiburg: Herder, 1975.

——. *Sein und Existenz.* Freiburg: Herder, 1965.

——. "*Being* and *Existence* in Scholasticism and in Existence-Philosophy." Trans. Robert E. Wood. *Philosophy Today,* 9, No. 1 (Spring 1964), 3–45.

——. "Heidegger und das Christentum." *Doctor Communis,* 4 (1951), 63–73.

——. "Das Sein selbst und das subsistierende Sein nach Thomas von Aquin." In *Martin Heidegger zum siebzigsten Geburtstag.* Ed. Günther Neske. Pfullingen: Neske, 1959. Pp. 180–94.

McCool, Gerald. *Catholic Theology in the Nineteenth Century.* New York: Seabury, 1977.

——. "Twentieth-Century Scholasticism." *The Journal of Religion,* 58 (Supplement 1978), S201–202.

Martin Heidegger zum siebzigsten Geburtstag. Ed. Günther Neske. Pfullingen: Neske, 1959.

Marx, Werner. *Einführung in Aristoteles Theorie vom Seienden.* Freiburg: Rombach, 1972.

——. *Heidegger and the Tradition.* Trans. Theodore Kisiel and Murray Greene. Evanston, Ill.: Northwestern University Press, 1971.

Mehta, J. L. *Martin Heidegger: The Way and the Vision.* Honolulu: The University Press of Hawaii, 1976.

Merleau-Ponty, Maurice. *The Phenomenology of Perception.* Trans. Colin Smith. New York: Humanities Press, 1962.

Meyer, Hans. *Martin Heidegger und Thomas von Aquin.* Munich: Schöningh, 1964.

Müller, Max. *Existenzphilosophie im geistigen Leben der Gegenwart.* 3rd ed. Heidelberg: Kerle, 1964.

Noël, L. "Les frontières de la logique." *Revue Néo-Scolastique de Philosophie,* 17 (1910), 211–33.

O'Mahony, James E., O.M. Cap. *The Desire of God in the Philosophy of St. Thomas Aquinas.* Cork: Longmans, Green, 1929.

O'Meara, Thomas, O.P. *Romantic Idealism and Roman Catholicism: Schelling and the Theologians.* Notre Dame, Ind.: University of Notre Dame Press, 1982.

Owens, Joseph. *The Doctrine of Being in the Aristotelian* METAPHYSICS: *A Study of the Greek Background of Mediaeval Thought.* 3rd rev. ed. Toronto: Pontifical Institute of Mediaeval Studies, 1978.

——. "Aquinas—'Darkness of Ignorance' in the Most Refined Notion of God." In *Bonaventure and Aquinas: Enduring Philosophers.* Edd. Robert W. Shahan and Francis J. Kovach. Norman: University of Oklahoma Press, 1976. Pp. 69–86.

Phelan, Gerard. "The Existentialism of St. Thomas." *Proceedings of the American Catholic Philosophical Association,* 21 (1946), 25–40.

The Philosophy of Brentano. Ed. Linda McAlister. Atlantic Highlands, N.J.: Humanities Press, 1976.

Pieper, Josef. *The Silence of St. Thomas.* Trans. John Murray, S.J., and Daniel O'Connor. New York: Pantheon, 1957.

Pöggeler, Otto. *Der Denkweg Martin Heideggers.* Pfullingen: Neske, 1963.

Powell, Ralph. "Has Heidegger Destroyed Metaphysics?" *Listening,* 2, No. 1 (Winter 1967), 52–59.

——. "The Late Heidegger's Omission of the Ontico-Ontological Structure of Dasein." In *Heidegger and the Path of Thinking.* Ed. John Sallis. Pittsburgh: Duquesne University Press, 1970. Pp. 116–37.

Rahner, Karl. *Hearers of the Word.* Trans. Michael Richards. New York: Herder & Herder, 1969.

——. *Spirit in the World.* Trans. W. Dych, s.j. New York: Herder & Herder, 1968.

——. "The Concept of Existential Philosophy in Heidegger." Trans. A. Tallon. *Philosophy Today,* 13, No. 2 (Summer 1969), 126–37.

——. "Thomas Aquinas on the Incomprehensibility of God." *The Journal of Religion,* 58 (Supplement 1978), S107–25.

Richardson, William, s.j. *Heidegger: Through Phenomenology to Thought.* The Hague: Nijhoff, 1962.

——. "Heidegger and Aristotle." *Heythrop Journal,* 5, No. 1 (January 1964), 58–64.

Rioux, Bertrand. *L'Etre et la verité chez Heidegger et saint Thomas d'Aquin.* Paris: Presses Universitaires de France, 1963.

Rousselot, Pierre, s.j. *The Intellectualism of Saint Thomas.* Trans. James E. O'Mahony, O.M.Cap. New York: Sheed & Ward, 1935.

St. Thomas Aquinas, 1274–1974: Commemorative Studies. Ed. Armand A. Maurer, c.s.b. 2 vols. Pontifical Institute of Mediaeval Studies, 1974.

Sallis, John. "Into the Clearing." In *Heidegger: The Man and the Thinker.* Ed. Thomas Sheehan. Chicago: Precedent, 1981. Pp. 107–15.

——. "Radical Phenomenology and Fundamental Ontology." *Research in Phenomenology,* 6 (1976), 139–50.

Schaeffler, Richard. *Die Frömmigkeit des Denkens? Martin Heidegger und die katholische Theologie.* Darmstadt: Wissenschaftliche Buchgesellschaft, 1978.

Schutz, Ludwig. *Thomas-Lexikon.* Stuttgart: Frommann, 1958.

Seigfried, Hans. "Kant's Thesis About Being Anticipated by Suarez?" In *Proceedings of the Third International Kant Congress.* Ed. Lewis White Beck. Dordrecht: Reidel, 1972. Pp. 510–20.

——. "Martin Heidegger: A Recollection." *Man and World,* 3, No. 1 (February 1970), 3–4.

——. "Metaphysik und Seinsvergessenheit." *Kant-Studien,* 61 (1970), 209–16.

Sheehan, Thomas J. *Rahner: The Philosophical Foundations.* Athens: Ohio University Press. Forthcoming.

——. "Heidegger, Aristotle and Phenomenology." *Philosophy Today,* 19, No. 2 (Summer 1975), 87–94.

——. "Heidegger's Early Years: Fragments for a Philosophical Biography." *Listening,* 12, No. 1 (Winter 1977), 3–20. Repr. in *Heidegger: The Man and the Thinker.* Ed. Thomas Sheehan. Chicago: Precedent, 1981. Pp. 3–19.

——. "Heidegger's 'Introduction to the Phenomenology of Religion,' 1920–21." *The Personalist,* 60, No. 3 (July 1979), 312–24.

———. "Notes on a 'Lovers' Quarrel': Heidegger and Aquinas." *Listening*, 9, Nos. 1–2 (Winter–Spring 1974), 137–43.

Siewerth, Gustav. *Das Schicksal der Metaphysik vom Thomas zu Heidegger*. Einsiedeln: Johannes Verlag, 1959.

Stallmach, Josef. "Seinsdenken bei Thomas von Aquin und Heidegger." *Hochland*, 60 (1967), 1–13.

Stegmüller, Friedrich. *Karl Braig (1853–1923)*. Offprint from *Oberrheinisches Pastoralblatt*, 54 (1953).

Stein, Edith. "Husserls Phänomenologie und die Philosophie des hl. Thomas von Aquin." *Jahrbuch für Philosophie und phänomenologische Forschung*, 10 (1929), 315–38.

Stewart, Roderick. "The Problem of Logical Psychologism for Husserl and the Early Heidegger." *Journal of the British Society for Phenomenology*, 10, No. 3 (October 1979), 184–93.

———. "Signification and Radical Subjectivity in Heidegger's *Habilitationsschrift*." *Man and World*, 12, No. 3 (August 1979), 360–77.

Synan, Edward, *Thomas Aquinas: Propositions and Parables*. The Etienne Gilson Series No. 1. Toronto: Pontifical Institute of Mediaeval Studies, 1979.

Theron, Stephen. "*Esse*." *The New Scholasticism*, 53, No. 2 (Spring 1979), 206–20.

Thomas of Erfurt. *Grammatica speculativa*. Ed. G. L. Bursill-Hall. London: Longmans, 1972.

Überweg, Friedrich. *Grundriss der Geschichte der Philosophie*. IV. *Die deutsche Philosophie des XIX. Jahrhunderts und der Gegenwart*. Rev. ed. T. K. Österreich. Berlin: Mittler, 1923.

Vaughn, Roger Bede, O.S.B. *The Life and Labours of St. Thomas of Aquin*. 2 vols. London: Longmans, 1872.

Volpi, Franco. *Heidegger e Brentano*. Padua: Cedam-Casa, 1976.

———. "Alle origini della concezione Heideggeria dell'essere: Il trattato *Vom Sein* di Carl Braig." *Revista critica di storia della filosofia*, 34 (1980), 183–94.

———. "Heideggers Verhältnis zu Brentanos Aristoteles-Interpretation: Die Frage nach dem Sein des Seienden." *Zeitschrift für philosophische Forschung*, 21, No. 2 (April–June 1978), 254–65.

Weisheipl, James A., O.P. *Friar Thomas d'Aquino: His Life, Thoughts, and Works*. Garden City, N.Y.: Doubleday, 1974.

Welte, Bernhard. *Auf der Spur des Ewigen: Philosophische Abhandlungen über verschiedene Gegenstände der Religion und der Theologie*. Freiburg: Herder, 1965.

———. *Meister Eckhart: Gedanken zu seinen Gedanken*. Freiburg, Herder, 1980.

——. *Zeit und Geheimnis*. Freiburg: Herder, 1975.

——. "La Métaphysique de saint Thomas d'Aquin et la pensée de l'histoire de l'être chez Heidegger." *Revue des Sciences Philosophiques et Théologiques*, 50 (1966), 601–14. Repr. in *Zeit und Geheimnis*. Freiburg: Herder, 1975. Pp. 203–18.

Zimmerman, Michael E. *Eclipse of the Self: The Development of Heidegger's Concept of Authenticity*. Athens: Ohio University Press, 1981.

——. "Heidegger and Bultmann: Egoism, Sinfulness, and Inauthenticity." *The Modern Schoolman*, 58, No. 1 (November 1980), 1–20.

INDICES

INDEX OF NAMES

INDEX OF SUBJECTS

INDEX OF GREEK TERMS